MINOTAUR

MINOTAUR

Sir Arthur Evans
and the
Archaeology
of the
Minoan Myth

JOSEPH ALEXANDER MacGILLIVRAY

HILL AND WANG

A division of Farrar, Straus and Giroux

New York

Hill and Wang
A division of Farrar, Straus and Giroux
19 Union Square West, New York 10003

Copyright © 2000 by Joseph Alexander MacGillivray
All rights reserved
Distributed in Canada by Douglas & McIntyre Ltd.
Printed in the United States of America
Designed by Abby Kagan
First edition, 2000

Library of Congress Cataloging-in-Publication Data
MacGillivray, Joseph Alexander, 1953–
  Minotaur : Sir Arthur Evans and the archaeology of the Minoan myth / Joseph
  Alexander MacGillivray.
    p. cm.
  Includes bibliographical references.
  ISBN 0-8090-3035-7 (alk. paper).
  1. Evans, Arthur, Sir, 1851–1941.   2. Palace of Knossos (Knossos).   3. Knossos
(Extinct city).   4. Excavations (Archaeology)—Greece—Crete.   5. Crete (Greece)—
Antiquities.   6. Minoans.   7. Archaeologists—Great Britain—Biography.
8. Archaeologists—Greece—Biography.   I. Title.

DF212.E82 M33 2000
939′.8—dc21   00-033606

FOR BOB—

one of the two essentials for intellectual freedom

Contents

Illustrations follow pp. 88, 184, and 280.

MINOTAUR

Introduction

Like most visitors to Knossos who want to see the remains of the earliest civilization in Europe, I first looked at the Greek archaeological site in a photograph. The fierce brown bull charging between dark columns on the stone bastion towering above the North Entrance Passage was projected onto the wall of a makeshift classroom in my Montréal junior college. "This is the evidence," the young lecturer informed us, "which Sir Arthur Evans discovered at Knossos, to prove the facts behind the myth of the Minotaur and the Labyrinth which Daedalus built for King Minos in Crete." He expected us to remember it only long enough to pass the quiz at the end of the week, but I've never forgotten it.

Six years of university and graduate school in archaeology passed before I stood in the Palace of Minos at Knossos and shared, like millions of tourists each year, that moment of enlightenment when you first see the downward-tapering, sooty-black painted columns and the richly grained beams in the great halls and dark passages. But then you reach out and touch, not the warmth of natural wood but the eerie chill of cement or, more precisely, reinforced concrete, once coated with a brilliant gloss but now cracked and chipped, or blown away, leaving only a dull hint of faded grandeur. But whose grandeur, and from when?

On the heels of this jarring encounter with the cold, hard facts followed bewilderment and disappointment mixed with a sense of betrayal and shame. I looked at the walls around me and realized I couldn't tell which ones were modern and which were ancient. And if I was confused, what about all those visitors who hadn't studied archaeology as I had? If Evans had literally constructed much of the palace, how much more had he fabricated?

I became Knossos Curator of the British School at Athens in 1980, three years after my first visit to Crete, and I began to re-examine Evans's work in detail, starting with his excavation of the earliest palace beneath the huge complex of state and store rooms set around the Central Court, now so familiar to tourists. My investigation concentrated on tangible artifacts like pottery and walls, but, as I worked through the excavator's notebooks and publications, I came to know the man who had done so much to reveal and revive Knossos. As I completed a technical manuscript for a report on the earliest palace at Knossos, I began to read Evans's personal letters and testimonials and entered the maze of social, political, religious, and artistic movements stretching back to a time long before his birth and culminating in his dazzling discoveries on the threshold of the twentieth century.

The myths that the ancient Greeks "literally believed and reverentially cherished," including the "fabulous incidents attached to the name of Minos," wrote the British member of Parliament and historian George Grote in 1846, in his universally accepted twelve-volume *History of Greece,* were "in the eyes of modern inquiry essentially a legend and nothing more." Five years later, Arthur Evans was born to prove him wrong.

"We know now that the old traditions were true," Evans declared almost a century later, standing beneath a bronze bust of himself, placed to mark his achievement in the western courtyard of the Palace of King Minos, the palace he had discovered on the site of the Knossian Labyrinth that Daedalus built to house the Minotaur—the monstrous result of Queen Pasiphae's lust with the Greek god Zeus in the guise of a bull. "It is true that on the old Palace site what we see are only the ruins of ruins," he conceded, "but the whole is still inspired with Minos's spirit of order and organisation and the free and natural art of the great architect Daedalos." Evans opened the twentieth century with the revelation that Knossos had really existed: he found it in March 1900 in

Crete, buried under the low hill where Greek tradition placed it. Excavating on and off for the next thirty years, he gave the world a new chapter in its ancient history, one he called Minoan.

Arthur Evans was "a man of paradoxes . . . flamboyant and oddly modest: dignified and loveably ridiculous . . . extravagant, yet by no means self-indulgent and in some things austere . . . always loyal to his friends," Joan Evans eulogized in *Time and Chance,* a biography of her half-brother forty years her senior. "He lived as the genius he was," her praise continued, "and a genius is a man whose mind works in so unusual a fashion that his truth to that vital working must be the only criterion of his life." Evans's genius was to notice something unusual about a place or thing and to let his unfettered imagination raise it from the mundane to the eternal. His childlike enthusiasm and stubborn insistence on revealing the truth blended perfectly with his willful independence and propelled his longing to substantiate the folklore and early myths of Greece.

Where did this longing come from, and why was it so important for Evans and his society? Born the first son of John Evans, a successful British paper manufacturer, in Herefordshire in 1851, Arthur John Evans was a "rich man's son," and so he could do largely as he pleased, but the source of the wealth that his freedom depended upon was also the cause of his yearning for something fantastic.

Evans grew up in a dull and sullied landscape of industrial England, where the random harmonies of nature had been replaced by man's geometry and harnessed to satisfy society's arrogant need to control its resources in the name of progress. He was surrounded by communities that, he felt, were enslaved by their nation's greed, by a delusive urgency to create a surplus, and by a mechanistic, materialistic world. The people who lived there had forgotten what it was like to live in the natural world, as the clock replaced the sun and the calendar the moon, as water came from a pipe and light from a wire. Evans shunned "modern conveniences," using electric light and the telephone sparingly—unless, like the automobile and airplane, they saved him time, a commodity he was obsessed with.

Evans refused to join his father's world of merchants and manufacturers, and he escaped from his social and familial responsibilities into his own world of adventure and discovery whenever possible. In spite of nearsightedness and total night blindness, and fear of water—"that uncertain element" which made crossing the English Channel so arduous for him—he loved exploring new places and meeting strangers. But the farther he journeyed from his native land, the more difficult it became for him to reassimilate upon his return.

Eventually, Evans created a world of his own, which was "exactly to his taste," as Joan Evans acknowledged, "set in a beautiful Mediterranean country, aristocratic and humane in feeling: creating an art brilliant in colour and unusual in form, that drew inspiration from the flowers and birds and creatures that he loved . . . a world which served to isolate him from a present in which he had found no real place." It was the perfect antidote to industrialized Europe and America, which, he felt, was trapped in the pessimism and anxiety about the future that prevailed then and were expressed in the works of Henry James, Joseph Conrad, and H. G. Wells, and in *Decadence* by Arthur Balfour, leader of the British Conservative Party and prime minister from 1902 to 1905.

Crete was where Evans needed to go to heal his wounds. The death of his mother when he was six years old left a vacuum in his life that was never filled, not even by his wife, who also died prematurely and left him bereft; they had no heir. Minoan Crete was no Garden of Eden, where women were guilty of introducing all that was evil, but a place where the sexes were equal; men controlled the affairs of state, but women ruled the hearts and beliefs of a society at peace with itself and its neighbors. Evans's Minoans, then, worshiped the Great Mother of all creation, and when destruction came it was at the hands of a masculine society, Homer's Achaeans, dominated by their vengeful patron—Zeus.

Evans's Minoans are an example of how an archaeological discovery occurs first in the mind, born of the thinker's need to prove something of vital importance to himself. Finding proof in the dirt is the final stage of a process of wish-fulfillment. We're rarely aware of archaeologists' inventiveness and creative ability. It's only with hindsight that we can guess at the abstract origins of an archaeologist's discoveries, which otherwise appear to be surprising and fortunate.

Joan Evans attributed Arthur's brilliant discovery of Minoan culture to his being in the right place at the right time. "He had set out to find a script," she romanticized, "but Time and Chance had made him the discoverer of a new civilization." Nothing could be further from what I believe about how Evans discovered Knossos or how archaeological excavations work. I maintain that every detail in an investigation must be treated as a deliberate and relevant part of a greater picture; otherwise we would limit our study to selected material that fits a preconceived notion or research plan. When, however, we allow for chance, we impose another kind of limitation, because we acknowledge that accidents occur and that some things are beyond explanation, and thereby we draw a line between what we decide is worth examining and what is beyond our interest or grasp. Accidents appear to be chance only until we explain them, at which point they cease to appear fortuitous. There is no such thing as a random encounter or a lucky find, then. If such a thing did exist, we'd have to abandon all hope of ever explaining anything. When Joan Evans rationalized her half-brother's discoveries as luck, she excused herself from having to investigate the most important aspect of her study: Evans's *active* work in conceiving and discovering Minoan civilization.

Most archaeologists take comfort in being impartial observers using scientific techniques, which, they believe, reasonably protects them from anything but a passive involvement with their discoveries. For them, archaeology is the process of delivering the past into the present; they are the messengers, and the artifact is the message. But this separation is an illusion. Evans was no simple errand boy; the message he communicated was as much from him as by means of him. Archaeologists are the progenitors as well as the midwives at the birthing process we call excavation. To understand this process, I should like to examine the connection between Evans, appointed by his society to search for certain specific and tangible truths, and the material evidence that came into his hands in Crete.

The heart of what I call relative archaeology is complex; that is, the study of the origins of this association between an artifact and its creator or finder is quite elaborate. I treat all archaeological discoveries as creative in their origin, rather like Michelangelo Buonarroti's views of his own sculpture; he believed he was liberating figures trapped in the stones of the Carrara marble quarries (images that were submerged or repressed aspects of his own personality) when he tangibly created them. I suspect that the great archaeologists, like Heinrich Schliemann at the site he believed was Troy, do something similar when they gaze beneath the earth's mantle in search of clues to their desired history.

Much of this creative process is dismissed as archaeological intuition, but what does this mean? To intuit is to receive knowledge by direct perception without reasoning, but this presumes that the knowledge is absolute in its truth. To say that Evans was intuitive about

Knossos is to assume that what he found was an absolute truth. I think that what he found was a relative truth, relative primarily to himself and then to those who wanted it most and who engaged him and his colleagues to uncover it, and it was truthful only for as long as the facts he delivered were necessary to support the desired history.

Archaeologists create a version of history, which in turn guides the archaeology in a circular motion that, ideally, is ever changing as each new discovery causes a new appraisal of the history. New discoveries change the direction of archaeology, which in turn produces new artifacts and new histories, which send the archaeologists in new directions, so that they never cover the same ground twice. There is no stasis in such a dynamic, no fixed point, and therefore no absolute historical truth. Instead, a succession of relative truths occurs, with relative histories that satisfy a set of changing requirements for a while. When Evans formulated his notion of what Minoan culture in Crete had been, he blocked this succession by insisting on an absolute and fixed history. Because of his exalted status, this history was largely accepted, but until after his death in 1941 it hampered the learning process. And he didn't restrict himself to antiquity: Evans was also a powerful and willful designer of modern nations, as his involvement in the creation of Czechoslovakia and Yugoslavia during the First World War demonstrated.

Evans's great discovery of the Bronze Age civilization of Crete, the Minoan civilization, earned him a place in history. But what of the Minoans themselves? They have become such an important element in so many conflicting ancient and modern political, social, and spiritual agendas that we seem to have lost sight of who these early inhabitants of Crete were. They're still classed as pre-Hellenic—a label that tells nothing about them, leaving them in a state of suspense, waiting to become something recognizable to us as "Hellenic." They're presented as the last bastion of matriarchal rule and as worshipers of the Mother Goddess—believers that nature is a loving mother fertilized by a heavenly father (Evans's early theory recently revised). This view holds that the Minoans survived into "proto-historical" times, when their conquest by bloodthirsty "Indo-Germanic" ancestors of a European male-dominated society ended their civilization. Recent scholarship relegates them to an even more fantastic realm than that of Minos: Plato's lost continent of Atlantis. Some suggest that Atlantis was Crete, submerged at the height of its power by a tidal wave from an eruption from the nearby island of Thera, a volcanic crater whose most recent and most devastating explosion, in the fifteenth century B.C., had extinguished Minoan civilization.

A century after Evans's discoveries at Knossos, the time has come to reconsider the circumstances in which this early Cretan society was reborn, if only to clarify the origins of much of what we still call Minoan. To do so, we must start with Evans himself, the product of his genes and his life experiences, and with his own search to explain aspects of himself—such as his explosive temper, which his mother called his volcanic nature, and his frequent and playful references to beastly lairs. Evans identified with the mythical Minotaur—an allegory for the monster in men—but what was his particular monster, which he worked so hard to contain in its lair and hide from public view? I suspect that it may have been the repressed "beastliness" of his homosexuality, which gave his life part of its powerful creative drive until he lost control of it in his later years. But Evans didn't exist in a vacuum, and so we must also reconstruct the social, political, and intellectual climate in which he developed and that compelled him to excavate Knossos.

This study in relative archaeology is a radical departure from the common view of how archaeology and archaeologists work. It requires us to change our perceptions of the field dramatically. In my view, archaeologists must cease to believe that what they are doing is to sort objectively through a confusion of facts to sustain a historical truth, and they must become much more aware of their truly creative interpretative work. They must be conscious of their active participation in the formative and recovery stages of the archaeological process. In the twenty-first century, they must ask more penetrating questions than their predecessors in the twentieth century did, both about their discoveries and about themselves. This is only part of a wider review of the bigger question of how we relate to the past from the only fixed point in time we know: the present.

1

Apprentice Archaeologist 1851–83

Fossilizing

Sir Arthur Evans jumped into the trenches at Knossos for the first time on March 19, 1894, six years before he began excavations there. "When I discovered the site," he recounted much later, "there was a little old wall at one end. That was all. I explored the surface very carefully, and picked up little bits of painted stuccos and scraps of pottery—enough to convince me of the wonder of it. I saw in the hands of the natives some pieces of clay tablets bearing signs of writing in an unknown language." Evans's account of the discovery of the Palace of Minos at Knossos, which earned him his exalted and much deserved place in archaeological history, fits well with his half-sister and biographer Joan Evans's explanation that he happened to be "in the right place at the right time." The truth of how archaeologists make discoveries, however, is far from the popular notion of random encounters and chance finds. We must take the time to examine the personalities and events leading up to these discoveries.

There's no denying Evans credit for his work in Crete and his discovery of the Minoans, who have become many things to many people, but the credit does not lie with him alone. The discovery of an ancient society and then the developing consensus of scholarly opinion regarding its meaning are born of collective efforts made by many people from assorted disciplines and backgrounds, though most often the one who takes the initiative and assumes the responsibility accepts the credit. For Knossos and the Minoans, Arthur Evans was that person. This study of his origins and experience will, I hope, show how the Minoans first appeared to Evans as an idea long before the ancient artifacts fell into his hands in Crete, and that he used those tangible proofs to write an entirely new chapter in human history and, simultaneously, to create a lasting monument that is one of the most visited archaeological sites in the world.

Arthur Benoni Evans, Arthur Evans's grandfather, was born into a curate's family near Ashbury, in southwest Oxfordshire, in 1781. Great Britain at the end of the eighteenth century was still controlled by a hereditary nobility that answered to a "divinely inspired" monarchy, but changes in England and in continental Europe precipitated by a rapid succession of breakthroughs in scientific experimentation and application, coupled with a renewed concern for human rights, were already being felt. The basis for this Enlightenment, as the philosophical movement of the time became known, was traced directly to the Italian Renaissance and thence to ancient Greece and Rome. The "scientific revolution" at the basis of the Enlightenment was a slow and painful process, beginning in 1543 with Copernicus, who, bolstered by his mathematical work, dared to place the sun at the center of the cosmos. Fiercely attacked by the Roman Catholic Church, the observations of Copernicus and his successors nonetheless slowly introduced a new awareness of the natural world, after centuries of steadfast belief in the divinely inspired nature of the universe as ordained in the Bible. The new evidence, tangible and verifiable by more than one witness, was labeled "scientific"—from the Latin *scientia*, meaning knowledge.

The seventeenth-century French philosopher René Descartes took the new scientific method to its limits when he expressed theories of deterministic and materialistic physics to support his belief that the universe was little more than a great machine. This Cartesian model of an absolute and predictable mechanism peopled by automatons found no discernible evidence for divinity. But clerics urged their followers to believe in the supremacy of the Bible's teachings, though they could not provide the tangible proofs required by the men of science, who were fast replacing them as society's keepers of the truth. An acceptable blend of divine and materialistic doctrines came with Isaac Newton's *Mathematical Principles of Natural Philosophy,* in 1687: Newton agreed that the natural laws of the universe were indeed mechanistic, but he believed that they exhibited the wisdom and power of the "Great Mechanic—God himself." Clearly, this was not a theory whose authority could be questioned freely in most circles, especially in the British climate of Christian evangelism, the strict adherence to the evangel, or "good message," of the New Testament. The basis for Newton's principles was "absolute, true and mathematical time," which could be observed and recorded by the pendulum, produced as a timekeeping device in 1657 and responsible for a proliferation of clocks, seen as symbols of progress, erected in public places throughout the United Kingdom. But where did man fit in this great machine? Predictably, theories of the human machine were proposed; the earliest came from the French physician Julien de La Mettrie, who in 1748 applied Descartes's notion that animals are thoughtless automata to humans in his *Man the Machine,* a pioneering work of modern materialism, which introduced the dispassionate and cold-hearted attitude fundamental to modern medical research.

The scientific revolution against religious authority erupted simultaneously with a revolution against secular control, voiced by Jean-Jacques Rousseau in his *Du contrat social* of 1762. Rousseau's assertion that "man is born free, but is everywhere in chains" helped to found the romantic cult of the common man; common people were starting to question the existing social hierarchy and to become politically conscious. The belief that the ideal state is composed of citizens who entrust the powers of government to an elected body of their representatives led to the doctrine of popular sovereignty that found expression in the American colonies' Declaration of Independence in 1776. The most graphic display of the popular will against the ruling elite came on July 14, 1789, when the common people of Paris stormed the Bastille prison there. The French Revolution was the catalyst for a series of major transformations throughout Europe, and marked the beginning of our modern age. The rights of the individual and the rights of nations to govern themselves became themes that underscored the policies of the coming centuries, beginning with the French constitution of 1791, which asserted, "Sovereignty is indivisible, unalienable and imprescriptible; it belongs to the Nation; no group can attribute sovereignty to itself nor can an individual arrogate it to himself."

Eight years later, Napoleon Bonaparte led a parliamentary coup and the constitution was his first target. Napoleon earned his authority from successful military campaigns in Italy, Austria, and Holland, where he removed the British from continental Europe, causing them to declare war in 1793.

The storms of the British war with Napoleon were never too distant for Arthur Benoni Evans, though he spent his early years in a remote and timeless part of Oxfordshire, steeped in ancient superstition: at the southeast end of the Vale of White Horse, beneath the huge stylized quadruped cut into the chalk hillside that gave the valley its name. The giant etching, which is believed to be the work of a local Celtic tribe called the Belgae during the Iron Age, sometime before the Roman conquest of Britain in 54 B.C., is no less puzzling now than it was in Arthur Benoni Evans's boyhood. Equally mysterious is the horse's location about three-quarters of the way along the ancient Ridge Way, which runs from Beacon Hill, north of London, for eighty-five miles to the enigmatic standing stones set in circles at Avebury, in Wiltshire.

Evans grew to maturity with his namesake, the Reverend Arthur Benoni Evans, a bachelor uncle in Gloucester with whom he was sent to live following his mother's death in 1788. It seemed only natural that he take priestly orders in his turn, which came in 1805 at Gloucester Cathedral, shortly after he completed his studies at St. John's College, Oxford. But he found the curate's lot not to his liking, least of all its meager financial reward, and so, using his father's connections, he became a professor of classics and history at the newly established Royal Military College at Great Marlow, a grand title that masked the truth that he spent his days drumming Latin grammar into the heads of the officers' sons who saw little need for the language in their aspirations to join Britain's armed forces.

Disillusioned with the military life and no doubt with his own circumstances as he neared the age of thirty, Evans sought release from his discontent in two brief attempts at satirical humor. The first, *The Cutter, in Five Lectures upon the Art and Practice of Cutting Friends, Acquaintances, and Relations,* printed in Old Bond Street in 1808, only thinly disguised his unhappiness and immaturity, though it might have appealed to others in similar downtrodden circumstances. For example, to a fading beauty Evans advised:

Associate with none of an age above four and twenty: become excessively sportive: talk of frocks, balls, boarding-schools and elopements: give to your remarks a smack of youth and inexperience. In pursuing this plan of conduct, you will make yourself so superior to those of your own age, that you will find it necessary to avoid their malignant insults by constantly "cutting" them to the quick. When any unforeseen disaster brings you into their company, attack them obliquely by frequent contemptuous glances; disregard them, as you do those who are older than yourself; and when asked, who they are, you may answer by a conjecture, that they are maiden aunts of the old lady of the house.

Even more cruel, and equally revealing, was: "If you are ashamed to acknowledge a poor . . . and dependent friend in a party, ball or rout, cut him for the whole evening; and, calling upon him the next morning, tell him how anxious you were to have introduced him to a very valuable acquaintance, but that you could not catch his eye; that you were engaged in a most agreeable party."[1]

The second volume, a satirical novel called *Fungusiana, or the Opinions and Table Talk of the late Barnaby Fungus, Esq.*, appeared a year later. Like the first, it exhibited the wicked side to Evans's temperament. Neither was so well received as to liberate the author from the drudgery of teaching, but almost certainly these books eventually fell into the hands of his grandson and namesake, Arthur John Evans, when he felt most dejected and impressionable; they might well have inspired him to respond to what he felt were life's injustices in a similar manner.

In 1812 the Royal Military College was transferred from Great Marlow to Sandhurst, near Aldershot, in Berkshire. Evans seems to have settled in to the new situation, and, with the promise of a future in teaching, however modest the returns, he courted and wed Anne Dickinson in June 1819. Their first child, a daughter named Anne for her mother, was born a year later; their first son, Arthur, named after himself and his favorite uncle, followed in 1822. By this time, however, Evans was requested to resign from Sandhurst. The defeat of Napoleon in 1815 and the onset of peace had brought about a reduction in the armed forces, and the Latin tutor of seventeen years was to be replaced by a young war veteran. What may have seemed to Evans an impossible situation at the time—a wife and two children to support and no pension—with hindsight can be appreciated as a positive reversal of fortune. Circumstance ejected the Evanses from a life of mediocrity. Anne

Evans called on some family connections to secure her husband a curate's post at Burnham, near Slough, and, the salary being meager, she also managed a loan to buy a large house and property on the main road between Burnham and Farnham Royal, where she and her husband set up a preparatory school for potential military cadets.

The combined salary and income from the students' families gave Arthur Benoni Evans his first taste of financial security, and he began to enjoy his role as master of a country estate. He found more time to pursue the activities that gave him pleasure, and he developed a passion for drawing. He spent long hours in his garden working up studies of trees in fine black chalk on rough white paper, or sketching in sepia. The "Cutter" receded into the dark past, and Anne Evans's diaries, kept during the years of unhappy drudgery until 1822, were dutifully destroyed lest they somehow re-appear at some future date and remind them of a time best forgotten.[2]

They were now living on the outskirts of London, and as the family fortune increased so, too, did the frequency of Arthur's journeys into the city. He became a regular client of the booksellers in Holborn Street who kept him abreast of the latest developments in learning and brought to his attention the revolution in thinking taking place in the world of natural history and geology, particularly the ideas of the French naturalist Georges Cuvier, who gained a great deal of notoriety with his *Recherches sur les ossements fossiles des quadrupèdes,* published in 1812. Cuvier had noticed petrified bones from very deep cuttings in the gypsum quarries in Paris's Montmartre, which were being mined for making plaster. He concluded that the bones belonged to a time before the biblical flood, as described in Genesis, since he could prove that they came from layers beneath those with impressions of marine species. Cuvier's assertions were the beginning of the modern study of vertebrate paleontology, and they went a long way to support the efforts of geologists in a growing argument with clerics over the age of the earth.

Less than two centuries earlier, in 1642, Dr. John Lightfoot, master of St. Catherine's College and vice-chancellor of the University of Cambridge, had declared with confidence, "Man was created by the Trinity about the third hour of the day, or nine of the clocke in the morning on 23 October 4,004 BC."[3] The text that gave Lightfoot his authority was the Judeo-Christian creation epic as set forth in the Bible, Genesis being the primary framework by which scholars explained the antiquity of the world around them. By the nineteenth century, however, the dates worked out by readings of Genesis were coming under the scrutiny of a generation of thinkers who were not men of the cloth and did not consider themselves bound by the Scriptures, but attended rather to a new form of evidence: scientific.

Evans began his own investigations in 1823 when he visited a local chalk pit, exploited for the same reasons as the Montmartre mines, near Box Hill, east of Dorking in Surrey. This was the same year his second son, John, was born. Evans returned on numerous occasions to look for the imprints of extinct species, or "fossils," as the geologists called them (from the Latin *fossilis,* meaning "recovered by digging").

Between 1830 and 1833, Charles Lyell's essential *Principles of Geology, being an attempt to explain the former changes of the Earth's surface by reference to causes now in action,* appeared in London. Lyell used the growing body of scientific observation from British and European scholars in what amounted to an entirely new history of the earth. He made a conscious, and determined, effort to remove the account from the realm of biblical speculation—"to free science from Moses," as he put it—and his work helped to expand the already deepening chasm between those who adhered to the Scriptures and those who considered themselves as adhering to a new, unbiased truth.

Lyell supported the growing consensus among earth scientists that one should view the planet's history as a long uninterrupted time of formation and uniform growth. This theory of "uniformitarianism" soon became accepted and preached like a religious doctrine, and it paved the way for the acceptance of the evolutionary theory that followed. In his uniformitarianism, Lyell was reacting to his tutor, the Anglican priest William Buckland, the first professor of mineralogy at Oxford, who championed "catastrophism" as the best way to explain the coming and going of species. Buckland believed that geological history was a sequence of periods separated by natural catastrophes that wiped out all species. Like Cuvier, Buckland chose as his model the biblical story of the flood, and he posited that God created new species following each one of these drastic geological events. The species whose fossilized remains were recovered from geological layers below the flood levels were classified as "antediluvian." Lyell did much to strengthen and develop the increasing consensus against catastrophism, but the simplicity of its *tabula rasa,* or "clean slate," as an explanatory model, especially for those who fear higher authorities, probably accounts for its periodic revival as an explanation for the "collapse of civilization" and its continued appeal to the scholar and layman alike.

The new belief in science was formulated by men who rejected the uncritical beliefs of the creationists and tried instead to explain the world around them according to verifiable human observations. Scientific method required that a theory be proposed clearly, in a language without ambiguity, and that it be possible to repeat all aspects of an experiment designed to test it. The popularity of the new ideas and the controversy surrounding them led to the establishment of the British Association for the Advancement of Science, which met for the first time in 1832. The British Association, taking advantage of the latest developments in engineering, used the railways to promote a truly British association, and met every year in a different city, the first being York.

Eventually, the private tutoring business dwindled, and Evans set his sights on more elevated seats of learning with more reliable sources of income. He first considered the headmastership of Rugby School, then that of the Edinburgh Academy, but in truth he was qualified for neither. In the end he secured an appointment as head of a new grammar school at Market Bosworth, in Leicestershire, and he moved the family there in the autumn of 1829. By 1832, Evans and his sons were making a regular habit of "fossilizing," as they called their search for ancient artifacts, in the local gravel pits and the nearby limestone rocks at Cloud Hill, but they gradually widened their investigations to the Wenlock shale pits at Dudley, west of Birmingham, and then up to the Peak district, where they marveled at the geological formations. The family outings to chalk pits and exposed geological formations seem to have had little effect on the eldest son, Arthur. In the family tradition, he was sent off to Oxford, where he barely succeeded, then returned home to take holy orders. The effect on John, by contrast, remained with him throughout his life and guided much of what he did in his private hours.

Another hobby also attracted Evans. In 1832 he acquired a cabinet to house a growing coin collection. At first he accepted gifts of old coins from friends and added them to a collection that increased proportionately with his assortment of fossils taken from the surface of ancient sites. But by 1834 he was in touch with London dealers and buying items to fill the gaps in his holdings. He concentrated on ancient Greek and Roman coins of intrinsic value and gave his earlier acquisitions, along with introductory texts and a cash advance toward the purchase of a new cabinet, to his son John, who shared his father's interest and formed his own expertise on British coins.

John Evans was deemed "too sensible and hard working for the class room or parish" by his practical mother, and in April 1840 at the age of sixteen he was sent to join the paper-making firm of his uncle and god-father, John Dickinson, at Nash Mills in Hertfordshire.[4] His position was clearly regarded as a family favor for several years, and he was not given much credit for his own efforts, but John worked hard at his duties in the paper mills and kept his social life to a minimum. Gradually, though, he began to notice his uncle's daughter Harriet, five months his senior. Her earliest recollection of him was of his "trudging up and down a ploughed field, bent nearly double, poring over the earth through his steel-rimmed spectacles in a search for fossils"[5]—not her idea of perfection, but she eventually seems to have returned his admiring glances. Her father was quite keen that she marry wealth and position, as any ambitious father of the time would have been, but eventually he gave in to his daughter's desires. After months of deep longing expressed in a secret correspondence, John and Harriet were married on September 12, 1850, and went off to Paris for their honeymoon; their first-born, a son, arrived a little more than nine months later.

The excursion to Paris took them along newly laid rail lines through the Somme, and on either side John observed the recent cuttings at the edge of the right-of-way and the geological layers they revealed. On their return homeward they had to wait between trains at Amiens, where John ran off to see the Gothic cathedral and its famous sculptures. He returned to Amiens nine years later without Harriet, but with a new mission.

A Perfect World

Arthur John Evans was born on July 8, 1851, into a self-proclaimed Golden Age. Two months earlier, Queen Victoria had opened the Great Exhibition at the Crystal Palace in London, a city that was considered by the English not only the center of the civilized world but, as a report in the *Times* on May 2 suggested, the closest thing in this world to paradise:

> There was yesterday witnessed a sight the like of which has never happened before . . . In a building that could easily have accommodated twice as many, twenty-five thousand persons, so it is computed, were arranged in order round the throne of our Sover-

eign. Around them, amidst them, and over their heads was displayed all that is useful or beautiful in nature or in art. Above them rose a glittering arch far more lofty and spacious than the vaults of even our noblest cathedrals. On either side the vista seemed almost boundless . . . Some saw in it . . . a solemn dedication of art and its stores; some were most reminded of that day when all ages and climes shall be gathered round the throne of their Maker . . . all contributed to an effect so grand and yet so natural, that it hardly seemed to be put together by design, or to be the work of human artificers.

England's material prosperity, gained from a surge in industrial production and from growing world markets that England dominated, gave the mid-Victorians a hitherto unprecedented self-confidence. The period between the Battle of Waterloo in 1815 and the outbreak of the First World War in 1914 has been called the Century of Peace, when Britain concentrated on its preeminence as the world's major power. With such prestige, however, came the need for Britain to understand its good fortune, if only so that the British might maintain it. Lord Macaulay's *History of England,* which appeared in 1848, set out to explain what elements of character had contributed to making England the most prosperous nation on earth. He began with this opinion: "The history of our country during the last hundred and sixty years is eminently the history of physical, of moral, and of intellectual improvement," a clear statement of the three primary tenets of the Victorian social agenda. The physical improvement could be related to industry and the work ethic; the moral improvement reflected the strict adherence by most Englishmen to a Christian evangelism, advocated by the Church of England and the Nonconformist chapels, with their commitment to the supreme authority of the Bible; and the intellectual improvement was evident across the broad spectrum of both the sciences and the humanities. Strict adherence to all three would lead to what the Prince Consort in 1851 described as "the great end to which all history points—the realization of the unity of mankind."[6] What would unify mankind, then, would be the universal adoption of those standards that made the English great: this was the guiding principle of British imperialism.

One aspect of Arthur Evans's character, which reemerged throughout his life, was apparent from the very beginning. Soon after his christening, his mother wrote to her sister-in-law Emma: "My Baby has a good deal of the Dickinson in him, indeed he has a double right to it, and I fear he inherits also a little of the Pepper, what your Father calls the 'Volcanic' Nature, but . . . I hope he has good sense and then a great deal may be done by training."[7] But no amount of training could contain the volcanic nature that erupted at key moments in Arthur's life and cast a shadow across the otherwise bright recollections recorded by his friends and loved ones.

In September 1851 the young family moved into the new red-brick house they built on the edge of Nash Mills village. Though it was made of the same material as the neighboring buildings, it was called the Red House for its radiance in the industrial landscape of blackened factories and the sooty homes near Abbot's Langley, north of Watford, on the gray waters of the Grand Union Canal; it was soon endowed with the family's inner light and warmth. John's study seems to have been one of the first rooms to be organized, as Harriet wrote to her brother, "Jack's library is quite a picture of comfort. It is a nice little room; one window opens towards Nash Mills Village (of which ours is now the first house in the row of Cottages), the other window looks towards the Mill. The length of the room is taken up with book-shelves very nearly filled."[8] It also contained the coin cabinets, now quite numerous, with their valuable contents. John seemed particularly taken by the examples from Sicily, perhaps because he knew his father was.

In 1848 John read a paper to the Archaeological Society on coinage in Britain before the Roman conquest. Its favorable reception marked the beginning of an intellectual career outside the halls of learning that had been denied him as a youth.[9] Then he tried his hand at archaeological excavation at the site of a nearby Roman villa. By today's standards it was little more than a documented treasure hunt; he worked up drawings of the pottery and the mosaic floor he uncovered, and presented his results in a lecture to an antiquarian meeting at nearby St. Albans in April 1852. His efforts qualified him for election to the exclusive Society of Antiquaries in December. The society, founded in about 1585 to establish a firm basis for British history, was as prestigious a gathering of like-minded individuals as John Evans could hope to impress. But his chief concern was the study of geology, and not solely as an intellectual pursuit.

John Evans found that his scientific observations could benefit the family business in disputes with the local waterway authority. The managers of the Grand Union Canal, a man-made arterial link between

London and the industrial cities of the north, through their drillings and diversions had been reducing the water flow necessary to supply the mills. John took it upon himself to investigate the geological reasons for the changing water conditions. As his research into soil and rock conditions and his skill at presenting his conclusions for favorable judgments in the law courts became known, he found himself in demand by other firms with similar problems. On one of many trips to give evidence, he shared a railway carriage with one Joseph Prestwich, who had been called in to represent the opposing party in the lawsuit. By the end of the journey both men realized how much in common they had. Prestwich was a prosperous wine merchant in London's exclusive Mark Lane who, like Evans, had taken up geology as a hobby. We aren't told how the case was decided, but the encounter on the train produced a lasting bond.

John's marriage to a Dickinson daughter had brought with it a promotion to junior partnership in the paper firm, less of a material reward at first than an opportunity for him to play a more active part in running the mills, which soon paid off as the paper industry blossomed due to the increased efficiency of the British Post Office. John and Harriet's growing prosperity brought with it the means to enlarge their family, which they did at a rate of about one a year. Two sons, Lewis and Philip Norman, were born in 1853 and 1854, and a daughter, Alice, in 1856. But the joys that accompany the miracle of new life were punctuated with bouts of illness; typhoid, scarlet fever, and pleurisy, often for months at a time, severely weakened Harriet's constitution.

In 1856 the Evanses moved into the large house where Harriet had grown up at Nash Mills. Here the children could play in a garden while Harriet sewed and read. John's library was now where John Dickinson's office had been, looking out across the drive to the mill. It was a grand room of elegant bookcases with latticed glass doors and two large safes for his coin collection.

By all accounts, young Arthur was a late starter. His grandmother in 1857 records in a note to Harriet the general feeling about his intellectual progress in contrast to that of his father at the same age: "Sorry to hear of the darling *Trot* being a bit of dunce . . . Now he has reached the mature age of six, I hope he will become ambitious of putting a little more into it."[10]

A second daughter was added to the family on December 19, 1857, but the nurse brought infection with her. Harriet, now thirty-five, again fell ill. Arthur was sent to Grandfather Dickinson's house, called Abbot's Hill, up the road. Years later his half-sister Joan, no doubt recording one of Arthur's most private confessions to her, recounted:

> He overheard the nurses talking and knew that she [his mother] was very ill; if she died, they said, someone was going to come from Nash House and throw gravel against the nursery window. He tried to stay awake, and listen every night; and on New Year's night he heard the sound he dreaded. Later he was taken to see his mother, where she lay so white and still. He knew he would never see her again, and studied and studied the features that were so familiar and so changed; he was determined that if he never saw her again he should remember her all his life.
>
> With her loss the world fell to pieces. When the children came home from Abbot's Hill, John Evans wrote in his wife's diary that they did not seem to feel her loss; more than seventy years later Arthur Evans was to write an indignant *NO* in the margin. Arthur was only six, . . . he had learned too young what bitter grief love could bring; and thereafter the innermost recesses of his heart were guarded by fear. He was never cold-hearted, . . . but he kept himself remote, . . . preferring impersonal relationships, . . . those who loved him would always be conscious of something enigmatic and hidden.[11]

A year later, John Evans, in a letter to his cousin Fanny Phelps, who was to become Arthur's stepmother, commented that his son was

> a very odd child, and though I am an Evans myself to a great extent, I cannot quite understand him. Think of him burying a china doll (with its legs broken) with a butterfly and some other things in the garden, and placing this inscription over them "KING EDWARD SIXTH and the butterfly and there cloths and things." Whether he had some notion about the resurrection or not I cannot say, but the Psyche element is very singular and the placing of the clothes in readiness for his re-existence looks like forethought.[12]

This curious episode and the buried time capsule labeled with the name of a king who reigned three hundred years earlier and with a butterfly, universal symbol of rebirth, is all the more striking when we know that the child went on to devote most of his life to uncovering what are essentially time capsules from much older civilizations. Already, he associated buried artifacts with buried history, and took part in the process by burying them himself.

Arthur's retreat led him into a world of reading and imagination. Arthur Benoni and Anne Evans had put together, as Anne boasted, "two most delectable volumes folio of coloured calico covered with an immense variety of little engravings and etchings of all descriptions, about 1,500 altogether," on learning that they were grandparents.[13] The grandfather Evans had passed on his interest in books, coins, and fossils to his son, and now he was passing something else on to the next generation, something he and his circle could only dream of or experience through the prose, poetry, and portraiture of adventurers in foreign lands who survived the hardships of exploration and translated their most cherished moments for a captive audience on the home shores. On many of his visits to London, Arthur Benoni Evans would peer through the window of a diorama containing tiny models of romantic places illuminated by gently swinging pendant lights to feign the motion of a dramatic sky, or he would gaze at a continuous picture in a cylinder at the Panorama and feel himself transported to the Swiss Alps, a street in Pompeii, or the mountains of New Zealand.[14] (He was too early by only a few years. In 1855 Thomas Cook recognized the needs of men and women such as he and organized the first of many tours for the intelligent traveler in Europe and the East.) In these etchings of romantic and exotic places like Athens, Nineveh, and Cairo, he was passing on a torch he had never truly held, the light experienced by the imaginary nomad. Young Arthur was profoundly affected by his grandfather's dreams of travel, the longings of a frustrated generation that gave Arthur a vision around which to construct his own future; he took it as his duty to become one of those wanderers his grandfather so admired, and he realized this ambition within the guidelines set forth by the rebellious dreamer.

Whatever books Arthur Benoni Evans hadn't given to his son John in life were bequeathed after his death in 1854. He once wrote, "I have some thousands . . . collected by my uncle and myself, as well as a curious and useful mathematical library of your grandfather's . . . I have too upwards of 100 Grammars of all languages."[15] The little study came to house an enormous collection of all manner of learning, and Nash

Mills became a paradise for the young reader. Arthur availed himself of the proximity of a world in print. One book in particular—Robert Walsh's 1828 *Narrative of a Journey from Constantinople to England,* filled with vibrant accounts of nations which, though within the geographical limits of Europe, were well beyond the grasp of the Victorian English in their customs and behavior—was so impressive that when Arthur's turn came to travel, this was the direction he took.

The year that Thomas Cook first took mature travelers to "the Continent" of Europe, Charles Kingsley published the first of a series of storybooks that transported generations of British children on even more distant and fantastic journeys. When not composing sermons as canon of Eversley in Hampshire, Kingsley wrote novels intended to awaken the social conscience of the British elite; he was a founding member of the Christian Socialist Movement, which aimed to correct the inequalities propagated by industrialism through the practice of Christian ethics. For his own children he composed a modern version of the Greek myths called *Heroes.* The fearless pursuits of Perseus, Jason with his Argonauts, and Theseus as told by the canon had such a universal appeal that the book went through several reprints, and Kingsley, because of his popularity, became canon of Westminster and chaplain to Queen Victoria. His link to the Evanses came with his induction into the Geological Society, where he and John were fellows. It was there that Charles Kingsley and John Evans came to know and admire Charles Darwin and his revolutionary notions.

Arthur Evans was among the thousands of adolescents who were first exposed to the Greek myths through Kingsley's *Heroes,* and the heroic quest that most engaged him was told in the last chapter. There, Kingsley recounted the exploits of Theseus, who volunteers to go with an annual tribute of seven youths and seven maidens sent by his father, the Athenian king Aegeus, to Crete, where, in revenge for the death of the son of King Minos at the hands of some unknown felon in the Attic kingdom, "Minos thrusts them into a labyrinth, which Daedalus made for him among the rock," Kingsley fantasized. "From that labyrinth no one can escape, entangled in its winding ways, before they meet the Minotaur, the monster who feeds upon the flesh of men." Though Kingsley left the origins of the monster obscure, he wrote elaborately about the achievements, exploits, and outcome of the architect Daedalus. He described how Daedalus makes for Minos, in addition to the labyrinth, "statues which spoke and moved, and the temple of Britomartis, and the dancing-hall of Ariadne, which he carved of fair white stone." But the cunning creator runs afoul of the monarch and is forced to flee. As Minos controls the land and sea, the inventor creates huge feather wings bound with wax for his son Icarus and himself, and they leap to their freedom from a mountaintop. But the boy flies too close to the sun, the wax melts, and he falls to his death into the sea which bears his name. The father continues his flight to Sicily, where he goes into service under King Kokalos, and where Minos tracks him down at the end of his days.

Kingsley enchanted adolescent Victorians with the story of how the Athenian hero Theseus wins the heart of King Minos's daughter Ariadne, who plots to help him in his quest: "I will give you a sword, and with that perhaps you may slay the beast; and a clue of thread, and by that, perhaps, you may find your way out again." So armed, Theseus is led away by night to the labyrinth, and is forced to enter

> into that doleful gulf, through winding paths among the rocks, under caverns, and arches, and galleries, and over heaps of fallen stone. And he turned on the left hand, and on the right hand, and went up and down, till his head was dizzy; but all the while he held his clue. For when he went in he had fastened it to a stone, and left it to unroll out of his hand as he went on; and it lasted him till he met the Minotaur, in a narrow chasm between black cliffs.
>
> And when he saw him he stopped awhile, for he had never seen so strange a beast. His body was a man's; but his head was the head of a bull, and his teeth were the teeth of a lion, and with them he tore his prey. And when he saw Theseus he roared, and he put his head down, and rushed right at him.

The agile Athenian steps aside and begins stabbing the monster as a picador wounds his adversary, and then pursues the wounded beast "through cavern after cavern, under dark ribs of sounding stone, and up rough glens and torrent-beds, among the sunless roots of Ida, and to the edge of the eternal snow went they, the hunter and the hunted, while the hills bellowed to the monster's bellow."

The imagery, topography, adventure, and horror of Kingsley's tale of Theseus and his Cretan perils never left Evans. Even before he gazed upon the slopes of Mount Ida with his own eyes, Evans sought out the

Minotaur and his lair in the Balkans. And once he did set foot on the shores of Minos's island, he rediscovered much of the Athenian hero's righteous determination in his own search for the labyrinth and its denizens.

The coins, fossils, rings, brooches, and books at Nash House were a form of escape for young Arthur from the world of unspeakable hardship that followed his mother's death. The hours he spent in solitary reading were an incubation period for what emerged when he left his private retreat of self-learning and joined his social class and generation at school.

Prehistoric Times

At the end of the eighteenth century, Danish historians had suggested that mankind's early history should be treated in stages reflecting innovations in weaponry and, as Hesiod had done for the early Greeks, they proposed a succession of ages from Stone, to Copper, to Iron. This tripartite system was formalized in Christian J. Thomsen's *Guide to Northern Antiquities,* an orderly catalogue of the National Museum in Copenhagen, an English edition of which appeared in 1848. It became a model for antiquarians throughout the world and remains in use today.

As the antiquarianism of the eighteenth century gave way to systematic inquiry and as dedicated, full-time archaeologists sought recognition among the emerging sciences, a number of definitions were posited to fix the limits of what they did and thereby justify themselves in the eyes of their fellows in learned society. One of the most comprehensive, eloquent, and instrumental was that formulated by Charles T. Newton. Born in 1816 and educated at Shrewsbury and Christ Church College, Oxford, Newton joined the Department of Antiquities at the British Museum in 1840 and gained firsthand experience of a wide range of artifacts from all over the world. His personal experience very much shaped the definition he read to the Oxford meeting of the Archaeological Institute on June 18, 1850:

The record of the Human Past is not all contained in printed books. Man's history has been graven on the rock of Egypt, stamped on the brick of Assyria, enshrined in the marble of the Parthenon—it rises before us a majestic Presence in the piled-up arches of the Coliseum . . .—it is embodied in all the heirlooms of religions, of races, of families; in the relics which affection and gratitude, personal or national, pride of country or pride of lineage, have preserved for us—it lingers on the lips of the peasantry, surviving in their songs and traditions, renewed in their rude customs with the renewal of Nature's seasons—we trace it in the speech, the manners, the type of living nations, its associations invest them as with a garb—we dig it out from the barrow and the Nekropolis, and out of the fragments thus found reconstruct in museums of antiquities something like an image of the past— we contemplate this image in fairer proportions, in more exact lineaments, as it has been transmitted by endless reflections in the broken mirror of art.[16]

Newton asserted that the function of archaeology was "to collect, to classify, and to interpret all the evidence of man's history not already incorporated in Printed Literature," and he regarded the evidence as threefold: oral, "spoken language, manners, customs"; written, "documents and manuscript literature"; and monumental, "remains of architecture, painting, and sculpture, and the subordinate decorative and useful arts." One who would undertake such an endeavor

> must combine with the aesthetic culture of the Artist, and the trained judgment of the Historian, not a little of the learning of the Philologist; the plodding drudgery which gathers together his materials, must not blunt the critical acuteness required for their classification and interpretation; nor should the habitual suspicion which must ever attend the scrutiny and precede the warranty of archaeological evidence, give too skeptical a bias to his mind.

For the archaeologist to do his work well, "he must travel, excavate, collect, arrange, delineate, decipher, transcribe, before he can place his whole subject before his mind."

Newton's broad view expressed the discipline as it developed at the time. His definition of archaeology very much suited the generation of John Evans and his colleagues, who were busy classifying the diverse evidence available from the great ages of Stone, Copper, and Iron. John Evans's father had encouraged the direction he would take, and his major contributions to Newton's grand synthesis were in two fields. The first was his studies of coins and medallions: between 1851 and 1872 he contributed forty-seven papers, for part of the time edited the *Numismatic Chronicle*, and served as president of the Numismatic Society. But it was his contribution to the second field that earned him his elevated status in the world of learning: his expertise in those chipped stone tools his father had first taken him to find at Box Hill became widely known, and his contribution to solving the problem of their age won him a place in archaeological history.

The new history of the earth as modern geologists told it had obvious implications for the history of man. Jacques Boucher de Crèvecoeur de Perthes, a man of means who was director of a customhouse at Abbeville, near the mouth of the Somme river in northern France, had been attracted to the chalky plateau of Picardy, where he collected fossils from the banks of the river. While Arthur Benoni Evans was introducing his son John to "fossilizing" in England, Boucher de Perthes began following the cuttings of railroad engineers who were digging a canal and laying a track near Abbeville. He observed the fresh-cut layers of chalk terraces thirty-three meters above sea level, and he set about classifying by type the species they contained. From layers beneath what he presumed were those indicating the Great Flood of the Bible, and mixed with the fossils of species such as the mammoth, the southern and straight-tusked elephants, and the early bison and rhinoceros—all long since extinct—he found examples of flints that, he realized, had been shaped by humans as primitive tools. Between 1830 and 1838 he displayed many of these worked flints in Abbeville. He also published descriptions of the objects and their contexts together with measured drawings in a five-volume series entitled *De la Création: essai sur l'origine et la progression des êtres* (On the Creation, an essay on the origin and progress of beings), which appeared between 1838 and 1841. His ideas were met with skepticism bordering on ridicule at the Académie des Sciences and the Académie des Inscriptions et Belles-Lettres in Paris. But he was not dependent on the academics' idea of his intellectual standing, and he persisted in his convictions, gave a public address at the Académie des Sciences in 1846, and privately published a new study, *Antiquités celtiques et antédiluviennes* (Celtic and antediluvian antiquities), in 1847.

In England, similar evidence was being presented by amateurs who received similar rebuffs from the experts. In 1797, one John Frere sent a notice to the Society of Antiquaries about some worked flints from gravel pits near Hoxne, in Suffolk. Frere found the tools with a huge jawbone of "some unknown animal" in a deposit beneath a layer of sand mixed with sea shells which, he believed, at one time must have been the bottom of the sea or a stretch of coastline. He commented that the "situation in which these weapons were found may tempt us to refer them to a very remote period indeed, even beyond that of the present world."[17] Frere's notice was published in 1800, but not given the attention it deserved until it was revived as part of a growing body of evidence collected by John Evans in 1859.

Evans, admitted as a fellow of the Geological Society in 1857, kept up with the claims from around the country that the products of human hands occurred in sediments that also contained the bones of extinct animals and so indeed lay beyond "the present world." Another such claim had been made by a Roman Catholic priest named Father MacEnery, who excavated in Kent's Cavern, near Torquay, between 1824 and 1829, and observed the remains of extinct animals with human products beneath a layer of stalagmite, or calcium carbonate deposited by the very slow process of water dripping from the ceiling of the cavern. He had presented his evidence to William Buckland, who declared that the stone implements were those of ancient Britons of the Roman period and that they had been cut into the stalagmite layer only recently and so their association to the extinct animals was fortuitous.[18] Very much an outsider, MacEnery did not force his views or publish his results; he died in 1841, disenchanted with the world of learning and with his belief in what he had seen with his own eyes. Only in 1858 did the Geological Society finally agree to sponsor and supervise excavations in the recently discovered Brixham Cave near Kent's Cavern under the direction of William Pengelly, a recognized geologist who specialized in his native Devonshire. The involvement of reputed scientists, including Charles Lyell, lent an air of respectability to the venture that made the conclusions very difficult to ignore. Pengelly found and, in a manner acceptable to the learned world, recorded that tools of humans were mixed with the bones of extinct animals beneath "a sheet of stalagmite from three to eight inches thick: and having within it and on it relics of lion, hyena, bear, mammoth, rhinoceros and reindeer"—exactly what MacEnery had observed.

John Evans's amazement at these discoveries and their consequence for human history was expressed in a letter to Fanny Phelps in late

March 1859. "Think of their finding flint axes and arrowheads at Abbeville," he exclaimed,

> in conjunction with bones of Elephants and Rhinoceroses 40 ft. below the surface in a bed of drift. In this bone cave in Devonshire now being excavated by the Geological Society they say they have found flint arrowheads among the bones, and the same is reported of a cave in Sicily. I can hardly believe it. It will make my ancient Britons quite modern if man is carried back in England to the days when Elephants, Rhinoceroses, Hippopotamuses and Tigers were also inhabitants of the country.[19]

Joseph Prestwich, spurred on by the results from Torquay, tried to organize a visit by the Geological Society to test the claims that Boucher de Perthes had been making at Abbeville. In the event, only his close friend John Evans was sufficiently motivated. On May 1, 1859, Prestwich and Evans met in Abbeville and the following day Boucher de Perthes led them to some of the nearby gravel pits where he had made most of his discoveries. They found nothing of note and so went to Boucher de Perthes's house to see his collection. Much impressed, Evans described it as "a complete Museum from top to bottom, full of paintings, old carvings, pottery etc. and with a wonderful collection of flint axes and implements found among the beds of gravel and evidently deposited at the same time with them—in fact the remains of a race of men who existed at the time when the deluge or whatever was the origin of these gravel beds took place."[20] They proceeded to Amiens, where they were shown an axe in position in a gravel pit and had a photographer record it, "so as to corroborate our testimony," and collected more examples from workers in the pit.

Prestwich and Evans returned to England and used what little time they could set aside from their duties to prepare a report for the scrutiny of their geological colleagues. It is important to recall that these innovators were outside the strict confines of the university. Here were a papermaker and a wine merchant preparing to present evidence provided by a customs official in order to prove to the learned academy that they had in fact seen what they claimed to have seen and that they were correct in their assumptions as to its meaning, that is, that human beings had lived on this earth for a far greater time than the clerics had allowed for. The weight of responsibility was immense, and Evans certainly felt it, though he was only able to draft his part of the report the day before the meeting of the Royal Society in London on May 26. He wrote to Fanny that he had sent his description of the flints to Prestwich to incorporate them into a lecture, but that Prestwich only had time to give "an indifferent abstract of it and his voice was hardly audible," and had also, "dexterously," managed to forget John's letter. And so, Evans reported, "I had to stand up and give an extempore lecture about these flint implements which I thought I got through very well."

The importance of the occasion and therefore Evans's cause for anxiety can be measured by his next sentence: "There were a good many geological *nobs* there, Sir C. Lyell, Murchison, Huxley, Morris, Dr. Perry, Faraday, Wheatstone, Babbage, etc. so I had a pretty distinguished audience."[21] He seems to have made a strong impression, as the next time he attended the meeting of the British Association in 1861 he was addressed as "Flint Evans," and by early 1862 he was elected a fellow of the Royal Society of London for the Promotion of Natural Knowledge. Founded in 1660, the Royal Society was the oldest scientific forum in Britain; prominent fellows had included the architect Christopher Wren, the astronomer Edmund Halley, and Sir Isaac Newton. With his election in 1865 to the Athenaeum, an exclusive London club named for the ancient Greek center of learning in the temple of Athena, John Evans the papermaker became John Evans the archaeologist.

Evans and Prestwich were now trusted members of the intellectual body whose opinions mattered, and what they said was revolutionary. The great antiquity of man, demonstrated using scientific procedures, became acceptable to the learned community. John Frere and Father MacEnery did not live to see their observations verified. As is so often the case, the keepers of perceived wisdom in any generation, the "wise men" who hold the power of intellectual veto, were unwilling to allow for rapid change. The establishment provides necessary checks and balances on radical new theories, but it also directs the course of future research; the result is that new bodies of evidence and new theories most often come from outside of the university establishment, and it takes at least one intellectual generation, or roughly twenty-five years, before they find sufficient adherents to topple the weight of opinion against them and allow for the reappraisal of their merits.

Boucher de Perthes survived the test of time and delighted in the triumph over his detractors in the French academy. In his *De l'homme an-*

tédiluvien et ses oeuvres (Antediluvian man and his works), published
in 1860, he reminded readers that a quarter of a century earlier, when
he had proposed his theory of the contemporaneity of man with "the
giant mammals," they had demanded more proof. Now his theory had
been tested and proven by British as well as French geologists. Curiously, Boucher de Perthes still saw the need for "the finger of God" to
explain the "convulsions of nature" delineated in the superimposed
strata. Evans and Prestwich likewise favored the catastrophic model;
their paper read to the Royal Society concluded that the "period of
Man and the extinct Mammals . . . was brought to a sudden end by a
temporary inundation of the land,"[22] a clear statement in favor of the
Great Flood, despite the growing acceptance of uniformitarianism
among their scientific colleagues.

The concept of a "pre-historic" period was introduced in 1833 by the
French pharmacist Paul Tournal, who defined it as the time from the
first appearance of man on the earth's surface to the beginning of
the "most ancient traditions" in the historic period, which for him was
the construction of Thebes during the Egyptian Nineteenth Dynasty,
roughly 1200 B.C.[23] Daniel Wilson, in his *Archaeology and Prehistoric
Annals of Scotland,* published in the year of Arthur Evans's birth,
brought the concept of prehistory to a British readership, who accepted
it as the time before written records of people and events. The further
refinement of Paleolithic and Neolithic, Old and New Stone Ages in
prehistory was added by the banker John Lubbock in his *Prehistoric
Times* in 1865.

The idea of a prehistoric stage presumed that human development
was uniform and predictable and that eventually all societies would
"achieve" the complexity that required them to keep written records.
The notion of uniform social development combined with the unifor-
mitarian view of the earth's geological history made Charles Darwin's
theory of natural selection proposed in his *Origin of Species,* published
in 1859, acceptable to naturalists. Darwin's success helped to solidify
his idea of a linear trajectory of human development, which included a
number of predictable stages from the wild ape to the modern *Homo
sapiens.*

The summer of 1859 saw further triumphs for John Evans, at age
thirty-six. On July 23, he married Fanny Phelps. She was thirty-two,
"rather small and a little plump," as Joan Evans reported, "graceful,
with long ringlets and beautiful small hands; accomplished, a good lin-

guist," and a brilliant pianist.[24] Arthur seems to have taken to his stepmother, who had no children of her own, though he would soon leave the nursery she took charge of at Nash House.

Pen-Viper

In September 1860, after a holiday with his father digging ancient pottery from the sea cliffs at Dunwich in Suffolk, Arthur Evans began his formal education. Though he was nine years old, he was considered small for his age and never grew much beyond four feet. He went to Callipers, a preparatory school near Chipperfield, run by C. A. Johns, a keen naturalist and field botanist who encouraged Arthur's love of nature and taught him to observe and classify species of plants and animals in the same way his father had showed him how to organize the products of human hands. Arthur learned to view the landscape with the eyes of a naturalist and delighted in the artistry of creation.

Arthur went to Harrow School in 1865. Initially created almost three centuries earlier to educate the poor children of Harrow, the school eventually allowed "foreigners" from other parishes to attend and by Arthur Evans's time had become one of the most prestigious independent schools of Great Britain, with such noteworthy alumni as Robert Peel, prime minister in 1834–35 and 1841–46 and founder of the British Conservative Party, and Lord Byron, the romantic poet-warrior who fought in the Greek struggle for independence.

Arthur was a young man with penetrating blue eyes, the left set deeper than the right, and thick black hair. As his half-sister learned later from his colleagues, he was recalled as being "small and rather insignificant; his short sight, for which he refused to wear proper glasses, made him carry his head in a rather peering way. Moreover, he suffered from an extreme degree of night blindness, so that in the winter terms at Harrow he needed a friendly guide to steer him to or from afternoon school."[25] His housemaster, the Reverend F. Rendall, seems to have thought him "not so very clever" and complained of his "dirt and untidiness."[26] Arthur began to use a walking stick, less for support than for feeling his way by thrashing it about his intended path. At some point he adopted a slender but sturdy cane which he called Prodger and which became one of his trademarks, as for some men cigars or pipes do. Prodger invariably pointed the way, figured in many a story of his life's adventures, and remained with him longer than any other of his cherished artifacts.

Evans's interest in the natural world, instilled by Johns at Callipers, was further encouraged and complemented at Harrow when, in 1865, the oldest society for natural history in a public school was founded and was addressed by such remarkable figures as John Ruskin, the prominent art critic, and Alfred Russel Wallace, the Welsh naturalist who founded zoogeography and for whom the evolutionary distinction between the fauna of Asia and Australia is named. Arthur became an active member of the society, gave talks on "Mosses" and on "The Antiquity of Man," and exhibited minerals, fossils, antiquities, and coins from his father's collection. To display his appreciation of one species, and no doubt to impress his classmates, he trained a grass snake to pass through his sleeves and emerge from under his collar during lectures. Snakes, both in the flesh and as symbols, continued to fascinate him throughout his life.

During Arthur's first winter break at Harrow, in January 1866, father and son set out for the Continent. Arthur had his first experience of the "horrors of middle-passage," as British travelers called the rough seas at the halfway point in the two-hour crossing from Folkestone to Boulogne, and never quite accustomed himself to being on what he thereafter termed "that uncertain element." They traveled for ten days in northern France, going from pit to pit in search of prehistoric implements, interspersed with business meetings for the father. A year later Arthur, at sixteen, was deemed mature and interested enough to hear his father read a paper at the Society of Antiquaries on the flints he'd been gathering in Ireland.

Only in his last year at school did Arthur Evans emerge from obscurity to become a memorable figure with a marked individuality. His colleague Gerald Rendall recalled that due to his poor eyesight, "the only athletic feat he admitted was 'jumping at conclusions' in a general information paper," but that he was "physically active, of disarming and engaging simplicity, instinctively rebellious against conventions," and possessed "an amused disdain of consequences."[27] Though normally associated with youth, these attributes remained his most distinctive characteristics throughout his life and led him into and then out of many a difficult and dangerous incident.

In the 1869–70 school year, Arthur joined with a friend, S. H. Hood, to resuscitate the *Harrovian,* to which he contributed a natural historian's view of "Harrow Animals." His catalogue included the *Aper domesticus,* or bore, *Canis ignavus,* the lazy dog, and *Rāna parasīticus,* the "toady" or "sycophant." A darker side, recalling his grandfather's un-

happy moments, emerged in the winter of 1869, when Arthur produced *Pen-Viper, a comic and satirical magazine,* a two-page quarto
sheet, which included the following advice to a would-be Harrovian:
"The first great thing you should do is to be as noisy as you can . . .
Then you shouldn't be squeamish about telling a few lies to the masters
. . . talk as much slang as possible . . . through reading as many two-
shilling novels as possible . . . Of course I needn't tell you that to work
at all in school . . . would be very much against you." This was all too
close to the voice of *The Cutter,* and it signaled an unhappy period in
Evans's life.

At Harrow, as at most schools charged with educating the nation's
gentlemen, students were forced to adopt the British obsession for classical antiquity, instigated largely by the effects of a London group called
the Society of Dilettanti. Founded in 1734, the Dilettanti supported archaeological research in Italy, Greece, and the Near East, and through
their publications sparked a popular interest in a subject otherwise restricted to the wealthy noblemen for whom the grand tour was a necessary component of their education. The area that had comprised
ancient Greece, well known through the writings of ancient authors,
since 1453 had been a part of the Ottoman Empire—the Muslim dominion founded in the fourteenth century by Osman I. Romantic and
largely Christian Europeans, who idealized Greece as the birthplace of
their own art and democracy, found this situation intolerable.

In many ways, the west European attitude toward the Ottoman Empire recalled that of the twelfth- and thirteenth-century Crusaders, the
Christians sent by the Pope to defend Christendom from "infidels,"
"heretics," and "schismatics" in the East. Initially conceived to assist
Christian Greeks against the Seljuk Turks in Asia Minor and to safe-
guard the pilgrim routes to the Holy Sepulchre in Jerusalem, the eight
Crusades became a confusion of ideals and politics, but always with the
manifest goal of recovering from Islam those places deemed as holy by
the Christians.

When Britain established a protectorate in the Ionian Islands, between Italy and Greece, in 1815, it provided a base for the philhellenes,
wealthy aristocrats who devoted their energies, their fortunes, and in
extreme cases—as with Lord Byron—their lives to the Greek independence movement. This movement sparked a war with Ottoman Turkey
in 1821 and led to the establishment of the new state of Greece at the
Conference of London in 1832. Perhaps the clearest statement of the

British identification with the ideals of philhellenism was Percy Shelley's "We are all Greek . . . But for Greece, we might still have been savages and idolators," from the preface to his great poetic work "Hellas."[28]

The glorification of classical Greek art and everything to do with Athens in the fifth century B.C. had been canonized for the modern era with the publication of Johann Winckelmann's 1764 *Geschichte der Kunst des Altertums* (History of ancient art), in which the Parthenon and its sculptures were exalted as the eternal standard by which beauty should be measured. Ancient Greek writers and philosophers were placed at the fountainhead of knowledge, and their works were considered the basis for all learning. Evans's "instinctive rebelliousness against conventions," together with the broadminded view of antiquity he shared with his father, brought him into conflict with Harrow's restricted horizons. He joined the debating society and took the firm stand "that the present system of classical education is carried to excess." But he knew that to continue being a member of the social elite and to attend the university his family had been associated with for generations, he would have to gain a proficiency in ancient Greek, though he refused to compromise himself completely and didn't learn the complex and difficult system of accents that guided breathing and pronunciation. In the end, Arthur did moderately well in most subjects and excelled, surprisingly, only in ancient Greek composition, though he remonstrated against the "tyranny of accents" by submitting his prizewinning verses unaccented.

When Evans left Harrow, Rendall, his housemaster, wrote on his behalf to the principal of Brasenose College, Oxford: "you will find him a boy of powerful original mind I think, if any questions in your matriculation examination should take him off the beaten track."[29] Evans rejected outright his father's invitation to join the family business as a partner, preferring instead to pursue the leisurely life of learning he felt was his due.

Evans took his contrary stance toward "the Greeks" with him to Oxford, where he matriculated at Brasenose in 1870. Dissatisfied with his tutors and the syllabus, in December 1871 he passed, without distinction, the "Mods," or Moderations—the first public examination, essentially a preparation for the much more demanding and specialized "Greats," a concentrated course of study in a specific discipline. The obvious course of study would have been that in which the university and his father placed great store and where his experience and expertise lay—the antiquity of man and the classics. Instead, he followed an un-expected direction and read for the recently established school of mod-ern history, whose Regius Professor, William Stubbs, was composing his *Constitutional History of England.* Evans cared little for Stubbs and his narrow scope of interest; another Oxford don was writing a differ-ent sort of history, called linguistic, which Evans found more appealing and, in the long run, more impressive.

Smiter of Pashas

The German philologist Max Müller, who began studying the Avesta, the Zoroastrian sacred text written in Old Persian, had moved to Ox-ford in 1849, where he became professor of comparative philology in 1868. Soon after Müller's arrival in England, the British East India Company engaged him to translate the "Rigveda," the most ancient of the Hindu sacred hymns, from Sanskrit, the classical language of India and Hinduism. Müller's English rendition introduced to British and European scholars the tale of the Aryans who migrated long ago into India from the northeast. (The literal meaning of the Sanskit word *arya* is "noble.") Müller's interest was in the spread of language and ideas, but it wasn't long before speculation about the Aryans' ethnicity began, and the migration in Hindu myth became a historical reality.

Earlier in the century, the science of historical linguistics had been merged with the science of folklore by two Germans, the brothers Grimm, who, in their pursuit of legal manuscripts of the Middle Ages, gathered the first systematic collection of folktales—now well known as *Grimm's Fairy Tales.* But the line between story and history vanished when Jacob Grimm, who observed the regularity of sound change in vowels and consonants from the various languages he studied, demon-strated the principle of the regularity of correspondence among conso-nants in genetically related languages—the basis for the linguistic law he postulated, which proved "all the nations of Europe migrated an-ciently from Asia." Grimm's simple explanation was the "irresistible im-pulse" to march from east to west.[30]

Max Müller waxed lyrical on Grimm's "impulse" in his 1859 *History of Ancient Sanskrit Literature,* stating that the "main stream of the Aryan nations has always flowed towards the north-west. No historian can tell us by what impulse those adventurous nomads were driven on through Asia towards the isles and shores of Europe," he admitted, "but whatever it was, the impulse was as irresistible as the spell which in our own times sends the Celtic tribes towards the prairies, or the regions of gold across the Atlantic." Müller's fantasy, essentially a foundational epic for European society, idealized those early adventurers as men of strong individuality and great self-dependence—in other words, perfect ancestors for the leaders of Europe's modern social movements.

The Indo-Aryan homeland was identified as the Caucasus, the steppes north and east of the Caspian Sea—a traditional boundary between Asia and Europe. The Aryan story soon became a key part of the historical imperative for asserting the overall superiority of the white, or Caucasian, racial type, believed to be the antecedent of tribes that migrated long ago from the Caucasus and whose acme was beheld in the modern Germanic race. The French diplomat and social thinker Joseph-Arthur de Gobineau championed the doctrine of Germanic supremacy in his *Essai sur l'inégalité des races humaines* (Essay on the inequality of the human races), published in four volumes from 1853 to 1855, in which he declared that a society's fate was determined by its racial composition. His thesis, that the Germanic Aryans would retain social superiority only if they retained racial purity and didn't dilute their genetic inheritance through mixing with inferior black and yellow strains, became the basis for the political movement called Gobinism at the end of the century; the German philosopher Friedrich Nietzsche used it to create his ideal of the *Übermensch*, or superman. But, already in 1869, the great German composer Richard Wagner began to weave elements of his nation's mythic superiority into his works drawn from the Teutonic tales gathered by the brothers Grimm. Much as Kingsley had done for the Greeks, Wagner dramatized the essential elements of Germanic and Old Norse myth, such as the sacred ash tree, Yggdrasil, at the center of the universe and the personification of natural forces, like the Valkyries and the Rhinemaidens, who fashioned a supernatural tool for ultimate enlightenment, the golden Ring of the Nibelung, from divine light. The tales were at the center of his operatic work *Der Ring des Nibelungen*, the drama of which culminates with the premature death of the warrior Siegfried, who symbolizes individual strength and outstanding courage. The operas brought the legends to the public at the time when Anglo-Saxons were themselves searching for clues to their highly evolved ethnic origins. Evans came to Oxford just as the Aryans marched from myth into history, and he was as proud as any other to proclaim his connection to them.

Arthur's first opportunity for travel came with the end of Trinity Term in June 1871, when he set out with his brother Lewis to spend the Long Vacation on the Continent. Intent on cutting a dashing figure, Evans left Britain in a dark cloak with a scarlet lining, but on the advice of a French customs official concerned that he might be mistaken for a spy and "shot down like a dog," he reluctantly hid the cloak in his case. This was only a month after the conclusion of the brief but bloody Franco-Prussian War, declared by the Emperor Napoleon III in July 1870 but incited by the Prussian chancellor, Otto von Bismarck, in an attempt to place Prince Leopold, of the Prussian royal house, on the Spanish throne. The defeat of France in that war marked the end of French hegemony in Europe and resulted in the creation of a unified Germany.

"At Amiens we at once found ourselves among the Prussians," Evans wrote home, "such fine soldiers and such excellent precision." He could see for himself Gobineau's Aryans, and was suitably impressed. Prussia's triumph over France was largely due to its well-trained and professional army, he believed, with its code of honor that was the ideal of British schoolboys. Arthur took his brother to the local gravel pits, where he was relieved to find that the "Prussians have not taken to flint collecting yet," but that, to his irritation, "they go about buying up all coins found and are seen everywhere after butterflies and insects." His notes on troop movements around Amiens, recorded in his first letter home from Paris, are early signs of a seemingly innocent and boyish amusement that landed him repeatedly on the wrong side of the authorities. At Versailles, the brothers attended a sitting of the National Assembly under the presidency of Louis-Adolphe Thiers, a shrewd politician who had changed his allegiance at the outset of the war and thus survived the transfer to Prussian administration, becoming the first president of the French Third Republic. A month earlier Thiers had led German troops against a workers' insurrection in Paris, effectively ending the aspirations of the French Socialist movement. Evans considered Thiers a deceitful turncoat, and, as his half-sister recalled, he retained "a lifelong distrust of the political capacities of the French nation" as a result of this visit.[31]

The young brothers set out from the disturbed but orderly Paris to the decidedly unstable states of Slovenia and Croatia, then within the dominion of the Ottoman Turks, whose waning authority left an impoverished rural society cut off from the rest of the world. The Balkans were terra incognita to the British; Evans was unprepared for anything or anyone that greeted him when he entered the small town of Kostainica, southeast of Zagreb. Here the enigmatic East met the familiar West: Turkish men wore dark baggy trousers with crimson scarves wound round their waists, blue sleeveless jackets richly embroidered with blue and gold, and bright red fezzes on their heads. Arthur returned to Oxford with a complete outfit, though there can't have been many suitable occasions when it could be worn. It was a constant reminder during the gray winter months at Oxford of the bright new world he had discovered in the Balkans.

Evans's earliest scholarly publication, "On a hoard of coins found at Oxford," appeared in the *Numismatic Chronicle* that year. To see one's name in print for the first time is a true landmark in the life of a scholar; Evans now joined an exclusive group of recognized specialists. That he accomplished this at the age of twenty, while still an undergraduate, demonstrated his confidence in the subject from an early age and his ability to communicate his thoughts decisively. It also showed what family connections, his father's, could do. It was the first of many contributions that displayed Arthur's capacity to notice and describe artifacts in minute detail. And numismatics taught him a manner of thinking that he extended to other disciplines. Like his father, he became interested in objects chiefly from owning them. He would write up reports on a class of artifact around the nucleus of one or more in his private possession. No matter how objective and scientific the treatment, the subjective element of an object's monetary value was always tangled with its academic worth and with the personal pride of the collector. A further confusion came from Evans's strong sense of proprietary rights over the identification and interpretation of the material.

The next Long Vacation, in 1872, provided another opportunity for travel abroad, and this time Arthur took his brother Philip Norman, who was still at Harrow. His letters home formed the basis for his first journalistic writing; they were published as "Over the Marches of Civilized Europe" in *Frazer's Magazine* the following May. In this article we experience in remarkable detail the bright world of the Carpathian Mountains, with their flora, fauna, and human populations meticulously observed through the wide eyes of two boys relishing each adventure—from sleeping in the rough to drawing their revolvers when crossing border lines in forests where they hoped no guards would appear to ask for papers they did not possess. Here was Walsh's *Narrative of a Journey* with a *Boy's Own Annual* flavor, spiced with incongruous comparisons that could only be made by an antiquarian. For example, Evans marveled at how the Wallachs of Romania prepared food in jars whose shape he likened to those that might have come from a Bronze Age barrow, or burial ground; and the mountain men, he observed, wore a "broad leathern dagger-belt round their waist indented with strange spiral decorations, and curiously reminding one of the bronze belts discovered in the pre-historic cemetery at Hallstadt[sic],"[32] the early Iron Age cemetery in northern Austria used from roughly 1100 to 450 B.C. Evans was more acquainted than most with the early costume and weaponry of the region, for his father had excavated at Hallstatt in 1866 and carried home fine examples of axes, knives, spearheads, and other artifacts engraved with the typical spirals of early European art.

Evans devoted himself to his studies throughout 1874, but broke down during exams and was unable to answer any question on history more recent than the twelfth century, which provoked some debate among his examiners. As at Harrow, he failed to distinguish himself, instead barely managing to get a "first" class degree, reluctantly signed in December by W. Stubbs and both history examiners, G. W. Kitchen and J. R. Green, thanks to the collegiate coercion of one of the modern history tutors, Edward Freeman, who saw some potential in young Arthur, and to the committee's awareness of his father's high standing in learned society.[33]

When he graduated, "Arthur Evans at twenty-four was a fantastically conceited young man who knew better than anyone how great were his especial gifts; and he set about using them, and making the world value them, as best he could," his half-sister recorded.[34] He was well aware of the comparison made at the time between himself and his father; J. R. Green, his examiner, referred to Arthur as "Little Evans—son of John Evans the Great."[35] In many ways he was a protégé of his father, trained by him from a young age in gathering and sorting artifacts of all descriptions and in extracting their historical value. But the inevitable comparison left Arthur little room to express his individuality. Unlike his father, who had worked hard to create positions of trust and respect in the two worlds of industry and learning, Arthur never felt the pressure to do so. He took for granted the stability of a comfortable home and obedient staff, the Oxford tailor who satisfied his expressive sartorial needs, the cobbler who monitored the wear and tear the traveler put to his fine hand-sewn boots, and the guaranteed allowance of £250 a year provided without question. Like many sons of wealth rebelling against conservative parents and the ease with which life's material advantages came, Arthur was drawn to the idealized humanistic views of William Gladstone. The "Grand Old Man of Liberalism," Gladstone, as prime minister from 1868 to 1874, led one of the strongest governments of the Victorian era; but it was his compassion for the lower classes, as shown by his stance against the oppressive landlords in Ireland, his charitable works for London's prostitutes, and his concern for the predicament of the underclass in Ottoman Europe in particular, that struck a resonant chord with the idealist in Evans.

So it was that Evans found himself, at the beginning of 1875, ill suited to academic research and looking for a direction in life. Dr. Henry Montagu Butler, headmaster of Harrow and always eager to promote his boys, suggested that Evans consider doing some real historical research: "You are one of the few Harrow men of the last fifteen years who might do so without presumption," he advised.[36] The study of modern history was a novelty in Britain, but had been a respected part of the curriculum at German universities for over a century, so Evans decided on a summer term at Göttingen under the tutelage of Professor Pauli, a colleague of J. R. Green and admirer of William Stubbs.

On the way to Göttingen, Evans stopped at Trier, where he was delighted to find diggers happily looting tombs in the Roman cemetery outside the city. This was a time when ancient relics were easily accessible to anyone with the inclination and resources to dig for them, and Evans, like many of his generation, was spoiled by this free access. The following day he hired his own workmen and joined in the plunder. "When we came to anything by digging I cut it out of the sand with a knife, and it was most exciting work," he wrote home.[37] The finds were numerous but hardly important: lamps, pottery, a corroded fibula (an ancient dress pin), and a number of coins.[38] His personal value system based on financial worth allowed him to treat as commonplace objects that modern archaeologists are obliged to record and publish in detail; the finds from Trier became his personal trinkets, which he packed into a large crate and shipped to his father.

Evans's summer term in Göttingen was spent less in pursuit of the past than in explorations of the present. His letters reveal his shock at the condition of the peasants in the surrounding villages; there he observed that the "fever-stricken inhabitants" lived in "indescribable filth" within "a few miles of a university with seventeen professors of medicine." The naturalist in him was especially offended by the state of the countryside: "wherever small holdings exist, as here and in France, so surely are trees and half the pleasures of life destroyed." Evans's ideal system was that of the squires in Britain: hereditary landholders charged by a central authority with overseeing agricultural production on large estates. What greeted him in Germany were the worst effects of a "squireless" society.[39]

In Göttingen he completed the groundwork for a more systematic return to the land beyond Zagreb; this time he had a passport and a plan. Pleased by the reception of his first travel story, he intended to turn the next foray into a more substantial piece of written work with modern illustrations, for which he bought a camera—broken early on and not used. He adorned his little notebook with the Bosnian coat of arms, and prefaced it with a list of useful Bosnian words, notes on government, religion, ethnic types, currency, and a précis of the prominent leaders and events in the agitated region's history.

During the second and first centuries B.C., the Romans conquered the Illyrian tribes in what is today Bosnia and Herzegovina, incorporating them into the province they called Dalmatia. The Goths drove out the Roman armies in the fifth century A.D. but in their turn were forced out early in the sixth century by the Emperor Justinian I, who claimed the territory for the expanding Byzantine Empire—named for the ancient Greek colony of Byzantium, which had become New Rome under Constantine the Great in A.D. 324, who later called it Constantinople, modern Istanbul. The last major population change had come with the Slavic migrations of the sixth and seventh centuries, when Croats settled in western, central, and northern Bosnia, and Serbs occupied what is now Herzegovina. Northwestern Bosnia was conquered by Charlemagne's Franks early in the ninth century but was returned to Byzantium in the tenth. Byzantine rule ceased in 1180 and Bosnia became independent for almost three centuries, until 1463, when Constantinople took charge once again, this time under the new authority of the Ottoman Turks, who only a decade earlier had conquered the great city on the Bosporus. Over the next century a large part of the native population converted from Christianity to Islam, as the economic and social benefits for Muslims became apparent.

Ottoman rule in the Balkans brought with it both enlightenment—as prosperous urban centers like Sarajevo and Mostar became centers of learning with great schools, libraries, and mosques built for the

Muslim inhabitants, who commissioned elaborate fountains and elegant bridges, many of which lasted until 1992–93, when they were deliberately destroyed by the Bosnian Croat militia—and the misery of
increasingly burdensome taxation on the rural population, especially
those who adhered to Christian beliefs. The recent effects of these
taxes, coupled with a particularly bad harvest in 1875, triggered the revolt that awaited Evans in Bosnia and Herzegovina. His half-sister later
likened his arrival to that of the storm petrel, a winged herald that
swoops over agitated waters, but this comparison only disguises the
fact that Arthur was aware of the impending trouble and made his
plans accordingly.[40] For the budding journalist, this really was a case of
going to the right place at the right time.

At the end of July, the very month when the insurrection against the
Turks broke out, Arthur joined his brother Lewis at Zagreb. They set
sail along the Save river, the boundary between Christian Croats on the
western bank, controlled by Vienna since the reconstitution in 1867 of
the Habsburg monarchy to rule Austria-Hungary, and the Muslim
Serbs on the east. The beginning of a succession of hostile encounters
with officials of various nationalities—the brash young Englishman
seemed to have a knack for this—came at their first stop in the town of
Brood. Despite his overtly British costume—a single-breasted jacket
with box pleats and a fitted belt, known as the Norfolk coatee and designed as a Victorian gentleman's country and sports wear, topped with
a Solar Topee, or pith helmet, which colonial soldiers in India wore—
the Austrian police, evidently untrained in contemporary fashion, arrested Evans and his brother as spies for Russia, which was currently
poised to enter on the side of Serbia and Montenegro in their struggle
against Turkey. They were detained until the mayor personally secured
their release.

The following day they crossed into Turkish Bosnia with a pass
signed by Dervish Pasha (high-ranking soldiers and civil servants in the
Ottoman Empire appended the Turkish honorary title of *Paşa* to their
names), the governor general, who had just declared a state of martial
law throughout the country. As the young men rambled south, the tension in the district intensified; by the time they reached Sarajevo, ar-
sonists had attacked the city's Christian quarter and British tourists
were billeted at Her Majesty's consulate. Arthur, ignoring the friendly
fetters of official precaution, soon found his way into the old quarter of
the city in search of curios; instead, he found himself once again facing

an Austrian authority. This time they got his nationality right but accused him of being a paid agitator, sent from England to whip up discontent among the Christians. The British consul intervened, and the
brothers were dispatched south to Mostar, named for its stone bridge
(*most* in Serbo-Croat) across the Neretva River, a masterpiece of Ottoman engineering built in the sixteenth century and destroyed in
1993. The consul arranged for them to join a caravan of sixty horsemen, who saw them safely through Herzegovina to Metkovic, near the
Dalmatian frontier.

Dalmatia, a name probably derived from the Delmata tribe of the
ancient Illyrians, is the narrow strip of Adriatic coastline, including a
sprinkling of islands, to the west of Herzegovina. The Illyrians entered
written history when Greek colonists began to settle the islands in the
fourth century B.C. and came into conflict with them. They appealed to
their Roman allies, who initiated the lengthy Roman-Illyrian wars,
ending in 155 B.C. with the fall of the capital at Delminium, after which
the province became Dalmatia. Between the Roman conquest and the
establishment of Venetian rule in 1420, the strategic coastal cities
passed through the hands of Greeks, Magyars, Tartars, Croatian and
Serbian princes, Venetians, Sicilians, and crusading Normans. Three
and a half centuries of Venetian prosperity and culture, called the Croat
Renaissance, lasted until 1797, when Venice was given to Austria, in
whose control Dalmatia remained, with the exception of a decade of
Napoleonic command from 1805, until the First World War.

The Evans brothers entered the ancient Illyrian homeland on a "flat
beetle-like craft" hired at Metkovic to take them down the Neretva
River to the Adriatic coast. The journey took on mythic proportions as
Evans recorded, "Just beyond Fort Opus ever and anon mysterious
boomings and bellowings are heard to proceed as from the inmost recesses of the mountain. It is, say those who have heard it, as the bellowing of a bull." The rational explanation of pent-up air in submerged
caverns occurred to him, but Evans preferred a version of Charles
Kingsley's beastly creation: "A veil of mystery hangs over the whole . . .
nothing but the portent is certain; and fearful as I am of giving publicity to ill-omened words, I cannot refrain from breathing a suspicion
that this unhallowed bellowing may proceed from some hideous Minotaur, caverned in his labyrinthine den."[41] Whether in earnest or in jest,
Evans revealed his fascination with the bull-headed monster long
before he saw Crete's Mount Ida or Minos's Knossos. The mythical

EVANS' 1873 ROUTE

ROUTE — - — - —
STATE BORDERS ————
RIVERS ⌇⌇⌇

metaphor for the repressed beast in man, manifested by his own "volcanic nature," haunted him, and did so for the whole of his life.

Once on the coast, Evans and his brother roamed southward through a countryside that intoxicated the naturalist in Evans with its "Southern vegetation" of vines, pale olive woods, and stately cypress trees, and with country villas "perfumed by gardens where roses and verbenas mingle with citron and myrtle of a more tropical flora." Ragusa, whose modern name is Dubrovnik, with its fine stone houses, Venetian churches, and the grand Palazzo Rettorale, succeeded in casting a spell on Evans as no other place had before:

> Here at last, after painfully exploring some of the turbid streams and runnels of the mediaeval civilization of Bosnia, we take our seat beside the fountain-head of Illyrian culture. This is . . . the "Athens of Illyria" . . . the sweet interpreter between the wisdom of the ancients and the rude slavonic mind, who acclimatized on Dalmatian soil the flowers of Greek and Italian genius . . . the "Palmyra between great empires" . . . the city of Refuge which received . . . the hunted remnants of Christian chivalry who, when Bosnia was trodden down beneath the hoofs of the Infidel, preferred exile to renegation.

Evans's rhetorical manner and poetic expression of idealized insight into the city's Norman history set the tone for much of his subsequent writing, especially when urging his readers to join him in his crusades against "the Infidel."

Evans returned to the less dramatic surrounds of Oxford in September 1875. He tried once more to win a place in one of the colleges, took the exams for fellowships at Magdalen and All Souls but, again, was considered as not the right sort of thinker, and in any case not well suited to the cut-and-dried world of academia. He spent the winter reliving his travels and recasting his impressions into a manuscript: *Through Bosnia and the Herzegovina on Foot, during the Insurrection, August and September 1875, with an Historical Review of Bosnia and a Glimpse at the Croats, Slavonians and the Ancient Republic of Ragusa.* A Dickinson family connection with the London publisher William Longman provided the outlet and John Evans provided the £100 subsidy to publish Arthur's first book, which duly appeared in June of the following year.

In this book, Evans re-created his discovery of the Republic of Ragusa as one of the great early centers of civilization and commerce, the
secret to its prosperity lying in the "sober genius of both the nobles and
people of Ragusa." And, as in his native land, "The governing classes
looked on their authority, not as a mere prize of birth, but as a sacred
trust"—no "squireless" rabble here. Not surprisingly, and much to the
delight of his British readers, he described a naval empire of traders
stretching as far as the Indian Ocean, which granted its citizens such an
overabundance of enlightenment that it seems to have spilled into the
hinterland: "The greatest glory of Ragusa lies neither in her wealth nor
in her princely hospitality, but rather in the civilizing influence which
she exercised over the most barbarous European member of our Aryan
family."

As all great ages must come to an end, Evans chose the great earthquake of 1667 for the final eclipse:

> It was half-past eight o'clock on the morning of April 6 . . . The
> inhabitants of Ragusa were mostly at home, or in the churches at
> morning prayer, when, without a moment's warning, a tremen-
> dous shock of earthquake overwhelmed the whole city and
> entombed a fifth of the population . . . Marble palaces—the accu-
> mulated embellishments of ages of prosperity—valuable libraries,
> archives, irreplaceable manuscripts . . . all alike perished. The sea
> left the harbour dry four times, and rising to a mountainous
> height, four times threatened to engulf the land. The ships in port
> were sucked into the vortex of the deep, or dashed to pieces
> against each other on the rocks. The wells dried up . . . The sky
> was darkened by a dense cloud of sand. The earthquake was suc-
> ceeded by a fire, and a strong gale springing up spread the flames
> over every quarter of the ruins. Finally, to complete the catastro-
> phe, the wild Morlachs descended from the mountains and pil-
> laged what remained. Ragusa never recovered from the blow.

The cataclysmic end to Evans's first recovered Golden Age is remarkably similar to the one he posited many years later in Crete, when he
next championed a center of civilization that also was submerged in
time beyond the memory of "the West."

An extraordinarily candid exposition of Evans's pomposity and
manifest racism against the landlocked Bosnians comes toward the end

of the book, where he sums up his hostile personal feelings thus: "Nature's gentlemen the Bosniacs certainly are not! . . . they have not sufficient tact to perceive when their impertinence or obtrusive curiosity is annoying . . . they never displayed gratitude . . . In these Illyrian lands I have often been addressed as *brat*, or brother . . . I . . . happen individually not to appreciate this *égalitaire* spirit. I don't choose to be told by every barbarian I meet that he is a man and a brother." We fully expect one of Evans's class and breeding to treat equality as a birthright, not something earned, but nothing prepares us for the shocking extreme he expresses at the conclusion to his assessment: "I believe in the existence of inferior races, and would like to see them exterminated."[42] To embrace the tenets of Gobinism is one thing, but to confess to a belief in the need for genocide is quite another; it exposes the darkest side of Evans's elitist presumptions. His personal interactions were minimal outside the restricted range of the men in his social circle; while he might become sympathetic to the nationalist aspirations of others, even the lowly "Bosniacs," he could not allow close friendships to develop.

The value of Evans's book lay in its myriad detailed observations, ranging from the pleasures of the natural scenery and its wild residents, among which Evans felt truly at home, to the explicit portrayals of the manners and costumes of the inhabitants of the region. The reviewer for the *Manchester Guardian* thought it was "a most opportune contribution to the geography, customs, and history of a country which suddenly emerged from the dimmest obscurity into the full glare of European observation." To Evans's great good fortune, its appearance in June 1876 coincided with Serbia and Montenegro's declaration of war on Turkey. The Sultan's reprisals against civilian populations, now in open revolt throughout the Balkans, became the topic of British public resentment against the Tory Parliament that refused to enter the conflict for fear of disturbing the status quo. Gladstone's fury against the government's apparent complacency exploded in a passionate speech on the "Eastern Question," in which he cited Evans's report of the Bosnian situation. The tone of his speech earned Gladstone, who left retirement and was swept back into power in 1880, the title "the scourge of Turkey," and the undying admiration of the young reporter, himself now somewhat of a scourge.

Suddenly Evans was treated as an expert on Balkan affairs, though he was still without work or direction. In a gesture of affection for his old friend John Evans, Joseph Prestwich, now a professor of geology at Oxford, contacted his nephew C. P. Scott, who had recently become editor of the *Manchester Guardian,* the Liberal newspaper outspoken in its support for Gladstone's stance against the Ottoman rulers in Turkey. Scott made Arthur Evans his special correspondent in the Balkans, an unpaid position providing only for a small sum to cover the cost of telegrams, but an official post nonetheless. In preparation, Evans went to London to meet with W. J. Stillman, the *Times'* Balkan correspondent. An American diplomat, writer, and pioneer photographer, Stillman was a veteran of ethnic conflict: ten years earlier, as American envoy to Crete, he had witnessed and reported vividly on the Cretan insurrection against Turkish rule and its bloody suppression in 1866—an experience that left a deep scar and engendered his mistrust of the Ottomans.[43] The seasoned observer assured the young reporter that there would be war, as Russia and Germany intended to create a South Slavonic confederation while Great Britain was keen to slow Russian expansion and so tried to maintain the status quo by supporting Turkey.

With war in the air, Evans set off for Trieste, then under Austrian control, on January 20, 1877. His guise was that of a journalist but his mission was a confusion of adventure writer, antiquarian, and relief worker. On the journey in 1875 he had met a Miss Irby, who had a Christian school in Sarajevo. Arthur had remained in contact with her and became secretary to the relief fund she had set up in Britain to help refugees, so, when he arrived with supplies and funds, he found himself well placed to gather the information he needed for dispatches and also managed to interview the insurgents.

It was never in his nature to be impartial. Still under the influence of Gladstone, Evans was sympathetic to the Slavic nationalist goal of democratic homelands and could never quite identify with the Muslims. Nonetheless, he found the hate and intolerance on both sides so extreme that it seemed to him the only way to bring peace to the region would be for the Austrian army to impose it by force. This he duly confided to his readers along with reports of civilian massacres at the hands of the Turks, which the British consul continued to deny or downplay.

The historian Edward Freeman, who had taken an interest in Evans at Oxford, was a leading figure in Miss Irby's relief fund. Freeman, born in 1823 and orphaned in infancy yet with sufficient family wealth never to have to worry about earning a living, had been brought up with the

strict ideals of the High Church and the Victorian acceptance of his
overall supremacy based largely on a historical link with the "Germanic
race." He had married his tutor's daughter, Eleanor Gutch, and had two
daughters, Margaret and Helen, before Eleanor's premature death. He
was best known for his six-volume *History of the Norman Conquest,*
which had begun to appear in 1867 and the last volume of which
would come out in 1879, though it had been largely completed by this
time.[44] Freeman was a very vocal member of a movement of historians
and politicians who believed in the rights of nationalities to govern
themselves. His case against "the Turk" was quite clearly stated in his
recently published *The Ottoman Power in Europe,* in which he used history to identify the ancient precedents for his chosen ideals and showed
himself a devoted missionary in the search for proofs to illustrate and
glorify the high level of culture and political unity of Gobineau's
Aryans. Freeman and Evans began a correspondence while the latter
was in the Balkans in 1877, and gradually Freeman came to exert a
strong influence over the young man, who in many ways was adopting
this self-styled country gentleman and outspoken scholar as a role
model.

Freeman came to inspect the relief work at Ragusa on June 18 with
his daughters. Whether one believes in love at first sight or not, it is certain that by the end of the month Arthur and Margaret had given their
hearts to each other. She was a very practical woman, three years his
senior, with a knowledge of ancient and modern languages and a comprehensive knowledge of history, having worked as her father's secretary for many years.

Margaret also shared her father's extreme views on the supremacy of
their race, though she didn't voice them as freely as he did. In a letter to
his naturalist friend W. B. Dawkins shortly after the visit to Ragusa,
Freeman wrote in praise of his young colleague, "We saw a good deal of
Arthur Evans in Dalmatia. He is sending wonderful things to your
Manchester Guardian." The same note continues, "I made some natural
history observations in Greece . . . You may find the tortoises in the
fields, and water-tortoises in the brooks, which later are said to stink as
a Jew."[45] Such observations seem to slip easily from the pen of one filled
with such righteousness as not to recognize his words as offensive. In a
lecture four years later in the United States, Freeman publicly expressed
the wish that every Irishman, the bane of the mid-Victorian British
elite, would murder a Negro, to whom he assigned a similar role for his

American audience, and be hanged for it for the greater good of the Germanic race.[46] When asked to explain his remark to an outraged public, he replied, "While all Teutons are very near to us, no European Aryan is very far from us."[47] Before setting out for Ragusa he had written to Evans regarding *Through Bosnia and the Herzegovina:* "I am reading your book more carefully than I did before. How you notice everything: things about fiddles and pots, which I should never think of, and things about noses and eyes which I always wish to notice, but don't know how."[48] The two seem to have agreed on those "inferior races" that troubled them both, and now Margaret could be called upon to form a bridge between them.

Evans returned to England in the autumn and set about lobbying conservative politicians on behalf of his Slavs. Margaret Freeman returned from Sicily, where she had been assisting her father in his research into the island's Norman history. They were soon formally engaged and spending much of their time together. Edward Freeman was delighted to approve of the union, as he conveyed the news in a letter at the end of March to John Meredith Read, the American ambassador in Athens: "My eldest daughter . . . is going to marry Arthur Evans, whose name you doubtless know as a smiter of Pashas."[49] Thus Arthur's anti-Islamic stance preceded him to the Aegean.

It was a heady time for the young couple looking forward to a lifetime together. They made frequent outings, including a trip to London in March to see the spectacular finds from the tiny hill in Turkey that the German archaeologist Heinrich Schliemann claimed was Priam's Troy, on display at Burlington House. How much of the glitter and romance of the Trojan exploit distracted the two lovers is not recorded. By the end of March, Arthur was off again to Ragusa, where he continued to report on the state of the conflict. He returned to England on September 19, 1878, he and Margaret were married, and by the end of October the couple was en route back to the Balkans. They settled in Ragusa in a modest home called the Casa San Lazzaro, overlooking the sea. Evans continued his journeys into the interior while Margaret stayed on the coast and tried to cope with the domestic wildlife—fleas, flies, and mosquitoes—and the strange food and languages. Her father, who had advised them against settling in such a foreign place, tried to find work for Arthur in Oxford.

In June 1879, Freeman wrote that an archaeological studentship was being funded in England for which Arthur should be an ideal candi-

date. Freeman had been approached to join the recently formed Society
for the Promotion of Hellenic Studies, which met for the first time at
Freemason's Tavern on June 16 with Charles Newton, now Keeper of
Greek and Roman Antiquities at the British Museum, presiding. The
society had grown out of the wish to create a British equivalent to the
French Association pour l'encouragement des études grecques (Association for the Promotion of Greek Studies), and the desire of a growing
number of British scholars to promote the study of ancient and modern Greek language and literature among a wider public than the educated elite. More than fifty members were elected at the first meeting,
including Freeman, and the raising of funds to provide studentships
was discussed.[50]

Acutely aware of his embarrassing succession of prior failures to get
Oxford fellowships, Arthur replied, "I have a mortal horror of Exami-
nations and that kind of thing, and do not want to compete unless the
probabilities of getting the post are on my side . . . Then again one feels
that what is wanted is a student of 'Classical archaeology' and that anyone who wasn't would probably have scant justice done to him at Oxford." His suspicions were well founded, for the studentship was indeed
intended to support Greek and only Greek archaeology. Arthur's reaction shows a deepening of his dislike of the Hellenocentric establishment. "It is quite evident that Athens and no other earthly site is
Newton's goal," he wrote, noting that the word "archaeology" should be
applied more universally and should include prehistoric Europe. He
continued, "Oxford, however, seems to have set itself to ignore every
branch of Archaeology out of its own classical beat."[51]

Margaret was unhappy in her exile from England, her friends, and
her family, and it began to show in the deteriorating state of her health.
She and Arthur both wanted children, but they seemed unable to conceive, and eventually she went to England for an operation. Arthur was
less than attentive; he did not accompany her. Instead, he wrote letters
detailing his exploits, which included more illicit excavations, even rob-
bing skulls from a neighboring church vault for an Austrian army doctor who was also the secretary to the Anthropological Society in
Vienna. His cavalier manner with the recently deceased was equal only
to his treatment of Margaret, a point his stepmother, Fanny Phelps,
made clear to him in a reproving note. She admonished him for his
continued wanderings while his "poor wife" needed attention, but he
brushed off the advice with no small amount of irritation, saying, "I

cannot help thinking that women more than men are always harping on the personal side of the question."[52] For Margaret's sake Evans should have heeded the mature woman's warning, but instead the self-absorbed young man, perhaps aware that he may have made an error by marrying and that his true sexual inclinations, not revealed until much later in his life, lay elsewhere, continued a pattern of neglect until it was too late to rectify it.

Arthur himself eventually fell ill from exhaustion in late 1880 and returned briefly to England for a rest. But by early 1881 he had persuaded Margaret to return to Ragusa. The Austrians in the Balkans were not all the same as the "noble" Prussians whom he had admired so greatly; and considering the Austrians little more than an efficient replacement of the Turks in their oppression, Arthur began a new crusade in favor of his underdog Slavs. He launched a campaign of outspoken criticism of Vienna, which increased in volume both in the British press and locally until he was arrested on March 7, 1882. Whether brash, naïve, or just plain foolish, he had encouraged public opposition to Austrian military rule in the Balkans and had been seen visiting with insurgents, one of whom when himself detained claimed that Evans had given gold sovereigns to his men to turn them against their own commander, who was siding with the Austrians. A shaken Arthur cooled his volcanic nature in detention while his friends and family pestered the Foreign Office to intervene. During the wait, Margaret, also under suspicion, was forced to turn over the letters he had written to her. Every bit her father's daughter she wrote that "you can imagine how I hated it the first day . . . would you like to see all your love letters read by a little Jew at your elbow?"[53] She found that the neighbors were even less friendly than before, and she came to hate her surroundings.

With the repression of the latest rebellion, to which Arthur had been linked, came his release and order to leave Austria on April 23 and never return. Ragusa, the city he had once proudly stated was by birthright a "city of Refuge" for the "hunted remnants of Christian chivalry," withdrew its promise of asylum; it could no longer afford to shelter the unpopular knight-errant. In any case, Evans had become too much a part of the modern history of the city and region to compose the detailed study of ancient Illyria he so longed to do. He would have to content himself with survey articles in the antiquarian periodical *Archaeologia* and entries on modern history in the *Encyclopaedia Britannica*.

Homer's Hero

The abrupt ejection from his beloved Ragusa and forced return to England in 1882 was a great shock and disappointment to the young idealist. It seems the modern world of Balkan politics was not where he belonged, though he continued his involvement from a safe distance. Determined not to resume his standing as "Little Evans—son of John Evans the Great," Arthur went with Margaret to Oxford, where they both had friends and he could begin to look for a position near her family. Arthur and Margaret set up home at Thirty-two Broad Street in the heart of Oxford in early January 1883.

Edward Freeman's health was failing—he complained of gout and bronchitis—but his hateful rhetoric and his belief in the superiority of the Teutonic race were as robust as ever. He had even taken to chastising students and colleagues alike for using words with a Latin base; now only pure German-based English, or at the very least Greek, could be employed in his presence.[54] As a historian concerned with current events, especially when they involved "the Turk," Freeman had been in correspondence with W. J. Stillman over the continued troubles in Crete as early as April 1881. Freeman's views on the matter of Cretan independence, a piece of the very complex puzzle known as the "Eastern Question," as Gladstone had called it in his famous speech, were clearly stated when he asked, "What will happen? Will anything come of a movement which I see is hinted at, for adding nothing to the kingdom, but giving a large autonomy—I hate the word in Roman letters, but I can swallow αυτονομία [autonomia], which I know the meaning of—to a much larger district of enslaved Greece? I should not quarrel with this, as my object is deliverance of the greatest number of Christian souls from the Turk."[55] His declaration of a moral crusade against "the Turk" permeated Freeman's writings, and like all Liberals he was appalled by his government's stance regarding Constantinople. In a note of October 1, 1882, he reminded J. Bryce, M.P., "Every time a British Minister treats the Turk as an equal, calls him Majesty, regards his susceptibility, and all that, the bondage of some bit of Christendom is prolonged."[56] This moral stance, though repulsive to objective historians, compelled Gladstone to offer Freeman the Regius Professorship of Modern History on March 24, 1884. Though it came late in his career, he was glad to accept.[57]

Soon after their return to Oxford, a correspondence in the *Times* appeared that reminded Arthur and Margaret Evans of those early days in their romance when they visited the Trojan exhibit at Burlington House. On January 10, 1883, it was reported that the most recent excavations in Turkey by Heinrich Schliemann had failed to confirm his hypothesis that the mound at Hissarlik was Homer's Troy and that the architectural history he claimed to have unraveled there was implausible.[58]

Schliemann had burst upon the scene only twelve years earlier. Born in 1822, he had spent the first part of his life in trade, with such success that by the age of forty he was a millionaire. Schliemann dedicated the second part of his life to realizing what he later recalled as having been his childhood ambition of discovering the sites where the human heroes of the Homeric poems, Achilles and Agamemnon, Helen and Menelaus, Odysseus, Penelope and Telemachus, had achieved their immortality, and thereby achieving his own. While Arthur Evans at the age of twenty had been busy discovering the intrigues of modern conflict in eastern Europe, Schliemann at fifty was embarked on a seemingly naïve search for the locus of one of the best known of ancient conflicts. In 1871, he sank his first trenches into one of the huge "tells," or mounds formed over many centuries of human occupational debris, that were known along the northwest Aegean coast of Turkey. Schliemann was soon able to declare to the world that he had found the walls that King Priam fought to defend against Achaean Greek aggressors led by Agamemnon: the mythical city of Troy.

Apprenticed to a grocer at the age of fourteen, Schliemann lacked a tutored education, and accepted uncritically the allegorical players in the metaphorical roles of the Greek myths and legends as literal histories, seeking their basis in physical reality. As one later historian put it, "Schliemann began his twenty-two year career as a working archaeologist with the firm conviction that not only was Homer in the *Iliad* to be read as if he were a reliable 'war correspondent' . . . but that the *Odyssey* was a mixture of Ordnance survey and log-book."[59] Had Schliemann had the privilege of regular education, he would have been taught that Greek history began with the first Olympiad, in 776 B.C., and that anything before that remained in the realms of myth and beyond the legitimate interest of the historian. George Grote, a London banker and parliamentarian, in his universally accepted twelve-volume *History of Greece,* published from 1846 to 1856, represented the learned view when he wrote of the Trojan War, "Though literally believed, reverentially cherished, and numbered among the gigantic phenomena of the past by the Grecian public, it is in the eyes of modern inquiry essentially a legend and nothing more."[60]

Schliemann's business acumen together with the power of his wealth gave him the determination and the resources to pursue his goal, legendary or otherwise. After his first visit to the Aegean in 1868 he declared his intention to find the palaces of his childhood heroes to prove that these immortal men did, indeed, once walk the earth. *Ithaque, le Péloponnèse, Troie. Recherches archéologiques* was published the following year.

His Trojan revelations began in 1871 with excavations into the mound at Hissarlik, which he declared concealed Priam's fair city. With more than a hundred unskilled hands in his employ he cut through the huge tell much as a greedy child attacks a Christmas pudding in search of its treasure and found a formation of levels built up over millennia. In a few months he removed tons of soil and recovered thousands of objects from what seemed to be a confusing mass of superimposed building remains. The most spectacular find was a hoard of gold jewelry, which appeared in May or June 1873. As with most discoveries of genuine value, suspicion shrouded this treasure from the outset. Schliemann reported that he had seen the twinkle of gold in a wall, dismissed the workmen for an extra rest period, and then, at great danger to himself because of an overhang, carefully extracted the 250 gold objects, which he called the Treasure of Priam. His Greek wife, Sophia, he recorded, wrapped the precious cargo in her shawl and together they removed the loot to their Athens home.

The publicity of the find brought with it the outrage of the Turkish authorities; though legally entitled to one-third of ordinary finds, Schliemann was required by law to turn over all important, singular, or "original" finds to the state, and his share was to consist only of "duplicates," a vague term to describe objects that occur in such frequency, or are so like others in a similar class, that they aren't worthy of being catalogued. In practice, exact duplicates were rare, but this convenient loophole in the law allowed officials to turn a blind eye to the export of minor artifacts. The Treasure of Priam, however, was no minor collection of artifacts; Schliemann appeased the Turkish state with a 50,000-franc compensation. But the circumstances of the discovery led to suspicion in scholarly Europe, where the treasure's authenticity was questioned. (It continues to arouse suspicion today, as we know now that Sophia was not at Hissarlik at the time, and Schliemann's diary shows him to have been in Athens when he made the entry.)[61]

Schliemann's decision to enhance his own prestige through the popularization of his discoveries touched a raw nerve with European scholars. He would never get from them what he desired most: induction into the prestigious Berlin Academy. Indeed Adolf Furtwängler, the powerful curator of the Berlin Museums—which had been gathering splendors from Greece, Egypt, and the Near East for more than a century, and whose reputation had been made on the study of the Bronze Age pottery that Schliemann found in great abundance—later declared, "He is and remains half-mad, a man of confused ideas who has no idea of the value of his discoveries."[62]

Schliemann's reception in England was quite different. Charles Newton, as doyen of Hellenic archaeology in Britain, was effusive in his praise of "the untiring enthusiasm and liberality of one man, whose achievement entitles him to the gratification not of Greece merely, but of all civilized races, so long as the human Past shall have any interest for mankind."[63] Schliemann's brash pronouncements and the vast golden treasure were featured in the popular press and excited the layman as well as the specialist. At Burlington House, in the presence of Gladstone, he and Sophia became honorary members of the Society of Antiquaries. There in December 1877 the Treasure of Priam was put on display to the delight of Londoners, who formed long queues to marvel at the glittering evidence that proved the discovery of Homer's Troy. Part of Schliemann's popularity and warm reception in England may have been due to his tenacity in the face of his stated humble origins. His early entry into business and his struggle for recognition in Europe, despite the obvious success of his endeavors, were solid points to his credit in the esteem of John Evans and his associates.

In 1874 Schliemann went to Mycenae in search of Agamemnon's palace. This small citadel in the northeastern Peloponnese, known to travelers for centuries by its massive walls of roughly hewn stones and attributed in Greek myth to the building skills of the Cyclops, is best remembered as the locality of the ill-fated House of Atreus, whose misfortunes form the bases for some of the best-known tragedies of classical Greek literature. The story recounts the murder of Atreus, King of Mycenae, by his nephew Aegisthus. His sons, Agamemnon and Menelaus, take refuge in Sparta, where they marry Clytemnestra and Helen, the daughters of their host, Tyndareus. Agamemnon returns to

Mycenae to reclaim the throne, and has a son, Orestes, and three daughters, Electra, Iphigenia, and Chrysothemis. When he is away laying siege to Troy, Clytemnestra plots with her new lover, Aegisthus, who kills the hero on his return; that death is duly avenged by Orestes. But the seat of these tragic sorrows was not the attraction; Homer's glittering references to Mycenae's "broad streets" and "wealth in gold" are what appealed to the treasure hunter in Schliemann.

Due to the adverse publicity surrounding his Turkish dealings, however, he wasn't able to begin digging in earnest there until 1876, after he had bought the support of the powerful Greek Archaeological Society by giving funds to pull down a medieval stone tower that was thought to mar the beauty of the marble buildings of the Athenian Acropolis. This act of vandalism, in our modern viewpoint, was one that Charles Newton boasted of taking part in.

Homer's golden epithet was soon proven to be accurate, as graves just inside Mycenae's city walls were opened and produced a treasure trove of gold and silver vases, jewelry and death masks, the first of which Schliemann declared to be that of Agamemnon himself. Thirty pounds of golden objects—this was how the trader described these priceless artifacts—were removed and sent to Athens, where they became the focal point of the National Archaeological Museum. The finds from these graves, now known as the Shaft Graves of Grave Circle A, excited the art world; with their beautiful representations drawn from nature and figures of elegant women in long robes, they were linked to the spirit of classical Greek art and instantly recognized as its precursors.

On the summit of the Mycenaean acropolis above the grave circle, Schliemann found the remains of a large rectangular building with a wide circular hearth at the center of a great hall; this he called the Megaron, after Homer's "large room" said to lie at the heart of an Achaean king's palace. There was no doubt in Schliemann's mind that Agamemnon himself had sat on his throne before that very hearth.

The dispute about Troy did eventually excite the British archaeologists, and in January 1883 the *Times* made the arguments for and against Schliemann's practices well known. Though the first edition of his *Ilios: The City and Country of the Trojans,* published in November 1880 in the language of his greatest admirers, had sold well, the reviews were generally poor.[64] Perhaps the most confrontational was one by an influential classicist named Richard C. Jebb, at the University of Glasgow, who attacked Schliemann's historical reconstruction of the successive cities, although the alternative he proposed was equally flawed and fanciful. Schliemann's reaction was to contact his small network of potentially friendly reviewers in Britain and bribe them to write replies to the accusations of Jebb and others. His greatest ally in this matter was the Reverend Archibald Henry Sayce, a fellow and tutor at Queen's College, Oxford, who, like Schliemann, was a diverse linguist; his greatest contribution was his Assyrian grammar, though he worked on a number of Near Eastern languages.

As a means of averting further accusations of wrongdoing, Schliemann hired Wilhelm Dörpfeld to lend credibility to his work. Dörpfeld, at twenty-nine, had made a name for himself by introducing the revolutionary concept of stratigraphical archaeology to the German excavations at Olympia, in the northwestern Peloponnese. He showed the older antiquarians how they could rely less on their extremely prejudiced estimates of the chronology of their discoveries by observing, as John Evans and his colleagues were doing in caves and ditches, the position of artifacts in the ground in relation to each other and to the buildings constructed for the Olympic Games over the centuries since 776 B.C. Dörpfeld's detailed recording techniques lent an air of science to what had been little more than a scramble for art treasures, and so Schliemann, hoping to acquire some of the new archaeological respectability, went to Olympia to recruit him in 1881. But the pragmatic Dörpfeld was unable to join him full-time; he had recently been appointed architect of the German Archaeological Institute at Athens, where he brought notions of engineering and materials to a field dominated by impractical observers trained only in art history. However, he did work on a contract basis during the 1882 season at Troy, where he showed Schliemann the technique of digging and observing the superimposed layers of historical periods separately, and so began clarifying many of the errors made during previous seasons of archaeological work. While Dörpfeld and Schliemann seem to have worked well together, the former was not in full agreement with the latter's history of the towns, and this became apparent in a letter he published in the *Allgemeine Zeitung* to refute the claims of a Professor Brentano in a pamphlet distributed in August 1882. Jebb seized upon this disagreement and adopted Dörpfeld's interpretation in a lecture to the Hellenic Society in October. The letters published in the *Times* in January 1883 drew further attention to the struggle Schliemann was having with a highly critical and hostile academic establishment.

Evans was having his own trouble with Oxford University. In March 1883 he wrote to Freeman that

> there is going to be established a Professorship of Archaeology and I have been strongly advised to stand. I do not think I shall unless I see any real prospect of getting it . . . to begin with it is to be called the Professorship of "Classical" Archaeology and I understand that the Electors, including Jowett [Benjamin Jowett, the vice-chancellor] and Newton of the Brit. Mus. (who prevented my getting the archaeological Traveling Studentship of old) regard "archaeology" as ending with the Christian Era. To confine a Professorship of Archaeology to classical times seems to me as reasonable as to create a Chair of "Insular Geography" or "Mesozoic Geology."

Freeman, with his typical malice, replied, "Every ass knoweth his master's crib, and they do it for what they call *Greats*. Of course all those people will make a stand against you, just because you know more than they do and go beyond their wretched narrow circle." But he urged Arthur to submit an application: "just to go in and tell them a thing or two, [even though] they will have some Balliol fool, suspending all sound learning at the end of his crooked nose, to represent self-satisfied ignorance against you."[65]

The post, called the Lincoln and Merton Professorship of Classical Archaeology, was offered to William Ramsay, well known for his explorations in ancient Anatolia, but Ramsay soon left for Aberdeen University. Percy Gardner, who had trained with Charles Newton at the British Museum, then accepted the appointment and brought the ancient world to generations of eager young minds, many of whom were drawn into the field as a result. One such convert was Max Mallowan, later excavator of Nimrud and director of the British School of Archaeology in Baghdad, who recalled that Gardner was "a tall upstanding figure, [who] lectured in a frock coat with winged collar of a type which must have gone back to the 1860s. He gave us of his incomparable store of learning with a permanently bored expression, in a monotone that somehow contrived to rivet our attention."[66] Gardner successfully performed the marriage between text and monument that gave birth to the style of classical archaeology practiced thereafter at Oxford, a union that Evans would never have attempted because of his broad view of world history and prehistory.

The arrival of spring 1883 brought with it the instinct to travel, and with Austrian territories being off-limits, the time had come for the Evanses to experience for themselves the ancient monuments that travelers had marveled at for centuries. Once again Arthur and Margaret left Oxford in the spring and returned to the Balkans, though this time their journey took them past the bittersweet coast of Dalmatia and farther south into a landscape well trodden in the minds of all students of ancient Greek literature but experienced by only a few. They arrived at the sacred oracle of Apollo at Delphi at the beginning of May, just in time for the celebration of spring. Margaret complained of the inferiority of the Greek monuments compared to those of her native country, but Arthur was spellbound as they rode through valleys scattered with bright red anemones, spurge, and yellow sage, and across mountain passes overgrown with all the necessities of an herbalist's kit, with the mixed perfume of sage, rosemary, and oregano rising from the horses' hooves.

Evans felt at full force the shock of this first encounter with the physical setting for the myths, tales, and brave deeds of the ancient Greeks. He also registered the link between the modern natives and their distant relations. "It is hard to imagine a more beautiful picture," Arthur wrote from the village of Stiris, near Delphi, where an Easter dance was in progress, "than this chain of girls in white and scarlet, slowly and stately in measure, as becoming the antiquity of their dance, tripping across the green—a winding glen bright with glowing corn behind them and above, the empurpled steeps, the snows, and cloudy veil of old Parnassus," the rocky height that dominates the heart of central Greece.[67] A week's carriage journey through Boeotia, across the saddle of Mount Helicon, home of the Muses, took them to Leivadheia, where they diverted northeast to Orchomenos to visit the site where Schliemann had gone in 1874 to uncover the citadel of King Minyas but found instead a large vaulted underground chamber that he surmised to be the mythical monarch's last resting place, long since looted. Their journey through the center of the Greek mainland continued to Thebes, once the seat of King Laius, best known for his murder at the hands of his unwitting son, Oedipus, who went on to marry his mother, ignorant of her identity. The ghosts of Greek myth multiplied as they rode into Attica and joined the path followed by Theseus on his way from the Peloponnese to claim his royal birthright in Athens before going on to gain notoriety in Crete.

In Athens they met with Heinrich and Sophia Schliemann in their new home, a neoclassical mansion completed in 1880, called the Iliou Melathron—the Palace of Ilion, or Troy. The visitor was never in any doubt of the owner's enthusiastic identity with ancient Greece: literary aphorisms were painted on the borders of the ceilings, and the walls were decorated with panels depicting not only the events of the Trojan War but also the events and heroes associated with its rediscovery in the modern age. The wooden floors incorporated patterns based on artifacts from Schliemann's excavations at Troy and Mycenae, a detail that Evans recalled and copied when he built his own private palace ten years later. The house was consecrated to the rediscovery of the mythical landscape of the Aegean, and its builder, at the age of sixty-one, had himself become a modern myth.

Evans was intrigued by Schliemann, and he later recalled being mildly amused at "the odd little man and his preoccupation with Homer" and his "spectacles of a foreign make."[68] Nonetheless, years later when it came time for Arthur to take his place alongside the great explorer, he would concede, "In Dr. Schliemann the science of classical antiquity found its Columbus."[69] Schliemann's discoveries, especially the gold work from Mycenae, were an instant success with Evans and left a lasting impression. Evans's growing opposition to the worship in Britain of classical Greek art attracted him all the more to these fresh images from a culture that preceded the glories of fifth-century Athens by several generations. In the gold and silver relief work, especially on the rings and carved gemstones, Evans saw Egyptian and Babylonian elements but something else besides, something indefinable but definitely exciting.

Schliemann left for Oxford soon after, where, with support from Sayce, he was made honorary fellow of Queen's College, and so could don scarlet robes to befit his flamboyant personality when he received his honorary doctorate at the Encaenia ceremony of June 13 and stood for the admiration of all in the Great Quad at All Souls College.

Arthur and Margaret sailed to the island of Aigina in the Saronic Gulf opposite Athens, and then to Nauplion, the first capital of modern Greece, in the northwestern Peloponnese. This was their first experience of Homer's "wine-dark" Aegean Sea, named for the Athenian king Aegeus, who threw himself off the cliffs at the tip of Attica in despair at the thought of losing his son Theseus to the Cretan Minotaur. From the harbor they rode up the Argive Plain to the great citadel at Mycenae, whose massive "Cyclopean" masonry supports a giant frieze sculpted in limestone high above the fort's entrance, with heraldic lions facing a column tapering downward, as if in defiance of the classical orders of architectural style—a stance not lost on this defiant observer. Gradually, Evans succumbed to the same unknown force that had beset Schliemann. Perhaps there *was* something to the odd little man's insistence on the mortality of Homer's heroes. Evans was being drawn into a new world, uncharted, untainted by the dogma of scholars, ripe for exploration and exploitation.

The Evanses remained in the Aegean region until September, when they returned to Oxford. Arthur set to work on writing up his notes on the sites and topography of ancient Illyria made during his residency at Ragusa. Meanwhile Schliemann, wishing to avoid the sort of hostile reviews he had previously received in Britain, approached Edward Tylor, keeper of the University Museum in Oxford, to review his new book *Troja* for the *Academy* in exchange for a gift of Trojan antiquities for the museum.[70] Tylor passed this dubious honor on to Evans, who fulfilled his obligations seriously and submitted a long and detailed assessment in December. Evans used the review to praise Schliemann, on the one hand, stating, "Faith has indeed, 'removed mountains,' and skepticism must henceforth reckon with the spade as well as with the shield. The indomitable industry and persistence of one man conquered; and we may now see mapped out before our eyes, by the hands of competent architects, a city which, if it be not the city of Priam, at least owes its disinterment from the grave of Time to 'the tale of Troy divine.' " But, on the other hand, Evans reminded the reader that "archaeology has perhaps little call to concern itself . . . with poetical topography," and expressed caution at Schliemann's identification of the site as Troy, preferring to call it "the hill of Hissarlik." But he emphasized that the excavations "have a profound and enduring interest in their bearing on the prehistoric past of the birth-places of Hellenic civilization."[71] He made the case for the origin of many vase forms of later Greece with those found at Hissarlik, but also pointed out similarities between the earliest pottery found there and that found in Swiss and north European sites, which, he ventured, "may turn out to have been an original heritage of Aryan peoples." These early Aryans were left in the dark, however, when he concluded the review with a stirring evocation of the origins of Hellenic culture in the Troad, where "a civilization quickened by Aegean breezes and expanded by an Eastern sun was already advancing to maturity at a time when Illyrian shores and Danubian plains were still slumbering in their Age of Stone."[72] This curious position, no doubt inspired by a desire to understand what came before classical Greece, was short-lived, as Evans delved deeper into the Aegean world during the next decade.

2

The Ancient Labyrinths 1883–93

A Home for Archaeology

The benefactions of centuries of Oxford alumni—with tastes ranging from local Anglo-Saxon and antique curios to "birds, beasts and fishes" brought back from Captain Cook's voyages to the South Sea Islands—had grown by the seventeenth century into an eclectic repository of disparate holdings that few in the university seemed willing to acknowledge, let alone deal with. When the Oxford astrologer and antiquarian Elias Ashmole added his bequest of botanical curiosities in 1677, the university decided to provide a building to house Ashmole's collection and all the others, and named it for their most recent benefactor. The collection languished for two centuries under low-paid keepers, the most recent at Evans's time being John Henry Parker, a local bookseller appointed in 1870. Parker was beyond his best years and rarely appeared at the museum. Meanwhile, Percy Gardner's appointment to the chair in classical archaeology and the movement to bring ancient Greece and her treasures to Oxford sparked a new interest in the Ashmolean as a proper teaching collection. Parker graciously offered his resignation, and the vacancy was advertised early in 1884.

Arthur Evans pulled the right strings and was elected to this position on June 17. The Ashmolean holdings were in such a shambles of chaos and neglect that it would take him the better part of a decade to set it all in order. And, while he may have thought that he had left battles with negligent or intransigent officials behind in the Balkans, Evans soon encountered the local tactics of delay or lack of cooperation on the part of the university's vice-chancellor, Benjamin Jowett, a renowned classical scholar and Plato expert who was also master of Balliol College, and to Evans little more than "a master of intrigue." But Evans's instinctive attraction to conflict had prepared him for Jowett's tactics, which, if anything, firmed his resolve to have his own way, as in the end he did. He insisted that the collection be comprehensive, and he fought against what he saw as "the absurdity of separating off as 'Classical' the remains of a few privileged centuries," and determined to incorporate all branches of art history and archaeology in the museum.[1]

On November 2 he gave his inaugural lecture, "The Ashmolean as a Home of Archaeology in Oxford." Although the address was designed to attract the attentions of both the university authorities, whose cooperation he needed as keeper, and potential donors and contributors, who were reminded of lacunae in the collections, Evans also informed his listeners of the current state of the new science of archaeology. "Our theme is History," he began, "the history of the rise and succession of human Arts, Institutions and Beliefs . . . The unwritten History of Mankind precedes the written, the lore of monuments precedes the lore of books." For his father's benefit he asked his audience to

> Consider for a moment the services rendered within quite recent years by what has been called Præ-historic Archaeology, but which in truth has never been more Historic, in widening the horizon of our Past. It has drawn aside the curtain and revealed the dawn. It has dispelled, like the unsubstantial phantoms of a dream, those preconceived notions as to the origin of human arts and institutions at which Epicurus and Lucretius already laughed, before the days of biblical chronology.

In deference to what he privately called the "Classical School" of Oxford, he added: "The Science of Archaeology . . . has recovered some at least of the monuments that men deemed irrevocably lost. By the patient collection of first hand materials, the pure gold of Hellenic workmanship has at last been cleansed and purged from its later alloy. We no longer see the image of the Hellenic genius darkly, as in a Roman mirror, but stand face to face with its undimmed glory."[2]

The "science of archaeology" in Britain had evolved a great deal since Evans had made his first field trips with his father a quarter of a century before. Colonel Augustus Henry Lane-Fox, a career officer, who was promoted to general and forced to change his name to Pitt-Rivers in order to take his inheritance, was formalizing the techniques of field excavation, a code of practice that would earn him the title of father of scientific archaeology. Pitt-Rivers combined ethnology, anthropology, and archaeology in a single pursuit, and he looked for proofs of his belief that the gradual evolution of species, theorized by Darwin, could be applied to a similar gradual evolution of culture. He was a colleague of John Evans through their association with the Anthropological Institute, and John, as president of the Numismatic Society, designed the medallions Pitt-Rivers used as permanent calling cards when he filled in his trenches.[3]

The advent of scientific archaeology brought with it a narrowing of Charles Newton's definition to suit the emerging specialization. In 1883, J. Romilly Allen in Cambridge wrote, "The basis of the physical sciences is exact measurement. Archaeology, then, may be said to be a science, the ultimate object of which is to deduce from the materials at its disposal a consistent theory of the history of man, as manifested in the works he has produced, and of the development of his civilization and culture in past ages." Therefore the role of archaeologist as specialist was "to collect these [fixed structures, movable objects, historical records] together, and decipher, translate, copy, and annotate . . . so as to be in proper form to hand over to the historian."[4] This split between field archaeology and history led to the present practice of developing methods, tools, and techniques of field archaeology for their own sake, which supports the current purist view that excavators are truly impartial observers of an intact past. Modern scientific archaeology purports to have all the answers but has forgotten the questions, which were posed by historical archaeologists.

To the great ages of man that John Evans's generation had first delineated could now be added the further refinement of the concept of social evolution. The year 1871 had seen the publication and wide readership of Charles Darwin's much awaited *Descent of Man* and Edward Tylor's *Primitive Culture*. Darwin's evolutionary thinking had a lasting impact on the Evans family; Arthur grew up with a "plaster maquette of the great man" that, his half-sister recalled, "loomed over the dining-room door at Nash Mills" to remind him of his father's friend.[5] Both books provided Arthur Evans's generation with a series of new subdivisions to add to their classification. Human history was now charted as a linear evolutionary process beginning with a stage of primitive hunting and gathering, which was called "Savagery," followed by the early farming stage, called "Barbarism," until "Civilization" was indicated by the use of writing. Still further subdivisions were made possible by a three-part progression from Birth and Maturity to Decay, supplied by the natural historian's concept of the cyclical pattern of life. The combination of these anthropological and biological determinist categories gave a paradigm for the "Evolution of Culture" with which historians and their archaeological cousins, for many generations to come, explained the rise, floruit, and collapse of civilizations.[6] Of course, Tylor's definition of civilization acted like a red rag to a bull in "civilized" Europe, and the search for the earliest writing on the Continent, begun with the concept of prehistory, gathered momentum. Among the first casualties were the vases and spindle whorls with incised signs from Schliemann's excavations at Hissarlik, which were "read" as a form of Greek as early as 1874.[7] John Evans later recalled that it was at this time he first formulated his theory of a system of "pre-historic" writing in Greece.[8]

There was a brief flurry of excitement in 1886 when Schliemann once again was dragged through the gantlet of scholarly doubt. John Evans presided over a much publicized meeting of the Hellenic Society in the rooms of the Society of Antiquaries in London on July 2 to which Schliemann and Dörpfeld had been summoned to respond to accusations in the *Times* of incompetence and false deduction.[9] Stillman, now Athens correspondent to the *Times*, had written two articles at the end of April in which he stated that the walls of the Mycenaean grave circle and therefore the famous burials themselves were far more recent than Schliemann had made out, and suggested that Schliemann's lack of archaeological training had led him to date a number of structures, including the palace at Tiryns, to a preclassical period, when in fact they were probably Byzantine. He called Schliemann's results "one of the most extraordinary hallucinations of unscientific enthusiasts which literature can boast of."[10]

What gave credence to Stillman's startling accusation was that he was supported in his observations by F. C. Penrose, the great architectural historian who had published the first measured study of the Parthenon, and H. F. Pelham, the Oxford ancient historian. The case against Schliemann, read by Penrose to an excited house, was clarified when Schliemann admitted that the walls in question at Tiryns were, in fact, those of a Byzantine villa left in position above the earlier remains, which had been covered over for their protection, and that the walls in question at Mycenae were indeed recent, in fact only ten years old, reconstructed by the Greek Archaeological Society in 1876 in order to stabilize the sides of the shaft graves, which had been dismantled during the excavation in order to extract every last fragment of gold.[11] Schliemann assured his followers that no deception was intended, and the proceedings ended peacefully with his exoneration.

The Ashmolean Museum was an ideal base for a man of Evans's self-absorbed and wandering inclinations. Though the keeper's salary was not generous, the conditions of residence were very liberal and the only firm commitment was to give occasional public lectures on the progress of research that might concern the holdings. Most appealing was that the keeper could and should travel to secure new acquisitions. His absence was so frequent and seemingly spontaneous that the assistant keeper, Edward Evans (no relation), delighted in telling callers that "The Keeper, Sir, is somewhere in Bohemia."[12] In truth, Arthur and Margaret made frequent trips to Italy and especially Sicily, where Freeman had embarked on a monumental history of the island in all periods and where Arthur carried further the Evans family study of coinage to the colonial cities of Syracuse and Tarentum. His article on the Horsemen of Tarentum, published in 1889, brought him acclaim in the fields of both ancient history and, her handmaiden, numismatics.

In creating a new Ashmolean Museum, Evans enlisted the support of Charles Drury Fortnum, of the Piccadilly grocery Fortnum and Mason, who was looking for a permanent home for his collection of ancient pottery and bronzes, majolica, Renaissance bronzes and sculpture. The gradual process of acquiring Fortnum's assorted "treasures" and persuading the selective collector to endow the museum with the funds necessary to create and maintain a world-class standard of display was one of Evans's most exhausting tasks, and took many years, but was one of his greatest achievements.

In November 1886 Arthur with his father and uncle Sebastian went to Aylesford in Kent to do as the family had done for over half a century—search for Paleolithic implements. But this time their attention was diverted to more recent finds from superficial layers, the mortal remains of some of John Evans's "ancient Britons" in the clay jars of a Celtic cemetery. What attracted Arthur was not so much the crude British ceramics but the metal objects found with them, for which he suggested a Greek or Roman source. Arthur set about locating objects that had come to light during previous explorations in the cemetery, and in September 1887 he returned to the site, hired six workmen, and directed one of the first systematic excavations of a Celtic burial ground in Britain. Evans had acquired some of the field methods of General Pitt-Rivers, who had started large-scale excavations, combining his skills as military officer and respected squire to inspire his team of agricultural workers to become archaeologists, on his estate at Cranborne Chase in 1880, and began circulating full and detailed reports in 1887. The difference between the thoughtless pilfering of antiquities from the tombs at Trier in 1875 and the clear records, with drawings of where the finds were located, and the respect given the artifacts at Aylesford, shows not only how much Arthur Evans had matured as a field archaeologist but also how much more respect he felt for the ancient Britons and their products than he did for Roman provincials in Germany.

Evans's newly found responsibility to archaeology was also expressed in his 1888 review of Julius Nane's book on excavations in Bronze Age barrows in Upper Bavaria, where, he observed, Nane

> has conscientiously explored, but he has also given a short account of the contents of each individual grave—a point of primary importance too often neglected by explorers whose relic-hunting zeal outruns their patience in keeping scientific record of their observations. How well one knows the result!—the inevitable Atlas, and *édition de luxe*—a museum "stuffed"—and a whole chapter in the remote history of an European race irrevocably mutilated![13]

It seems that Evans was ready to atone for his poor performance at Trier.

At Aylesford he found six undisturbed urn-burials and gathered together other artifacts from the site in a detailed catalogue and analysis that displayed his wide breadth of knowledge, from current trends in European archaeology to classical Greece, Rome, and beyond. Three of the burials had roof slabs with holes large enough to penetrate with a human hand. Evans drew a parallel between these and the mortuary chests of the Natchez Indians of the American Northwest, an illustration of his continued interest in ethnographic parallels from around the world.[14]

Evans used the Aylesford results to initiate a new synthesis of Celtic art and society. He began to formulate ideas on the links between the Mediterranean civilizations and the early societies of the British Isles, and in February and March 1888 presented his first impressions in a series of lectures on late Celtic art and culture. A full account of the excavation and its implications was read to the Society of Antiquaries of London on December 5, 1889, and March 20, 1890, and published as "On a Late-Celtic Urn-Field at Aylesford, Kent" in the society's periodical the following year. But, as he became drawn to the eastern Mediterranean, Evans combined his knowledge and curiosity about Celtic art with what he saw in the early cultures exposed by Schliemann, culminating eventually in his impression of Celtic art, which owed much of its vitality to Evans's evaluation of Mycenae and the Aegean civilizations.

Another, less tangible aspect of Celtic society attracted Evans. On December 6 he gave a public lecture, as one of his duties at the Ashmolean, on Stonehenge and its likely function.[15] He incorporated a synthesis of Indo-Aryan and Teutonic religion to explain the great circle of capped standing stones by suggesting that the monoliths with their impossibly heavy capstones were erected to encircle a sacred tree, an allusion to Wagner's Yggdrasil—the ash at the center of the world. Evans was much taken by the worship of trees, and of the more enduring symbol of the tree's strength—the stone pillar. He accepted both as key symbols in a prehistoric European belief system, which he constantly attempted to verify in the archaeological record.

Late in 1888 Evans acquired for the Ashmolean a collection of "Phoenician" seals from the Reverend Greville Chester, who had worked on excavations in Palestine. The seals are thumbnail-sized devices made in red and green jasper, amethyst, carnelian, and other semiprecious stones, often translucent, always pierced for suspension, and engraved with tiny scenes of surprising complexity, given their size. They were used for ensuring that access to places or documents could be controlled, in much the same way that seals were used throughout history. Evans the numismatist was excited by the miniature scenes on the gems he held up to the close scrutiny of his eyes, but Chester's collection, gathered in the bazaars of Greece and the Middle East, also included an assortment with peculiar, inscribed but illegible, characters, which enhanced their charm enormously.

Schliemann's excavations had proven an Aegean origin to much of what was classed previously under the generic "Phoenician" label, and, in 1883, the German art historian Arthur Milchhöfer suggested that the source for many of the seals found by Schliemann at Mycenae and Tiryns, then also known as "island stones" because of their frequency on the Greek islands, was Crete. Evans saw that the symbols on the stones, which Chester had acquired in Crete, were similar, though not identical, to signs that his Oxford colleague Sayce had recently recognized as Hittite, and that they also resembled Egyptian hieroglyphics, though they were somehow different. At first, the engraved stones were little more than a curious enigma to Evans, but in a few short years they became the focus of his attention, when it became clear to him that they were a key part of an emerging and very appealing historical puzzle, of which he was the first to understand the full importance.

The Egyptian Labyrinth

Among the most popular acquisitions that began pouring into the Ashmolean Museum at Evans's instigation was a share of the discoveries from Flinders Petrie's excavations in Egypt. Two years Arthur's junior, William Matthew Flinders Petrie, grandson of the British navigator Captain Matthew Flinders, an explorer of Australia, had had a similar early exposure to archaeology. As a grown man he recalled being horrified when he witnessed at the age of eight the destruction of a Roman villa on the Isle of Wight; no doubt this was the catalyst for him to develop the excavation and recording techniques he is credited with introducing years later into Egyptology.[16]

Flinders Petrie started digging in Egypt under the auspices of the newly founded Egyptian Exploration Fund in 1882, the year Evans was ejected from Ragusa. He was revolted by the wanton destruction of ancient sites and regarded his predecessors as little more than looters. This is hardly surprising, as the first modern scientific expedition to Egypt was combined with Napoleon Bonaparte's invasion of the country in 1798, as part of a strategy to cut off the British from their eastern trade routes. The artists and architects whom Napoleon brought with him made thousands of measured drawings of the monuments and art, which they published between 1809 and 1828 in the *Description de l'Égypte,* making an abundance of new documentation about ancient Egypt available to scholars and to the public. The result was a period of "Egyptomania" in Europe. But Napoleon's tenure was short-lived; his army was defeated by a combined British and Ottoman attack in 1801. The British tried to hold a strategic post in Egypt but were themselves evacuated in 1803, when the Ottomans took control. After a series of riots in Cairo and a military coup, an Albanian lieutenant, Mohammed 'Ali, assumed power and controlled Egypt from 1805 to 1849. 'Ali opened the country to Europeans and consular agents, and adventurers began to remove antiquities, which they sold abroad to create the great Egyptian collections in European and American museums. Even scientific expeditions were sponsored by the foreign museums, which expected objects worthy of display in exchange for their patronage.

One of the most accomplished explorers at the time was the German philologist Karl Lepsius, a lecturer at the University of Berlin, who from 1843 to 1845, under the patronage of Frederick William IV of Prussia, led an expedition to Egypt and the Sudan. Lepsius found the evidence that dated the pyramids to the beginning of Egyptian history and found the first evidence to portray the character of King Akhenaten, also called Amenhotep IV, the controversial pharaoh who instituted the worship of one god when the ancient Egyptians revered many. Lepsius was the first to measure the Valley of the Tombs of the Kings at Thebes, and recorded countless inscriptions throughout a country whose ancient history was just beginning to emerge from the sands on either side of the Nile River.

Egyptian history was based largely on a fragmentary papyrus acquired by the king of Sardinia in 1824, only two years after the French linguist Jean-François Champollion began publishing his decipherment of ancient Egyptian scripts. The papyrus, known as the Turin Canon because of its current home in the Regio Museum there, lists all the Egyptian kings up to the end of the Hyksos period, roughly 1550 B.C., with the numbers of years they ruled, and astrological observations of the dawn rising of the star Sothis (our Sirius) so that the dates can be computed with accuracy by modern astronomers. Champollion's success at decipherment was due to the discovery, during

Napoleon's invasion, of a trilingual inscription in three ancient writing systems—Egyptian demotic, hieroglyphic, and ancient Greek—on a stone, near the town of Rosetta, northwest of Alexandria in the Nile Delta. This Rosetta Stone gave Champollion the Greek equivalent, which he could read, of the illegible cursive "demotic," or popular script, and the formal "sacred carving"—the literal Greek meaning of "hieroglyphic," which to the ancient Egyptians was "the gods' words" of the priestly class.

Lepsius collected many more transcriptions of historical documents, and in 1849 his *Chronologie der Ägypter* (Egyptian Chronology) was published. Though much dispute over details arose among scholars (and continues to plague them), Egypt's ancient history, as told by the Egyptians themselves, began with the unification of Upper Egypt, the entire Nile valley as the river winds through the desert south from Aswan (near the First Cataract and modern Lake Nasser, created by the Aswan Dam) to Cairo, and Lower Egypt, the triangular Nile delta region, distinguished by broad expanses of fertile soil replenished yearly by the flooding of the Nile and bounded by the Mediterranean Sea to the north. Menes accomplished this feat and founded the First Dynasty around 3200 B.C. The hereditary monarchs of the Fourth Dynasty, who built the great pyramids at Giza, began the Old Kingdom, which started around 2680 B.C. and ended with the last of the Sixth Dynasty rulers around 2258 B.C. There followed an interregnum and division of power called the First Intermediate period until 2134 B.C., when the country was unified under the central authority of the Eleventh Dynasty, based at Lisht, near the Fayum, a large fertile region south of Cairo. This Middle Kingdom period, comprising the Eleventh and Twelfth dynasties, lasted from 2134 to 1786 B.C., then gave way to the Second Intermediate period, when the Delta region was occupied by foreigners called the Hyksos. Around 1550 B.C., Ahmose, a forceful ruler, rose to power, drove out the Hyksos, and united Egypt once again, initiating the Eighteenth Dynasty of the New Kingdom, a period of renaissance in the arts and literature that lasted until around 1100 B.C. and the Third Intermediate period.

Despite the thorough philological work carried out by Lepsius and his contemporaries, Flinders Petrie was highly critical of their field techniques. Without any guidance from his employers, who themselves had no training, he developed his own procedures of archaeological excavation and recording, based on the principles recommended by Pitt-

Rivers for British archaeologists. These fundamental principles, which became the standard for the Near East, were (1) care for the monuments being excavated and respect for future visitors and excavators, (2) meticulous care in the actual excavation and the collecting and description of everything found, (3) detailed and accurate survey and planning of all monuments and excavations, and (4) complete publication of results as soon as possible.[17] As Dörpfeld had done in Olympia, Petrie was the first explorer in Egypt to conduct stratigraphical excavations of tell sites, the great earthen mounds formed by humans building, destroying, and superimposing new structures for thousands of years on the same spot. By recording the stratigraphy of the mound, Petrie established a chronological sequence for the artifacts—primarily decorated pottery, which, he noted, changed in style through time—recovered from a succession of layers. In general the lower the layer, the older the artifacts it contained. The artifacts themselves were given a new status, as he urged that *all* finds should be studied and classified regardless of their monetary value. The result was the first of a series of typological and stylistic classifications of Egyptian artifacts made of many different materials and set within a reliable, chronological framework.

Petrie's new techniques allowed for the addition of earlier periods not charted in the official history, which he called Pre-Dynastic, but the major museums were not ready to acknowledge the importance that he gave to the primitive pottery and stone tools of his new period. When he selected a series of "duplicate" objects from the early cemetery of Naqada for the British Museum, he was told they were "unhistoric rather than prehistoric." Arthur Evans, wasting no time, gratefully acquired them for the Ashmolean's Egyptian collection, along with the lion's share of Petrie's exported finds.

Petrie's revolution in Egyptology not only redefined how Egyptian history was to be recovered but also had profound effects in neighboring countries. He took bright young students along on his expeditions and gave them the field training that would ensure a high quality of work done by the next generation of archaeologists. One such beneficiary was David George Hogarth. Born one of eight children of a Lincolnshire vicar in 1862, Hogarth came from a family that was not wealthy, though descended from the eighteenth-century painter William Hogarth, so he worked for his successes.[18] Hogarth attended Winchester School and went to Oxford, where he was elected to a fellowship at Magdalen College and was a tutor there in 1886–93. In 1888, he was working at Paphos, in Cyprus, where he came to respect a local field technician named Gregóri Antoniou, of Larnaca, whom he described as his mentor and in whom he placed a great deal of his trust. Then he was put in charge of the Egypt Exploration Fund's excavations at Queen Hatshepsut's temple at Deir el-Bahari in Thebes for the next three years. He later recalled that "largely through becoming known to Petrie, and living with men who had served apprentice to him, I had learned to dig."[19] Thus, Hogarth's Egyptian training transformed the practice of archaeology in the Aegean when, as director of the excavations at Phylakopi, in Melos, in 1898, he introduced the concept of stratigraphy and classification to a world still largely recovering from Schliemann's treasure hunt.

In 1888, Petrie conducted large-scale excavations in the Fayum near the Middle Kingdom capital of Lisht, where Lepsius had looked for the monuments described by Herodotus, the fifth-century-B.C. author of the earliest history of Greece, by Pliny the Elder, the first-century-A.D. soldier best known for his *Natural History,* and by Strabo, the first-century-A.D. geographer and historian. Once Petrie successfully identified the remains of the pyramid at Hawara as that of Amenemhat III, one of the great monarchs of the Middle Kingdom, he looked to its south in search of the funerary temple reputed to have been one of the wonders of ancient Egypt. Again, with ancient writers to guide him, he sank trial pits over a large area and was able to report in June, "The site of the Labyrinth is now fixed beyond reasonable doubt." In Egyptian, the world "labyrinth" means "the temple at the entrance of the lake." The site was east of the Lake of Moeris and so seemed correct; Petrie concluded that "after seeing the country it is certain that the description of Strabo cannot agree with any site but that by the pyramid at Hawara." Mud brick buildings, which Lepsius had mistakenly thought were the remains of the labyrinth, Petrie showed, by carefully recording the pottery they contained, to be a Roman village. When he excavated below them he found that "they were resting on a mass of fine white limestone chips. All over an immense area of dozens of acres . . . I found evidences of a grand building. In every pit I dug there was the flat bed for a pavement either of clean flat sand, or usually of rammed stone chips, forming a sort of concrete. Over this bed in a few cases the pavement itself remained; while in all parts was a deep mass of chips of the finest limestone lying upon it." He resolved that "there is no other site geographically for the Labyrinth; and there is no other building known to us to which such extensive remains could be assigned. This is the case for it; but of more direct evidence I fear none will ever be obtained, the destruction having been so thorough and entire."[20]

According to Herodotus, the entire building, surrounded by a single wall, contained twelve courts and 3,000 chambers, 1,500 above and 1,500 below ground. The roofs were wholly of stone, and the walls were covered with sculpture. On one side stood a pyramid about 243 feet (74 meters) high. Herodotus himself went through the upper chambers but was not permitted to visit those underground, which he was told contained the tombs of the kings who had built the labyrinth and the tombs of the sacred crocodiles. But Pliny, in his *Natural History,* stated that the labyrinth became the site of later quarrying for its fine stone, so it was hardly surprising for Petrie to find more than six feet of stone chips across a vast area and little else.[21] Did Petrie's readers, upon accepting his identification, then make the required leap of faith and believe all the rest of Pliny's account?

Pliny described Hawara as the first labyrinth, and mentioned a second built along the same lines in similar "white marble," with 150 columns on the north Aegean island of Lemnos. He quoted the early Roman archaeologist Varro for the location of another at the tomb of Lars Porsena at Clusium, in Etruria (now thought to be in the mound at Poggio Gajella, near Chiusi). But it was the fourth that most excited the interest of the British elite, well schooled in their ancient authors: the notorious Labyrinth crafted by Daedalus on the lines of the Egyptian original and built for King Minos at Knossos in Crete.

A report by such a respected figure as Flinders Petrie bore an unquestioned stamp of authority, and his identification of the labyrinth at Hawara still remains intact more than a century later. Evans, who very much admired Petrie and respected his opinions, was intensely affected by the announcement. Much more impressive than Schliemann's insistence on the truths behind the Homeric tales was Petrie's conclusion that he had found the Egyptian labyrinth; by implication, the others existed and could be revealed by the spade. Evans was forced to review with a new respect and excitement the evidence for the Cretan maze, which formed the basis for Charles Kingsley's tale, as he considered the implications of finding the Labyrinth of Daedalus.

Another radical aspect of Petrie's work was that it provided the dating evidence required to locate Schliemann's Aegean discoveries in the firm historical framework of the Egyptian Dynasties. The Mycenaeans were regarded as pre-Homeric and therefore earlier than 850 B.C.—the traditional date given for the composition of Homer's epics, but a finer chronology had not been accepted. After his first seven years of exploration Petrie wrote with his usual assurance that "it is Egyptian sources that must be thanked by classical scholars for revealing the real standing of the antiquities of Greece. Without the foreign colonies on the Nile, they would still be groping in speechless remains, which might cover either a century or a thousand years, for aught that could be determined in Greek excavations."[22] Petrie showed that the Aegean pottery found in Egypt, in particular the diagnostic types of transport jar with the false neck and double handle that were typical of Mycenaean Greece—classified by Adolf Furtwängler and G. Loeschcke in 1886 as *bügelkanne*, or "stirrup jar" to the English—had a history of development from about 1400 to 1050 B.C. for which a parallel development could be tested in Greece. But Petrie's evidence went back further to a time as yet unexplored in the Aegean. In his seminal study of 1890, "The Egyptian Bases of Greek History," he proposed, "The civilization of Mykenae was no sudden apparition; it must have had centuries of preparation; and we now turn to what came before its time."[23] During his 1889 and 1890 campaigns at Kahun, a site at the entrance to the Fayum, in the rubbish heaps of the Twelfth Dynasty town he found finely made and decorated pottery that he suspected was of Aegean origin, though he noted, "The style of the painting is much more like the savage neatness of Polynesian ornament."[24] He placed the context somewhere between 2500 and 2000 B.C. and stated his belief that the inhabitants of the town were mostly foreigners.

Petrie then "ventured a working hypothesis," which established the direction of Aegean studies for the next half-century:

> The whole of the early civilization . . . known as the "Mykenae period," is a branch of the civilization of the bronze age in Europe, with but little contact with the East . . . The fruit of this civilization, and its power, is seen in the vigorous wars which it made on Egypt . . . if this were the case in the second millennium B.C. . . . and if at that time the luxurious and beautiful objects found at Mycenae and Tiryns were being made, what wonder is it if this culture were already rising a thousand years earlier?[25]

His hypothesis was that a wave of outsiders had poured into Egypt at that time, as there were similar, well-documented phenomena in the

Sixteenth Dynasty—the invasion of the Hyksos—and later in 1200, 1100, and 1000 B.C., with the loose confederation known as the Sea Peoples. Petrie concluded his article with a provocative statement: "we have pushed back the hazy and speculative region to before 2000 B.C., and shown some reasons for looking to a rise of European civilization before 2500 B.C."[26] Petrie, then, gave impetus to the theory that the Aegean civilizations were European in origin, that they had invaded Egypt at certain intervals and affected Egyptian art, and that there must be a predecessor equally rich to the "Mykenae period" that remained to be uncovered in Greece. A further incitement came in 1892 when he declared of the Mycenaeans, "We begin to see a great past rising before us, dumb, but full of meaning."[27]

Flinders Petrie was appointed Edwards Professor of Egyptology at University College in London in 1893, and, through his close connection with the Ashmolean, he exerted a strong influence on Evans, one of the scholars who found his provocation most appealing and responded accordingly.

At the same time, a tall, striking, and highly motivated young man presented himself at New College in Oxford. John Linton Myres was born in Preston in 1869, read classics but also combined chemistry, physics, and geology into his fields of interest at Winchester School and had taken charge of the school's collection of fossils and antiquities, mainly from Cyprus. Myres came up to Oxford in 1888, where he was initially unimpressed by his lecturers but kept up his scientific interests by working in the University Museum. Then, in 1891, Myres first visited Greece; it was the turning point in his life that led him to Evans. His trip began in Marseilles on a Greek torpedo boat that took him through the Peloponnese in a series of adventures that brought him to Athens, where he stayed at the British School. The journey showed him that he could place the histories he had been reading in a living topography; that Greece was "a real country, exceptionally constituted, and inhabited still by a people who retained much of their ancient habit and outlook."[28] Myres returned to Oxford in the autumn, fired with a thirst for knowledge of the Hellenic past. With David Hogarth, who was lecturing on prehistoric Greece, Myres formulated a research topic on "Oriental Influences on Prehistoric Greece." The following year he took his "first" in Greats and won the Burdett-Coutts Scholarship in Geology at Magdalen, and a Craven Fellowship. The requirements of the Craven were to travel and study abroad, and the timing couldn't have been better. Myres had been introduced to Flinders Petrie, who had shown him the Aegean wares from Kahun, and when Myres asked why the great Egyptologist suspected them to be Aegean, the prophetic response was to go to the Aegean and find more of them![29]

On September 22, 1890, Arthur's stepmother, Fanny Phelps, died. John Evans, now sixty-seven and widowed a second time, seemed inconsolable. Arthur responded with the offer to return to the family home at Nash Mills, but his father, with the wisdom and suspicion of ancient Kronos, politely refused what he saw as a takeover bid on his estate and position as head of the household. There was also the matter of Margaret and her high-handed treatment of the staff at Nash Mills, where her involvement in running the household on one occasion had been so oppressive that, as Joan Evans later related, when she left, the butler celebrated "by playing a carillon with a broomstick on the spring bells, one for every room, that hung in the kitchen passage."[30]

Arthur had become fed up with his life in Oxford and had made it known that he intended to move on from the Ashmolean, where by now he felt he'd done all he could do. He was concerned that the damp climate was the cause for a new round of illness to which Margaret succumbed late in 1890. The specialists diagnosed tuberculosis, but Evans, who, as his half-sister recalled, "had a Victorian contempt for germs," was confident that fresh air and Mediterranean sunshine would be the ideal therapy, and so he moved her to Torre del Greco, in Italy, and thence farther south to Taormina in Sicily for the winter.

Not far from where Arthur took Margaret to prolong her life, Heinrich Schliemann's came to an unexpected and painful end. Schliemann had complained of periodic deafness in his left ear and sought the advice of a surgeon at Halle in Germany. He was operated on in mid-November 1890, and after a month's frustrated convalescence went to Berlin, where he saw his old friend Dr. Rudolf Virchow, to whom he announced his next archaeological destination—the Canary Islands. However, the ear operation was not a success. Schliemann went to Paris, but complications had set in by the time he reached the city, so any further plans had to be postponed, and he decided to go home to Athens. By the time he reached Naples, where he planned to take a boat to Piraeus, the infection in his ear was spreading to his brain. Schliemann stayed in Naples for medical treatment but, while walking on Christmas day, collapsed in the street, alone and unrecognized by the passersby who stopped to help. The following day he died.[31]

Arthur and Margaret read of the great explorer's end with mixed feelings. Here was the example of a man the same age as their fathers, who had lived a life full of adventure from joining the California Gold Rush to being shipwrecked off the Dutch coast and stranded in Panama, who had become fabulously wealthy from the indigo trade in Russia and from profiteering in the Crimean War, who spoke at least fifteen languages, ancient and modern, but who in spite of all this would have remained unknown had he not chosen a different course halfway through his life. At the age of forty-seven Schliemann had set out to prove a point about the tangible truths underlying some of the world's oldest stories, and he had succeeded in convincing a skeptical world of his belief. They read of the triumphant return of the hero's mortal remains to his adopted homeland of Greece, and might have been reminded of Theseus, whose bones were brought to Athens in the fifth century B.C., and they read of the state funeral accorded to the German who had shown modern Greeks their Homeric past at a time when they most needed to be reminded of heroic deeds. Speeches were read to the assembled mourners in the salon of the Schliemann home, where the body was exhibited with copies of the *Iliad* and *Odyssey* on either side and a bust of Homer presiding over the procession of well-wishers from the Greek royal household, government, academy, and archaeological services and societies. Schliemann's funeral on January 4 ended at his final resting place on the highest part of the oldest cemetery of modern Athens, with a direct view across to the Parthenon. Here, the newspapers reported, as a final reminder to the assembly of mourners, "the grey-headed Nestor of Neo-Hellenic literature, M. Rhangabé, recited some farewell verses . . . in the measure dear to the deceased, the Homeric hexameter, and breathing a faith in the historical reality of the Homeric world equal to Schliemann's own."[32] Evans may have been amused by the pomp and ceremony accorded the amateur archaeologist, but he was also developing an awareness of the important field Schliemann had opened up and the vast amount of archaeological business he had left unfinished.

In June 1891, Arthur returned to Oxford refreshed and apparently less determined to quit the Ashmolean. Ever since he had been an undergraduate he had been drawn to a place on Boars Hill, west of town, where the view seemed to be endless in all directions and the evening sun gave the distant spires of the Oxford colleges a magical radiance. At the northern end of the hill was a hollow sheltered by forest—oak to the east and pine to the north and southeast. Now, twenty years later, Evans decided to live there. By September he was investigating the purchase of a sixty-acre estate, which his father, who would provide the capital, considered "overly-expensive" and "overly-extensive," upon which he was planning a house that was "over-large." Evans's scheme was postponed but not abandoned while he occupied himself with the machinations of Oxford committees and the miseries of Margaret's health. For the latter, they spent the winter at Bordighera and early spring in Alassio, both fashionable resorts on the Italian Riviera.

The Cretan Labyrinth

On February 3, 1892, Evans left Margaret by the sea and went to Rome to meet the man who would guide him through the Cretan Labyrinth. Federico Halbherr was "an Italian of Alpine stock, slight and wiry, austere and devout; his simple and friendly manners, his disinterested love of his work and his enthusiasm for travel made him at once a congenial friend."[33] Halbherr's name had become synonymous with the ancient history of Crete through his recent and much publicized discoveries, starting in 1884. British intellectuals had followed his early progress through the enthusiastic dispatches of Joseph Hirst in the *Athenaeum* and, more recently, through Halbherr's own detailed accounts in 1888 and 1890. He had also begun to summarize his Cretan travels as a series of short descriptive notices in the *Antiquary* the previous November. Evans wanted to know more about the island at the center of both the ancient tales of heroism against a bitter monarch and the modern reports of bravery against the cruel regime of His Imperial Majesty Abdülhamit, Sultan of the Ottoman Empire; Halbherr knew both stories very well and briefed Evans thoroughly.

The Dutch philologist Karl Hoeck had gathered ancient literary sources on Crete, from the earliest Greek poems to the Roman writers, in three volumes called *Kreta*, which appeared between 1823 and 1829; this was the first modern scholarly account of an island he never visited himself.[34] The second volume, *Das Minoische Kreta* (Minoan Crete), dealt with the myths, but also the earliest reliable references, beginning with the ancient Greek historians. Herodotus in his *Histories* recounted how an expedition of Cretans followed King Minos to Sicily in his pursuit of Daedalus, and Thucydides in his preface to *History of the Pelo-ponnesian War* told of how King Minos was the first to rid the Aegean Sea of pirates and to "rule the waves"—his rule a thalassocracy, or con-trol of the sea—thanks to a powerful navy. But, in 1846, George Grote, in his *History of Greece,* was adamant with regard to the low value of the Cretan stories for the historian: he dismissed Thucydides' account of the thalassocracy of Minos as a conjecture "derived from the analogy of the Athenian maritime empire of historical times, substituted in place of the fabulous incidents and attached to the name of Minos."[35]

Then, Schliemann's identification of Troy at Hissarlik, and especially his revelations at Mycenae, went a long way to change the understand-ing of Greece's ancient history, so that even the Homeric poems were being read, albeit with caution, as history. For Evans and Halb-herr, Crete entered written history with certainty in the writings of Herodotus and Thucydides, in the fifth century B.C., at the same time that the Athenian philosopher Plato admired her ancient institutions in his *Laws.* Aristotle in his *Politics,* a century later, recalled that the Cretan caste system of his own day was based on that introduced by Minos; for these philosophers, at least, Minos was a historical figure and a great le-gal reformer. In their day, however, Crete was not unified, but separated into city states, which formed leagues, often at war with each other, un-til the Roman conquest of 67 B.C., when the new masters established a capital for the joint province of Crete and Cyrenaica (Libya) at Gor-tyna, in Crete's Mesara region, the island's largest and most fertile plain at the center of the southern coast; they knew the desert tribes of North Africa wouldn't cross the sea to attack their administrative buildings and temples. At the center of Crete's northern coast, the Romans built a port town called Heracleium, starting the long and turbulent history of the town known legally since 1898 as Herakleion, the island's main port for Aegean and northern trade.

Roman reforms of the third century A.D. separated Cyrenaica from Crete, which became part of the Eastern Roman empire when Con-stantine the Great founded his capital at the ancient Greek city of Byzantium. Constantine converted to Christianity in 312, and his new city gradually became the religious and political center of the Byzan-tine Empire.

Crete remained under Byzantine rule until 823, when the Saracens, Muslim pirates named for a tribe originally from the Sinai Peninsula, stormed the island and occupied Heracleium; they renamed it Kandak, the Arabic word for the great ditch they dug around the city for protection. For over a century Khandax, as it came to be known, boasted one of the most prosperous slave markets of the Mediterranean, until Nikiphoros Phocas reconquered Crete for Byzantium in 960. The merchants of Venice then bought it from Boniface, marquis of Montferrat, to whom it was allotted with the Latin conquest of Byzantium during the Fourth Crusade, in 1204, and called both Khandax and the island Candia.

The Republic of Venice ruled Crete for more than four centuries of cultural enlightenment; the Venetians promoted schools of the arts (one of which prompted the painter Doménikos Theotokópoulos, better known as El Greco, "the Greek," to further his studies in Venice) and built huge fortifications, fountains, and other public works reflecting material prosperity, but, as always, at a high price. The profits came from an oppressive system of taxation and forced labor, which prompted frequent revolts, not only by the natives against their masters but also by the Venetian colonists against the republic. The Cretans appealed to the republic's rival, Genoa, for salvation from Venetian rule, but without success. Then they turned their hopeful gaze to the east and sought help from the Turks, but the Ottomans had their own problems. Following the death of Suleiman the Magnificent in 1566—best known for his patronage of the arts but also credited with conquests in Europe and North Africa—the Ottomans suffered military defeats and internal social, political, and economic conflict, until the dynamic rule of Murat IV, who, from 1623 to 1640, spurred new conquests.

The revitalized Ottomans responded to the plight of the Cretans, who got more than they bargained for: one hundred warships carrying fifty thousand Ottoman troops arrived in 1645 at the commencement of open war with Venice. The Ottomans captured Canea (modern Chania), a fortified port on the northwestern coast, and then moved east to the next sea fort at Rethymnon in 1646. Two years later they arrived at the center, installed their cannon atop the highest hill south of Candia, subsequently called the Fortetsa, and began a reign of terror over the city that lasted twenty-one thunderous years. The Venetians fought hard for their last possession in the eastern Mediterranean, even sending a fleet against Constantinople, but the empire triumphed over the republic, and in September 1669 Candia surrendered to the Turks.

The Cretans were now subjects of the Sublime Porte, the center of the Ottoman government (from the French translation of Turkish *bâbiâli*, or Sublime Gate, the official name of the grand portal giving access to the block of buildings in Constantinople that housed the state departments). At first, Ottoman rule suited the islanders; forced labor was abolished and more than a quarter of the population converted to Islam. Crete became a popular source of honey, wax, almonds, chestnuts, raisins, and wine, as well as an assortment of textiles in wool, cotton, flax, and silk. But, as the fortunes of the empire waned in the late eighteenth century, Crete, like other outposts, suffered from cruel governors and increased taxation. The first great revolt came in 1770, led by the fierce Sphakiots from the rugged southwestern region called Sphakia, but it was suppressed. Then again in 1821, the men from Sphakia rose against the Turks when revolution in central Greece, which led to the formation of an independent Greek kingdom, stirred up nationalist feelings among the Greek Cretans. United with the mainland Greeks by language, Christian orthodoxy, and sentiment, they took control of the countryside, forcing the Muslims into the cities until Mohammed 'Ali, of Egypt, arrived at the sultan's request and reduced the island to submission in 1824.

France, Great Britain, and Russia, known then as the Allied Powers, agreed in the Protocol of London of 1830 that Greece should be an independent kingdom but that its size should be kept small and manageable; so Crete was ceded to Egypt when Greece gained her independence in 1832. Mohammed 'Ali appointed the Albanian Mustafa as governor, and the island saw a rare period of civil obedience as Mustafa encouraged agriculture by improving roads and ensuring safety in rural areas by charging an Albanian police force to maintain order, which they did by suppressing banditry. Even after Crete was returned to Turkey, in 1840, Mustafa retained his governance until 1852, when he moved to Constantinople as grand vizier—an exalted position, second only to the sultan in authority, which included the right to demand and obtain absolute obedience. This concept of acquiescence was lost on the Christian Cretans, who made their own demands: equal rights and privileges with the island's Muslims; these were conferred by imperial decree on condition that they lay down their arms. But by 1864, the promised rights had still not materialized, so the sultan was petitioned by an assembly of Christians. In reply, he ordered the Cretans to render unquestioning obedience to the authorities, causing further tension until May 1866, when the first pan-Cretan assembly met and drew up another petition to the sultan, this one complaining of the ever increasing taxes. Again the reply from the Porte was hostile, so the assembly met in August and urged open revolt against Turkey and unity with Greece. Additional Turkish troops arrived in Crete in September and for two years swept through the island, causing severe damage to rebel and peaceful civilian alike. The revolt was brutally suppressed, but it prompted the Porte to compose the Organic Statute of 1868, which granted rights to the native Cretans, including the provision for a council-general elected by the populace, essentially the first constitutional government in the island's modern history. But the concessions were slow in being implemented, and a decade of unrest followed until Austria convened the Congress of Berlin in June 1878 at the conclusion of the Russo-Turkish War.

The Congress of Berlin was dominated by Prussia's Chancellor Bismarck, who satisfied the interests of Austria-Hungary by allowing it a mandate to occupy Bosnia and Herzegovina and thereby to increase its influence in the Balkans; and by Foreign Secretary Lord Salisbury, who saw to British interests by occupying Cyprus, by denying Russia permission to enlarge its naval force, and by maintaining the Ottoman Empire as a European power (even though it had been shorn of many of its European territories), a policy that was disputed by British philhellenes. Greece was not formally invited to take part, but the sultan was encouraged to reopen dialogue with George I, King of the Hellenes. Crete was to remain under Turkish dominion, but the Sublime Porte undertook to enforce the Organic Statute of 1868, and a new agreement was negotiated and signed at Halepa, a suburb of the new Cretan capital at Chania, on October 25. An elected Cretan Assembly then came into being with forty-nine Christian and thirty-one Muslim deputies; a Greek Christian, John Photiades, was appointed governor-general.

The Pact of Halepa also contained important new privileges for native Cretans. Article XV stated, "It shall be lawful for the inhabitants of the island to found literary societies, printing presses, and to publish newspapers in conformity with the laws and regulations of the empire." A Greek literary and scientific group called the Association of Friends of Education, which had been established in Candia, in 1875, on the model of the well-known Greek Philological Syllogos in Constantinople, now became a legal body by imperial decree, and from 1879 on, it elected a yearly president. Two medical doctors, Sphakianakos and Zaphirides, were followed by the head of Candia's gymnasium-school,

Harriet Ann Evans (née Dickinson) c. 1857, the year she died and left Arthur Evans, age six, without the "active center of his world" (JOAN EVANS 1943)

John Evans c. 1855. Deemed "too sensible and hard working for the classroom or parish" by his practical mother, John "Flint" Evans, Arthur's father, made a fortune in the Dickinson family paper mills and entered academia as an amateur antiquarian (JOAN EVANS 1943)

Arthur John Evans c. 1867. A young man with penetrating blue eyes, the left set deeper than the right, and thick black hair, Evans was reserved at Harrow School and remembered for only one athletic activity: "jumping at conclusions" (ASHMOLEAN MUSEUM)

Arthur John Evans in 1878. Evans left Oxford "a fantastically conceited young man who knew better than anyone how great were his especial gifts," his half-sister Joan Evans recalled (ASHMOLEAN MUSEUM)

Margaret Freeman in 1877. She married Evans in 1878 and "was a helpmate such as few have known," he fondly recollected after her premature death in 1893 (JOAN EVANS 1943)

Farewell party for Arthur and Margaret on the eve of their move to Ragusa in 1878 (ASHMOLEAN MUSEUM)

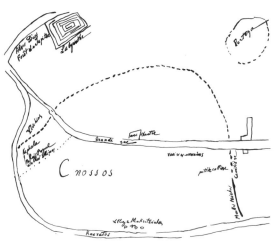

Sketch map of "Cnossos" by Minos Kalokairinos, the first modern explorer of the site in 1878–79, showing the "Great road" from Candia passing the "Kephala" with its "Royal Palace of King Minos" and the "Forest of Jupiter" at the entrance to the "Labyrinth"
(after Kopaka 1995, Fig. 5)

Sketch plan by Kalokairinos of the "Royal Palace of King Minos" showing the location of the large jars, or pitharia
(after Kopaka 1995, Fig. 7)

Sketch map of Candia and the Knossos valley at the time of Evans's first visit in 1894 (after Mariani 1895, with English additions)

Sketch of a Cretan pithos, a large ceramic storage jar, from Kalokairinos's excavations (after Fabricius 1886)

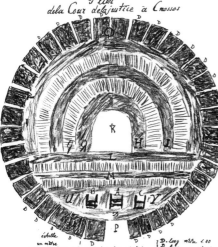

Kalokairinos's fanciful reconstruction of the "Court of justice at Cnossos" in the area later identified by Evans as the "Throne Room" (after Kopaka 1995, Fig. 8)

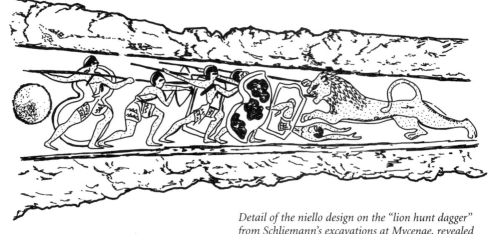

Detail of the niello design on the "lion hunt dagger" from Schliemann's excavations at Mycenae, revealed during conservation to show the high quality of the Mycenaeans' metallurgy and the liveliness of their art (after Evans 1930a, Fig. 71)

Detail of the "silver siege rhyton" from Mycenae. Evans commented that the "subject well known in Oriental Art is found here for the first time in Mykenaea," where, he fantasized, "A freer more democratic spirit here breathes," because the outcome of the battle was unknown (after Evans 1930a, Fig. 52)

Scenes on the pair of gold cups found by Tsountas at Vapheio. One scene reminded Evans of Homer's phrase "writhed as a bull that herdsmen in the mountains have bound with twisted willow branches," and he extolled it thus: "The art displayed is astonishing & seems to belong to a much later period. No schematism or slavish adherence to received tradition in the ancient forms (Compare archaic Greek art !!!)" (after Evans 1930a, Fig. 123)

The Keftiu, with long flowing locks and red skin, were shown bearing tribute of Aegean artifacts to the Egyptian king in the tomb of one of his nobles, Menkeper 'ra-senb, at Thebes. Evans thought that their red skin tone was due to "the Egyptian way of rendering the rosy European cheeks," and concluded that they were Cretans (after Evans 1928b, 746 Fig. 482)

Youlbury, the home Evans built in 1894 on Boars Hill, near Oxford, which at its greatest extent comprised twenty-two bedrooms, five bathrooms—one with a sunken Roman bath in marble—a library, study, dining and sitting rooms, all of grand proportions (PAUL HASKINS)

Evans seated (left) with Hazzidakis (center) and Halbherr, Savignoni and Mariani standing. He learned much from the pioneers of Cretan archaeology (ASHMOLEAN MUSEUM)

The entrance hall at Youlbury with a Renaissance-style barrel-vaulted ceiling and a tiled floor with a rectanglar labyrinth pattern flanking a Classical Greek Minotaur

Engraved scene on the Ring of Knossos, bought in 1894. Evans saw "a kind of stone worship that still survives in India and elsewhere to the present day. The god, brought down by ritual and incantation, is seen descending on the sacred obelisk that thus becomes his temporary dwelling-place, or, in Biblical language, a Bethel" (after Evans 1901c, Fig. 48)

Fragment of a stone vase from Knossos. "At first," Evans noted in 1894, "I thought it was a bit of some kind of Roman relief ware, but to my astonishment I found it was Mykênæan, with part of a relief representing men perhaps ploughing or sowing—an altar?—and a walled enclosure with a fig tree: a supplement to the Vapheio vases and contemporary in style!" Evans converted the horned cult object atop the built platform, long known to Egyptologists as the hieroglyphic sign for the horizon, to a new concept, which he called the "Horns of Consecration" (after Evans 1901c, Fig. 2)

The four-sided stone seal that Evans bought at Palaikastro in 1894. He was the first to recognize the importance of the engraved symbols (after Evans 1894e, Fig. 35)

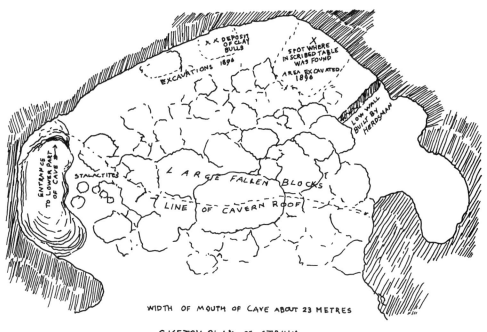

Evans's sketch plan of the cave at Psychro in Lasithi, where he conducted illegal excavations in 1895 and 1896 and found small bronze double-axes like those Schliemann had suggested symbolized Zeus Labrandeus, which he took as proof that this was the Diktaian Cave where Zeus was nurtured (after Evans 1897a, fig. 26)

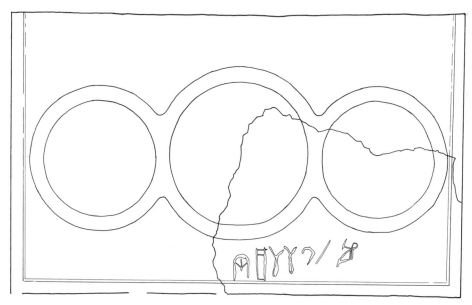

The inscribed graffito on the rim of the Psychro stone table gave Evans the first tangible proof of his theory of the linear scripts of early Greece. He re-created the table as a three-part offering table used in a ritual performed in honor of the Cretan Zeus; the three bowls were for milk and honey, sweet wine, and water, mixed to commemorate the nourishment provided by the mythical Amalthea (the goat) and Melissa (the bee) for the infant Zeus (Evans 1897a)

View of Kalokairinos's trenches on Kephala at Knossos at the outset of Evans's excavations in 1900. "Here at a place called τα πιθάρια [ta pitharia] are the remains of Mykênæan walls and passages," Evans noted of the earlier trials when he first saw the site in 1894 (ASHMOLEAN MUSEUM)

Evans and Duncan Mackenzie, his superintendent at Knossos, keep a close watch over the Cypriot Gregóri Antoniou and a Cretan digger
(ASHMOLEAN MUSEUM)

Gregóri Antoniou, "the most expert tomb robber of the Levant," surrounded by his team of expert Cretan diggers
(ASHMOLEAN MUSEUM)

The centuries of soil over the Palace were removed in wicker baskets and sent to the "shoots," or spoil heaps, in wheelbarrows
(ASHMOLEAN MUSEUM)

Professor Michelides, then Bishop Dionysios of Chersonissos, who presided over the creation of a library and organized lectures to raise educational standards among those of Greek descent. The Syllogos, as it came to be known, very soon embodied two major aims: to aid and advance Christian Greek education in Crete, and to fight for unification with Greece.[36]

In 1883, the presidency came to Joseph Hazzidakis, another doctor but also a philologist, who had first come to Crete two years earlier and had become intrigued by the island's antiquities.[37] He saw that strong, continuous leadership was required and used his authority to guide the Syllogos from its idealistic origins to a position of practical authority. Hazzidakis, born on the island of Melos, had been educated in Athens and Germany and, like any European man of letters, also spoke excellent French. He became a strong proponent of Cretan-Greek nationalism.

At the time, all antiquities of note discovered in Crete could be required to be sent to the Imperial Museum in Constantinople, since the island was subject to the laws of the Porte. Hazzidakis and the Syllogos took it upon themselves to enforce the will of the Cretan Assembly's Greek Christian majority, who believed that the safest place for the island's ancient monuments was in the bosom of "mother earth" until such a time as the Turkish troops in their garrisons at the major port towns were removed from the island and, with them, the danger of artifacts being looted. Hazzidakis was the prime mover behind Crete's first modern museum, which was established during his first year in office under the watchful gaze of the Christian god—in a building in the courtyard of Aghios Minas cathedral in Candia. This was the first formal attempt to protect the island's antiquities from export and to create an archaeological museum. Hazzidakis, in his Greek nationalist fervor, defined the course that Cretan archaeology was to take, and his motives were quite clear: the Muslim population had no place in the new version of ancient history that the Syllogos set out to write. The strong Greek-Christian bias of the Syllogos resurfaced when an attempt was made to burn down the museum twenty years later, but by then it was far too late; the Ottomans and their culture had effectively been written out of the selection process that historians undertake when they choose their evidence and praise the relative merits of one period over another.

At that time, the corpus of ancient Greek inscriptions was being supplemented at a brisk pace by discoveries in continental Greece, so Halbherr's tutor in Rome, the great Latin scholar Domenico Comparetti, sent him to search the Greek islands and Crete, in 1884.[38] The year before, the French School at Athens had sent Bertrand Haussoullier, and the Germans had dispatched Ernst Fabricius for the same reason. The Syllogos was eager to encourage foreign interest in their Greek past but equally concerned that the strict guidelines for the protection of the antiquities deemed worthy by the Cretan Assembly be enforced.

In the five months from June to October, Halbherr gathered no fewer than 166 previously unpublished inscriptions. At first, he was satisfied with collecting inscribed stones lying about on the surface and searching the building blocks in recent monuments for traces of earlier materials that had been reused—a practice that brought him into conflict with suspicious clergymen, who feared having to dismantle their churches for the greater glory of the Syllogos and its mission. But Halbherr was reminded of the potential wealth of buried treasure when one day his horse stumbled against a piece of marble sticking out of the path.[39] Close examination of the offending object revealed a flat surface with letters leading into the ground. Soon after, a peasant let him know that in a channel used by the water mill at Gortyna, another foreigner had once picked up large stones with the sorts of inscription that seemed to interest the young Italian. Halbherr followed the lead and arrived to find that the sodden course could be inspected because the mill was shut down for repairs and the water diverted elsewhere. This was the site that the French explorer Léon Thénon had described in 1868 and from which he had removed two inscribed blocks (now in the Louvre).[40] Halbherr worked furiously in the mud to uncover as much as possible before the repairs on the mill were finished. He was able to expose and read parts of a legal code inscribed on a semicircular wall about thirty meters long and two meters high, which he thought might be the back wall of an ancient court of justice, where rules literally had been written in stone for all to see above the judge's heads. The parts he could make out by brushing away the mud in the channel seemed to deal with debt and inheritance laws, but before he could be certain he almost lost his life when the makeshift dam was removed and the channel filled once again with water. No amount of pleading with the practical miller could persuade him to divert the runoff elsewhere, so Halbherr rode in haste to Candia and brought Hazzidakis. Long and drawn-out proceedings with the miller were eventually resolved by

Domenico Comparetti, who bought the entire property and compensated the owners for their loss of a working mill.[41] What was gained was arguably the most important inscription ever found in the Greek world. Fabricius was called in to help, and the scholars prepared a joint publication of the oldest legal code in Europe.[42] The inscription became known as "The Law Code of Gortyn," the site is visited by thousands of tourists annually, and Halbherr's place in archaeological history was assured.

The significance of a legal code from Crete, famed in antiquity as the domain of King Minos the Lawgiver, was not lost on Evans, though he did not share Halbherr's enthusiasm for Greek and Roman inscriptions. The code outlined the proper behavior and human rights in a just society of ancient Crete, which included the surprising element of inheritance being through the female line.[43] Mothers administered property on behalf of their daughters in a truly matrilineal system, for which, it was surmised, there must have been an earlier matriarchal precedent, an idea Evans found most appealing, though what interested him much more was the Italian's knowledge of the discoveries at the ancient site of "Cnossos," where Halbherr conducted trial excavations in 1885.

Thanks to the sultan's concessions in 1878, only two years after Schliemann's discovery of the Grave Circle at Mycenae had excited public interest in a pre-Greek past and its golden glow, a man named Minos Kalokairinos, in Candia, gained the approval of the owners of a low knoll in the valley of the Katsambas river and began the modern search for the legendary city of Minos.

Minos Kalokairinos, born in 1843 on the Greek island of Kythera, south of the Peloponnesus, completed one year of law school at the University of Athens before quitting and going to Paris to study languages. After his father's death of cancer in 1864, he took over the family's business interests in Crete. At the time of Halepa, Minos Kalokairinos was dragoman to the British vice-consul in Candia, who was his older brother Lysimachos. The dragoman—from the Arabic *tarjuman*, or *tercüman* in Turkish—was a local interpreter in countries where Arabic, Turkish, and Persian were the official languages and where, due to the religious ban on Muslims using the languages of non-Muslim peoples, the pashas needed local intermediaries. Inevitably, the dragomans acquired considerable political influence, since they were intimately involved in sensitive negotiations, and acquired quasi-diplomatic status, but they also carried the stigma of complicity with the Sublime Porte; as the modern Cretan historian Theocharis Detorakis says, "they tended to be avaricious, mean and unhesitating oppressors of their fellow nationals and Christians."[44] Kalokairinos, by all accounts, was none of these; nonetheless, he was regarded with suspicion by Greek and foreigner alike.

In December 1878, Kalokairinos went to the hill known locally as tou Tseleve he Kephala, a toponym that combines the Greek κεφάλα (*kephala*), or "headland," and the Turkish *tselevi*, "landowner" or *bey*; in English this became the Squire's Knoll. The site had been known as the ancient city of Gnosus (Knosos) for centuries, and foreign travelers had been taken to see the remains of the fabled city there as part of a tour that also included the Grotto of Zeus and the Labyrinth of Daedalus.[45] Edward Lear, the Victorian painter and poet, taken on just such a tour in 1864, recorded, "The site of Knossos possesses water and trees and plenty of aidhonia (in Greek αηδόνια—nightingales), but except for scattered masses of brickwork, little remains."[46] This "brickwork" included the traces of a hillside theater and of an enormous Roman basilica recorded in a plan by Onorio Belli in 1586 and then brought to the attention of modern readers by Edward Falkener in 1854.[47] Belli was in no doubt that he was at the ancient city of "Gnossus," as it was quite common to find there ancient coins with the word ΚΝΩΣΙΟΝ (*Knosion*), or the more frequent abbreviation ΚΝΩΣ (*Knos*), on the obverse and a version of the maze or labyrinth symbol on the reverse. Belli had not found any traces of the Labyrinth of Daedalus, but then he hadn't expected to, since Pliny had written that nothing of the famous structure remained. Besides, most travelers in search of the Labyrinth were taken to a large, complex underground quarry on the slopes of Mount Ida, near Gortyna, and urged to enter the dark subterranean dungeon where they might find a Minotaur lying in wait. One such traveler, Bernard Randolph, in 1680, added the graphic and unsavory detail that his party's "curiosity did not invite us to see it, for were it not true, as in probability 'tis not, the noisome smells are enough to stifle one."[48]

As a collector himself, Kalokairinos was well aware that local shepherds and farmers had been finding "island stones" on the hillock for generations. Before modern collectors had taken an interest in these stone seals, Cretan women had threaded the brightly colored gems and worn them around their necks during the fertile years of motherhood, for they were believed to contain talismanic or magical powers to ensure lactation—hence the local name γαλόπετρες (*galopetres*), literally meaning "milk-stones." They were worn hanging on the breasts during lactation and otherwise slung around to the back to draw the milk back in. The Kephala was well known as a source of these distinctive stones, extremely important to a population that explored all means to combat a high rate of infant mortality.

Kalokairinos seems to have waited until the winter weather cleared, and in April 1879 he returned to the Kephala with twenty workmen for three weeks of intensive digging before he was stopped by order of the Cretan Assembly.[49] He found the traces of a rectangular building measuring thirty meters east-west by sixty north-south, which included on the west side a storeroom with huge ceramic jars, five feet tall and rather like something out of Ali Baba and the Forty Thieves, called πίθοι (*pithoi*). On the south side were entrances into the hillside that seemed to lead to basement rooms where, he hoped, he might find treasure on the scale of Schliemann's recent discoveries at Mycenae. When the exciting news of Kalokairinos's success spread to the Cretan Assembly, it quickly called a halt to his work. The reasoning, which Kalokairinos accepted, was that he might begin to reveal the sort of enviable artifacts that would almost certainly be removed from Crete to Constantinople.

In a collection of notes written down twenty-two years later and intended as the basis for an excavation report, which he never completed, Kalokairinos identified the building on the Kephala as "le Palais Royale du Roi Minos."[50] To the north of the palace, the remains of what he thought was a circular chamber twelve meters in diameter were identified as "la Cour de la justice à Cnossos," complete with thrones for three magistrates near the rounded entrance; a large underground stone quarry at Ayia Irini, about a thousand meters south of the Kephala, became, for him, the Labyrinth. Here, Kalokairinos speculated, Athenian prisoners, including Theseus, were marched through a wooded area, which he called the "Forest of Jupiter," and imprisoned. The underground maze, he speculated, was carved out of the earth by Daedalus when he removed the stone to build the palace on the Kephala. Whatever the mythical associations were, it was clear that the regular plan of the walls on the Kephala, the pottery shapes and designs, and the painted wall plaster were all reminiscent of the palace on the acropolis at Mycenae, just published by Schliemann as the seat of Agamemnon.

Kalokairinos's discoveries and his willingness to share them with all interested parties made the Kephala site at Knossos the object of considerable attention over the next few years. Soon after the digging was interrupted, Photiades declared in the Cretan press the need for a museum of antiquities to be established in Candia.[51] This publicity and Kalokairinos's own family affiliation with the British Consulate in Candia ensured that word of his successful exploits spread rapidly in diplomatic circles. By the end of the month, Thomas Backhouse Sandwith, British consul in Crete since 1870, who had helped negotiate the Pact of Halepa and thus enjoyed good standing on the island, implored Charles Newton at the British Museum to consider visiting the Kephala with a view to initiating British excavations. Sandwith, like most diplomats at the time, was an avid collector of antiquities and had formed an important collection of early pottery from a cemetery at Rhodovani, in western Crete. In a letter of April 27 he reported to Newton that Kalokairinos "opened a large chamber containing some 20 jars ranged in rows . . . Besides the jars, many fragments of broken pottery which seem to be of Phoenecian ware . . . were found." Sandwith's motive is clearly stated in the postscript to his letter, which declares, "There could not be a better opportunity of excavating than now before Crete passes out of Turkish hands, in case you think Gnossos a good field for the purpose."[52] But, Newton, already by 1879 the "*Doyen* of Hellenic studies in England,"[53] was very much tied up with the establishment of the Hellenic Society in Britain, which met frequently during May and had its inaugural meeting, over which he presided, on June 16 of the same year.[54]

Bertrand Haussoullier of the French School at Athens was shown Kalokairinos's finds and wrote the first scholarly account of the discoveries on the Kephala.[55] His report, which appeared in 1880, concentrated on the early style of the painted pottery Kalokairinos had unearthed and drew attention to its similarity with pottery from elsewhere in Crete, but also with material from Rhodes and Thera, previously called Phoenician and Pelasgian and now called Mycenaean due to its abundant occurrence at Mycenae. Haussoullier was cautious about the date of the *pithoi*, but proved beyond any doubt that the early building on the Kephala and its decorated pottery belonged to the same time period as Mycenae.

Haussoullier seems to have acted quickly, as Sandwith wrote to Newton on February 24, 1880, "The French School of Antiquaries at Athens has just made a proposal . . . to undertake some excavations at Gnossos

... on the condition of leaving to the authorities of the island whatever antiquities they may discover ... I know that Photiades Pasha is anxious to found a Museum of Antiquities at Candia, and I should think he will jump at the offer." Ever the diplomat, he added, "I thought you would like to be informed of this, though I hardly think the Museum Authorities would desire to thwart the proposal of the French School."[56] It seems, however, that Photiades may not have jumped at the offer, or if he had, he wasn't able to convey his enthusiasm to the other members of the Cretan Assembly. The French claim seems not to have existed when the next suitor presented himself for consideration.

W. J. Stillman had left Crete in 1868, much affected by the horrors he witnessed during the insurrection of 1866. He regarded the unhappy time he had spent as American consul at Canea—two years of hardship and house arrest—as the reason for the onset of the fatal illness that claimed his much beloved son, John, and for the mental breakdown and suicide of his wife, Laura Mack, in Athens in 1869. Nonetheless, Stillman retained an interest in Cretan history and returned in 1881 under the authority of the Archaeological Institute of America to appraise Kalokairinos's trials on the Kephala and pursue the possibility of American excavations on the site.

Stillman's report to the Archaeological Institute was filled with news, not of his own glorious exploits, as might have been expected, but rather of Kalokairinos, who once again eagerly shared his discoveries at Knossos, perhaps hoping that a foreigner might have more influence with Photiades and the Cretan Assembly than he had had. Stillman was the first to provide a detailed plan and description of the Kephala excavations.[57] He reported that before the work had been interrupted, Kalokairinos had "laid bare some remains of ancient walls. They are, though what is left of them is only about six or seven feet in height, of very great interest, being constructed of huge blocks of hewn stone, gypsum, and sandstone, and the very small portion uncovered shows a narrow passage which gives me the impression of an entrance into the city. The structure is the earliest sample of the style commonly known as Hellenic that I have ever seen." On a subsequent visit he noted that the rain had washed clean the walls with the cut blocks and exposed incised marks in the form of double-axes, a star, and a gate. Kalokairinos also told him of the large oil jars, or *pithoi*, which he had found there. North of the storerooms Stillman was shown another excavated pit, which contained what seemed to him to be part of the same building but with "what appears to have been an adytum [inner sanctum, usually of a temple]. It is furnished with stone seats (?) which are about six inches in height." This was Kalokairinos's Courthouse. Stillman's description ends with the enticing speculation that he was "at a loss to attribute this work to any other period or any other use than that which would belong to the Daedalian Labyrinth . . . The importance of the discovery, if its supposed character be maintained on further excavation, is patent." To Stillman, the whole complex on the Kephala was the Cretan Labyrinth.

Stillman worked out an agreement with the landowner to begin excavating, with the assurance of Photiades Pasha that he would not have a problem gaining official permission. He had applied for a firman, or letter of approval, from the Porte in Constantinople through the American minister there, but eventually the application was turned down, apparently on the advice of Photiades. Though the bitter Stillman later speculated that the difficulty had been that he "had not offered to give his excellency [Photiades] the coins that might be found in the excavation,"[58] he was also aware of the difficult position that Photiades was in vis-à-vis the Cretan Assembly. The pursuit of his alternative proposal, the Cave of Zeus on Mount Juktas, six kilometers south of Knossos, was also abandoned when new disturbances ensued after the murder of two Muslims at Gortyna and the predictable retribution against Christians in Candia. Another circumstance, which Stillman couldn't have anticipated, was the appointment that year of Osman Hamdi Bey to direct the Imperial Museum in Constantinople. Hamdi Bey actively set out to form a collection to rival those of the imperial museums in Europe and was only too eager to acquire important Cretan antiquities, as Photiades and the Cretan Assembly were well aware.[59]

Stillman's report on the discovery of the "Daedalian Labyrinth" at "Gnossos" contributed to the growing excitement over the Kephala excavations that eventually reached Heinrich Schliemann, who predictably turned his insightful gaze to Crete. On January 7, 1883, Schliemann wrote to Photiades about obtaining permission to excavate Knossos, without even having seen the site.[60] He had enjoyed friendly relations with Photiades when the latter had been Turkish ambassador in Athens, and so Schliemann fully expected him to see the request through the Cretan Assembly. As Crete was Turkish, Schliemann agreed to abide by the rule of Turkish law and content himself with one-third of the finds. Photiades, no doubt anticipating the hostile reaction of the

Christian majority in the Assembly and thinking of the new museum that he and Hazzidakis proposed for Candia, recommended that Schliemann offer to give everything of importance to the state, retaining only some "duplicates" by agreement with the local authority, as the new Greek law stated,[61] and anticipating the expected changes in Turkish antiquities law forbidding the export of all antiquities, which were to take effect in the next year. Aware that even this concession was unlikely to bear fruit, Schliemann understood that he would have to appear in person in Crete in order to lobby the members of the Assembly when they met in session in April and May. But this was the time he had set aside to be honored in Oxford, and so Crete had to be put off. The next year Schliemann received permission to excavate at Tiryns in the spring, and in 1885 he went to England to receive a medal from the hand of Queen Victoria herself on behalf of the Royal Institute of British Architects.

During October 1885, Halbherr went to Knossos and excavated part of a Roman building at a location called στο Κατσούνι (*sto Katsouni*), near Makryteichos, a small hamlet north of the Kephala.[62] The results of a few days' digging were enough to convince him of the importance of ancient Knossos, and he proposed to his professor, Comparetti, that the Italians acquire the site for exploration. Comparetti declined the suggestion of initiating new work in the small town of Knossos, and chose to concentrate his resources on the great Roman provincial capital at Gortyna.

The revelations at Knossos and Gortyna, which Halbherr and the Syllogos, Haussoullier, and Stillman reported to the learned world and interested public, sparked a renewed fascination in the ancient history of Crete. Warwick Wroth quickly published a study of the Cretan coins in the British Museum,[63] which showed that as many as thirty city-states of the Hellenistic period, from about 220 B.C. until the Roman conquest in 67 B.C., minted their own coins and used mythological figures associated with their region as emblems. The design on the Gortyna coins, a woman seated on a bull's back, was chosen to commemorate how Zeus, in the form of a bull, lured Europa, the Phoenician maiden, onto his back and sped across the sea to the Mesara plain. A geometric or concentric maze pattern with a star at the center on the coins from Knossos was connected to Asterion, which had been associated with the Minotaur depicted on the obverse; and the appearance on the coins of Phaistos of figures such as Talos, the man of bronze whom

Diodorus Siculus, the first-century-B.C. Greek author of a forty-volume universal history, tells us traveled the limits of Crete regularly to ward off intruders, reminded scholars of some of the lesser known myths of the island. The *Athenaeum* review of Wroth's study praised the work but pointed out, "The true interest of Cretan history lies, so to speak, in the prehistoric period, of which the events are represented to us in confused, distorted, and extravagant legends."[64]

It wasn't until May 1886 that Schliemann, accompanied by Dörpfeld, was able to go to Crete. His first impressions are recorded in a letter of May 22 from the hamlet of Makryteichos to his friend Max Müller in Oxford. Unlike most other visitors at the time, Schliemann could make firsthand comparisons with other "prehistoric" buildings, in particular the one that he and Dörpfeld had cleared just the year before; he wrote to Müller that the Kephala contained "a vast edifice similar to the prehistoric palace at Tiryns, and apparently of the same age, for the pottery found in it is perfectly identical with that found in Tiryns and in the royal sepulchers at Mycenae."[65] In the same year, Ernst Fabricius published a detailed report on Kalokairinos's excavations and concurred with Haussoullier that the date of the building and its contents was the same as that of the palaces at Mycenae and Tiryns.[66]

No longer in any doubt about the site's importance, Schliemann renewed his efforts to secure the rights to dig. In the meantime, though, the power over Crete's antiquities had shifted from Photiades to Hazzidakis, who had decided to hold on to the presidency of the Candia Syllogos after his 1883 term, and thus emerged as the most influential defender of the island's Greek heritage. Schliemann no longer saw the need to address the Assembly in person; instead he would try to convince Hazzidakis to do so on his behalf. Hazzidakis was not entirely honest with Schliemann about his chances for approval from the Assembly,[67] but in any case there were problems with the landowners to be sorted out. Schliemann worked hard at striking a bargain with the owners, as the *Athenaeum* regretfully reported on October 16, "Dr. Schliemann still finds impediments in the way of his much-looked-forward-to excavations in Crete. He intended to excavate a hill on the site of Cnossus, but the proprietor has lately died, and the guardians of his children will not allow any digging unless Dr. Schliemann is willing to buy up all their property—nearly the whole site of Cnossus—for several thousand pounds."[68]

The "whole site of Cnossus" seems to have covered a vast area and comprised a largely derelict and undesirable agricultural estate, as the *Athenaeum* of November 6 hinted, in its continued coverage: "Dr. Schliemann has returned to Athens from his unfortunately bootless errand to Crete."[69] It seems the Turkish authorities in Constantinople had told him to come to his own terms with the landowners, "but that he must pay 1,000*l*. as a guarantee that he took nothing from the excavations." One thousand pounds was considered an extravagant indemnity even to Schliemann. Evidently the Turks had learned their lesson, for, the report continued, "His former conditions in the Troad, that he should have all duplicates, were considered far too lenient, as real duplicates were found never to occur, there being always some variety between the specimens, however slight." The Cretan Assembly refused to expropriate the property for the state, as was the practice in mainland Greece, so the owners, seeing themselves in a strong position, asked £4,000. "True, there were two thousand olive trees growing on it," the report conceded, "but the sum was ridiculously exorbitant, and they insisted on his taking more land than he really wanted. The site fixed upon by Dr. Schliemann is an artificial eminence occupying the center of ancient Gnossus, and quite away from the modern scattered hamlet, on which archaic remains had already been discovered." Schliemann felt he was being tricked into buying the entire valley, including the hamlet of Makryteichos, and he balked, both at the demand and at the price. The report concluded with the wistful lament that Schliemann had seen in the Kephala "a huge building peeping, but what it was— whether a Megaron, as he hoped, or a temple—he could not tell, and thus he was obliged to go away without having dug his spade into the ground."

Schliemann didn't visit Crete again until February 1889, when he made a last attempt to secure Knossos. Again he gazed at the subterranean building on the Kephala with the hope of unveiling its mysteries himself, but this time he boasted in a letter to his friend Virchow that since it was only 55 meters long and 43.30 meters wide he could clear it in one week with a hundred workmen,[70] the sort of claim that would have made Dörpfeld blanch. Still, he couldn't come to an agreement with the landowners. It seems he suspected them of trying to cheat him by listing more olive trees than the property contained, a common Cretan ploy to this day. This was Schliemann's last attempt to acquire the Kephala and his last visit to Crete; his death in 1890 left the field open for the next suitor.

Within four months of Schliemann's funeral, the French scholar André Joubin secured from one of the landowners of the Kephala an option to excavate for two years. Soon after his appointment to the directorship of the French School at Athens, Théophile Homolle had sent Joubin to Crete to carry out explorations in the manner of Halbherr and Fabricius, but with specific instructions to reclaim the site for France since its importance had first been made public by Haussoullier, before the Germans could reassert a claim.[71] Further social unrest prevented Joubin from conducting any work in 1890, and he was recalled to Athens at the end of May. Nonetheless, the *Antiquary* that autumn promised, "The French School has completed its contract with the proprietors of the ruins of the large ancient building of Cnossos, in order to excavate them; the works are to be completed in two years."[72] As Halbherr brought Evans up to date in February 1892, the position was that the French School had consulted those who might have had prior claims to the site, including Halbherr himself, and that it now fell to Joubin to commence modern scientific excavations on their behalf at Knossos.[73]

Evans's meeting with Halbherr was one of the major turning points in his career. Disillusioned with museum work and longing to expand his horizons, Evans began to look with greater interest at the world Schliemann had unwittingly brought to light on the Greek mainland, and Kalokairinos had begun to reveal in Crete. If Petrie's prediction of an important forerunner to Mycenae was to be believed, and Milchhöfer's theory about the original home of the inscribed "island stones" in Crete was to be tested, Halbherr was the ideal guide. Evans stood to benefit most from the Italian's knowledge of the landscape and antiquities of a place that to most was still a mystery, little more than the traditional home to fanciful legends, an enchanted isle peopled with the grotesque characters of fantastic myths. The seeds of new ideas were sown in Rome, but the season was not yet right. There was still much to consolidate in England before considering any new ventures abroad.

Civilized Strangers

Edward Freeman had gone to Spain early in the year while Margaret and Arthur were in Italy. There Freeman contracted a mysterious fever—it turned out to be smallpox—and died at Alicante on March 16. This was a severe blow to his daughter, whose own state of health was feeble. In the Evans household at Nash Mills, by contrast, there was a positive reversal of fortune. John Evans made Queen Victoria's Birthday Honours list in June as a Knight Commander of the Bath, and soon after the new title of "Sir John" came a new wife. Maria Millington Lathbury entered his life when he approved her attending a meeting of the Antiquaries, otherwise not open to women, as a guest of the speaker, F. C. Penrose. John had been urged by friends and family to consider remarrying, but had protested that he wasn't interested in "old ladies and children." Maria was neither. In her mid-thirties, she was a recent graduate of Somerville College, Oxford, where she had read Greats, and she knew Arthur and Margaret. Her specialty was ancient Greek dress, and she had been to Greece to study representations that formed the basis for a book she was preparing on the subject.[74] A brief romance ensued and John and Maria were married on July 9, 1892.

Arthur returned to Oxford, leaving Margaret in the summer sunshine at Dover. His first concern was to move to Boars Hill to escape what he had decided was in many ways an unhealthy climate. Early in October he took Margaret for a brief visit to the site of their future home for her approval. There they strolled in the woods, and he might have related to her how the hill got its name. Local legend tells that a scholar wandered up from Oxford one sunny afternoon to find a quiet place to study. Suddenly a wild boar charged from the woods intent on devouring him. The scholar armed only with his reading stuffed his precious edition of Thucydides' *Peloponnesian War* into the beast's jaws and choked it to death.[75] Arthur would have relished the reference to one of the classics being put to a practical use after all.

Margaret approved the location and Arthur pressed his father to help acquire the sixty acres and the peace of mind it represented. Finally, John Evans agreed, and they closed the deal at the end of October. Arthur made his first home on the site by cutting off the tops of pine trees about eight feet from the ground, setting a platform on the stumps, and building a wooden cabin with a wide verandah all around on the platform. He was intent on lifting Margaret well away from the damp ground, but also may have considered the possibility of unpredictable encounters with the local wildlife. The cabin was to be their home while the permanent house at the heart of the estate was built. Satisfied that all was in order for the next phase of their life in Oxford, Evans collected his wife and returned to Italy for the winter.

Margaret stayed at Bordighera with her sister while Arthur went to Sicily to complete the fourth volume of his late father-in-law's *Sicily*, a final tribute to his teacher. Arthur seems to have written about one-quarter, but he had influenced a large portion of it, as Freeman himself had admitted.[76] The younger man's supplements were noted in reviews and heralded as having "much more historical insight, a much truer instinct of the things that are important in history and of the way to find them out, than Freeman ever had."[77]

With the completion of the Sicily volume, Evans was now free to consider his next objective: the island Halbherr had introduced him to. In January 1893 he wrote to his assistant at the Ashmolean to send his personal copy of Milchhöfer's *Anfänge der Kunst* to him in Italy, as he began his detailed study of the "island stones."[78]

In the middle of February, Evans went to Athens, where he had arranged to meet with John Myres at the British School. Myres had arrived in Athens for the autumn 1892 term and had been making the most of his fellowship awards by traveling extensively throughout Greece. He took Evans to Shoe Lane, in the flea market below the Athenian Acropolis, where they haggled with the antique dealers. "I have got a very beautiful little Mykenaean gold bead," Evans wrote to Margaret. "I found it amongst a lot of rubbish. Item, a Mykenaean short sword, in three pieces, but it will put together and they are almost unknown out of Greece."[79]

In the Athens flea market, Evans made the first great personal discovery of his career, the one that is often cited as the decisive turning point in the otherwise routine life of the meticulous scholar and museum curator. With Milchhöfer's images and his own memories of the tiny Phoenician seals that Greville Chester had donated to the Ashmolean four years earlier still fresh in his mind, he now held new types in his hands, which the merchants assured him were Cretan, and he quickly acquired them as his own. As Evans gazed at the semiprecious stones with their odd inscriptions over the next few months, he engaged in the same process of intellectual alchemy he had learned from his father for coins and other objects: once the ancient artifact was acquired personally, it assumed a far greater significance than it could ever have had in a museum case or someone else's collection. It gave the collector-scholar the cherished nucleus around which to build a theory, which would both explain the artifact in an ancient context and add to its importance in the modern context, thereby enhancing its value in every way. The gestation period for Evans's new theory about the stone seals, which greatly affected Aegean studies and guided him into the second, much more rewarding half of his life, had begun.

At the National Archaeological Museum in Athens, Myres introduced Evans to the antiquities he had been studying, and they were able to examine closely the amazing objects that Schliemann had found at Mycenae, which had attracted Evans a decade earlier. But more important than those gold masks first publicized by Schliemann were the treasures subsequently recognized during the less glamorous, but no less exciting, aspect of archaeology, which follows on from the spadework. Schliemann's preoccupation with counting and weighing the gold objects, which had come from the ground as gold usually does, requiring little more than a soft brush to expose their splendor, left the remainder of the finds in need of the careful, patient, and time-consuming cleaning away of layers of dirt and corrosion, which the Athenian conservator Athanasios Koumanydes undertook in order to reveal their secrets.

Museum conservators are the unsung heroes of archaeology. Quietly cleaning and consolidating ancient materials in laboratories, they can spend hundreds of hours on a single object that the field archaeologist lifted from the excavation site in a matter of seconds. Metals especially present problems: silver turns black after several years, and bronze develops a green patina, or protective layer, then begins to flake and decay. The conservator can never stop the process of decay, but tries to slow it down long enough for us to appreciate an ancient work of art.

Koumanydes meticulously cleaned a collection of bronze daggers from Grave Circle A at Mycenae and discovered that many were inlaid with gold, silver, and copper, and some were decorated in the intricate niello technique, which is smoothing a black mixture of sulfur and silver or copper into shallow recesses left in the cast metal, then heating it to bond. He was the first modern man to see the magnificent lion hunt scenes and patterns with animals or flowers—essentially painted in metal, which made connoisseurs notice Mycenaean art and its creators, placing their skills on a par with the finest metallurgists anywhere in the world.

Even more striking to Evans, though, were the fragments of a silver vase from Mycenae with a gold-plated rim decorated with tiny human figures in repoussé technique, that is, pushed out from the inside to form a low relief, then chased, or engraved, for added detail. Only a few fragments survived from a vase that stood about 12 inches high, but enough to show a scene featuring two slingers standing before kneeling archers, all naked, in active defense of a town where women are seen gathered on the parapet. In a series of rough notes, probably written then and there,[80] Evans recorded his initial, excited impression: "The subject well known in Oriental Art is found here for the first time in Mykenaean. But it was known to Homer and Hesiod. cf. descriptions of shields of Achilles & Herakles." Evans discounted the suggestions that other scholars had made that the vase was of Egyptian or Syrian origin; he preferred to place the fine workmanship firmly in the Aegean, again citing the sixth-century Boeotian author of the *Theogony*—the earliest survey of the Greek myths: "In both Hesiod's treatment of the subject and that on our silver vessel there is a difference from the Egyptian & Assyrian etc. There the enemy is wholly overthrown—(generally the besieged). Here tho' we unfortunately see one side, it is evident from the action of the women that the combat is still doubtful. The object of the artist—like Hesiod—was simply to represent the heat of the battle." Evans marveled at the emotional impact of the scene, in which, he felt, "A freer more democratic spirit here breathes"—a concept that, for Evans, distinguished the European Mycenaeans from their Asiatic contemporaries.

Still more, and greater, marvels were being added to the repertoire of Mycenaean art. Some years before, Schliemann had intended to excavate a circular tomb near Sparta, but when Sayce went on reconnaissance he reported that it had been too severely plundered and so he left it.[81] A young Greek archaeologist, Christos Tsountas, who had taken over Schliemann's excavations at Mycenae in 1886, then followed up on the Spartan lead and conducted a rescue excavation in the ruined tomb near Vapheio, on the site of Pharis, in 1888. Tsountas found that Schliemann's instinct had been correct and the looters had missed the greatest treasures yet found in all of Mycenaean art—two gold cups, each about 4 inches high, with repoussé and chased designs of such unique vitality and exquisite detailed execution that they continue to astound the art world.[82]

The first of the Vapheio Cups, as they are known, shows a hunt for wild bulls with a net stretched between trees in which one beast has been snared while another attacks his pursuers and a third escapes at a flying gallop through a landscape with palm trees. The second cup shows domesticated cattle in a landscape with olive trees. Evans recorded these cups in precise detail and marveled at their composition, though of the first one he noted, "the position of the bull is not very natural & the position of the bull charging behind with its body is not happy. Nor is the position of the man in its horns well judged." Nonetheless, he conceded: "Otherwise the art displayed is astonishing

& seems to belong to a much later period. No schematism or slavish adherence to received tradition in the ancient forms (Compare archaic Greek art!!!)."

A growing number of scholars were beginning to see that the artifacts, images, and ideas in the art of the Mycenaeans could be associated readily with events and possessions described in the Homeric poems. For his part, Evans likened the domesticated scene of the capture on the peaceful second cup to the passage in the *Iliad* that relates how the warrior Adamas, speared in the stomach by Meriones, "writhed as a bull that herdsmen in the mountains have bound with twisted willow branches." For the bellowing of the bull on the violent cup, he recalled another grisly death, this time Hippodamas speared in the back by Achilles as he leaped from his chariot to flee: "His life left him as he bellowed like a bull dragged to the altar of Poseidon."[83]

Evans, only a decade earlier, had been reluctant to heed Schliemann's insistence that the Mycenaeans were Homer's heroes, but now he greeted the new realm of Homer's Mycenaeans with wonderment. In an unpublished manuscript entitled "Notes on the Origins & Affinities of Mykênaean Culture," he began: "The Mykênaean Culture springs like Aphrodite from the sea. It rises to the sight full grown—on European soil it seems to land a civilized stranger in the midst of barbarians."[84] It was as though Evans saw Europa stepping from the bull's back, or a glorious female figure springing from the brow of Schliemann, much as Athena emerged from the head of Zeus in Greek myth.

Evans's loose notes, most likely made in February 1893, display a period of rapid conversion to the extraordinary fact of early Greek art at Mycenae, but they also provide insight into the direction his observations were leading him in: "All points to S. W. A. Minor as origin. source of Myk. pop. Crete as centre of Earliest Greek state. Minos may have played great part in spreading this culture."[85] The legendary Cretan king was becoming a historical figure, and the roots of Hellenism were to be found in Crete.

Of Marguerites and Mountain Heath

With his suitcases full of new acquisitions and his head swimming with fresh ideas, Evans left Athens for Italy in early March 1893 to be with Margaret. He may at last have realized the severity of her condition, but it was too late. On Saturday, March 11, Margaret was "seized by a violent paroxysm of pain, and died in an hour or so, holding Arthur's hand to the last," his half-sister recorded.[86] Margaret's link to her father broken only a year earlier, she had tried to organize Freeman's papers with a view to publishing an account of his life and a selection of correspondence, but she had been too weak, and so handed it on to a family friend, a Reverend William Stephens, who eulogizes her devotion in his preface to Freeman's *Life and Letters*: "Never was a daughter fonder or prouder of a father than she was; never did a daughter labour more assiduously than she did to help on work which was to perpetuate her father's memory."[87]

The funeral took place on Sunday afternoon; Margaret was laid to rest in the English corner of the cemetery at Alassio, beneath a tombstone commemorating her devotion to her father, to whom "she had once been as a right hand," and to her husband: "in wild travel, through troublous times, and in quiet study—she was a helpmate such as few have known. Her bright energetic spirit, undaunted by suffering to the last, and ever working for the welfare of those around her, made a short life long."[88] For her grave, Evans made a wreath of marguerites, scented broom, and white Mediterranean heath, the inspiration for a poem he kept to himself:[89]

To Margaret my beloved wife

Of Margarites and mountain heath
    And scented broom so white,—
Such as herself she plucked,—a wreath
    I wreathe for her tonight.

Flowers of the sunshine & the fells
    Where we together roved
And one—the eye of the day that spells
    The name of my beloved.

For she was open as the air
    Pure as the blue of heaven
And truer love—or pearl so rare
    To man was never given!

"I cannot yet fully realize the blow which has fallen me . . . I do not think anyone can ever know what Margaret has been to me. All seems very dark, and without consolation," Evans wrote to his father.[90] He was never again to marry or come as close to a woman as he had to her. He had been deeply affected by his mother's early death and was of a generation who gave their hearts to one woman and never again. He and Margaret had tried unsuccessfully to have children and placed the blame for their failure firmly on her, even though his neglect of her, not to mention his repressed desires for young men, which surfaced later, may have been more than a little responsible. Now she was gone and he was alone. His fathering instinct was to reemerge when he later found material stability and security and adopted two boys, but for now whatever emotions he had expressed through Margaret were locked away in what his half-sister dubbed "the secret fortress of his heart."

Along with Margaret went many aspects of Evans's early life. The completion of the Sicilian history had been their last project together, and was his last link with that island, now too closely associated with death and the spirits of departed loved ones.

After a mourning period of three days, Evans set off northward to Parma, whence he explored Terramare and the Ligurian caves in search of clues to a Neolithic society of cave dwellers,[91] then on to Zagreb, to revisit the site of his first Balkan adventure, perhaps trying to recapture the moment when he was a brave, uninhibited young student, so many years before. He was back in Oxford by June and sought refuge in the solitude of the Boars Hill cabin, the treetop nest he had built for Margaret.

Soon after the loss of Margaret, the family gained a girl for Sir John and Lady Evans, named Joan, after her father. Arthur shared his discomfort at the news with Charles Fortnum, perhaps because he himself had not succeeded in paternity and his father, a sprightly sixty-nine-year-old, accomplished it with ease. Eventually Evans came to accept his half-sister and found much of his lost wife's competency, as well as a close confidante, in her.

The tone of his outward emotional expression was set by the notepaper he commissioned: the traditional white with a wide black band at the edges and an elephant at the letterhead to commemorate his loss and affirm his intention never to forget her. Evans continued to use the black border in all his correspondence, as a barrier to any would-be intruders upon a person who had decided on a course of privacy in all matters, for the rest of his life. He was forty-two years old—a failed journalist, banned from Austria; a failed husband, now widowed without an heir; and a notoriously strong-willed but hopelessly idealistic opponent of tyranny. But above all else, he was tired of administration and the endless fund-raising for the Ashmolean, and fed up with his dealings with the Oxford establishment, whose closed academic circles he couldn't break into, due to his unwillingness to conform. He was ready for life to take a new turn, and the most appealing direction was that illuminated by Halbherr. The way was being prepared by the youthful industry of John Myres, who was already exploring the broad avenues opening up to a brilliant new world with its clues to an early civilization "quickened by Aegean breezes."

3

Candia 1893–1900

Mycenaean Hieroglyphs

As Arthur Evans began his long, lonely journey north across Europe in mid-March 1893, clutching firmly in his grip the seal-stones he'd found in Athens, engraved with the clues to his next incarnation, an excited John Myres set about clearing the way for the next stage in Evans's life. Evans and Hogarth had instructed Myres to use his fellowships to conduct a survey of prehistoric sites in Greece and the islands, and to carry out an exploration of possible prehistoric sites on Crete.

The archaeological survey, essentially visiting ancient sites, noting visible remains and listing them by suspected periods of occupation, was postponed when Myres hurt his knee and had to recuperate at the home of the philhellene Edward Noel, in Euboea; he described the estate as having the feudal atmosphere of an English country house set in the middle of a Greek village. Myres studied the modern Greek language during his two-month convalescence and familiarized himself with local customs. One that most impressed him was the Orthodox Easter ceremony: the commemoration of the resurrection of Christ by light and fire, he recounted many years later, might not have happened this particular year had he not heard the priest mutter under his breath that the matches to light the candles were damp; the resourceful Englishman passed a dry box through the screen between the painted icons, to the cleric's heartfelt relief, and heard the soft whisper, "Thank God, so Christ *will* rise after all."[1] The following day the men took part in a distinctly Orthodox Christian event, the "Shooting of Judas" in the churchyard, a ceremony surrounding an exploding dummy that was vilified and referred to as the Jew.[2]

Myres had recovered sufficiently by May to respond enthusiastically to a request from W. R. Paton, an Aberdonian who had married Olympitis, the beautiful daughter of the mayor of the Greek island of Kalymnos, and had received as part of her dowry a farmstead on the Turkish mainland at the ancient site of Myndus, in the region of Caria, to assist with the survey he planned to conduct of the ancient monuments on the Turkish peninsula of Halicarnassus and Myndus, near Bodrum on the Aegean coast. Myres set out from Piraeus, the harbor for Athens, late in May, made several ports of call across the Aegean, enjoying the sorts of adventures that seem to present themselves to inquisitive youths, and eventually sailed into the harbor of Kalymnos, where Paton lived. One of the Dodecanese, in Greek literally the "twelve" islands, which are scattered down the southeastern Aegean coast of Turkey, Kalymnos was famous for its sponge fishermen. Myres recalled being "surrounded by a flotilla of little boats manned by naked copper-coloured boys, looking like animated bronze statues as the ancients would have known them." He learned that "they were the children of sponge-fishers . . . their parents used to throw them into the harbour at a year old: if they floated and came ashore they would make good sponge-fishers; if they sank without a trace it was good riddance."[3]

Myres worked with Paton for two months, walking the hills of Caria and finding as much to interest him among the ancient ruins as among the modern Carians and their lifestyle. He was a keen observer and participant (in sharp contrast to Evans, who always remained aloof and kept his distance), and gained a detailed firsthand knowledge of the Anatolian coast and the adjacent islands, which was to come in handy when he was recalled to the area to serve his country twenty years later.

The Caria survey ended in late July, and Myres set sail for Crete. The previous December he had written to Thomas Sandwith, now retired from his consular duties in Canea, asking for advice on how best to conduct his search for prehistoric sites. The ex-diplomat's reply had spelled out what he recalled of the rules of Turkish law regarding antiquities, which "allows only duplicates to be kept by the finder, all originals, except in the case of small pieces of jewelry, being claimed for the Museum of Constantinople." As the Turkish authorities had discovered with Schliemann, the term "duplicate" allowed for much leeway on the part of those deciding the relative merits of antiquities—which should remain in the country of discovery and which might be allowed free passage abroad. Sandwith continued his advice to the young explorer, cautioning,

> There is a further division of the spoil between the Govt. the proprietor of the soil and the finder. But this law, not being one of the unalterable character of the Medes and Persians, is subject to modification in practice . . . A greater obstacle to the explorer of antiquities lies in the patriotic jealousy with which certain educated Greeks in the chief towns regard the foreigner. There exists an inchoate Museum in Candia, to which these Cretan gentlemen are anxious that all objects of archaeological interest should find their way, but in as much as the Turkish authorities would prefer to send such to Constantinople, the former discourage the search after antiquities till such time as the island should pass under Greek rule, which cannot be said to be within measurable distance.[4]

Sandwith supported the official British government view that the Ottoman authority, flawed as it might be, offered more stability in the eastern Mediterranean than would new nationalist governments working out the problems of power after generations of subservience to outsiders.

At Sandwith's recommendation Myres contacted his successor as consul in Crete, Alfred Biliotti, who assured him that he should have little difficulty traveling in most parts of the island and offered to help with letters of introduction and supplies. Myres found that since Sandwith had retired, new "Regulations concerning Antiquities" had been published by the Turkish government: since 1884 the export of *all* works of art from Turkish territory was forbidden. To complicate matters, the Candia Syllogos adopted the recent Greek law stating that all ancient objects belonged to the state. Whoever wished to excavate in Greece had to pay the expenses of a government inspector and was allowed to take only drawings or casts of the discovered objects out of the country.[5] But, to his relief, Myres also found that the new Turkish regulations were virtually unenforceable and for the most part ignored.

In Candia, Myres stayed with the British vice-consul, Lysimachos Kalokairinos, older brother of Minos the dragoman, and the three of them rode out to the Kephala, where Minos explained his findings to the young English scholar. At the Syllogos, Hazzidakis proudly showed Myres the growing collection of antiquities, and one group of artifacts immediately caught his eye, or so he recalled many years later. "A few days before, a peasant had brought down a basketful of potsherds from the Kamares cave, high on the south side of Mount Ida," he wrote. Myres recognized the similarity with those that Flinders Petrie had sent him off to find more of, and here he could safely prove their Cretan origin, as there seemed to be great quantities from the cave; also he was certain of their date, since similar pieces had been found in a nearby tomb with an amethyst scarab of the Egyptian Twelfth Dynasty—a perfect fit with Petrie's date for the Kahun material. Recognizing the importance of this correlation, Myres made color drawings, took the next steamer for Athens, and within six days was comparing his drawings with the Egyptian finds in the British Museum in London.[6] The correspondence was exact. In September he presented his discovery of what he called "Kamares Ware" to the British Association and thereby provided, as Petrie had predicted, one of the most reliable means of assigning to the discoveries in Crete a historical time period, albeit one calculated in Egyptian terms.[7]

Soon after his return to England Myres set about trying to gain permission to excavate in Crete. Unlike Evans, he had no private income but was confident that Oxford, the Hellenic Society, and the British School at Athens would willingly provide funds. He wrote to Biliotti in October, asking him to get permission from the authorities: "I propose to begin at Gnossos but want to get a general leave to make trial-diggings at such other sites as I may find promising during my next journey. And if possible, the leave should be got from the Government on the spot, so as not to encounter the authorities of the Constantinople Museum, who will ruin everything by demanding the transference of the Government share to Constantinople."[8] The brash youth seemed to be either ignorant of or unconcerned about any prior claims to excavate, and to be assuming that he could undertake a fairly grand program of research. But Halbherr, simultaneously, was being courted by the Archaeological Institute of America, and it seemed to some that he wanted to dig Knossos; Ernest Gardner, director of the British School at Athens, cautioned Myres on November 1, "I hope that he won't go and anticipate you at Gnossos, there is plenty of room in Crete, but these annoying things do happen sometimes."[9] Myres wrote to Hazzidakis for clarification and was told, "As things are today I think it impossible for an excavation permit to be granted in Crete." He tried to explain the difficulties the Cretans were having with Constantinople and asked him not to try to get permission for the next three months at least.[10] So Myres turned his attention to Cyprus, which was under Turkish sovereignty but, since the Cyprus Convention of 1878 between Britain and Turkey, was administered by the British government as part of the British guarantee to preserve the sultan's Asian possessions from threat by Russia, and therefore easier for British archaeologists, who set up the Cyprus Exploration Fund, to excavate there. Myres joined the British Museum excavations at Amathus in the spring of 1894, and over the next decade became one of the leading specialists in Cypriot early history. Myres had been the eighth in a line of distinguished investigators to try to reveal the mysteries of the Kephala, but, as those before him had discovered, the time was not yet right.

Arthur Evans had arrived in Oxford in the summer of 1893 and supervised the construction of his first permanent house on Boars Hill, while reviewing proposals for the new Ashmolean Museum; it was a time of building for the future. In September, he read a paper on the discovery of an ancient British pile-settlement near Glastonbury to the British Association. Pile-settlements were first discovered after a drought in 1853, in Switzerland, when Alpine lakes fell to an unprecedented low and the waterlogged, wooden remains of ancient dwellings built on piles driven into the lakes' bottoms were revealed, and dated somewhere between 3000 B.C. and the Roman conquest in the first century B.C. These so-called Lake Dwellings, now thought to have been houses set over marshland near the lakes, were heralded as typically early European, and so Evans was delighted to draw attention to the early arrival of a respected form of civilization in Britain, which he now placed three centuries before Julius Caesar's conquest in 55 B.C. He theorized that Belgic tribes had first brought European ideas to Britain as early as 300 B.C., a point he clarified in a long letter, published in late September in the *Times*: "Greek and Italian Influences in Præ-Roman

Britain." Evans added his newly formed ideas on what he suspected to be the "northern effects" of the Mycenaean art that had so beguiled him in Athens:

> Here it is impossible to do more than allude to this far-reaching chain of cause and effect, the links of which, as I hope to be able eventually to show in the most conclusive manner, form a direct connection between the highest development of ancient British or late Celtic art as seen in the earliest illuminations and goldsmith's work of Christian Ireland on the one hand, and, on the other, with the most ancient ornamental system of the Hellenic world—the art of Mykenae.[11]

Evans believed that the use of spirals as decorative motifs in both regions was concrete evidence of some form of contact; and this theme—of early Greek civilization, for which the art of Mycenae was fast becoming the beacon, and its effects on prehistoric Britain—allowed him to unite the two ancient worlds he most admired: his own Britain and Homer's Aegean.

On November 27 Evans gave his first lecture on his newly adopted Mycenaeans to the Hellenic Society in London, about an odd assortment of goldware and jewelry that had come into the possession of the British Museum the previous year, "A Mykênæan Treasure from Ægina."[12] Curiously, he still retained the anachronistic spelling and accents for ancient Greek words, such as Mykênæ for Mycenae and Knôsos for Knossos, which was in keeping with the strict rules of language "purity" dictated by Edward Freeman. These continued to appear in his notes long after his father-in-law's influence might well have faded, and long after editors at the close of the nineteenth century had modernized the transcriptions to suit the typewriter and printing industries.[13]

Evans used the occasion of his formal entry into Aegean archaeology to air his views on the Greek and Turkish "Regulations concerning Antiquities" forbidding the export of all works of art from those countries:

> Opinions may well differ as to the propriety of removing from the soil on which they are found and to which they naturally belong the greater monuments of Classical Antiquity. But in the case of small objects, made themselves for commerce, and free from the

same local ties, the considerations, which weigh under other
circumstances, lose their validity . . . This, it is true, is not the
standpoint of the Greeks, or, for that matter, of the Turkish Government. But the theory that the present occupants of Greece or
the Ottoman possessors of the Eastern Empire are the sole legitimate heirs even of such minor monuments of ancient culture is
not likely to commend itself to the outside world. 'Twere hard indeed that not so much as a plaything should come down to us
from the cradle of our civilization![14]

The contrast between Greek "occupants" and Turkish "possessors"
was a clear statement of his personal preference regarding ethnic prece-
dence and historical imperative, and it pleased his colleagues in the
Hellenic Society. As far as antiquity was concerned, the "playthings"
that Evans had enjoyed since childhood were exactly those things he
wished to export from Greece for his continued enjoyment as an adult.
"The laws by which not even a coin, or a jewel or a vase is allowed to
find its way beyond a certain privileged zone, while frivolous in themselves and powerless to secure the object that they have in view, inflict a
permanent injury to science," he continued, pointing out that the
strictness of the laws forced the illicit recovery of artifacts and the
removal of any archaeological context. No curator of a European
museum hoping to increase its endowment through archaeological activities in the Aegean was willing to accept the conditions in Greece and
Turkey. Instead, they would search for ways to circumvent the authorities.

The stylistic parallels that Evans listed for the gold jewelry were
drawn from his knowledge of Egyptian, Syrian, Greek, Italian, Sardin-
ian, Central European, and even Caucasian art. In the end he concluded that the treasure was indeed "Mykênæan" but belonged to about
800 B.C., when, he said, the great days of Mycenae had passed but some
artistic traits had survived on the island of Aigina. This view is no
longer supported, as his own later Cretan discoveries showed the group
to be much earlier.[15]

During the discussion that followed his address, Evans made the
startling announcement of his discovery of a "Mykênæan" system of hieroglyphic writing. Since his return from Athens, he had reexamined
Greville Chester's "Phoenician" seals given to the Ashmolean in 1888,
and he had compared them to some of those published by Milchhöfer

with scratched signs, of which Adolf Furtwängler in Berlin had sent
him impressions. Evans added to the discussion his own recent acquisitions from Shoe Lane, which remained his personal property, as well as
those that Myres had bought in Crete and donated to the Ashmolean.[16]
He claimed he had sufficient evidence of some sixty symbols to establish that there was indeed a "native Greek" script and that the inscriptions resembled the hieroglyphic scripts of Egypt and Anatolia but
were quite independent. His father's lessons in classification showed
him how to divide these symbols into three types, which, he suspected,
represented stages of development from picture to hieroglyph to linear
script.[17] This first fruit born of the seeds of the Athens flea market
might have come as a surprise to many, but not to John Evans, who
now saw that his wish to promote the European ancestors from the
lower leagues of barbarism to the exalted ranks of civilization was fast
approaching reality. Arthur's discovery made all the more urgent a trip
to the rumored source of the inscribed gems. "I am getting very restless
and want a good run!" he wrote to Charles Fortnum in November.
"Nothing will content me but to go round by Sicily to Crete"—from
the well trodden to the unknown.[18]

How Are the Mighty Fallen!

Evans set off for the Mediterranean as soon as weather permitted, arriving in Cairo in February 1894. Though unhappy in modern Egypt
and suffering from malaria, he used the occasion to supplement at
firsthand an already quite detailed knowledge of the art and archaeology of the country with a careful study of its ancient hieroglyphic
scripts, deciphered by Champollion seventy years earlier. In many ways,
Evans, too, was a student of Flinders Petrie and owed much of his view
of ancient Egypt's cultural and political domination of the ancient
Near East to Petrie's authoritative summaries.

   In March, Evans sailed to Athens, then found passage on the Austrian Lloyd's *Juno* for Crete. *Juno*—as the Romans called Hera, wife of
Zeus—bore Evans on his first journey to the land where he would "explore what lay behind the traditions of Minos and Daedalos, and of the
fabled Labyrinth, together with the quest of a still earlier form of writing,"[19] as he recalled later, though at the time he set aside only a fortnight in which to do so.

   It was on the Ides of March 1894, a full year after Margaret's death, that Evans gazed for the first time upon the seemingly inhospitable landscape that had given birth to the histories, mysteries, and clues to the new world that had come to obsess him. Out of the morning mist rose the great Lefka Ori, or White Mountains, in the west, as the *Juno* swung in from Melos and began its journey from the north and west across the top of Crete, the direction that most travelers were to take in both the physical and metaphorical senses during the next century of exploration.

To the maritime viewer, Crete appears to stand in the Aegean Sea like the top of a great bull charging westward. Its four mountain massifs with hard, blue-gray limestone at the core explode from the sea and climb suddenly to 2,200 meters in the White Mountains at the far west, then go even higher, to 2,456 meters at Psiloritis, the pinnacle of the Idaean range, into which the White Mountains blend above Rethymnon. Psiloritis, the ancient Mount Ida, is the highest peak on the island and the focal point of legends both ancient and modern; it was the obvious setting for Kingsley's Theseus to pursue the Minotaur. There's a break in the middle of Crete linking the rolling hills of the northern center, where Herakleion (Candia) sits, with the Mesara plain on the southern coast. Here, Ida's foothills mingle with the beginning of the Diktaian range, which there rises to the east in a ring around the Lasithi plain, a concealed plateau 900 meters above the sea. Another sudden break occurs at the Gulf of Mirabello, where the port of Aghios Nikolaos is nestled on the north coast, giving way to the sharp, almost impenetrable rise of the Thryphti range above the port of Siteia, which tapers off gradually into the Sea of Egypt at the island's eastern flanks.

Sunrise revealed the profile of Mount Juktas, a solitary point in the otherwise rolling foothills of the Idaean range at the island's very heart, and Evans could make out the great forehead, pointed nose, and endless beard of the dead god Zeus, reclining from north to south, who the Cretans claimed was buried there—one reason the Greeks, to whom Zeus was immortal, regarded all Cretans as liars. This distinctive profile should have been enough to vanquish the previous twenty-four hours of travel sickness. Soon, the old *vapori*, as the Greeks called a steamer, slowed at the shelter of Candia harbor, with its grand stone vaults erected by the Venetians standing to attention along the shore while the Lion of St. Mark, symbol of the republic's patron saint, on the small peninsular fortress surveyed the small landing craft that jostled to meet the new arrivals and compete for their custom. Evans soon found a

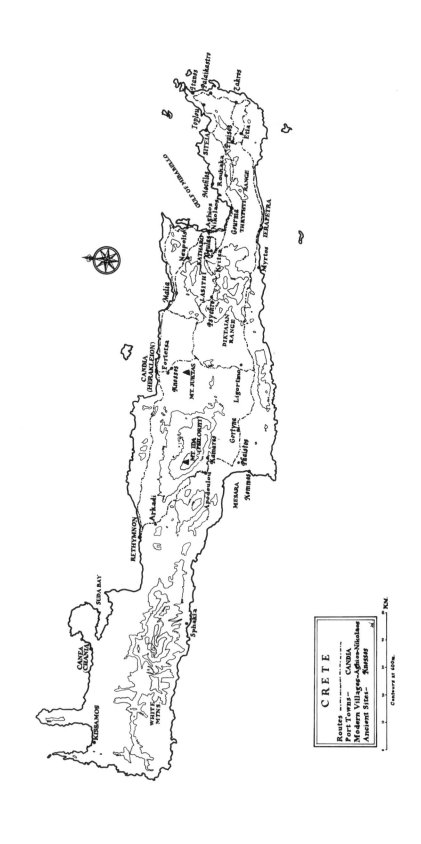

CRETE

Routes ----------
Port Towns— CANDIA
Modern Villages—Aghios-Nikolaos
Ancient Sites— Knossos

Contours at 600m.

room overlooking the harbor and set out to discover for himself the city of Candia.

The route up from the harbor took him past the great church of St. Titus, first Christian bishop on Crete, said to have been appointed by St. Paul himself when he was shipwrecked on the island's south coast during the Roman occupation of the first century A.D.[20] Next on the left he passed the Loggia, an elegant structure of the early seventeenth century built by Francesco Morosini, one of the last Venetian governors, who was also responsible for the fountain that still bears his name in the little square opposite, at the north end of the marketplace— Evans's first destination. In the narrow alleys of the bazaar, crowded with tiny stalls, Evans sought out the antique dealers and bought no fewer than twenty-two early Cretan seal-stones for one and a half piasters apiece (a piaster being one-hundredth of a Turkish pound), the total cost being roughly one-quarter of a British pound at the time: an amazingly low price by any standard.

Evans looked for Halbherr but was frustrated to learn that both he and Hazzidakis were in Canea. The next day he visited the Russian vice-consul, Ioannis Mitsotakis, who had been involved in looting the Cave of Zeus on Mount Ida shortly after its discovery by shepherds in 1884, and who had amassed quite an impressive collection of votive offerings—including ancient Greek arms and armor, a popular form of dedication by warriors to Zeus in gratitude for a victory—before the Syllogos intervened and sent Halbherr with one Mr. Aerakis, from Candia, to excavate in the summer of 1885.[21] Mitsotakis was willing to part with his plunder and sold Evans twenty-one seal-stones, but far more important than all the gems on offer was an object that must have made Evans's hands tremble.

Mitsotakis had a gold ring like those Schliemann had found at Mycenae and Tiryns, but this one, he said, came from Knossos. The excitement that must have surged through Evans as he held the precious metal would have been hard to conceal. Here was a golden clue forged in some remote antiquity. To him, the scene engraved on the ring seemed "to illustrate a kind of stone worship that still survives in India and elsewhere to the present day. The god, brought down by ritual and incantation, is seen descending on the sacred obelisk that thus becomes his temporary dwelling-place, or, in Biblical language, a 'Bethel.' "[22] On the left of the obelisk Evans could make out a shrine-like building enclosing a tree, perhaps like the sacred ash tree Yggdrasil, the tree of life at the center of the Teutonic myths. As he slipped it onto his little finger he might have felt the power of Alberich or Wotan, or their local equivalents, Prometheus and Zeus. In the Germanic legend, possession of the Ring of the Nibelung symbolized gaining some sort of enlightenment, a deeper awareness of oneself and one's mission in life. Evans quickly acquired the Ring of Knossos and later referred to it as one of his "most precious spoils" from Crete. Like other clues he felt the need to own, the ring acted like a magnet for further artifacts which he used to construct a world of ideas, his earliest composition of what Cretan religion might have been, and to make a link between the Rhinemaidens and their natural cousins in the forests of Crete. The power of the ring seems to have given Evans the confidence of a Siegfried in his future ventures, though with less tragic results than for the Germanic hero. Though the object was technically an important cultural artifact and should have gone into a museum, he kept its power for himself for the next forty-four years.

Next, Evans made his way to the cathedral of Aghios Minas, where, in the courtyard to the left of the main entrance, was the small building that Hazzidakis and the Syllogos had converted into a museum. A year before, the Italian traveler Vittorio Simonelli had been enchanted by the little museum in one long room, describing it as "a real surprise. A veritable treasure house of bronze objects, inscriptions, vases, worked stones and marble sculpture." The prize pieces were the bronzes from the Cave of Zeus which Halbherr had rescued from Mitsotakis. When Simonelli had asked his guide if there were plans to enlarge the collection, the reply was that they were biding their time; they considered it "better to wait a little while longer, in any case no one can better preserve an ancient monument than the earth which has done such a good job for so many centuries."[23] His guide was repeating the opinion shared by the Greek Cretans, as Myres had most recently discovered, that any excavation now would only benefit the Imperial Museum in Constantinople. The danger was real, as Evans in his turn heard the rumors that Hamdi Bey threatened to come to Crete with a view to exploring its archaeological sites in person.

That afternoon Evans made the acquaintance of Minos Kalokairinos and inspected his collection of finds from the excavations at the Kephala. Evans was very impressed indeed by the pottery, which, he observed, had "very good Mycenaean designs," but he was dubious about the merits of their discoverer, who, he recorded in his diary, "has views as to his remote ancestor!"[24]

Whether because of his long-standing disrespect for self-made men who took to science, or because of a more personal issue with him, Evans found it difficult to credit Kalokairinos with the discovery of Knossos, and was eventually to write him out of the site's modern history. But for now, he humored the dreamer with his unbelievable tales of King Minos holding court with his magistrates in the circular Courthouse by the Royal Palace at Knossos, and took advantage of his expert knowledge of the region. Impatient to visit the source of all he had heard about from Halbherr, Stillman, Myres, and now Kalokairinos, Evans hired a local guide named Poulakakis on the fifth day of what he had planned to be a brief visit, and on March 19 set out for Knossos. The six-kilometer ride took them through a countryside coming to life after a wet winter. It was all new yet somehow familiar to Evans, perhaps from imagined journeys; this route was one he would travel regularly for the most creative and eventful part of his life.

They left Candia through the Kainoriou Gate of the Venetian fortress and crossed the great Saracen moat on a narrow bridge to the south bank, where they met with a ragged assembly of sad souls banned from the city streets: the lepers, who exhibited their deformed extremities in hopes of evoking the sympathy of affluent travelers. Evans was moved by their hardship and shared some of his good fortune. From the south bank, the route took them up slippery clay slopes and through a landscape consecrated to death: here were the fields that the British traveler Bernard Randolph, in 1680, just eleven years after the defeat of Venetian Candia by the Turks, described as "like a new plow'd field, where you cannot walk, but must see pieces of dead men's bones."[25] Now some order had been established, and it was a sprawling Muslim cemetery. About ten generations of Cretan Muslims, including the many Greeks who had embraced the Muslim faith in order to secure a share in the island's administration, lay buried here on their native soil. Some had lived and died in the land they labored on and loved; others had died during insurrections against Turkish rule. The tall, gleaming white markers stood for only as long as there were caretakers who cherished the memories of the lives described in the cursive script; they were destroyed and used for building blocks when Christians ravaged the cemetery early in the twentieth century. Farther along Evans and his guide came to a smaller, walled-in burial ground where flowers bright with the colors of new life in a field of death attracted their notice. Here the Christians had buried their dead, and continued to do so long after the Muslim memorials were desecrated.

Their first stop was at the Turkish monastery, or Tekke, at Ambelokipi, a large estate with vineyards that marked the northern boundary of ancient Knossos. The dervish welcomed them with traditional hospitality and enlightened Evans on the nature of the tensions among the locals. There were serious divisions within his own Muslim community, he explained: the peasants were happy to associate with their Christian counterparts and would in all likelihood become Christian themselves, but the "town Mohametans are a proud and exclusive caste" and given to the sort of fanaticism that fueled the fires of hate.[26] As he had been in Bosnia, Evans was drawn to the plight of the country folk, and he was to look for ways of bridging the gulf, but at the same time he could never fully abandon the mistrust and loathing that Freeman had instilled in him for "the Turk."

They left Tekke refreshed and soon entered a landscape where rocky crags gave way to a man-made formation of weathered brick and stone protruding from the hillsides and vineyards; these were reminders of Rome's claim to Crete's wealth at the time of Christ. The track took them through the heart of an ancient ghost town, the Colonia Juliana, past Belli's great basilica and through the orchestra of the theater where Roman immigrants had spent summer evenings immersed in timeless tales told as human drama, most probably including the stories that they knew had originated in their new home, perhaps even in their own fields. Evans would have been well aware of the same tales as he followed the track. Rounding the last bend in the road, he was shown his objective, down in the river valley to the left, but at such a distance he could see little without squinting. Instead, he let himself imagine the low protuberance jutting out from a gentle slope on the west side of the river, as numerous predecessors had described it. The party descended the slope, tied their horses to the trees at the route's edge, and walked out across the knoll, which was "brilliant with purple white and pinkish anemones and blue iris," to Evans's delight.[27]

Evans jumped down into the collapsed trenches that Kalokairinos had opened fifteen years before. He cleared away the weeds and for the first time ran his fingers across the cut signs in the sandstone blocks, so well described and illustrated by his friend Stillman in 1881. Halbherr and Myres had been quite right! This was the source of all that had come to attract him to this island at the far reaches of Europe. It was a moment of recognition he returned to often during the succeeding years, especially after the whirlwind of publicity that came with the rise of Knossos to international importance and his own subsequent fame, so much so that it became something of a mythic moment in his own mind. It's interesting to contrast his statement made more than thirty years later to Vera Hemmens, a British journalist, and the events as he recorded them in notebooks and publications nearer the time.

"I first explored the site of the palace of Minos in 1894, the first time I visited Crete," Evans recalled to Hemmens in September 1926:

> As soon as I cast my eyes on it I felt that it was all important because it was the centre of all the legends of ancient Greece. When I discovered the site there was a little old wall at one end. That was all. I explored the surface very carefully, and picked up little bits of painted stuccos and scraps of pottery—enough to convince me of the wonder of it. I saw in the hands of the natives some pieces of clay tablets bearing signs of writing in an unknown language.

This simplified version of his first-person-singular "discovery" of Knossos was well suited to the public's romantic image of archaeology, but it couldn't have been further from the truth. In his diary at the time he recorded:

> The site of Knossos is most extensive and occupies several hills. The Mykênæan akropolis however seems not to be the highest but that to the south west . . . Here at a place called τα πιθάρια [ta pitharia] are the remains of Mykênæan walls and passages (where the great pots, Pithoi, were found) noted by Stillman and others.[28]

It was no happy coincidence of "Time and Chance," then, as his half-sister later fantasized. Evans had been aware of the importance of Knossos since Stillman's report of 1881, thirteen years earlier, and by the time he stood in the trenches on the Kephala he had read reports by a long succession of scholars who had already gathered evidence that allowed them to formulate conflicting theories about the site's date and identification. He had met with the site's first discoverer, and he had handled the "little bits of painted stuccos and scraps of pottery" recovered by Kalokairinos in his home, not lying about on the surface. His relationship with Knossos had less to do with fortune than with conscious decision. Evans wanted to dedicate his efforts to revealing ancient Knossos because he believed this would help him answer his question about the origins of the Mycenaeans. He knew he was the ninth in a line of distinguished suitors, all of whom had failed before him, but that afternoon he set his mind on the prize.

On the way back to Candia, Evans and his guide stopped in the hamlet of Makryteichos and Evans's seemingly innocent call for *antikas* brought forth "a remarkable fragment of a black basalt vessel. At first," he noted, "I thought it was a bit of some kind of Roman relief ware, but to my astonishment I found it was Mykênæan, with part of a relief representing men perhaps ploughing or sowing—an altar?—and a walled enclosure with a fig tree: a supplement to the Vapheio vases and contemporary in style!"[29] Here was his second solid link, after the Ring of Knossos, to the greatest treasures of Mycenaean art, but again found on Cretan soil—and at Knossos.

Evans had arrived that morning at the Kephala with a certain amount of skepticism, especially after the conversation with Kalokairinos, but he left convinced of at least one thing: he wrote in his diary that the walls "are very complex as far as one can judge from what is visible to the eye, but were hardly as Stillman supposes the Labyrinth itself. (Later: No, on further examination I think it must be so.)"[30]

The following day his friend Halbherr arrived from Canea with Hazzidakis, and they gave him a detailed tour of the little museum. They spoke of future excavations on the Kephala site, and Hazzidakis "poohpoohed" André Joubin's claim, according to Evans. The option that Joubin had secured in 1890 for the French School at Athens to excavate at Knossos had been with only one of the four landowners, and had also been for only two years, which time period had elapsed. There was also the more serious matter that Joubin had blotted his copy book, as far as the Greek Cretans were concerned, by going off to Constantinople to help Hamdi Bey to catalogue the recently completed Imperial Museum and thus was persona non grata. As Evans recorded, "Hadjidakis [Hazzidakis] and all the Greeks here are much averse to Joubin having any finger in the pie now that he has become a Turkish employé and an underling of Hamdi Bey."[31] Evans lost no time in substituting himself as the best candidate for the position.

On the afternoon of March 21, Halbherr and Kalokairinos took Evans back to the Kephala site and also showed him around the other antiquities in the Knossos valley. That evening he entered into a formal discussion with Hazzidakis, not about acquiring the right to excavate as others had done—that would come later—but about acquiring the land on which the site stood. Evans the collector knew well the privileges that came with ownership and set in motion the scheme that would win him his greatest prize. Their talks continued the following day, and they finally agreed that Hazzidakis would bargain with the one proprietor who seemed willing to sell and would buy one-quarter of the property on Evans's behalf, thereby giving him the right to force the purchase of the remainder of the property. Evans then promised to raise the full amount in England through a body he would create: "the 'Cretan Exploration Fund'—at present non-existent."[32]

Evans then set off on an expedition to explore Crete for himself. He left Candia on March 23, going west toward Rethymnon. On the way he found that the roads and all the bridges were in disrepair. "Even in the towns I did not meet with anything that could be called an inn. Thanks to periodical insurrections, half of most of the villages is composed of blackened shells, and as a rule little earth-floored huts supply the only accommodation, though I found the inmates hospitable and obliging."[33]

In Rethymnon he sought out Halbherr's guide, Alevisos Papalexakis, and engaged his services. As his proposed excursion was to take place during the Christian Orthodox Lenten fast before Easter, "when the common garden snail becomes the chief support of orthodoxy," Evans was delighted to have found "a muleteer who can jug a Cretan hare and convert into soup an occasional fowl . . . an invaluable auxiliary." But his greatest praise was for Alevisos's "real nose for antiquities"—hardly surprising, as the Cretan had guided visitors for at least a decade and was well acquainted with the ancient monuments scattered throughout the island's rugged landscape.[34]

Evans found more examples of early gems at a goldsmith's shop in Rethymnon and noted with growing awareness and excitement: "The proportional importance of Mykênæan remains strikes one at every turn. The legendary days of Minôs, thalattocracy of Idomeneus and the Hundred Cities were the great days of Crete."[35] Here indeed was the island of Homer's enchanting description that only a generation earlier had been regarded as little more than a fascination, a fabled tale with fantastic characters. Now Evans was being swept back into a poetic landscape, and try as he might to remain rational, the more he saw, the more he allowed himself to consider the possibility that true history was concealed beneath the myths.

Homer's Crete, as described by Odysseus in the guise of a wandering Cretan chief, was "a land . . . in the midst of the wine-dark sea; fair, rich and sea-girt is she . . . In her is a countless multitude of men, and ninety cities. Among these is the great city of Knosos, where Minos, confidant of Zeus, ruled for nine terms." Of the Cretans themselves he sang, "Intermingled are their languages, one with another. Achaeans are there, great-hearted Eteocretans, Kydonians, Dorians, and lordly Pelasgoi."[36] As Homer tells it, Idomeneus was the son of Deucalion and grandson of Minos—himself a son of Zeus. It was he who led the Cretan navy, third only in number to Agamemnon of Mycenae and Nestor of Pylos, to the war that united the Achaeans against Troy, and he returned home with his entire force intact.[37] Did Evans convince himself that the Cretan landscape was indeed that of the poem? Were these tumbled-down and overgrown walls the ancient dwellings of the poet's remembrance? Was it to this very island that Idomeneus returned victorious from Troy only to become lord over a population defeated by disease and a land that was soon cursed with famine and pestilence? If so, Evans was witness to the circularity of history as he confronted illness and hunger wherever he went.

Evans and Alevisos left Rethymnon on March 27 and climbed the western foothills of Mount Ida to the monastery of Arkadi, where they were received by the Abbot Gabriel, whom Evans described as "a jovial man on whom the lenten fasting sits uneasily," and on whom recent events sat with even less ease.[38] The abbot related the story of the indiscriminate massacre there of 550 men, women, and children who had fled the coastal towns in search of sanctuary, a horror that Stillman had witnessed during the insurrection of 1866. At the end of the assault, when it was clear that all was lost for the Christians, the abbot had lit the storehouse of gunpowder and blown the place up. Evans was told that only one monk had survived, and saw for himself that the once great Venetian church was reduced to rubble.

The more Evans traveled through the landscape of burned-out farmsteads and villages and heard tales of internecine conflict and disease—leprosy seemed to resurface on a regular basis—the more he was reminded of the contrast between the "great ages" of civilization and the seemingly inevitable slide into despair that followed. The countryside, like the towns, still contained vestiges of the great artistic floruit of the Cretan renaissance, when Venetian authority had brought with it education and aesthetics, but huddled within the collapsed framework of the Republic's attempt to rule the islanders was a people for whom Evans could muster little respect, though occasionally he did spare a little sympathy.

His journey took him to the Asomatos monastery and thence to Apodoulou, where he stayed with the local priest:

> He was old and lame, and his lair was near the fire in a little earth-floored room, where as I sat sheep walked in and out, and now and then an intrusive pig; while an unexpected coney-kin came out between my legs and I found that there was a whole litter of rabbits under his reverence's berth. The guest room on the opposite side of a sort of rough porch was better, though the sheep and lambs had free entry and apparently slept with the women and children in a further sanctum into which I did not penetrate . . . Apodoulo had been burned during the insurrection of '66 but the inhabitants had fled. It is still, as village after village that one passes here, half composed of ruins.[39]

The next day Evans attempted to climb to the Kamares Cave, where the pottery made famous by Myres had been found, but he was stopped on the lower slopes by a strong north wind and word that the cave, in any case, was filled with snow. The wind drove them down into the Mesara plain, where Evans was eager to explore a hilltop identified with ancient Phaistos. Homer relates how Idomeneus, in his rise to power before the Trojan conflict, killed Phaistos—perhaps a reference to some ancient conflict between Knossos and this place.[40] But Evans saw little to confirm the poet's assertion of a once great city on the low hill he was shown, and he moved on, leaving the discovery of the site's importance, second only to that of Knossos, to Halbherr.

They searched for the site of Agios Onouphrios, which Halbherr had said was in the neighborhood of Phaistos. Seven years before, a child had picked up a piece of gold on the hillock and caused a frenzy of illicit digging that produced objects of the period then called the "Worship of the Isles," as the finds included little white marble statuettes similar to those found on the Cycladic islands of Melos, Amorgos, Keros, and Thera, and thought to be associated with an early form of veneration. These were first studied in the 1830s by the German scholar

Ludwig Ross, who grouped them in what he called an *Inselkultur* (island culture) and ascribed them to a time well before that of the Phoenicians, later Schliemann's Mycenaeans; the distinctive idols are now considered to be hallmarks of the Early Bronze Age in the Aegean. The Syllogos investigated the site in 1888 and found it so full of human bone and the decayed remnants of weapons of war that they concluded it must have been the site of an ancient battle.[41] Whatever its true identification, Evans's decision would have to wait, as he was unable to locate the hill (now interpreted as a funerary site), and so moved on to Gortyna, where he hoped to meet with Halbherr. His Italian friend was himself off exploring some other region, however, and so Alevisos showed Evans the remains of the great Roman city with its famous inscription and the Christian basilica of St. Titos.

They traveled east to Myrtos, and then along the Libyan Sea coast to Hierapetra, where once again Evans was moved by the degradation to comment, "How are the mighty fallen!" The Roman city of Hierapytna had been one of the jewels of the ancient Mediterranean; Evans was quite familiar with its elaborate coinage and the two remarkable sarcophagi that Captain Thomas Spratt, the naval surveyor engaged by the British admiralty to map the coast of Crete, had bought here in 1861 and sent to the British Museum. But systematic looting and destruction by local landowners had reduced a mighty city, "once sovereign of this part of Crete," to "a miserable townlet in the last stage of dilapidation and deadrot."[42]

From Hierapetra they traveled northeast to Praisos, where Halbherr had gone in 1884 and discovered an inscription "in a strange alphabet of some unknown tongue."[43] As Homer located the homeland of the Eteo, or "True," Cretans in the east, Praisos, it was surmised, might have been their center, and the "strange alphabet," still undeciphered, could be in their language, Eteocretan.

Alevisos then led Evans across a dry, windswept plateau atop the Thryphti range and down into the Zakros valley, which seemed an earthly paradise by comparison. A fountain at the head of the vale created "a very oasis, with murmuring millstreams, olives, carobs, figs and rich vegetation of all kinds, peach and apple blossom, poplars in pale spring green, tall cypresses standing out against the grey background of limestone crags."[44] Within this magical setting they explored a rock shelter at *stous Anthropolithous*, "the place of stone ones," and picked up clay figurines of humans and animals. Evans imagined here a "sacred grotto," or nature shrine.

At the coastal plain of Palaikastro, or "old castle," Evans climbed the conical promontory which, with its ancient remains, gives the area its name. But he failed to take note of the ancient town there, called Roussolakkos, or "the red hollow," well described by Halbherr,[45] though he acquired a gemstone engraved with dolphins and still coated in gold leaf, which, he recorded, "Shows the way in which the dark unornamental stones were treated and confirms my idea that the fragment of the stone vessel from Knossos with the reliefs was originally plated with gold. In this practice we get the origin of the Mykênæan gold reliefs like the Vapheio cups."[46] Here Evans also bought a four-sided stone seal engraved with symbols the importance of which he was the first to recognize: his long hours in the saddle gave him the time to consider fully the meaning of what he was seeing and where the objects he was acquiring fit in his developing theories of an early form of writing, earlier than ancient Greek. By the time he reached the town of Palaikastro, where the three- and four-sided gemstones he had bought elsewhere were said to abound, any lingering doubts that may have existed about his identification of the symbols they displayed being a complex system of writing in hieroglyphs had completely vanished.[47]

"Thanks to a happy accident of Cretan superstition," he wrote, he was able "to collect a considerable number" of the stone seals. As Halbherr had warned him, "the women called them 'milk-stones' and wore them round their necks as charms of great virtue." Undaunted, Evans

therefore made a house-to-house visitation in the villages, and by one means or another prevailed on many of the women to display their talismans. I soon discovered that ladies of a certain age were not altogether averse to parting with their "milk-stones" for a consideration, but with the younger women it was a more delicate business. In some cases I succeeded in swapping stones of smaller archæological value, the lactiferous qualities of which, however, I could safely guarantee. But not unfrequently all permission was useless, and the only reply was, "I would not sell it for ten pounds! Don't you see my baby?"[48]

Leaving the coast they wound their way up through limestone ridges to a hidden plateau where Christian monks had sought refuge in the twelfth century and built the first chapel of what became the Toplou monastery, named for the Turkish word for cannon, of which there was a single example. Halbherr had come here a decade earlier and recorded the ancient inscriptions gathered by industrious monks over the centuries from the collapsed shrines in the nearby coastal ruins and built into their own sacred architecture. He had identified the ruins of Erimoupolis, or the "deserted city," with ancient Itanos—famed in antiquity as the gift of Mark Anthony to Cleopatra. One large stone set into a chapel wall recorded the arbitration by the Magnesians of northern Greece in a dispute over the rights to the temple of Diktaian Zeus, a Cretan predecessor of the head of the Greek pantheon, said to be somewhere between the territories of Itanos and Praisos. Evans was witness to a contemporary attempt at arbitration and praised the abbot, whom he found caring for the comforts of two Muslim travelers. Ten years later, a British scholar searching for the temple characterized the monastery with less charity thus: "The place is frightfully medieval; they are dirty and ignorant and fond of wine and keep a dwarf to amuse them."[49]

Down the weathered ridges from the Toplou monastery they made their way to the easternmost port town of Siteia, established at the base of a small Venetian fort. This tiny outpost had been sacked in 1538 by the famous Barbarossa, grand admiral of the Ottoman fleet, as part of his successful campaign to take control of the eastern Mediterranean Sea and give the sultan a thalassocracy. Evans found a new town growing up around a small harbor and stayed long enough to secure more gems from the locals before going inland on April 13.

The wilds of Crete, more than the coastal towns and their sad histories, seem to have especially fascinated Evans. High atop the Thryphti Mountains they passed through Roukaka (now called Chrysopigi) and "ascended a wild limestone gorge overlooked by the heights of the Affendi Vounou range, the lower parts bright with yellow oxalis and higher up among the rocks many tall yellow arums. From the top of the pass (1 hr) a beautiful view opens of the blue waters of the Gulf of Mirabello and the snow clad heights of Dikte beyond."[50] Evans became addicted to the natural beauty of the island on his first journey and made a point of taking long treks into the wilderness, even in later years, after he committed himself to large-scale excavations at Knossos.

On the western slopes of Dikte, looking out over the Gulf of Mirabello, they found Kritsa, "the largest village in Crete" and "the starting point for . . . by far the most imposing . . . ruined primeval city, now known as Goulàs, from the Turkish word for a tower, of which the ancient name is still lost in the mist of time. The city, indeed seems to have been deserted before the dawn of history." Evans was completely taken by this rugged, unexplored acropolis. "The general effect is stupendous: the whole height which culminates in a rocky point to the N.E. is strewn with heaps of Cyclopean ruins." The site had long been known by travelers; recently Halbherr had hoped to interest Schliemann in exposing its secrets, but to no avail.[51]

Repeated wanderings about the hills of Goulas convinced Evans that he had found a palace of the Homeric period:

> Upon a second and hitherto undescribed acropolis on the summit of which were the lower walls of a building the hall or *megaron* of which shows close points of comparison with more than one building of the Sixth or Mycenaean City of Troy— the true Homeric Pergamos. For vastness of extent the ruins of Goulàs are surely unrivalled among the primeval remains on European soil ... The glimpses of the neighbouring coastland bring home to us the fact that we are within hail of the chief harbours of Eastern Crete, looking out towards the island stepping-stones to Asia Minor. There can be little doubt that future research and much-needed excavation will reveal in Goulàs a principal centre of ancient Aegean civilization.[52]

Evans staked a finder's claim on the second acropolis at Goulas, as he was eager to take his place alongside Schliemann as a discoverer of Homeric cities, but his primary focus remained Knossos, where ancient sources and modern exploration converged to guarantee rich rewards to the excavator.

On April 24, Evans returned to the Knossos valley with Halbherr and Kalokairinos to explore the slopes on the eastern side and to look into the rock-cut tombs of the Roman period at the head of the valley at Spilia; these were near the path leading up a narrow gorge to the great underground cavern at Ayia Irini, which Kalokairinos believed to be the inspiration for the legend of the Labyrinth, though Evans would have none of it. His image of the ancient maze was that written by Pliny and found by Flinders Petrie; Stillman's identification of it with the structure on the Kephala hill was much more suitable than with this man-made quarry hidden away in a dark gorge.

The fortnight's travel originally planned had turned into the most productive forty days of Evans's life. On April 25 he sent a note to the

Athenaeum with the conclusive announcement of his discovery of a "Mycenaean system of writing in Crete and the Peloponesse." His hypothesis formed around his discoveries in the Athens flea market a year earlier gained new support in the form of the inscribed stone seals he had obtained in almost all parts of the island. He could now report a catalogue of more than eighty different symbols belonging to at least two separate scripts, one pictographic and the other linear and alphabetic. "The evidence supplied by these Cretan finds shows that long before the time when the Phoenician alphabet was first introduced into Greece the Ægean islanders, like their Asianic neighbours, had developed an independent system of writing." The same scripts were used on the Greek mainland, he suggested, but, "Crete seems to have been its chief centre, and there can be little doubt that they were made use of by such members of the Hellenic stock as came within the range of the 'Mycenaean' culture." The letter ends with a provocative conclusion: "I do not think that it is too much to say that the σήματα λητρά [*semata legra*, or 'baneful signs'] of Homer are here before us."[53]*

There is a tendency to suspect an archaeologist who finds what he looks for, but at the same time to dismiss one who doesn't. Evans had set out for Crete to test a theory proposed at the end of November. Now, only five months later, he had succeeded beyond even his own wildest imagination at proving it to be true.

Minoan Crete and Mycenaean Greece

Evans returned to England in May 1894 triumphant and with a new mission: he focused all of his energies on the Kephala. First, he needed to secure the land under his name, and then he had to convince the Cretan Assembly to permit him to excavate.

He wrote up a popular summary of his journey for the *Times*, which began with an explanation of Crete's importance in antiquity:

---

*These signs are referred to in the *Iliad* (6:168), the only reference to writing in the Homeric poems. Proetus, as Hippolochus tells it, inscribed them on a "folded tablet" and gave them to the heroic Bellerophon to take with him to Lycia, where he was to show them to Iobates, father of Anteia, Proetus's wife. The signs are pernicious because they instruct Iobates to kill Bellerophon (which he is unable to do once the hero proves his noble birth and worth). This tale—and the reference—would have been well known to Evans's readers.

Crete may be described as the half-way house between two continents. Thrust forth into the eastern Mediterranean with its southern front looking out on Libya and Egypt, and the two extremities
reaching forth towards Greece on one side and Asia Minor on the
other . . . its unique position made it of old the natural meeting
ground of European and Egypto-Oriental elements. It is this fore-
gathering of East and West that gives the archaeology of Crete an
interest of far more than the local range. In ancient art the offspring of this intercourse is embodied for us under the legendary
name of Dædalos.[54]

Evans's most pressing needs were thinly masked, if masked at all. He
was eager to highlight the importance of archaeological exploration in
Crete so as to benefit the Cretan Exploration Fund, which he had
promised Hazzidakis would be forthcoming, and he fully expected
compensation for the purchase of his share of the Kephala. Evans's note
continued, "Sufficient remains, indeed, have been made known to show
that Crete came well within the range of the Mycenaean civilization.
But, compared with the mainland of Greece, research in this direction
is still at its beginning, and the yet more primitive periods of Cretan
antiquity are still shrouded in the deepest darkness."

Evans also wanted to draw popular attention to the island's strategic
importance as the link between east and west, and to create a sense of
urgency among British politicians to intervene in the Christians' struggle against the Muslims and to help eject "the Turk" so that his own exploration of Knossos might begin. The letter continued:

The most surprising thing . . . is that the Turkish Government,
which "cares for none of these things," has suddenly developed an
extraordinary interest in the monuments of classical antiquity.
The Governor, Mahmoud Pasha, has in fact, as I learn from
Canea, seized more than one recently discovered statue and
packed it off to Constantinople, to the no small indignation of the
more intelligent and influential Cretans, who wish to keep their
monuments on the island.

Evans then boldly listed the numerous "precious spoils" he acquired on
his travels throughout the island, confident that this was an acceptable
practice for a Westerner and a Christian.

In September Evans presented to the British Association in Oxford a full, detailed account of his discovery in his paper "On a New System of Hieroglyphics and a Præ-Phoenician Script from Crete and the Peloponnese" and with it a whole new "pre-history" of Greece. Evans's address opened with a statement born of Edward Tylor's definition of civilization: "In the absence of abiding monuments . . . throughout what is now the civilized European area there must once have existed systems of picture-writing such as still survive among the more primitive races of mankind." As possible examples Evans mentioned instances of painted or etched signs in Denmark, Lapland, the Maritime Alps, and along the Dalmatian coast, which he likened to those of Cherokees or Zulus: "It is impossible indeed to suppose that this European population was so far below even the Red Indian stage of culture as not to have largely resorted to pictographs as an aid to memory and communication." He urged his listeners to allow for "strong *a priori* reasons for believing that in Greek lands where civilization put forth its earliest blossoms on European soil," an early system of writing

> must have been in the course of working itself out. For we now know that in the South-Eastern part of our Continent there existed long before the days of Phoenician contact an independent form of culture . . . now conveniently known as the Mycenaean civilization. Is it conceivable that in the essential matter of writing they were so far behind their rivals on the Southern and Eastern shores of the Mediterranean?

The answer he hoped his audience would have at the end of the lecture should have been a resounding "no," and he went on to "demonstrate that as a matter of fact an elaborate system of writing did exist within the limits of the Mycenaean world, and moreover that two distinct phases of this art are traceable among its population. The one is pictographic . . . like Egyptian hieroglyphics, the other linear and quasi-alphabetic."[55]

In an attempt to predict what languages might be found in the scripts, Evans mapped out a history based on Karl Hoeck's comprehensive analysis of the ancient sources in *Das Minoische Kreta* (Minoan Crete). Only a decade earlier he had cautioned against Schliemann's identification of the mound at Hissarlik as Troy, saying "archaeology has perhaps little call to concern itself . . . with poetical topography."[56]

But now it seems, poetical topography had become a branch of science. The major events that left their impression on tradition could, he said, be set out in the following sequence: the death of Minos in Sicily was followed by widespread depopulation in Crete; the arrival of Dorian, Achaean, and Pelasgian settlers from Thessaly occurred in about 1415 B.C.; then came the Trojan expedition led by Idomeneus, followed by a second widespread depopulation from disease; and the arrival in Crete of more Dorians.

Evans used the term "Minoan Crete" as Hoeck had in the broad sense meaning the period of the characters figured in the myths, and he argued that the Mycenaean monuments on Crete belonged to that time. As the mythical title gradually took on a historical validity for him, he began to speak of "præ-Minôan times" as the period before the Mycenaeans.[57] Soon the titles acquired geographical significance for him, and he began to distinguish between " 'Minoan' Crete and Mycenaean Greece."[58]

The fifth-century historian Herodotus had claimed that all of Crete had once been occupied by "barbarians," that is, people whose language sounded like "bar bar" to the Greeks.[59] When Homer listed the ethnic peoples of Crete he sang of the "great hearted Eteokrêtes" as an indigenous stock, and so, Evans now suggested, the pictographic or hieroglyphic script, which he suspected was the earlier of the two, represented a language for which he could "provisionally give the name of Eteocretan." For the linear script he prophesied that "there seems every reason to believe that this quasi-alphabetic group of signs represents the typical form of Mycenaean script," for there were also examples found in the Peloponnese at a time he believed to be before the Dorian conquest reported by Herodotus and Thucydides, and so it followed that "among those who used the curious Cretan script of Mycenaean and earlier times there may well have been men of Hellenic speech."[60]

Further clues to the ethnicity of the early Cretans were forthcoming from outside sources. Flinders Petrie's excavations in 1892 at the new town of Akhenaten, at Tell el-Amarna, had produced Mycenaean pottery in such quantity that the palace at Mycenae and by association the building at the Kephala could be placed with complete confidence within the time of Egypt's Eighteenth Dynasty, most precisely to the thirty-seven years ending about 1380 B.C. with the death of the "Heretic King."[61] Depicted on the painted walls of the tombs at Thebes of the dynasty's nobles were a group of foreigners with long, flowing locks, whom the Egyptians called the "Keftiu" and who were shown bearing tribute. Modern scholars first identified them as Phoenician, based on Homer's description, but as the Mycenaeans and their culture emerged, it could be suggested that the ancient visitors to Egypt closely resembled the figures on the Vapheio Cups and that the gifts they bore resembled objects found at Mycenae. Evans developed the theory further, observing that "the ruddy hue of the Kefti chiefs in the Theban paintings,—which seems to be the Egyptian way of rendering the rosy European cheeks,—as well as their dress and facial type are clearly non-Semitic."[62] As he now extended Mycenaean civilization to include Crete, the islanders might also be seen to come under the title. Max Müller had shown that the Keftiu were probably to be associated with the Isle of Kaphtor, of Hebrew tradition, whence came the Philistines. This led Evans to speculate that Kaphtor was Crete and that the later Philistines may have been "a return wave of Europeanized Semites."[63]

Yet another role that Evans believed his early Cretans played was as intermediary between the great culture of Dynastic Egypt and the beginnings of civilization in Europe. He traced the earliest spiral-form decoration in Crete to Egyptian scarabs of the Twelfth Dynasty, a time, as Petrie had shown, when the Cretans were in close contact with the pharaohs, so the Cretan spirals were the prototypes for those found at Mycenae. "We can thus . . . trace . . . the origin of that spiral system which [was] afterwards to play such an important part not in Mycenaean art alone but in that of a vast European zone . . . Already at that remote period Crete was performing her allotted part as the stepping-stone of Continents."[64]

This comprehensive reconstruction of early Cretan history is all the more remarkable when we consider that Evans had only spent forty days on the island four months prior to giving the lecture, and modern archaeological excavations there would not take place for another six years. The crowded landscape that he painted from ancient tradition and his own modern sensitivity was both rational and fantastic, and included a heavy dose of wishful thinking. For example, he elaborated on how one myth, the one that recounts "the 'adoption' of Minôs by the son of the Dorian chief, after the settlers had seen a second generation grow up on Cretan soil, certainly points to a gradual and bloodless amalgamation of the Hellenic and indigenous elements." He believed this showed that his "own researches into the prehistoric antiquities of

Crete have brought home . . . the great homogeneity . . . of Mycenaean culture . . . common to the whole island."[65] His audience was well aware of the stark contrast between the bloodless amalgamation of his re-created past and the bloody segregation of the present Cretan population, and may have been touched by his idealistic attempt to coax the ancient precedent of peaceful coexistence into the modern arena of discord.

At the end of September 1894 Evans was searching for ways to a peaceful coexistence of his own with the university authorities in Oxford. He had begun to dismantle the old Ashmolean and was trying to amalgamate the old and the new, but he encountered nothing but obstacles. He concluded his keeper's report for the year with a snipe at his Oxford adversaries: "When all arrangements, both in the Ashmolean Museum and in the University Galleries, are completed, it will dawn upon members of the University that it possesses art-collections of a most unusually varied kind. Indeed, many a town on the continent with well-known museums will rank in this respect below Oxford."[66] A sympathetic Fortnum wrote in commiseration, "I sometimes wish I had nothing to do with Oxford; they are an obstructive lot. My old friend Hope was disgusted, Ruskin was disgusted; and I seem to be on the road, and you with me, to the same state of disappointment and dissatisfaction with the powers of the University."[67]

One consolation for Evans was the completion of his new house on Boars Hill, which he called Youlbury, for the ancient name of the field below it. It was a grand "palazzo" whose main entrance opened into a long hall with an Italianate niche with shell volute at the end of a double colonnade supporting a Renaissance-style barrel-vaulted ceiling and flanking a tiled floor with a rectangular labyrinth pattern, like those in Gothic cathedrals, but with a minotaur, based on a classical Greek vase painting, at the center. Neither the house nor any plans of it survive, but at its greatest extent it comprised twenty-two bedrooms, five bathrooms (one with a sunken Roman bath in marble), a library, a study, dining and sitting rooms, all of grand proportions. Over the highest part of the house Evans erected an ironwork tower, like the one recently completed by Alexandre-Gustave Eiffel for the Paris Exhibition of 1889, with a large platform that afforded a spectacular view of the surrounding downs beyond the forest, which he left largely intact, clearing only pathways between the oak and pine trees. He designed a garden of rhododendrons, azaleas, and heaths near the house, and by damming one end of a hollow built a clay-lined lake to replicate the serenity of an Alpine glade. On September 21, Evans invited Fortnum to be the first of three generations of archaeologists and friends who came to know Youlbury as their spiritual center.

Folklore and Poetical Topography

Evans tackled a different body of tradition on November 21, 1894, when he was inducted into the Folk-Lore Society and read a detailed study on "The Rollright Stones and Their Folklore." His previous work on Stonehenge had suggested that the sacred tree of the Aryans stood at the center of the great stone circle.[68] Now he investigated another well-known ancient monument in the British countryside, the Rollright Stones in north Oxfordshire. He set out historical and etymological arguments for linking the name of the ancient circle with the Song of Roland, thereby uniting "the old British stock," or his father's "ancient Britons," with the Celts in Brittany and Iberia. This was a theme that ran parallel with and at times overlapped that of the "indigenous Cretan stock" and their effects on early Europe.

In the spring of 1895, Evans was back in Candia, and on Monday April 15, he and Alevisos began another journey into Cretan "præhistory," this time with John Myres, whom Joan Evans depicted as "a Ulysses of twenty-six, black-bearded and quick-spoken, learned in many lores and a fit companion for Homeric adventure."[69] Hazzidakis accompanied them as far as Knossos, where Evans was delighted to visit the Kephala and to pick up more bits of pottery and tiny fragments of wall paintings. They climbed the Acropolis hill to the west and lunched in an open field overlooking the Kephala. At one point Evans turned to Myres and said, "This is where I shall live when I come to dig Knossos."[70] It was only four years since he had decided to build his primary residence on Boars Hill. Now the typical Cancer, with his need for domestic stability and eager to combine research with comfort, started planning his country estate. As we have seen, Evans had a way of successfully converting mental images into reality, and the exact spot he chose that day later became the site of his Cretan home.

The southeast route from the Knossos valley took them up into the rich rolling fields of the foothills of the Diktaian range and thence into the steep gorge known as the Tomb of Tsouli—a pass named for Tsouli, a Turk who, modern legend recounted, made the women of Lasithi dance before him—an insult of such magnitude in Crete that the Lasithiotes ambushed him in the pass, severed his head, threw the corpse into the gorge and sent the gruesome mask of their revenge back home in the saddlebag on his mule.[71] From the pass, the trail dropped suddenly into the huge plain of Lasithi, hidden from below by a ring of stone. They stayed in the village of Psychro, the source of some bronze objects Evans had acquired the previous year in Candia. The locals had found clay and bronze figurines in a cave above the village in 1883, which Halbherr and Hazzidakis then visited in 1886 to try to recover some of the site's archaeological history before it was entirely lost.[72] Evans and his party found that little had changed: "It being the holiday-time of the Greek Easter, a large part of the male inhabitants of the village were engaged in grubbing in the interstices of the boulders."

Most interested in what they were finding, Evans surveyed the spacious cavern with a view to serious exploration but concluded, "The huge masses of fallen rock with which almost the whole of the vast entrance hall of the Cave is strewn, preclude anything like systematic excavation on a large scale within the Cave except at enormous expense."[73] But this didn't preclude unsystematic excavation and suddenly Evans felt compelled to "assist at a small excavation which produced a variety of prehistoric relics."[74] His defiant stance against the antiquities laws of both Greece and Turkey seems to have removed any moral impediment to his obeying either those of the Turkish government or the Cretan Assembly, and so, despite his public condemnation of "explorers whose relic-hunting zeal outruns their patience in keeping scientific record of their observations,"[75] Evans joined the looters.

Among the artifacts that the joint group of "Helleno-British grubbers" acquired were small bronze double axes similar to those Schliemann had found at Mycenae and to others unearthed in the Idaean cave near Rethymnon. Similar in shape to the modern double-headed lumberjack's axe, these were a few centimeters wide and made from thin sheets of metal, which made them entirely symbolic; Schliemann suggested that the motif symbolized Zeus Labrandeus,[76] one of the earliest forms of the chief Greek deity—worshiped primarily in Anatolia. These new artifacts, which hinted at an early cult of Zeus, seemed to force the conclusion that the Psychro cave was, in fact, the *Diktaion Antron*, or Diktaian Cave, identified by the ancient Greek mythographer Hesiod as the birthplace of Zeus. But Zeus would have to wait. Evans was eager to move on and take young Myres to see the true objective of the journey—his Homeric citadel at Goulas.

They went through Aghios Giorgos, then up and out of the plain toward Katharo. Here they were treated to "one of the grandest panoramas to be seen in Crete, embracing the mountains of Siteia, the promontories that jut out from the low intervening tract and include the site of Minoa, to the conical height of Axos and the ranges of Mirabello."[77] The modern Myres ordinarily photographed the monuments they visited while Evans employed the more traditional art of sketching to create his own aide-mémoire. But in this case Myres created a wide panorama in pen and ink that covered the 180 degrees from west to east; it shows his own need to comprehend the general topography before being comfortable examining any elements within the landscape.[78] Very much anticipating the fortress at Goulas, and observing at a number of points leading from the plain the remnants of "Cyclopean" masonry, like that of the Mycenaean strongholds in Greece, Evans concluded that they belonged to "a fortified road of primaeval antiquity leading down to the rich Kritsà valley, dominated by what, so far as existing remains allow us to judge, was the greatest city of Mycenaean Crete."[79]

They spent three and a half days in an excited frenzy of discovery, picking up pottery shards, sketching walls, mapping and photographing the site, and generally convincing themselves of its commanding position in the region. Of the fragility of its domination Evans was in no doubt. As he surveyed the complexity of fortifications in the region he observed,

> it is interesting to remark that already at this remote period Crete presented a phenomenon only too familiar to us at the present day: the combination, namely, of lines of intercourse engineered at a great expenditure of skill and labour, with huge defensive works proclaiming that the neighbour of to-day was as likely as not to become to-morrow a hostile invader. We might be on the Vosges instead of the Cretan mountains.[80]

As though to balance the euphoria of discovery, Evans then returned to Candia and reentered into the frustration of bargaining with the proprietors for the remaining three-quarters of the Kephala site.

By May 20, Evans and Myres were back in Oxford and had completed an account of their discoveries entitled "A Mycenaean Military Road in Crete" for the *Academy*. This was the first and last time that Evans ever allowed another signature on a paper of which he was sole or part author, only this once in a publication record that eventually amounted to more than 150 notes, articles, and books. How are we to read this? Was the experienced forty-four-year-old offering an equal share in the credit of their research to his twenty-six-year-old protégé as an enticement? Could he have regarded the young scholar as his equal for one brief moment? Or was there a trace of guilt at having removed from the young man's grasp the prize of the Kephala, which he had worked so hard to secure years before Evans took an interest?

At a meeting of the British School at Athens in July, presided over by the Prince of Wales in St. James's Palace, it was announced that the British government promised it a substantial endowment over five years. But even more relevant to Evans was the sentiment expressed in a letter the great statesman William Gladstone read out to the participants, in which he declared his delight at learning that the school would include prehistoric Greece in its purview. "Greece herself offers to us a richly stocked field," he noted, and "the work of Schliemann in the peninsula may only have been the first fruits of an abundant harvest" of rich discoveries.[81] The days of competing with the classics, it seemed, were over. Mycenaean Greece was now a recognized field, and Evans was determined to be a major figure in it.

That summer, the Académie des Inscriptions in Paris was hosting a series of meetings to discuss the recent publication of an important new book on Mycenaean art, the sixth volume in an authoritative history of ancient art, in which Georges Perrot and Charles Chipiez concluded that the great treasures of Mycenae, Vapheio, and other Greek sites were created there during the time of Homer's Trojan tales and were, therefore, the beginnings of Greek art. The most hostile reaction to this idea came from Wilhelm Helbig, whose 1884 book about the Homeric epics concluded that the movable art such as the inlaid niello daggers and *repoussé* metalwork found at Mycenae and elsewhere in Greece was in such marked contrast to the in situ monuments, like the Lion Gate, that they must have been made outside Greece; what had come to be called Mycenaean art was to him none other than Phoenician.[82] Others argued that the human figure as depicted in Mycenaean art, best displayed in the Vapheio Cups, was in marked contrast to the principles of Phoenician, Assyrian, and Egyptian art because of its "energetic effort to express, by forms of excessive slimness and flexibility, the ideas of heroic strength and activity . . . essentially preserved through all periods of Greek art." This was a point that Evans agreed with, though the consensus view that placed the origins of the Mycenaeans in northern Greece was at odds with Evans's beliefs, which were leading him in exactly the opposite direction.

In the paper Evans read to the British Association in September 1895, "On Primitive European 'Idols' in the Light of New Discoveries," he tried to pull together all the nude female figurines of the Aegean Islands and Greece and evaluate their origins in relation to the Chaldaean underworld goddess Sala, Istar to the Babylonians,[83] to show how they spread into Europe across the Bosporus, through Thrace and across the Danube river to the Carpathians. This was an idea in direct opposition to that of Salomon Reinach, director of the archaeological museum at St. Germain, in France, an authority on European prehistory who had recently proposed that it was the early European "Aphrodités" who inspired the Mediterranean images.[84]

Evans had been corresponding with Reinach since 1888 and shared his strong dislike of the scholarly world's obsession with the "School of Hellas"—Reinach was formulating a theory of indigenous European social and artistic development without the influence of classical Greece. On one matter, however, Reinach took exception with Evans: he was a firm opponent of the early European racialist theories that had begun to spring up, particularly in Germany. While Evans was strongly influenced by works like Dr. Otto Schrader's 1890 *Prehistoric Antiquities of the Aryan People*, Reinach criticized that book: "to speak of an aryan race existing three thousand years ago is to put forward a gratuitous hypothesis; to speak about it as though it still existed today is quite simply to talk nonsense."[85] Evans may not have been as outspoken a supporter of the Aryan revival as his late father-in-law, but he was certainly more than sympathetic to the view of the superiority of the Germanic or Teutonic race whose traditional homeland, he believed, was Europe.

Reinach published two long articles in 1893–94 in which he elaborated on his opposition to the common belief that early civilization in western Europe came about due to Oriental influence. Reinach proposed that the greater part of Europe shared a common civilization that owed little if anything of its progress to its contemporaries in

Egypt, Palestine, Syria, and Babylon. He adopted the Swiss philologist Adolphe Pictet's suggestion of a European origin for the Aryan group of languages. Pictet in 1859 had begun what he called "linguistic palaeontology," in effect treating words or, more precisely, nouns as archaeological artifacts to be discussed in terms of meaning and origin like any physical artifact.[86] Reinach used these and more conventional, tangible evidence to contradict the prevailing opinion that favored Iran as the cradle of the Aryans, and claimed that bronze work in Europe, for example, must have come from the "Celtic Islands of the West," in other words Great Britain, where the necessary alloy tin occurred in abundance in Cornwall. He brought Schliemann's Mycenaeans and the rest of early Aegean civilization under his European umbrella, whose center was in northern or central Europe.

Many of Evans's ideas were so close to those of Reinach that the latter even accused him of plagiarism, to which Evans took umbrage; he was able to discount the charge in private correspondence.[87] But it couldn't be denied that Reinach's thesis had a profound effect on Evans's thinking and very much appealed to his notions of an early European society struggling for self-determination against the forces of large empires in the East.[88] The parallel currents in the ancient and modern worlds sometimes crossed the time barrier so easily during the next few years that the barrier itself became all but meaningless in Evans's mind.

Evans spent much of the autumn composing his thoughts on the origin of Celtic art for lectures that he delivered to the Society of Antiquaries of Scotland in December 1895. His father had been asked to deliver the prestigious series but deferred to his son's greater knowledge. The syllabus shows that Evans went to a great effort to prepare six long, minutely detailed lectures delivered at teatime on alternate days from December 10 to 20 at the National Portrait Gallery in Edinburgh. In them Evans displayed a sweeping range of knowledge, taking the listener from the earliest Celtic art and its origin in the "great days of Mycenae," following its trajectory and development through Illyria and the Adriatic cultures into northern Italy and the "Transalpine Celtic" countries, eventually crossing into Britain and finally ending in the land of his spellbound audience, where refugees from the Roman conquest kept the Celtic traditions alive until they could reemerge under the influence of "Celtic Christianity." Myres recalled that the lectures "were prepared with great care, lavishly illustrated, and faithfully summarized in *The Times* and *The Scotsman*, but when they were repeated in Oxford, the audience, never large, faded away; and they were never published."[89] Evans found it difficult to interest Oxford in the ancient Britons, as they might have seemed a crude and dull offshoot of the classical world that continued to dazzle.

Evans's struggle to unite the disparate collections of the Ashmolean under one keeper and to get some assistance in the form of a junior position was finally resolved, and on February 4, 1896, he proclaimed, "Victory at last! Victory all along the line!" The whole of a new building was to become the new Ashmolean; and the appointment of an assistant keeper, to alleviate his duties, was being considered.[90] Soon after, Evans, much relieved, departed for the Continent he knew so well and set a course for the island he longed to know better.

Divine Support

April 1896 found Evans back in Candia urging Hazzidakis to pursue the owners of the Kephala for an agreement to a full sale. While the designated representatives bargained on his behalf, the explorer once again set out in search of pieces to fit into the puzzle of Crete's early history.

Eager to resume the previous year's treasure hunt at Psychro, Evans traveled to the Lasithi plain, where he found his arrival had been anticipated. One of the young men he had "grubbed" with in 1895 had returned to the cave with the spring thaw of 1896 and dug down to the stone floor in one open area. He showed Evans "several clay bulls and figures of the usual Mycenaean class obtained through his dig, together with several plain terra-cotta cups," but, Evans recalled, "as a matter of comparatively minor importance, he informed me that he and a friend . . . had found at the bottom of the hole a 'broken stone, with writing.' It may be readily imagined that I lost no time in securing the stone and also in ascertaining on the spot the exact circumstances of its position."[91] It was part of a rectangular stone vessel "bearing part of an inscription clearly cut in characters about an inch high, arranged in a single line, belonging to the same Mycenaean script as that of the seal stones and of a type representing the linearisation of originally pictographic characters." On the top of the vessel, which had two of three sunken depressions still preserved, he could make out nine characters of what he approximated from the stone's original dimensions might have been an original eighteen. "That we have here to deal with a regular inscription no human being will doubt," he declared in his first report of the discovery and his explorations in the *Academy*.[92] Without paying the expenses of a government inspector and fully intending, in bold defiance of the law, to take away more than the drawings or casts of what he recovered, he "at once arranged to continue the excavation."[93]

The inscribed vessel, which Evans called an offering table, had been found at some depth against the far wall of the cave's "Atrium" opposite the entrance. "I dug out a space of sixteen square metres," he reported, "all round down to the rock which in most places lay somewhat over two metres below the surface." The rest of the table was not recovered, but, "about 1½ metres down, we found a continuous layer containing what appeared to be a sacrificial deposit of bones, horns and ceramic objects, imbedded in ashes and charcoal."[94] The pottery and votives were of the same type said to come from Mycenaean deposits elsewhere in Crete, and so he concluded that the "sacrificial layer" and therefore the inscribed "dedication" were indeed of the Mycenaean period.

The stone vessel provided the first tangible proof of his theory about the use of writing in early Greece, so Evans had to make it available for others to consult and presented it to the Ashmolean Museum for public display. It was the first personal possession he parted with in this manner. He exalted its message, still illegible, declaring,

Here, then, on European soil, in a sanctuary historically Greek, we have a formal inscription dating, at a moderate computation, some six centuries earlier than the earliest Hellenic writing known to us, and at least three centuries older than the earliest Phoenician. The fact is the more interesting since, during the period to which this specimen of prehistoric script must be referred, the Syrian Semites, as we know from the Tell el-Amarna Tablets, were in the full use of the cuneiform characters.[95]

Evans's proposed interpretation of his find made free use of Greek folklore about Crete: "The threefold receptacle of the Diktaean Table suggests some interesting analogies with a ritual usage which goes back to the earliest religious stratum of Greece." When Odysseus asks Circe how he might get to the unseen land, or Hades, she directs him to a point beyond the stream of ocean where he must dig a measured pit and pour a three-part offering to all the dead, the parts being milk and honey, sweet wine, and water.[96] Evans proposed:

> The heroic and chthonic character of the primitive Zeus-worship of Crete makes it probable that a similar usage may here also have obtained, and in the very cave where according to the legend the infant Zeus has been fed by the Nymphs with "mingled milk and honey" (*Diodorus* v. 70) the offering of μελίκρητα [Cretan honey] would have been especially appropriate. We are, indeed expressly told that the ritual performed in honour of the Cretan Zeus set forth the miraculous preservation of the infant and his nourishment by Amalthea [the goat] and Melissa [the bee].[97]*

The plan that Evans made of the cave's atrium showed the space for the most part filled with large fallen blocks. The stone collapse, taken with his remark that "the breakage of the 'table of offerings' was itself, in all probability, due to the fall of some rock from the roof of the cavern,"[98] hinted that the rest of the table remained to be found. His report inspired others to search the cave for the missing part of the inscription and gave hope that more written documents would be found preserved beneath the "vast ruin heap" of stone, a hope that was realized a few years later by a French rival.

On the completion of his first Cretan excavation, Evans crossed the Lasithi plain and climbed to the great pinnacle, appropriately called Karphi, meaning the "nail," at the plain's northwest limit. Below the peak he opened an ancient grave and removed its contents without a second thought.[99] About three hours on, northeast of Karphi, he came to the plain of Omales, where, he marveled, "In a wilderness of rock, beneath an ilex wood, where the Cretan wild-goat is still occasionally seen, was one of the most interesting primitive settlements that it has ever been my fortune to explore. It might be described as a 'town of castles.'"[100] He explored six of possibly eight small fortified hilltops, the

---

*The rite continued to have a practical component in Crete, as the later excavators at Palaikastro found. A workman severely injured in a stone collapse there was wrapped in the warm hide of a freshly killed goat and fed with milk and honey as though to patch his wounds from the inside.

largest of which, called Phrouria, or "forts," he designated the "mother" stronghold at the center of a συνοικισμός (*synoikismos*), or community, of fortified dwellings.

Returning to the Lasithi plain, Evans was shown another cave, at a place called Trapeza, above the main town of Tsermiado, where bones and pottery had been found in the past. He reported,

> With the aid of some villagers I accordingly made an exploratory excavation. We dug in two places . . . The floor here and throughout the cave was strewn with human bones and fragments of pottery—the result of earlier "tumultuary" grubbing on the part of the peasants. My dig produced many similar relics . . . steatite beads and pieces of gold ornaments, including a gold tube and two leaf-shaped pendants of Mycenaean date, together with part of a miniature votive double-axe.[101]

Perhaps it was the remoteness of the place that relaxed his guard; Lasithi rides high above the coastal plains and their large port towns, where three-quarters of Crete's population lived. Or Evans was encouraged by the impunity with which his ragged shepherd hosts raided the ancient sites, and was swept back into the feeling he experienced at Trier twenty years earlier—the excitement of personally removing ancient clues from the earth's matrix and taking possession of them instantly without debate or remorse. So confident was he in his actions that he noted most of his illegal discoveries and the irresponsible manner in which they were brought to light in his published reports. But some he did not, at least not initially. It took the passage of a quarter of a century before he revealed one of the great finds from Psychro, a remarkable bronze tablet with a mysterious scene of a dancer with a bird and fish beneath the sun and moon with symbols Evans couldn't yet recognize.[102]

Evans left Lasithi by the eastern route and entered the territory he had come to call "Mycenaean Dikta." Diodorus relates a Cretan tradition that when Zeus grew to adulthood he returned to his birthplace at Dikta, whence he had been taken to the Diktaian Cave, and founded a city. In Diodorus's time the city was deserted, though its ruins were still visible.[103] As Evans surveyed the heights of Goulas and convinced himself of its importance, he concluded that this must be Dikta, the city of Zeus. Three years earlier, Halbherr, on the basis of his readings of the ancient geographers and inscriptions, identified the site as one of two towns called Lato, this one being the inland settlement called Lato *mesogeios* (inland), and the nearby fishing village of Aghios Nikolaos being the modern successor to the ancient port of Lato.[104] But, Evans pointed out, "The only difficulty, indeed, in identifying Goulàs with the 'inland Latô' of classical times is the almost total absence on the site of any relics of the historical period."[105]

Evans used this visit to verify notes made the previous year with Myres and to prepare the final publication of their joint research. He convinced himself of the great antiquity of the remains, and of the sacral character of a small stone enclosure that he called a "hypæthral," or open-air shrine, and likened it to one in Cyprus dedicated to Aphrodite of Paphos, an integral part of his emerging reconstruction of the early Cretans' cult practices. Unlike the previous year's *Academy* report, the article he submitted to the British School at Athens bore his own signature, and it went to great pains to isolate the contributions made by himself and John Myres.[106]

Evans left Goulas for the north shore and soon came to "Gurnià, a pre-historic *polichna*, with remains of primitive houses adapted to later hovels, and traces of roads supported by Cyclopean masonry,"[107] he noted. But any intuition he may have had about a site's date and importance seems to have failed him here in these two cases. Goulas was later shown to belong almost exclusively to the Hellenistic period, and Gournia turned out to be one of the best preserved of Crete's Bronze Age towns.

Traveling up into the hinterland of the Thryphti range, Evans crossed the remote, windswept upland valleys calling at small, fortified hillocks, which he likened to the ones at Omales; he realized that in Mycenaean times Crete must have been covered with these military outposts, but this evidence of a well-defended hinterland, so well preserved along his route, was ignored when the time came for Evans to re-create Minos's Crete, a peaceful kingdom, after the excavations at Knossos.

Turning west, Evans took the southern route, along the flanks of the Diktaian range rising abruptly from the Libyan Sea. Near the Muslim village of Ligortino, on the site of a Mycenaean town, the local schoolmaster had excavated a group of "beehive" tombs. The villagers were wary of Christians, but Evans appealed to the schoolmaster's hospitality by pleading fatigue and so was able to rest in the shelter where some of the schoolmaster's finds were stored. Thus he could sketch most of the artifacts, including a lentoid (lens or lentil-shaped) gemstone "showing female votary at shrine containing sacred tree & below crescent moon = Astarte? ('Pasiphae'?)."[108] Pasiphae literally means "the shining one," and Evans was making the association between the Babylonian Venus and the wife of Minos, mother of the dreaded Minotaur. The numerous vases "of good Mycenaean period" from the tombs included a *larnax* (clay coffin) decorated with waterfowl, one of which "holds a worm in its beak while another is seen darting after a butterfly."* Evans likened a waterplant in the scene to the Egyptian lotus and concluded, "There can be little doubt that a whole series of riverside motives that appear in Mycenaean art are due to the same Egyptian source . . . the same Nilotic origin," though the designs on these particular *larnakes*, he felt equally certain, reflected "the local schools of Cretan art."[109]

Evans saw the strong Egyptian artistic influence in Crete as inevitable: "This accumulating evidence of early intercourse with the Nile Valley cannot certainly surprise the traveler fresh from exploring site after site of primeval cities which once looked forth from the southern spurs of Dikta far across the Libyan Sea, and whose roadsteads, given a favourable wind, are within forty hours' sail of the Delta."[110]

As he gazed out across the shimmering sea, Evans was struck by the close proximity of North Africa and was forced to record another of his cross-temporal observations; this one set the stage for his next adventure:

> At the Monastery of Haghios Giorgios . . . a sight awaited me which vividly brought home another geographical relation of this central island, and one which should never be left out of account in considering its ancient history. Outside the monastery gates was a group of Arabs from Benghazi soliciting Christian alms. Like many of their poor co-religionists, they had come over in small trading vessels from the Tripoli coast, to spend the summer in seeking alms from village to village, for the most part in the Mohammedan districts of Crete. The close commercial relations

---

*Evans was unable to acquire the finds, most of which were later bought by the French traveler Charles Clermont-Ganneau and sent to the Louvre. The gem, however, disappeared and Evans's sketch is all that remains.

of Crete with Cyrene in classical times are attested by the abundant discovery throughout the island of Cyrenaean coins. The more ancient connection with the Libyan tribes awaits illustration.[111]

On May 6, thanks to the tireless negotiations of Hazzidakis, Evans paid out 30,000 piasters (£235) plus expenses for one-quarter of the Kephala; it was a glorious victory. He acquired a share in what was to be the greatest of all his possessions, and held a bargaining position that no other interested party could match. He could also use his share of the estate to force the sale of the remainder, which is precisely what he instructed Hazzidakis to do. The Knossos valley was to be his own modest equivalent to the Rivers Estate, the property General Pitt-Rivers had taken over at Cranborne Chase in 1880 and continued to manage as an agricultural holding while conducting archaeological explorations. But Evans still had much to do before he could achieve the absolute control Pitt-Rivers enjoyed.

The next obstacle was the permission from the Cretan Assembly to excavate. Evans knew that the Ottoman administration had to be driven from the island before he might be allowed to excavate on the grand scale that the Kephala would require, so, from this point onward, he began to concentrate on the moment when the Kephala could be his to do with as he saw fit and proper with no possibility of interference.

Meanwhile, the Christian Cretans, as though to oblige, were on the verge of another uprising. Less than three weeks later, on May 24, the streets of Canea once again filled with insurgents, and a final swing of the pendulum to sweep the Christians toward political power began. As Ottoman authority waned, the modern nations engaged in their well-rehearsed intrigues at dividing the spoils at an early stage so that no single power could exert exclusive influence. There was a fear that Crete might become another jewel in Queen Victoria's crown to bridge Cyprus and Corfu, but France, Italy, and Russia stood by to curb Britain's appetite for Greek islands. Meanwhile, Her Majesty's Government was keen that Crete not be swept into the Greek net, as many of the Aegean islands had been, and encouraged support for Turkish rule there. The British public was outraged. One irate news correspondent declared,

There is nothing in the English situation more unexpected than the Tory policy toward the Cretans. There is a meekness, a tameness, a disposition to agree at any cost with almost anybody . . . All around Crete Britannia rules the waves. Not a Turkish soldier or a Turkish vessel can be moved without her permission . . . [but] . . . Fierce threatenings are issuing from all the chancelleries, not against Turks, but against Christians. It is not the villainous old Sultan who is exciting diplomatic rage, but the Christians whom he has robbed and murdered for two centuries.[112]

The philhellenic sentiment of Britain's educated elite, blended with their absolute faith in the Christian gospels, was strong, but the power politics of the eastern Mediterranean was stronger—for the time being, in any case.

Evans, back in Oxford by late May, began informing readers of the *Academy* of his exploits, discoveries, and impressions in a series of five breezy notices published in June and July:

The golden age of Crete lies far beyond the limits of the historical period: its culture not only displays within the three seas an uniformity never afterwards attained, but is practically identical with that of the Peloponnese and a large part of the Aegean world. Communications were infinitely more regular and extended; the density of the population, supported by both agriculture and maritime enterprise, was far superior to that of any later period of Cretan history. It was, indeed, the island of the "Hundred Cities."[113]

And what to call this Golden Age? Evans was now confident that "the great days of Crete [were] those of which we still find a reflection in the Homeric poems—the period of Mycenaean culture, to which here at least we would fain to attach the name 'Minoan.' "[114] Before long he used "Minoan" to describe a fixed block of time, the period of the island's greatest achievements, but for now he and his colleagues more commonly employed "Mycenaean."

The Ring of Knossos, like so many of his acquisitions, became the nucleus for a bold theory. At the meeting of the British Association in Liverpool on September 17, 1896, Evans presented his first thoughts on "Pillar and Tree Worship in Mycenæan Greece."[115] The worship of fetishes—that is, inanimate objects with conjectured inherent magical powers, such as sacred trees, belemnites (fossilized bones), and meteoric stones—which had become a part of the hypothetical Aryan religion,[116] inspired his suggestion that "the worship of deities in aniconic [symbolic] shape as stone pillars or as trees" was a major part of Mycenaean religion. His search for the enclosures to contain sacred trees in British henge monuments had now been extended to Crete, where he believed he had found a similar enclosure at Goulas and could see the same represented on gold rings and seals, implying an association between Cretan nature worship and the Teutonic religion centered around the sacred ash tree.

The sacred stone—or, as Evans preferred, baetyl, based on the Greek βαίτυλος (baetylos), probably derived from the Semitic Bethel, or House of God—represented in aniconic form the supreme god in his Mycenaean religion.[117] Evans borrowed Schliemann's suggestion that the double-axe motif symbolized "Zeus Labrandeus,"[118] and suggested that the objects found at Psychro "may actually embody the presence of the god himself," as "His actual image in the anthropomorphic shape was not needed by the religion of that time." This stated, he then had to explain the human and animal representations in Mycenaean art and the great numbers of plastic representations at the sacred sites he had been exploring. He concluded, "The great mass of votive figures found in the sacrificial deposits of these Cretan caves bear no distinctive attributes of divinity. They seem . . . to be simply miniature representations of human votaries and their domestic animals, who thus, according to a widespread practice, placed themselves and their belongings under the protection of the higher powers."[119] His devotion to this idea of "higher powers" and his belief that there had been a ban on their anthropomorphic representation relegated most of the human and animal figures in the growing body of early Aegean art to the rank of mortal votaries, where many are still classed a hundred years later.

The bird as a symbolic emissary between god and man was expressed by Evans as being "the Dove Cult of Primitive Greece," which he hypothesized on the basis of dove figures on the rims of bowls and the wild doves used by soothsayers in the cult of Zeus at Dodona.[120] His suggestion of the dove as a divine "agent of inspiration" was a clear reference to the dove symbolizing the Holy Spirit in the Christian Trinity. Likewise, the double axe, to Evans, became a precedent for the Christian crucifix. He pointed out the coincidence in Cretan caves for votive offerings to a cult of Zeus and the nearby chapels to Aphendi Christos, Christ the Lord, commenting, "It looks as if in all these cases we had to deal with the same primeval cult of the Cretan Zeus-Minôs, and the later assimilation of the surviving *religio loci* to that of 'Christ the Lord' is very suggestive . . . The abiding piety of the land of Minôs has simply transferred its devotion from the giver of the old law on Ida to the giver of the new."[121] No consideration was spared for other prophets. Evans's Christian family tradition merged well with his suggestion of an apparent Orthodox Greek "revival" of earlier cults.

The Yoke of Asia

As president of the anthropology section of the British Association, Evans read a moving address to the September meeting in Liverpool that seemed again to take no account for historical time, for he placed the modern "Eastern Question" facing the Great Powers in an ancient, almost eternal, setting. His position was quite clear, if the chronology a bit obscure, as he compared "the civilization of the Hittites in Anatolia and North Syria," whose "native elements were . . . cramped and trammeled from the beginning by the Oriental contact," with "prehistoric Greece," where "the indigenous element was able to hold its own, and to recast what it took from others in an original mould. Throughout its handiwork there breathes the European spirit of individuality and freedom."[122] Without the slightest ambiguity, he stated his political motive in his conclusion:

> To Crete the earliest Greek tradition looks back as the home of divinely inspired legislation and the first center of maritime dominion. Inhabited since the days of the first Greek settlements by the same race, speaking the same language, and moved by the same independent impulses, Crete stands forth again to-day as the champion of the European spirit against the yoke of Asia.[123]

There can be little doubt that he was appealing to the Great Powers to intervene on behalf of the Greek Christians in Crete and to remove the Ottoman yoke.

In November Evans read a paper on "Further Discoveries of Cretan and Aegean Script" to the Hellenic Society, in which he listed his most recent acquisitions. Once again he aired his intensifying views regarding the "European aspect" of early Cretan society. Evans reminded his listeners that the engraved signs were "found in upright columns as well as in a horizontal order, and in some cases the lines apparently follow one another in boustrophedon fashion [as the ox turns in plowing], alternately from right to left and left to right."[124] This was an obvious parallel to later Greek inscriptions, also called boustrophedon, and in marked contrast to the cursive Arabic script of the Ottomans; Evans considered being upright and on-the-level as traditional European qualities, while cursive or "running" characterized, in his view, Eastern society both ancient and modern.

The highlight of Evans's address was the report on his illicit excavations at Psychro and the discovery of the inscribed libation table, which, he declared, "stands alone among the written records of our Continent." He now revealed his subdivision of the Cretan scripts into three classes: the first and earliest was of "seal-stones presenting designs and characters of a linear kind," the second of seals with pictographic style designs, and the third and latest of the "Eteocretan seal-stones with a more conventionalized pictographic writing."[125] The classification was based entirely on his idea of how script should have developed, as there was no archaeological stratigraphy available to prove that one class was earlier or later than another. Nonetheless, the order and classification, once set out in table form, was difficult to alter later, even when stratigraphy, which he later revealed, showed the order to be false.

Religious and ethnic troubles in Crete had intensified after Evans left in 1896, and by early 1897, war between Greece and Turkey seemed imminent. In February 1897, Greece sent an expeditionary force to occupy the island in the name of King George, essentially to encourage the Christian Greeks to believe they could and should rise up with impunity against the Turks. Muslim fervor was whipped up in response by the arrival of one Kalil, "a member of the Sultan's negro guard, who had distinguished himself in the Armenian massacres at Constantinople," so Evans would later learn, and who proceeded to go to the Muslim villages "stirring up the faithful to do the same by the Cretan Christians."[126] The Great Powers agreed to police the island and to ensure that Crete would move toward true autonomy and not become a part of Greece. France occupied Siteia and the east, Britain established a cordon around Candia and the center, Russia did the same at Rethymnon, while Italy took charge of Kissamos and the far west. The strategic capital at Canea and Suda Bay became an international protectorate. The Greek force was withdrawn in May, but the summer heat fed the fires of revolt well into the autumn.

Crete's turmoil was reported throughout the world. In London, readers of the *Illustrated London News* learned that "Turkish soldiery, by all accounts, have displayed in this island a remarkable decline of their old military quality, behaving more like brigands, in cruel orgies of massacre, outrage, and plunder," but, equally, that "murders and other outrages have been perpetrated by some bands of Greek insurgents belonging to a rude highland race, and not subject to any discipline or military command."[127] Evans and Myres heeded the omens and kept away from Greece and Crete in 1897.

David Hogarth, by contrast, reacted quite differently to the promise of armed conflict. Hogarth had been appointed to the directorship of the British School at Athens, effective in the autumn of 1897, and he found himself without purpose that spring. A British correspondent in the Balkans, faced with having to cover the upheaval in Macedonia and Bulgaria, asked him to help report on the Cretan insurrection. "His actual correspondent, a Greek," Hogarth later recalled, "was colouring his despatches to London white and blue. Would I replace him awhile? My temptation was brief. I had never been in Crete, and a scholar may rarely watch war."[128] The scholar's first taste of war, the one that gave him an appetite for bloodshed, came on the day of his arrival in Canea in early March. From the deck of the steamship he watched a village burn and its occupants fight each other on the surrounding slopes:

> It was a small and desultory affair, from which less than a score of killed and wounded men were borne back at evening to the gates—patient Anatolian peasants for the most part, who had long served out their due time and fought without heat or reasoning why. Along with them came the corpses of two or three *bashibazuk* Cretans, Greek in feature and Greek in speech, Moslems by chance and all but ignorant of the faith they had died to uphold.[129]

Hogarth, due to his intimate experience of the ways of people in Cyprus, Egypt, the Levant, and Anatolia, seemed to take a particularly dim view of Greek Orthodoxy. He believed that

> No Greek may answer surely for any other Greek, since individualism and intolerance of discipline are in the blood of the race. In the stormy history of Levantine religious warfare you may note

one unvaried law of consequence. Where the Moslem has prevailed, the votaries of the two creeds have resumed peaceful life as
of old, the Christian knowing that Moslems act under orders as
one man, and that when Islam is triumphant its Gibeonites are
secure of their lives. But if Christians gain their freedom, the
Moslem leaves the land of his birth. For whatever pledges the new
authorities may give, he knows for his part that, since Eastern
Christianity supplies no social discipline, each Christian will act
on occasion as seems best in his own eyes.[130]

Hogarth's preference for the Muslim's company over that of the Christian Greek continued throughout his years in Greece, and he passed it
on to those he tutored later in Oxford.

Hogarth also found favor in the way the British were acting out their
medial role in a delicate situation. He recorded his admiration for Sir
Herbert Chermside, the British commandant, who, he felt, "sustained
the British name for cool courage and quiet discharge of duty in those
unquiet weeks."[131] In Candia, Hogarth became close to his country's
military units, preferring to pitch a tent near a mountain battery on the
town's ramparts rather than risk an encounter with smallpox, which
was spreading throughout the squalid neighborhoods down in the
town. His days were spent evaluating the official reports and riding out
to the rebel lines to make his own observations. "On these excursions,"
he recalled a little over a decade later, "I visited Cnossus for the first
time, and dreamed of digging in the Palace of Minos, some of whose
lettered stones already stood revealed. Indeed I was offered a squad of
sappers, who might begin the search there and then." He turned down
the offer, neither in deference to one of the site's owners—Evans, who
was also his colleague at Oxford—nor indeed out of any particular
compliance to the laws of state or the code of his discipline; instead, he
"refused it for lack of time and in distrust of soldier diggers."[132]

The Great Powers held sway over Crete's destiny and tried to maintain some sort of law and order throughout 1897, as one British sailor
later recalled with an equal mixture of boyish glee and adult horror:

Each nationality had its own way of punishing the blood-thirsty
native. The Italian shot them on sight; the French chopped their
heads off; the Russians whipped them to death—all without a
vestige of a trial. But the British—good old solid British—

brought them on board the battleships, imprisoned them in cages composed of torpedo nets on the mess-deck and solemnly tried them by Court-Martial. Afterwards we hanged them—solemnly, and in the face of all men; and I don't think there was a man among us who felt sorry for these degraded beasts whose murders had been so fearful.[133]

Hogarth had bidden farewell to Crete forever, or so he thought, in May 1897. But, despite his feelings toward the majority of the population, he soon returned as a leading player in their search for the island's "pre-classical golden age."

Evans used the interval to expand his frontiers in North Africa. On the premise of exploring "prehistoric Triliths" or "Great Stone Temples," which he showed to be oil presses of the Roman period, he met Myres in Tunis at the beginning of March and they explored the Libyan interior until they aroused the suspicion of the Turkish authorities and were marched back to Tripoli. Evans was using the same passport issued for his earlier adventures, and the "intimate notes on Austrian military dispositions scrawled on the back," as Myres later recalled, were enough to convince a local official that their business was not scholarly.[134] But the most compelling reason for the journey was to investigate the recent suggestion that proto-Egyptians were of Libyan origin.

Flinders Petrie's excavations at Naqada, in the upper Nile, had produced a cemetery of "pre-historic" Egyptians who seemed to belong to what came to be called the New Race, which Petrie believed existed in Egypt before the well-known Egyptians of the Pharaonic period arrived in conquest from the southeast.[135] The New Race, or so Evans thought, were "to be identified with the people of the Oases—the Tahennu or Tamahu, a race of Libyan stock." The appeal of this theory to Evans and his own race was that the Libyan Berbers comprised members of a "white-skinned race—so European in its affinities."[136]

Evans and his colleagues were much impressed by Giuseppe Sergi's 1895 *La stirpe Mediterranea*, published in 1901 in English as *The Mediterranean Race*. Sergi's thesis, that the people living on the Mediterranean littoral were a distinct race responsible for the great civilizations of Greece and Rome, which he later elaborated to prove that the Etruscans kept the European Aryans out of Italy,[137] demonstrated that the early Mediterranean societies were neither Aryan nor Semitic but somewhere in between. The early Libyan stock, which Evans came to admire, could be counted, by virtue of geography, among Sergi's Mediterranean race, and because of their "European" affinities, they seemed the most desirable source for the indigenous Cretans. But Libya's modern authority was one Evans knew and despised from previous encounters with its bureaucratic equivalents in the Balkans, and so he was relieved to depart, as he wrote to Fortnum on April 18, and find himself "safe out of the hands of 'Turks, heretics and infidels.' "[138]

Cretan Guardian

Evans returned to Crete at the end of March 1898 with Myres and Hogarth. The revolt was officially over, and the Great Powers strictly maintained law and order. The three archaeologists revisited the Kephala, which they found undisturbed, and reestablished their links with their Cretan colleagues, before Myres and Hogarth left to organize that year's excavation campaign on the Greek island of Melos. As director of the British School, Hogarth assumed responsibility for the first major excavation by a British team at the prehistoric Aegean town site of Phylakopi—a project that he later described as "the uneventful excavation, which it fell to me to conduct in Melos."[139]

Evans stayed on in Crete continuing his research; at first he found that it was best carried out as he had done twenty years earlier in similar circumstances in Bosnia: he assisted a British humanitarian mission with the delivery of sacks of barley to the most damaged villages. As in Bosnia, he was compelled to report to the *Manchester Guardian* a situation with which he found fault, but this time his encounter with authority was not with agents of the Austrian or Ottoman empires, but with those of Her Majesty's Dominions, of which he was a loyal subject.

Evans did not share Hogarth's admiration for the British authorities in Crete. Outraged at their policy of cooperation with the Turkish government, he referred to Colonel Sir Herbert Chermside, whom Hogarth held in such esteem, as the "British Assistant Pasha" of the "Turco-British *régime* in Candia." His rage peaked following the arrest and imprisonment of his muleteer, Herakles, as they entered the British cordon around Candia when they returned from an exploratory journey to the east. Herakles, a native of Siteia, did not have the required pass to enter Candia. He had been engaged for travel in Siteia and probably intended to return home after leaving Evans at the Candia frontier, but Evans probably tried to convince him to carry on into the British territory. It is quite likely, as later reports suggest, that Evans was trying to coax him to continue on a journey he had not planned for. Chermside happened to be passing the checkpoint at the same time, witnessed Herakles' reluctance to proceed, and ordered him to report to the police. Evans continued on his own into the town of Candia, but when his muleteer failed to report, he went to find him. The police, on finding that Herakles was without travel papers, had locked him up. With a display of the sort of single-minded arrogance that Evans seems to have enjoyed exhibiting even more as he aged, he located the prison, insisted on having the door opened, found Herakles, and, as he told the *Manchester Guardian,* "gave him my hand, and was proceeding to lead him out when we were forcibly held back by the armed police." Herakles feared for their lives, but Evans revealed his "volcanic nature" and behaved as he had come to think he should in such circumstances. "Sundry experiences," he reported, "in some of the most remote and barbarous parts of the Turkish dominions have taught me that a similar assumption of authority, and even the discreet resort to physical force, often succeeds with these gentry when persuasion and argument are useless." What he hadn't bargained for was dealing with his traditional foe on what was temporarily British soil. "The Turk here, under British protection, takes a very different count of 'European' pretensions,"[140] he conceded, and so Herakles remained in a foul dungeon until Evans could rectify the situation.

Recalling his own incarceration in Ragusa at the hands of the Austrian authorities, and, in all likelihood, quietly shouldering some of the blame, Evans tried unsuccessfully to contact Chermside in person, then wrote him a stiff note of disapproval. An equally stiff reply from the commandant's aide-de-camp and secretary inquired: "Do you think that a single Englishman, who thinks he can do what he chooses for his own purposes, is to be permitted to dictate to Turkish and British officials?" It is clear what Evans thought the answer to that seemingly rhetorical question should be and that he and Her Majesty's agent disagreed. So he sought the assistance of the British vice-consul, who took him for an audience with the Turkish governor, Edhem Pasha. Evans's appreciation of the governor's "shrinking glance, sour expression, and long narrow face, sallow and wrinkled as last year's pippin," made it clear that any negotiations would be strained, if not useless. In fact, they proved to be worse than useless. The pasha, unable to find sufficient cause to keep the muleteer, "with true Turkish shiftiness, entirely changed his ground," Evans related. "Did I not know, he said, that this Christian came from Sitia? Many Turks had been killed in Sitia; and this creature of the Imperial Butcher began forthwith, with every affectation of horror, to go through a very realistic pantomime of throat-cutting."[141]

Evans's overt force of will and bloodymindedness not only had failed but had dramatically worsened the situation. In twenty-four hours Herakles was transformed from an illegal immigrant into a mass murderer. His mules were to be confiscated and his own life would soon follow, or so his guards began to taunt him. Now Evans had to resort to his wits and act quickly. He drafted a telegram to the French Commandant in Siteia in which he related his version of the story and told of the British commandant's lack of authority with the Turks. Chermside intercepted and censored the telegram, as Evans knew he would, and granted an audience. Though Evans was clearly in the wrong, he managed to smooth the ruffled colonel's feathers long enough to secure Herakles' release to British troops, who put him on a boat back to Siteia.

Evans's happy resolution of this dangerous situation, albeit one of his own making, was heralded as an act of extreme heroism among the Christians in Crete, while he continued to revile the British for cooperating with the Turks in letters to the *Manchester Guardian*. He held up the French and Russians by contrast as shining examples of "correct" behavior: "They are there to prepare the population for the new order of things, and enforce upon the Mahometans the first and most necessary lesson, that Europe is now master." Never one to mince his words and fully aware of their impact, he declared, "They openly proclaim the fact that Prince George will come, and that the Turkish troops will be withdrawn."[142] The "smiter of pashas" had once again found a creative outlet and stood to benefit greatly from the title in Crete.

All was not one-sided, however, in the bloody civil war that threatened to deplete the island's population. There was plenty of tangible evidence for the barbarous actions taken by the Christians in the island's east that had so incensed the Muslims of Candia. In the village of Etia, near Siteia, Muslims had taken refuge in their mosque but were tricked into coming out and then slaughtered. When Evans surveyed the scene, he reported that the mosque had been left undisturbed until he

> entered its unhallowed precincts . . . The clothing of the wretched villagers, which they gathered together for their flight and left when summoned to their doom still covered the whole floor—bright bits of Oriental covering amidst festering rags, horsehair bags that contained their scanty stock of food, a green strip from the turban, perhaps, some descendant of the prophet.[143]

Five years later, Charles Trick Currelly, one of the excavators at Palaikastro, heard the full story. (Currelly had been assistant to Flinders Petrie in Egypt and was to become a founder of the Royal Ontario Museum.) He recalled that the excavation's

> labour came from about three-quarters of a mile away. The people were very merry and very devout, and I found them attractive: it was very interesting going to church with them and watching their intensive piety. It was hard to realize how truly bloodthirsty they were. One day two men turned up who did not belong to the village, but who wanted work. Their chief recommendation was that they had recently killed two Mohammedans. This led to the discussion of the part that our workmen had played in the troubled times only five years before. Some distance over the hills was a Mohammedan village. The Mohammedans were unsuspecting, and had no watch; when they heard the first volley fired they sprang up in total darkness, of course, as their little lamps are difficult things to light. Parents grabbed their children and what weapons they could find, and all ran to the mosque.
>
> Once assembled there, they found themselves very badly armed, and therefore called for a parley: they offered, in return for the sparing of their lives, to march away leaving behind them everything they possessed—their fields, their animals, their implements and their household gear—everything but what they had on their backs. These terms were accepted, and our villagers swore on the Gospels that they would be truly carried out; but they demanded that all arms should be passed through the mosque windows so that the Mohammedans, when they came

out, would be completely unarmed. The weapons were handed over, and the Mohammedans were told to come out and form a line to march away. They came out and drew up in line, the mothers with their babies, the old people helping with the children, and the men carrying some of the smaller ones. As soon as they were well in line, our people let loose with their new guns and killed them all except one little girl, who ran out from the line towards the Christians. A small boy, who had followed his relatives to the Mohammedan village, tripped her and threw his dark cloak over her, and the little girl was wise enough to lie hidden till all was over.

At another village not far away a similar massacre took place, but there the Christians took the Mohammedans to a cliff, stuck a knife between their shoulders, and dropped them over one at a time.[144]

Evans found that the civil war was even further complicated by jealousy among the Christians. The men of Kritsa, the largest of Crete's villages at the time, and Evans's base while investigating Goulas, comprised a band of "some six hundred warriors armed to the teeth" formed into squads, as Evans reported, "who, in return for pecuniary consideration offered to protect the more peaceful peasants of the adjoining districts, though these were not very long in discovering that their real object was to secure a principal share in the plunder of the Turkish villages." It was the men of Kritsa, "under their redoubtable chief Tavlàs," who were responsible for the worst of the Christian massacres, but also for one of the strangest exploits of the insurrection. Jealous of the way the neighboring town of Neapolis had become the administrative center of the eastern part of the island, they decided to lodge a protest in the only language they knew: they marched against the town fully intent on destroying it, but were kept away by the Neapolitan forces, though many lives were lost in the siege.[145] Hogarth might have cracked a wry and knowing smile as he read Evans's dispatches.

A Golden Age

Evans enticed his readers with descriptions of the particularly enthusiastic celebrations to mark the feast of St. George in 1898 due to the proposed nomination of Prince George, second son of King George I of Greece, as high commissioner for the Powers in Crete.[146] The Christians saw this appointment as the first step toward their unification with Greece, but the Great Powers insisted that Crete should remain independent. Bureaucratic delays ensued until early September, when British servicemen were killed by Muslims during a riot in Candia, and the British government found it could no longer support a policy of maintaining the status quo; Great Britain finally joined the chorus of European nations against the Porte. The last of the Turkish troops left Crete on November 14 and Prince George arrived at Suda Bay on December 21.

An Athenian correspondent waxed "white and blue" as he reported that, "after being torn for twenty-five centuries by civil war, foreign conquest, and oppression of the darkest description, Crete has suddenly attained liberty and good government, under a ruler of her own race and language."[147] The Greeks laid a historical claim to Crete dating back to the time of Periclean Athens in the fifth century B.C. and would insist that the island's true race and language were Greek. Nonetheless, Prince George worked hard to promote peace in Crete, urging both Christians and Muslims to put the past behind them and work together: a tall order indeed, which neither side could easily obey. Instead, most Muslims who refused to convert to Christianity sold their property for the equivalent of boat fare to the Anatolian coast, as Hogarth had predicted.

Prince George was very much in favor of archaeological exploration in Crete, but was concerned that it be closely regulated. There could be no talk of excavation until the laws regarding the export and recovery of antiquities could be agreed upon and written into the planned Cretan constitution, as Hazzidakis informed Evans early in 1899.[148] In the same letter he broke the news to Evans that he had lost Goulas to the French, who were, after all, in charge of the Mirabello region and thus outside Hazzidakis's influence. It was under French protection that Jean Demargne had gone to the Psychro Cave in 1897 and, much to Evans's chagrin, recovered more fragments of the famous inscribed libation table.[149] Now the same scholar set his sights on Goulas and the Greco-Roman city of Itanos, near Siteia, in the far east.

The French School was equally eager to begin excavations at Knossos. As the last public declaration of explorer's rights had been made by André Joubin, Théophile Homolle, director of the French School, was surprised to learn that Evans, meanwhile, had quietly jumped the claim, so a heated correspondence in the spring of 1899 flew between Homolle and Evans, with Hogarth, as British School director, caught in the middle. Hogarth, eager to avoid a diplomatic row, tried to play down the value of Knossos: "I have no great enthusiasm for the deep, expensive and Romanized site of Knossos," he wrote Evans, "but I will stand by you, if you want it, to the utmost limits of international courtesy." Eventually, Homolle, unwilling to play the "groundskeeper's dog," as he put it, retreated.[150] Evans's tenacity worked for him, but his most important card, part ownership of the Kephala, had won the round. Next he had to get the permission to excavate from the new high commissioner, and acquire the remainder of the property.

Evans arrived in Canea on March 22, and met with the prince three days later. Long past were the days when an individual like Schliemann could excavate an ancient site on his own behalf; the Cretan government insisted that exploration rights be granted to recognized institutions, as stated in Greek law. Evans introduced himself as the representative of the Hellenic Society and the London Committee of the British School at Athens, with a brief to "secure certain sites in Crete for British archaeological exploration." In truth, he represented his own interests. Evans was most concerned to secure "the ancient mound called Kephala on the site of Knôsos," but he also argued for ancient Lyttos and the Psychro cave, the Kamares cave, the cave of Hermes Kranaios, and the sites of Zakros and Kalamafka in the east; these were all sites either deemed important from his own observations or mentioned by ancient authors in connection with mythical figures.

Hogarth joined Evans to lend support to his demand for the Kephala, but the shrewd planner had little need of assistance. As Hogarth later put it: "Arthur Evans had long laid his plans, and, with the forethought of a genius, cast his bread on troubled waters by buying a Bey's part share of the site." The prince was aware of the French claim to Knossos but, as Hogarth recounted, "when others, who coveted Cnossus, put forward moral rights, he alone could urge the convincing claim of sacrifice, and the Cretans, for whom he had done so much in their hour of danger, upheld his cause in the hour of freedom."[151]

While awaiting the prince's decision, they traveled in eastern Crete "pegging out claims for future digging" in a landscape scarred by acts of vengeance. Hogarth was saddened by the destruction and lamented that "many villages lay gaunt skeletons of ruin; where olive groves had been, blackened stumps and pits bore witness to the ethnicidal fury of religious war in the Near East, which ever uproots the staple of the foeman's life, after it has killed the mother and her babe."[152] In the interim the prince approved Evans's request to excavate the Kephala "as soon as you can produce a legal right to the ground," read the victorious note of April 14. Now Evans could plan the first large-scale, modern excavations at the hill that had beguiled so many before him. But not a spadeful of dirt could be shifted until he acquired the remainder of the property and the legal status of the anticipated finds was clarified.

The Cretan government worked through the summer formulating a new constitution that in the end was based largely on that of Greece. Hazzidakis and the new secretary of the Candia Syllogos, Stephanos Xanthoudides, a Greek philologist and strong supporter of the move for unification with Greece, drafted a version of a law to protect Cretan antiquities, to be considered by the prince. Not surprisingly, the antiquities law passed in early August was almost identical to that passed in Greece a few weeks earlier. The Greek archaeological law of 1834 had been useless at curbing the flow of antiquities from the country. Indeed, dealers in Athens openly boasted of their ability to fill orders from foreign museums for all sorts of Greek antiquities.[153] The new law made the possession and exportation of antiquities a criminal offense; as all antiquities in Crete were to remain in the sole custody of the Cretan government, this meant that the acquisition of artifacts by foreign museums, the primary motive for most archaeological explorations, was strictly forbidden. Evans may not have been happy with the law, but he was not too fussed, either, as he rarely allowed affairs of state to affect his own affairs and always found ways to circumvent their laws. He also had a personal assurance from Xanthoudides that "not-wanted specimens" could be exported—finds the Syllogos felt were unworthy of their concern.[154]

With the antiquities regulations firmly in place by mid-August, the era of modern archaeology in Crete began immediately. It is no coincidence that the academies of Italy, France, and Britain assumed the dominant roles; their protectorates of the present were transferred imperceptibly to the past. Halbherr, on behalf of the Italian School, with Hazzidakis, started to clear the Agora at Gortyn. Demargne, for the French, enticed by Evans and Myres's promise of a fortified Mycenaean acropolis at Goulas, was joined by Xanthoudides, for the Cretan Association.

Hazzidakis had been hounding the owners of the Kephala estate on Evans's behalf and by mid-August had obtained their agreement to sell the remaining three-quarters for £200. The coincidence of their agreement with the passing of the new antiquities law betrayed the owners' eagerness to sell quickly and at a reduced price because of the potential loss of the property's value, as the antiquities it undoubtedly contained would no longer go to the new owner. But this was of little concern to Evans, who knew that an arrangement to suit his needs as regards the Ashmolean could always be worked out far from the gaze of customs officials. The purchase agreement Hazzidakis secured was legally binding and removed the last obstacle from the road to Knossos. Evans had fought long and hard since the afternoon of March 19, 1894, when he had made up his mind to acquire the Labyrinth of Daedalus. Now it would be his.

The time had come to make the Cretan Exploration Fund a reality. Prince George agreed to be patron, Evans and Hogarth were directors, and Myres the secretary. Their aim was to raise £5,000 to cover the full cost of British excavations in Crete and to reimburse Evans for the cost of the Kephala, but British newspapers were full of the war that Great Britain was losing to the Boers in South Africa, sparked off by the British attempt to enlarge its garrisons in the gold-mining district of the Witwatersrand, in the Transvaal. One event in particular, the Boer siege of the British post at Mafeking, begun on October 14, captured the public's imagination, as the press reported daily on the firm resolve of Colonel Robert Baden-Powell, who held the attackers off until mid-May 1900, thereby achieving heroic status but effectively diverting attention away from any other news. The Cretan Fund collected the disheartening total of £510, of which £100 was from Arthur and his father.

Hogarth, sensing Evans's disappointment with the Cretan Exploration Fund, wrote on January 1 of the new century to offer a share of his dig supplies, which cost £16, but Evans had already decided on which necessities he couldn't do without. His order, placed with the Junior Navy Stores in London and totaling almost four times that of Hogarth, reads, as one biographer writes, "like the contents of Rat's wicker luncheon basket in the *The Wind in the Willows*: In one case was packed 24 tins of Ox Tongues, 3 of Pressed Beef, 36 of Turkey and

Tongue Pâtés, 2 of Ham, 12 Plum puddings, 12 Guava Jelly, and 20 tins of Sardines. There were fourteen cases in all and the total cost was £56 1s. It is not altogether surprising to find . . . 12 bottles of Enos' Fruit Salts amongst the Quinine pills."[155] Evans knew what to expect in Crete and had no intention of roughing it to satisfy the public's perception of the rugged explorer.

Evans stood on the threshold of a new world at the beginning of the new century. All was set for his greatest adventure: his work at the Ashmolean was complete, and his assistant keeper, Charles F. Bell, was a reliable young man whom Evans was grateful to leave in charge; Youlbury was a firm home base from which to explore the world; and the Kephala was all but his. His mind was filled with the obscure history of Knossos and the great age when King Minos reigned over the entire Aegean Sea. Flinders Petrie had provided the absolute framework of the Egyptian Twelfth Dynasty for the formative period and the Eighteenth Dynasty for Crete's golden age. To their Egyptian contemporaries, the Cretans were the Keftiu, and to their neighbors on the Palestinian coast they were Kaphtorites. To this golden age Evans assigned the great art of the Mycenaean period depicting the worship of trees and pillars as surrogates for the true gods of the Indo-Aryan-Teutonic religion they spawned later in Europe.

There is a very real danger in all disciplines that a new theory, once it is proposed, gives direction to all subsequent research, certainly by its original designer but also by those who find it believable, suitable, or even expedient to the verification of their own theories. Evans's conclusions to his first detailed study of early Cretan history and society became the platform upon which all subsequent constructions and reconstructions were based. Ideally, a scientific scholar periodically reviews the status of the factual evidence relating to his theories and rejects those parts that can no longer be supported. However scientific Evans may have considered himself, his thinking was evolutionary, and so, too, was the way in which he constructed his ideas. His building-block approach increased the risk that he might eventually lose sight of the highly tentative foundations for his theories in the realms of possibility and grant them a basis in fact, which was not always warranted. In science, the transition from theory to law is a long, drawn-out process of experiment and verification by international consensus. The humanities, by contrast, rarely promote ideas according to this stringent system. Rather, the interpretation of tangible evidence may be accepted as probable or likely for as long as a consensus finds a use for it as part of a greater explanation of human behavior—but no longer. This ensures that there is a constant review process as the body of consensus itself changes along with its requirements. But Evans's "instinctive rebelliousness against conventions," which he could maintain thanks to his financial security, allowed him to operate outside of the body of consensus to which he would otherwise and should have been accountable. Instead, he remained aloof, rarely reviewing his evidence. And even when he did, changes of heart were the exception rather than the rule.

4

Knossos 1900–1907

Pre-Hellenic Crete

Evans sailed to Candia the first week of March 1900, eager to get an early start on the season, and though he arrived during one of the worst storms in living memory, he found the population filled with the optimism of the new century in a new and independent country. The spring of 1900 brought the hopeful dreams of reconstruction following one of Crete's longest and bitterest nightmares. No one denied that the scars of the recent hostility would take long to heal, but Prince George and the new government were determined that they must. The future could only be brighter, though the new Cretan administration still looked to its distant past for the inspiration to guide them through this difficult transition. Evans was pleased to find that they issued a series of postage stamps commemorating their mythical heroes, as the ancient towns of Crete had done on their coins.[1] The 1-drachma stamp had an image of Talos, the giant man of bronze who defended Crete against all invaders by hurling huge boulders at any stranger who approached the island's shores.[2] Minos on his throne, the engraving based on a coin from Knossos, sat in enlightened judgment on the 2-drachma stamp, while the 5-drachma stamp depicted the more recent myth of St. George slaying the dragon. The portrait of the saint's mortal counterpart, Prince George, in full military regalia, was on stamps of various lower denominations for internal circulation.

The juridical responsibilities for the new country fell to Prince George's minister of justice, a thirty-five-year-old Cretan lawyer and journalist named Eleutherios Venizelos, a member of the Cretan Assembly and the head of the recently formed Liberal Party. Venizelos, an outspoken Greek nationalist who later became prime minister of Greece and the most influential Greek politician of the century, made it clear that the Cretan Assembly had no intention of maintaining the island's independence; the popular cry was "Enosis" (union), and unity with Greece was their goal. This heartfelt aspiration by Crete's majority dictated the purpose and direction of all archaeological activity, as the elucidation of Crete's early Greek history became the sole focus of the new fieldwork and its results. Even the Minoans, whom Evans associated with Homer's Eteocretans and therefore placed ahead of the Greeks in time, became "pre-Hellenic," which meant that their study was important only so long as it showed what aspects of their culture survived into or even gave birth to the subsequent Hellenic culture. They were treated as the roots of Hellenism and as such provided modern Europeans with their own earliest "high civilization" in contact with, but quite distinct from, those of Egypt and the Near East. As "forerunners of the Greeks," the Bronze Age Cretans would be studied not for their own sake, as a complex and potentially multicultural society at the crossroads of the eastern Mediterranean, but as the originators of those aspects of Greek culture that were symbolic of the greatest achievements of Europe. Winckelmann had ordained over a century earlier that representational art adhering closely to realism, followed by planned architecture on a grand scale, was best executed in the Athenian Parthenon. The Minoans, then, like the modern Cretans, were unlikely to see their independence from Hellas and Europe.

Evans's first task was the long-awaited transfer of funds for the remaining three-quarters of the estate at Knossos; then he and Hogarth set about repairing the Turkish bey's estate house on the river's edge below the Kephala hill for use as a storeroom. "It is somewhat ramshackle, and we are busy giving it a drastic disinfecting and internal whitewashing, but it is a truly oriental abode with a kind of cascade fountain in the principal reception room and a small aqueduct running through the house," Evans wrote his father on March 7.[3] Hogarth found more "civilized" lodgings for them in Candia, as there was a dan-

ger of malaria in the Knossos valley, and hired a housekeeper and butler.

Then came the task of organizing the dig itself. Hogarth was wary of
Evans's lack of field experience and uncertain about the success of their
collaboration. "I have made digging so much my trade," he had written
to Evans a year earlier, "that I have various ways and methods (largely
of course learnt from Petrie) which I consider essential and must apply
for myself, under no more than very general direction from home. I
have earned, I think, the right to have a pretty free hand as to where I
dig and how. That is all. We can work together—you and I excellently."[4]
But now he was less convinced about their ability to share responsibility: "Could only work on terms of I find, and Evans observes," he wrote
in his diary on March 8, "but naturally E. doesn't like that." Hogarth
was quite certain that Evans was incapable of running the dig, and
noted, "Had it out with E. about Kephala—impressed him with size of
site and impossibility of working it alone. Suggested Mackenzie."[5]

Duncan Mackenzie, born in Rosshire, Scotland, in 1861, a graduate
of Edinburgh University, where he studied philosophy, and a recent
Ph.D. in classical archaeology from Vienna, was a tall, lean "Scot with
an inaudible Highland voice, a brush of red hair, an uncertain temper,
[and] a great command of languages," Joan Evans recalled.[6] Only
ten years Evans's junior, Mackenzie had earned a sterling reputation as
a field archaeologist at Phylakopi, in Melos, where he was the only
trained professional present throughout the entire campaign from
1896 to 1899.

The fourth of nine children born to a gamekeeper, Mackenzie depended on scholarships and salaried work for his livelihood, and he
never achieved financial security, largely because of his inability to control funds when they came his way. He had been on a yearly grant of
£50 while working on the Phylakopi finds, but ran afoul of the British
School at Athens when he obtained separate funding to pursue research
in Italy in 1899. The school quickly instructed him to remit the debts
he had run up for accommodation in Athens and insisted that "he at
once [hand] over to the committee his diaries and notes relating to the
excavations at Phylakopi 1896–1899 (inclusive)." An argument ensued,
and Mackenzie ran off to Italy with the dig notebooks. Hogarth knew
he was "hard to pin down to rules and dates," but recommended him as
"an attractive fellow and a first-rate archaeologist."[7] Evans gave in to
Hogarth's wisdom, and wired Mackenzie in Rome: "Could you come

superintend under my direction important excavation Knosos, personal not School affair terms four months sixty pounds and all expenses paid to begin at once." The clear statement of a private
enterprise not connected with the British School, as well as the handsome salary and benefits, were sufficient to lure Mackenzie away from
his course of study in Rome. His reply of March 16 was typical of what
Evans came to appreciate as the Scotsman's directness and economy of
words: "Agreed coming next boat."[8]

So began a thirty-year partnership that was a mixture of collaboration and codependence. Evans was the nominal director, while Mackenzie ran the excavations: supervising the men, keeping the accounts,
and writing the excavation daybooks on which Evans based his publications. But Mackenzie was never in a position to protest what at times
seemed an injustice—he needed Evans's financial support while Evans
couldn't do without his technical expertise. Evans called him "my lieutenant," but Mackenzie's chances of promotion were severely limited, if
nonexistent; he had no hope of rising in Evans's world, where status
was determined by birth and social standing—not by ability. Mackenzie was assuming a position similar to his father's on the Fairburn estate, in Scotland.

Evans took more of Hogarth's sound advice and, wishing to avoid
the sort of criticism that dogged Schliemann for most of his archaeological career, engaged an architect from the outset. The choice was
straightforward: David Theodore Fyfe. Born in the Philippines in 1875
and trained in Glasgow, Fyfe, who eventually became director of the
School of Architecture at Cambridge University, was then on a traveling studentship from the School of the Architectural Association in
London to Greece in 1899. He had duly impressed Hogarth, who recommended him to Evans, and, as joint directors of the Cretan Exploration Fund, they appointed him as architect for all their Cretan
projects.[9] The young trainee never had the freedom of expression that
Dörpfeld enjoyed with Schliemann, and so never found himself in a
position to contradict his master—another lesson Evans had taken to
heart from Schliemann's experience.

"If the labourer, who is a fool, cannot see what is being turned over
under his eyes," Hogarth cautioned Evans, "you at his side will see it no
better because you are not turning it over." Hogarth believed in educating the diggers on an archaeological excavation and interesting them in
what the archaeologist hoped to find, thereby increasing their chances

of success.[10] He sent for "the most expert tomb hunter in the Levant," a term for which we should read grave robber and looter of antiquities, his trusted Cypriot retainer, Gregorios Antoniou. Better known as Gregóri, the Cypriot displayed an "uncanny knowledge of the wild plants which betray 'antikas' in their roots," as John Myres later recalled.[11] Gregóri's task was to put his talents to the test and find the ancient burial grounds that Evans and Hogarth presumed were in the vicinity of the Kephala. Unlike habitation sites, tombs produce the intact antiquities that most appeal to museum curators and their public, like whole vases and jewelry, just the sort of boost the Cretan Exploration Fund needed.

Hogarth and Gregóri, with a small team of hardy diggers, began on March 13 to search the slopes of the Knossos valley surrounding, but never encroaching upon, the central mound of the Kephala hill, which was reserved for a very different sort of operation and would wait for Evans, who in turn awaited the arrival of his superintendent. For two months Hogarth supervised trials, that is, test pits measuring one meter by two, dug down to bedrock. These gave a glimpse of what might lie beneath the surface and allowed him to identify tombs or decide if an area might be rewarding for future large-scale excavation, for instance if traces of a fine building were found. The trials were dug to great depths, ten meters in some areas, until the natural soil or rock levels were reached, undisturbed by human occupation and thus devoid of artifacts. When the workers put the soil back into the pits, they left them without any indication and kept no precise map of their locations, simply moving on to the next spot that tweaked Gregóri's interest. These confusing pits are known now as "Hogeys" to the modern archaeologists who have the misfortune of encountering them during excavations in the Knossos valley.*

The Palace of Mycenaean Kings

On the morning of Friday, March 23, Evans, Hogarth, and Fyfe were helped into the wooden saddles of their tiny donkeys and rode through the long, dark tunnel of the Kainoriou Gate in the Venetian ramparts of Candia and began their journey to Knossos along a route that would

---

*The term was coined by Philip Mudd, who found his fair share on the Stratigraphical Museum excavations of 1978–80.

become as familiar to them over the next thirty years as any track they had known in their native Britain. They crossed the bridge and followed the dirt trail as it climbed the slopes to the south where the silent glare of high-pillared and turban-topped marble tombstones in the sprawling Muslim burial grounds followed their progress. A little farther on they reached the Christian cemetery, where they recalled their own countrymen who gave their lives during the recent troubles and now lay in one corner. The track then leveled out on a low ridge above the Katsambas river, high with the winter's rain and flowing against them down toward Trypiti and the sea.

The route took them past the foot of the Fortetsa ridge from whose heights the Ottomans had rained down terror on the Venetian stronghold of Candia. More recently, British naval cannon together with the guns of France, Italy, and Russia had thundered in their turn for shorter though no less terrifying bursts, ushering in this next chapter in Crete's history. But all was silent on that morning in the spring of a new century. Forces of a different nature gathered ahead of them on their path.

A crowd thronged around the taverna, a small single-storied stone building in the Cretan vernacular style on the slopes north of the Kephala. Muslims and Christians of both sexes and all ages had turned up from as far away as Lasithi, a full day's hike, hoping to be chosen by Alevisos, whom Evans engaged as foreman.* With preference given to those who had helped Evans in his Lasithi digs, Alevisos selected diggers, shovelers, barrowmen, and waterboys, and washerwomen to clean the finds, and told them that the workday stretched from sunrise to sunset. Then, at eleven o'clock, Evans finally staged the moment that he had rehearsed in his mind for six years. The party of archaeologists, followed by thirty-one of the keenest and ablest of those to survive the recent devastation, proceeded down the slope and walked out onto the Kephala headland. "For us, then, and no others," recalled Hogarth, "Minos was waiting. Over the very site of his buried Throne a desolate donkey drooped, the one living thing in view."[12] They drove away the beast, a poor substitute for the Minotaur Evans might have expected to guard the hill's secrets, and began reversing the process that had created the mound. The men set up a tent, borrowed from the British mil-

---

*I assume that this is the same Alevisos Papalexakis with whom Evans had traveled the island in 1894–96, though it is nowhere stated.

itary, where Evans found shade, and ran the Union Jack up a short flag-pole as a reminder that this was now British territory.

To the Cretan peasants, the foreign archaeologists were like sorcerers possessed of supernatural talents, including the ability to see through the earth's crust and know what lay beneath it. Evans later enjoyed telling the story of how, in anticipation of cleaning the finds and keep-ing the team watered, he commanded that a well be dug near the Kephala, indicating the spot with Prodger, his walking stick. Alevisos scoffed and some of the locals, who had worked the Cretan soil all their lives, asserted that it was the last place anyone would look for water. Evans's temper flared; he wielded Prodger like a magic wand and stuck it in the ground where he commanded the men to dig. Before long they came upon the top of an ancient well, from which they removed the antiquities all the way to the bottom where, to Evans's great delight and the peasants' eternal amazement, they found a spring which, when cleared, filled the well. From that point on, the workers accepted that their master had divine powers.[13]

All field archaeologists who have devoted the time, energy, and capi-tal to acquire a site and then have fought for the permission to excavate it, also suffer the anxiety of wondering, at that crucial moment of breaking ground for the first time, just exactly what they will find. Evans had given six full years of personal expense (and of an energy far in excess of that of most mortals) for the privilege of telling these thirty-one workers to remove the rich agricultural soil from the hillside in search of clues to a history that most of them would not compre-hend, let alone feel part of. They all faced the risk that within a few hours they might have removed only a thin layer of eroded soil and ex-posed a solid rock outcropping scattered with worthless potsherds. They might find that Kalokairinos had found all there was of impor-tance in 1879. Evans might learn that he had chased off the other suit-ors only to find the bride barren of promise and her dowry worthless. These are the risks that excavators take. But by the end of the first week any worry that he might have had was gone and forgotten forever. In-stead, his mind filled with mythic personalities and he recorded with childlike enthusiasm his first impressions of the treasures that began to pour forth from the distant past—so distant as to be almost unrecog-nizable.

"Kephala," reads the first page of his diary, which Evans wrote in short bursts, often without participles, and apparently after the fact—

the dates he used don't always correspond to those in Mackenzie's notes. Evans's record begins, "March 23 Began dig 31 men (8 piasters a day)." Mackenzie, whose boat landed at midday, arrived at the site in the early afternoon and began the detailed excavation records with "Day-book of the Excavations at Knosos—1900 Duncan Mackenzie," in bold script on the first page. His first entry, "The excavations by Mr Arthur Evans on the acropolis of Knosos began this forenoon with 31 men and foreman at work," sets the style for all subsequent records. "Knôsos," in the style of Freeman, was the preferred spelling; it was how ancient authors referred to it and how the Greeks and Romans named the place on the coins minted there. But there was a linguistic theory suggesting that place names with *ss* and *nth* were of greater antiquity than those with clear Greek roots, and so Evans, eager to establish the pre-Hellenic status of his site, soon converted the name to Knossos. Mackenzie's early pages are written matter-of-factly, describing the soil texture and colors, every bit the work of the well-trained, scientific archaeologist. Evans, in sharp contrast, was interested only in noting remarkable objects, and his selection gives a clear account of what he considered important.

Any archaeologist's daybook records the first appearance of objects and architecture usually well before they are understood within the greater context of their time and place. It's a provisional registration of the artifacts brought into the excavator's time—a sort of rebirth certificate issued before the character of the object is fully established. The British explorers on that dusty knoll at the far reaches of their civilized world couldn't have imagined the lasting importance of their entries, which they scrawled for themselves and never intended to be more than aide-mémoire for a final published account. Half a century later, their empirical remarks about the shattered finds, many of which when cleaned and restored were recognized as some of the most powerful images we possess from antiquity, were scrutinized by critical scholars and treated like holy scripture composed by wise men or prophets. Yet the innocence and youthful enthusiasm of Evans's notes seem to be almost naïve to the modern reader. On the second day, he sketched a tiny figurine and wrote "A. T. C. [terracotta] image," and called it the "Aphrodite of Knôsos!"—a reference to the "primitive European idols" he had studied in 1895. But, he noted, the workmen called it a "Stavros," a Christian crucifix, as they, too, participated in the search for identifiable and meaningful symbols. Mackenzie dryly noted that the same object, which is now recognized as a Neolithic figurine, was "An earthen ware hand-polished and incised figurine of a female without legs but with the broken surface, where they joined the body, traceable." The different appraisals, expectations, and desires among the director, his superintendent, and their employees, established on the first day, became a theme of the early years at Knossos.

At Hogarth's suggestion, the Kephala dig began with two days of testing the hillside to find a place without antiquities over which to "shoot," as he put it, the large spoil-heaps of dirt anticipated from the upper part of the tell, where Kalokairinos had exposed the storerooms with the large jars. Excavation "shoots" resemble the great artificial mounds one sees near the openings of mines, for, like miners, archaeologists discard what doesn't interest them and keep only the raw materials deemed necessary to manufacture their desired history.

Soon, human remains began to appear at the northern limits of the property. Mackenzie pointed out that the "head W." and "feet E." suggested Christian burials. "It was indicated by one of the men that the hands were folded over the pelvis and that accordingly the tombs must be Christian." Evans quickly decided to eradicate any possible motive for antagonism between the Muslim and Christian workers, which, if allowed to flare up, might interrupt the excavation. "These graves probably late but don't answer to modern Turkish or Christian," he declared. Mackenzie also eliminated any potential problem with the clear dismissal of the "tombs which afford no positive evidence of any interest from the point of view of the excavation." Evans had seen enough ethnic conflict in his life, and so the nameless mortal bones joined the spoil heap of discarded facts in the shoots.

The test pits on the surrounding slopes went on for a dull week with few finds until the second Thursday when "Excavation was . . . begun on the top of the acropolis," in what Evans described as his "assault on the central stronghold on the height."[14] His strategy was to locate the limits of the main building that Kalokairinos had found by excavating down to the highest floor level. Once inside the ancient walls, the character and quantity of the finds began to change dramatically. On Friday, March 30, Evans wrote, "Today two remarkable objects turned up." The first was a stirrup jar, or *bügelkanne*, a vase form whose shape was well known from Schliemann's excavations at Mycenae. It "seems to show that the most typical of Mycenaean vase-forms is of Cretan extraction," he proclaimed. Even Mackenzie was excited by the "false-necked amphora," which was probably, he wrote, the "original form." Both men were aware of how important such a find was to help prove that the origins of Mycenaean and, by extension, European society lay in Crete.

The second "important find," Evans noted, "was a kind of baked clay bar—rather like a stone or bronze chisel in shape—though broken at one end—with a script on it and what appear to be numerals. It at once recalled a clay tablet of unknown age that I had copied at Candia also found at Knossos. Also broken. There is something like cursive writing about these." Now even Mackenzie was thrilled and recorded that it "proved to be nothing less than a Mycenaean inscription incised on a terracotta object like a knife sharpener [whetstone]." But for once, Evans and Mackenzie were on an equal footing with their illiterate foreman and workers: the inscription was illegible to all.

During the Sunday break, when the workers returned to their villages, Evans made his own sketch plan of the walls coming to light. His playful side added curls to the edges to suggest a pirate's treasure map, like those in *The Boy's Own Annual*, complete with *X*s to mark where he had found buried treasure. Eager for more examples of script, he hired seventy-nine men when work resumed on Monday morning, and the wicker baskets, previously used to carry away the soil, were supplemented by new iron wheelbarrows to speed the process.

The conflicting views of what was being found during the first two weeks—affected by Greek myths, early Christian symbolism, and modern scientific archaeology—were nowhere more evident than when the first large-scale human representations appeared. On April 5, Evans recorded:

A great day! Early in the morning the gradual surface uncovering of the Corridor to E. of "Megaron" near its S. end revealed two large pieces of Myc. Fresco . . . One represented the head and forehead, the other the waist and part of the skirt of a female figure holding in her hand long Mycenaean "rhyton" or high funnel shaped cup . . . The figure was life size with flesh colours of a deep reddish hue like that of the figures on Etruscan tomb & the Keftiu of Egyptian paintings. The profile of the face was of a noble type: full lips, the lower lip showing a slight peculiarity of curve below. The eye was dark and somewhat almond [shaped] apparently partly in profile out-facing as Egyptian shaped. In front of the ear is a kind of ornament and a necklace and bracelet are visible. The arms are beautifully modeled. The waist is of the smallest . . . It is far and away the most remarkable human figure of the Mycenaean Age that has yet come to light.

It is clear from his sketch that Evans thought the figure was of a buxom woman. By April 10 he had named her: "I think that the 'Ariadne' had fallen from the forehall of the Megaron." His mind was filled with Schliemann's drawings of the Mycenaean-Homeric Megaron, a central building with a large hearth like the ones at Mycenae and Tiryns, but here the walls were decorated with fine paintings—portraits, it seemed, of their most famous occupants.

Mackenzie remained unmoved. He recorded:

It turned out to be the head, life-size of a human figure (youth) with the right hand holding the handle of the same vase. A little later part of the body including the left arm and hand came into view . . . The figure was bare to the waist. Round the waist was a blue band with double spirals in black on a red ground over blue. The hips were covered with a tight fitting loin-cloth with a complex system of rosettes . . . the legs below the level of the loin-cloth were not preserved.

No allusions as to gender, though both "youth" and "loin-cloth" suggest the masculine without being in obvious opposition to his master.

A burly, genial, and ambitious boy called Emmanuel Akoumianakis, who had come to Knossos to sell cherries to the workers but quickly attached himself to the excavations, had caught Evans's eye.[15] Manoli (the Greek diminutive for Emmanuel) was eager to please and so volunteered to guard the site at night against looters. His reaction to this fresco, more than the others, illustrates the excited tension that gripped everyone at Knossos: "At night Manoli 1st to watch fresco," Evans noted. "Believed by him to be saint with halo! His troubled dream— Saint wrathful—wakes and hears lowing and neighing—something about—but of ghostly kind—φαντάζει [fandázi]—it spooks!" Manoli was caught somewhere between fear and adoration. He had been deeply affected by the only art in his experience, the paintings in Greek Orthodox churches, and his reaction best expressed what the Cretan Christians were hoping to find at Knossos, and recalls Schliemann's workmen and their reverence for the gold "mask of Agamemnon," which they took to be a Christian icon, at Mycenae.

The painted figure played on Evans's mind for days; on April 13 he wrote:

> The chief event of the day was the result of the continued excavation of the bath chamber. The parapet of the bath proved to have another circular cutting at its East end and this was filled with charred wood—cypress—these openings were evidently for columns. On the other side of the North wall was a short bench, like that of the other chamber, and then separated from it by a short interval a separate seat of honour or throne. It had a high back, like the seat of gypsum, which was partly embedded in the stucco of the wall. It was raised on a square base and had a curious moulding below with crockets (almost Gothic!) Probably painted originally so as to harmonize with the fresco on its side. This was imperfectly preserved, but showed the upper foliage of a palm tree (No! reeds) and a part of another of a reddish brown colour on a pale ground.

Evans concluded that the suite "seems to be the women's bath and the isolated throne seems to show that it was the Queen's—Ariadne's bath." Mackenzie made no mention of Ariadne as he described clearing the bath and the "chair or throne" with his characteristic distance from all but the concrete evidence.

While it may be desirable to excuse Evans for the childlike enthusiasm driving his vivid imagination and to hope that his decidedly unscientific contemplation was restricted to a diary of private observations, this was not the case. When the young American archaeologist Harriet Boyd, the first woman to dig in Crete, visited on the afternoon of April 11, Evans was as uninhibited with her as he was with his diary. She recorded: "Intense excitement as in the presence of Dr. Evans a workman removed the last earth from the 'oldest throne in Europe,' and the stone chair stood forth intact."[16] She later wrote that Evans "Immediately named [the chair] in sport 'the throne of Ariadne.' "[17] Boyd was so impressed by the great British scholar that she assumed he was joking about the fabled princess and her bath, but he wasn't. When it came to verifying the Greek myths, Evans was serious, as on April 13, he noted, "Near corner of N. W. Chamber . . . a curious Myc. fragment of steatite showing gate of building with round cavities round doorway ... above are part of a lower limb of a *couchant* bull ... ? Minotaur over gate of Labyrinth!!"[18]

The elaborately decorated chamber became a "Throne Room," but whose? Evans remained ambivalent for some time about the royal seat's ancient occupant: "Here truly was the council chamber of a Mycenaean King or Sovereign Lady," he first reported in the popular *Monthly Review*.[19] But eventually he ceded authority to King Minos.

By April 10, the soil from many parts of the site was being poured through wire sieves so that no fragment of wall painting or inscription was lost. To his great delight, Evans soon found what he was looking for:

One result [of the sieving] was the discovery of what I had always hoped to find—the clay impression of a Mycenaean signet [ring]. It bore a bold but somewhat imperfectly executed design of a lion in a contracted position, with a star-like object on the fore shoulder ... The clay impression had been pinched in by the thumb and finger at the side and below. A part of the back had broken off showing a hollow where the string had passed through, some small strands of which, spirally woven, were visible. Nearby were found four small bronze hinges, which evidently had belonged to the box which it had sealed. There was also found a piece of charred wood with carving, probably a part of the coffer itself.

The unexpected abundance of delicate finds forced Evans to engage the services of a professional conservator. From the Candia Syllogos he brought in Ioannis Papadakis, experienced in Byzantine-style wall paintings, and put him to work on the "Ariadne." Papadakis carefully dug around the fragments, undercutting them as they lay on the ground, then applied gypsum plaster, like that used to make casts, to the underside. When the plaster dried the fragments could be lifted safely, though they became very heavy, so Manoli was called in to carry them down to the storeroom by the river, which he did with great ceremony, holding them high above his head. Papadakis also had to deal with the inscribed tablets, many of which "crumbled away" when the workers tried to lift them. Unlike Babylonian or Hittite tablets, which were intentionally baked like pottery for transport and storage, the tablets and clay sealings at Knossos owed their survival to a great fire that had evidently swept through the palace, partially baking the heaps of records, which otherwise would not have been intended to last. Papadakis employed the same method of coating the underside of the fragments with gypsum plaster, letting them dry and then lifting them. Even so, some of the precious inscriptions were lost when nocturnal rains broke through the roof of the storeroom and by morning had reduced the tablets to "a shapeless mass of clay."[20]

"You may imagine my satisfaction on coming here," Evans reveled in his first cable, sent April 6, to the *Times* in London, reporting that he was "gradually peeling off the superficial layers" of what was "certainly a palace," and finding "in several chambers a whole series of clay tablets with incised writing . . . Yesterday we found a clay bath-like receptacle in a chamber, with a whole deposit of tablets and fragments."

John Evans, on reading the news the following morning, reacted instantly by sending £500 to Arthur personally—the equivalent of the entire endowment of the Cretan Exploration Fund. Evans gratefully responded on April 15 with exhilarating news:

> The great discovery is whole deposits, entire or fragmentary, of clay tablets analogous to the Babylonian but with inscriptions in the prehistoric script of Crete. I must have about seven hundred pieces by now. It is extremely satisfactory, as it is what I came to Crete seven years ago to find, and it is the coping stone to what I have already put together. These inscriptions engraved on the wet clay are evidently the work of practiced scribes, and there are also many figures no doubt representing numerals. A certain number of characters are pictographic showing what the subject of the documents was. Thus in one chamber occurred a series with chariots and horses' heads on them, others show vases etc.[21]

Though Evans had predicted that he would find evidence for writing, even he was shocked by the overabundance of his great discovery.

John Myres used the *Times* cable to stimulate public interest and drum up further support for the Cretan Exploration Fund. He began a lively report in the *Oxford Magazine* with this reminder:

> It has long been known that the site of Gnossus was one of the most promising which remained unexplored . . . that the mound

called Kephala concealed the remains of a prehistoric palace, like that of Mycenae or Tiryns; and that on the walls of this palace were engraved a number of symbols belonging to the Aegean system of pictographic writing. But probably few people ventured to hope that Kephala would yield more than the ordinary spoil of a good Mycenaean site, least of all that it contained the archives of an Aegean state. It was in every way appropriate that the discovery of this mass of Aegean writings should fall to the lot of Mr. Arthur Evans. He was the first to point out the existence of the Aegean system of writing at all . . . and it is to his energy and persistence that we owe . . . the ample share of Cretan sites which the government of Prince George has assigned to British excavators.[22]

Thus it was that Myres, who had tried so hard himself to dig Knossos and had subsequently done so much to pave the way for Evans, now stood aside and let his colleague take credit for the discovery that made him one of the most influential archaeologists of the century.

On Monday, April 16, thanks to Evans's father's generosity, the work force was increased to ninety-eight eager pairs of hands. Suddenly the exploration looked less like a scientific experiment than an army of ants moving in and out of the ground as the workers swarmed over the hill. The digging was now entirely within the palace, as the complex of walls was called.

As work proceeded along the western limits of the building, Evans noted on April 18, "Here we have a whole series of narrow passages (or chambers) some ending blindly. The whole plan very labyrinthine." To Mackenzie the narrow passages remained a "system of galleries," which, he noted, "had been previously excavated partially in the course of an excavation by M. Kalokairinos." Evans was less objective when he recorded, "We are just entering Minos' excavations & in the first of his corridors running N. bits of tablets begin to occur—which shows how careless the dig was." What it also showed was that Kalokairinos, like Schliemann at Mycenae and Tiryns, didn't recognize tablets or sealings because he wasn't looking for them; so, too, Evans himself hadn't understood the importance of the tablet shown to him in Candia in 1896.[23]

The annual resurrection of the youthful Christian god at Easter forced a welcome pause in the digging between Holy Thursday and Easter Monday, April 19–23, but then work was further delayed by a strong south wind blasting sand-filled gusts from the North African desert, the excavators' first experience of the notorious Cretan sirocco. Evans used the interim to compose his initial report, "The Palace Archives of Mycenæan Cnossus" (the pre-Greek spelling now the rule), which he sent to the *Athenaeum* on April 23. Still smarting from the bureaucratic entanglements of the previous seven years, he reminded his readers that nothing comes easily: "After encountering difficulties of every kind I at last succeeded, only a few weeks since, in securing the remaining part of the site," but his tone changed when he described his findings: "The results already obtained have more than confirmed my most sanguine hopes . . . The building itself is certainly a palace of Mycenaean kings, indeed it may be confidently said . . . that hardly a scrap of anything later than the great days of Mycenae . . . has yet come to light."

Evans was eager to point out where he believed his discovery stood in relation to the other well-known archaeological revelations in the public's awareness:

Of the fresco painting and stone carving of that period the remains excel anything of the time yet found on the mainland of Greece. The royal bath room, with its central throne, preserved like a piece of Pompeii, shows a luxury unknown to Mycenae itself. But of even greater interest than these artistic relics is the discovery . . . of clay tablets . . . the perfect analogues of the cuneiform tablets of Babylonia, only in this case engraved with records in the Mycenaean script.

Only one month after the excavations had begun and three weeks since he discovered the first tablets, Evans boldly proclaimed:

These palace archives of Mycenaean Cnossus not only prove to demonstration that a system of writing existed on the soil of Greece at least six centuries before the introduction there of the Phoenician alphabet, but they show that already at that remote date this indigenous system had attained a most elaborate development. These inscriptions are the work of practiced scribes, following conventional methods and arrangements which point to long traditional usage. Yet this development has been arrived at on independent lines; it is neither Babylonian nor Egyptian, nei-

Women wash the pottery shards in the Central Court at Knossos, while the male diggers break for water (ASHMOLEAN MUSEUM)

After a quick wash, tons of smashed pottery were piled in heaps to dry near the soil "shoots," here shown under British military protection (ASHMOLEAN MUSEUM)

Ioannis Papadakis, experienced in conserving Cretan Byzantine wall paintings, was employed by Evans from the outset to excavate and treat the Minoan frescos and to recompose the smashed pottery, including the huge storage jars (ASHMOLEAN MUSEUM)

Cretans were accustomed to seeing human-sized pottery jars, so these Minoan examples in the palace stores, pictured here with local women, were familiar (ASHMOLEAN MUSEUM)

Evans looks on as Mackenzie studies pottery selected from the drying piles in the yard of the small workhouse and storeroom south of the Palace (ASHMOLEAN MUSEUM)

Evans, Fyfe, and Mackenzie pose with some of the restored artifacts in the yard of the workhouse (ASHMOLEAN MUSEUM)

Evans holds a stone rhyton like a Keftiu; the extended nail on the little finger of his right hand was his "pocket excavator's tool" (ASHMOLEAN MUSEUM)

Hogarth and Evans in their Candia (Herakleion) house. Hogarth castigated Evans for living at too high a standard and frightening away donors to the failed Cretan Exploration Fund (ASHMOLEAN MUSEUM)

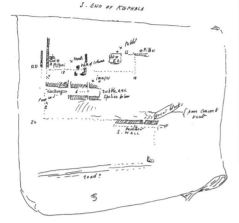

Evans's first sketch plan of Knossos, April 1, 1900, looks like a pirate's treasure map with x marking the treasures (after Evans's 1900 notebook, p. 13)

Evans sketched "the Ariadne," noting: "The eye was dark and somewhat almond [shaped] apparently partly in profile out-facing as Egyptian shaped" (after Evans's 1900 notebook, p. 19)

The Cup-bearer fresco as it was first observed in situ on April 5, 1900; "A great day!" wrote Evans in his diary. "Early in the morning the gradual surface uncovering . . . revealed two large pieces of Myc. Fresco . . . One represented the head and forehead, the other the waist and part of the skirt of a female figure holding in her hand a long Mycenaean 'rhyton' or high funnel shaped cup." He dubbed her "the Ariadne fresco," noting that "the figure was life size with flesh colours of a deep reddish hue like that of the figures on Etruscan tomb & the Keftiu of Egyptian paintings" (ASHMOLEAN MUSEUM)

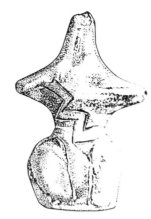

Evans's sketch of the "Aphroditi of Knôsos," March 26, 1900, with a later drawing of the Neolithic clay figurine (after Evans's 1900 notebook, p. 3)

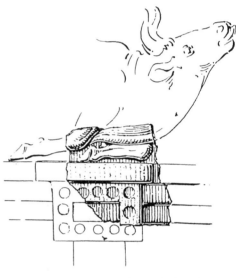

Evans's sketch of his "couchant bull . . . ?Minotaur over gate of Labyrinth!!" and his later reconstructed drawing of the fragment of a stone rhyton (after Evans's 1900 notebook, p. 34; and Evans 1921a, 688 Fig. 507)

Evans's sketch of the first inscribed tablet published from Knossos (after Evans 1900b)

By April 10, 1900, the diggers had revealed a "seat of honour or throne," Evans noted in his diary; he immediately named it "the throne of Ariadne" (ASHMOLEAN MUSEUM)

Evans gazes at the Throne Room complex, which he first reported "truly was the council chamber of a Mycenaean King or Sovereign Lady," eventually bestowing authority on the legendary King Minos (ASHMOLEAN MUSEUM)

The sunken chamber opposite the throne, which Evans thought "to be the women's bath and the isolated throne seems to show that it was the Queen's—Ariadne's bath," until he put Minos in charge, and called it the "lustral basin" (ASHMOLEAN MUSEUM)

A fanciful reconstruction of the Throne Room by E. J. Lambert (ASHMOLEAN MUSEUM)

The gypsum West Façade of the Palace as Evans first revealed it in 1900 (ASHMOLEAN MUSEUM)

The West Façade as reconstituted by Evans and Doll (ASHMOLEAN MUSEUM)

Emmanuel (Manoli) Akoumianakis, whom Evans affectionately called "my mountain wolf," stands near the first pillar encountered at Knossos in 1900, widely publicized to prove the sanctity not only of the pillar itself but of the incised double-axe symbols, which, Evans proposed, "stood as the visible impersonation of the divinity . . . Temple images in human shape were unknown" (ASHMOLEAN MUSEUM)

Reconstructed painting of
the Cup-bearer fresco
(Evans 1928b, Plate XII)

The "Prince of the Lilies" was born of
disparate fresco fragments united to
satisfy Evans's need for an earthly
authority at Knossos: his "Priest-King"
(Evans 1928, Plate XIV)

"Mais ce sont des parisiennes!"
exclaimed a French scholar in
1901, and the name stuck to one
figure in what is now called the
Camp-stool fresco. He suffered a
coup de foudre (love at first
sight) with his earliest glance at
La Parisienne, with "that ruffled
hair, that provocative lock on the
forehead in a 'hook your heart'
curl, that enormous eye and that
sensual mouth . . . stained with
violent red, that red, blue and
black rayed tunic, that flood of
ribbons tossed back in the
manner of 'follow me, young
man' " (Hood and Cameron
1967, Plate F1)

Reconstructed drawing of the miniature fresco that
Evans insisted "supplies indeed a vivid record of the
kind of elevation, which here would have confronted
the spectator," with "these décolletées ladies" who
appeared to Evans to be "fresh from the coiffeur's
hands with hair frisé and curled about the head and
shoulders" (Evans 1930, Plate XVI)

When what is now called the toreador fresco
appeared in 1901, Evans called these figures "girls
attired like Mycenaean cow-boys." They quickly
became the envy of the growing suffragette movement
in Britain and America (Hood and Cameron 1967,
Plate IX)

Evans's "Goddess on the Peak" impressed onto a clay sealing found in 1901 became Artemis with her bow to the Greek Cretans who put her on a stamp of their own

The Cretan Post Office adorned the 3-drachma note of 1904 with a view of Evans's excavations in the "Labyrinth," the Minoan spiral motif, and a heroic Cretan archer on the right taking aim at the "Minotaur" from Kato Zakros to the left

View of the Knossos excavations from the east at the end of the 1901 season (ASHMOLEAN MUSEUM)

General view of the Knossos excavations from the north, showing the observation tower in the West Court and temporary roof over the Throne Room (ASHMOLEAN MUSEUM)

ther Hittite nor Phoenician: it is the work on Cretan soil of an Ægean people. It is the fitting product of a country to which all later Greek tradition looked back as having supplied the earliest model of civilized legislation.

Evans penned these words in the dingy study rooms on the southern slopes of the Kephala hill, just below the excavation, while the workers were still brushing the soil away from tablets accidentally baked more than three thousand years earlier, and before any major archives had appeared. He would have done well to leave behind his premature ideas of early Cretan history, formed during his travels in the previous century. Instead, his first impressions remained the basis for his later conclusions on the nature of the inscriptions he found, and this became one of the main obstacles to his ever reading the documents that had led him to Knossos in the first place, and whose importance he had been the first modern man to realize.

A hasty note to Salomon Reinach contained just what the staunch European "aboriginalist" wanted to hear: that Evans had found a library of clay tablets inscribed in an indigenous script, which proved that writing existed in the "Hellenic world 500 years before Homer and before tradition places the Trojan War."[24] News of the exciting finds spread quickly, and, as Evans claimed international rights of discovery, Minos Kalokairinos spent the Easter observance drafting his *Guide de L'Antique Ville de Cnossos. Rapport des fouilles faites à Cnossos en Avril 1877 par Minos A. Calocairinos qui a découvert Le Palais Royal ou Le Megaron du Roi Minos et Le Fameux Labyrinthe situé près de Cnossos dans le bois sacré de Jupiter. Héraclion, le 23 Avril 1900.*[25]* But Kalokairinos's claim was too little and too late, and written by a man whose heart and spirit had been broken during the final bloody uprising of September 1897, when he had lost both his son and his brother. A fire set by insurgents had burned his Candia house to the ground, consuming his notes and those finds he hadn't already donated to museums. Also gone was the friendly, egalitarian spirit with which he had introduced the modern world to the marvelous potential of the Kephala hill.

---

*Guide to the Ancient City of Knossos. Report on excavations at Knossos in April 1877 made by Minos A. Kalokairinos who discovered the Royal Palace or the Megaron of King Minos and the famous Labyrinth situated near Knossos in the sacred woods of Jupiter. Herakleion, 23 April 1900.

Try as he might to convince the public that he had been the first explorer at Knossos, the affluent, influential, and outspoken Evans now occupied the throne and took his place on the first page of the history books of the twentieth century.

Excavations resumed on Wednesday, April 25, and the long wait was quickly forgotten when a clear link with dynastic Egypt appeared. As though in response to Flinders Petrie's petition for diplomatic links between Crete and the pharaohs, a small diorite statuette was found just below the ground surface. Entranced as he was with the art of Tell el-Amarna and well aware of the abundance of Mycenaean pottery and artistic influence found there, Evans immediately assumed the figure to be Akhenaten, the heretic, monotheistic king himself. Here, or so Evans thought, was the Eighteenth Dynasty connection linking two golden ages of the ancient world. Even Mackenzie was uncharacteristically excited, referring to the discovery as one of "capital importance." The Egyptian link was vital to Evans; throughout his notes he likened the style and colors of the Knossos frescos to those that Petrie had found at Tell el-Amarna. But which was the direction of artistic influence—Egypt to Crete, or the other way around?

When the fragments were cleaned over the Easter break, the "Ariadne" portrait became a less specific "girl fresco," but the quality and quantity of the painted plaster seems to have overwhelmed Papadakis, so Evans sent to Athens for the best-known conservator and artist in Greece. Emile Victor Gilliéron, born in Villeneuve, Switzerland, in the same year as Evans, had studied art at the academies in Paris and Munich and moved to Athens in 1877 after Schliemann's brilliant discoveries at Mycenae.[26] Gilliéron became a popular draftsman with the archaeological community at a time when photography was both expensive and uncertain, and in any case black-and-white images could hardly capture the brilliant essence of severely damaged objects. Gilliéron made it clear from the start that he planned to earn a living from archaeology.[27] He commanded large fees, but in return produced some of the most enduring watercolor reproductions of objects otherwise impossible to imagine because of their poor state of preservation. One such image was his restoration of a wall painting depicting a "man dancing on a bull" from Schliemann's excavations at Tiryns, where he was employed in 1884.[28] It so appealed to the scholarly and popular eye that Schliemann pasted it on the front cover of his report. When the Candia Syllogos conducted rescue excavations in the Idaean Cave, they turned to Gilliéron for help—restoring the cracked and corroded bronze votive objects, some with complex scenes from Greek mythology, to new lives as paintings. Now Evans turned to him to help revive a whole new gallery of art. Gilliéron had been visiting Crete before Easter and dropped by Knossos to investigate the rumors of Evans's success. Intrigued by the finds and swayed by Evans's bargaining power, he traveled to Athens briefly to cancel other arrangements, and then returned to Crete, where he joined the team for an extended stay. Gilliéron was determined to bask in the radiance of Evans's success, as it would ensure his own fame and fortune.

On May 3 and 4, pieces of another painted puzzle slowly began to appear and form themselves into an illustration to accompany the text in Evans's mind. As the fragments came together, Evans wrote of a dancing girl in his notebook, no doubt based on his eagerness to see "Ariadne's dancing floor," which Homer said Daedalus had built for the princess at Knossos, but Evans later inked over these first impressions and added in the margin that it was a boy and he had stopped dancing to become a "Saffron Gatherer." Later, when the fragments were cleaned, he admitted, "The dancing girl proves rather to be a boy gathering flowers & stooping over a basket." It wasn't until many years after that that the figure of a blue monkey was finally identified.

Dörpfeld, with a retinue of fifty-two eager followers, visited on May 7. So concerned was Evans to make the right impression on the greatest figure in Mycenaean archaeology that, as Mackenzie recorded, "Up till mid-day little real excavation was carried on except in the galleries it having been necessary to sweep all floors clean in view of the visit of the Germans." Dörpfeld was excited and intrigued by what his colleagues had to show him, and, though he declared that the "bath room" opposite the throne was a fish tank, Mackenzie was nonetheless grateful for the experienced scholar's confirmation that the pottery, and therefore the building, belonged to the Mycenaean period. Evans was not impressed with Dörpfeld's interpretation of the sunken chamber, since he was certain it was a royal bathroom. "Why such elaborate means of approach by steps?" he protested to his notebook, "& would 'royalty' come to sit near a stinking open tank—such as a receptacle of this kind would have become in the hot season?"[29] Evans was slow to change his mind about his interpretations, if ever, especially once he had stressed a particular point of view in print.

On the same day, Hogarth and Gregóri completed their full circle of the valley. They had started searching for tombs on the Gypsades hill, directly south of the Kephala, then moved to the slopes to the west, near the river valley in the north, and finally they explored the steep Ailias hill that rose above the Kephala to the east. Eight weeks with the foremost tomb robber of the Levant had failed to produce even a single early burial in the vicinity of the palace. Instead, they found plenty of evidence of the large town surrounding the central building, which Evans was bringing back to life at its nucleus. But what of the afterlife? Hogarth threw up his arms and conceded that "after two months' search I fear I leave the solution of the Knossian cemetery problem but little advanced."[30] Evans and Gregóri revisited the problem years later and succeeded by looking further afield.

"The cry is still they come," Evans gleefully reported on new inscriptions to his father. "I have just struck the largest deposit yet, some hundreds of pieces. I doubt if it will be possible to bring out any originals." He started to worry about how to study the great quantity of finds, as he couldn't select and export chosen pieces as his colleagues in Egypt and the Levant did. "I do not expect that I can get back to England till the second week in June, and how to get through the material, none of which may leave the island, is a problem."[31]

The new Cretan government had upgraded the status of the Candia Syllogos and given it permission to make a new museum in the old Turkish barracks to display its collection. The Syllogos quickly arranged for the display of the multitude of new finds—the overabundant first harvest reaped by the foreign excavators who had so eagerly joined in the search for Crete's historical treasures. Halbherr went to the hill at Phaistos, which Evans had surveyed but dismissed as worthless in 1894, and began clearing a large building very much like the one on the Kephala and in every way the worthy rival that Homer had sung about. Harriet Boyd, on Evans's suggestion, was working on the windy crags of a tiny peak called the Kastro, or "castle," near Kavousi, on the eastern side of Mirabello Bay, where she uncovered "the home of a highland chief of Homer's time"; by this she meant the Greek "Dark Age," the period that evidently had no major art, following the great days of Mycenae and before the well-known archaic and classical Greek periods.

Simultaneously, Hogarth went to the Lasithi plateau in search of adventure and the "mythic birthplace of the Father God of Crete," and he found both.[32] After blasting away the stone collapse that had prevented

Evans and Myres from exploring the Psychro Cave more fully, he pene-
trated the previously unexplored lower depths of the grotto, and ravaged the inner sanctum by offering his workers extra rewards "for the
better objects," thereby inciting a "frantic energy" in them which, he
confessed, produced "a grotesque sight, without precedent in an archaeologist's experience" as men, women, and children clung to the sta-
lactites while smashing at them in order to get at the votive offerings
the Cretans had left there thousands of years earlier. The desecration
brought five hundred new artifacts to the Candia Syllogos[33] and notoriety for Hogarth among the Cretans.[34] He preferred the company of
Arabs, later recalling, "The peasant Greek is neither brute nor butterfly;
but this he is—a man who is essentially inert, a man born physically
outworn. The whole race, as it seems to me, is suffering from over-
weariness. It lived fast in the forefront of mankind very long ago, and
now is far gone in years; and in its home you feel that you have passed
into the shadow of what has been, into an air in which man would
rather be than do."[35]

By May 16, Evans was certain he had entered the Minotaur's domain. At the north and west entrances to the palace, the diggers had
found huge, life-size frescoes of bulls done in *gesso duro*, the three-
dimensional lifelike realism of lime plaster in high relief. "What a part
these creatures play here!" he exclaimed in his notes. Equally impressed
was one of the Muslim workmen who, as he brushed away the soil and
the bull's great horns and lifelike flaring nostrils rose from beneath the
soil, screamed, fearful that he had disturbed either a "djin"—like the
one in Aladdin's lamp—or the devil himself. "Was not some one or
other of these creatures visible on the ruined site in the early Dorian
days," Evans later mused, "which gave the actual tradition of the Bull of
Minos?"

Evans hired one hundred and fifty workers on Monday, May 21, for
a final frenetic week of intensive digging during workdays that now
lengthened as spring turned to summer. But he himself was not present
for most of the time due to a severe bout of malaria.[36] His last entry for
the year, that very May 21, dealt with the discovery of his first inscriptions in the pictographic script, hitherto known only from the seal-
stones he had acquired in eastern Crete. The last pages of his diary,
undated, have rough sketches of the signs carved into the soft limestone blocks of the palace—the "mason's marks" that Stillman had
first noted twenty years earlier. So the direction and recording fell to

Duncan Mackenzie alone. Modern excavators, trained to observe and record everything, recoil in horror at the thought of so many diggers excavating for ten hours a day under the supervision of one man; it's little wonder that inconsistencies appeared in his notes as Mackenzie tried to keep track of the find places of the hundreds of objects surfacing daily.

Unfortunately, the greatest problem was with the stratigraphical position of the most important finds: the inscribed tablets and sealings. Evans kept a separate notebook with fine drawings and descriptions of the inscribed tablets and where they were found, but even this was inconsistent because, when they first appeared, Evans and Mackenzie were satisfied that they belonged to the Mycenaean period, and so their records lack precise stratigraphical observations. When the building grew in complexity with each new room they opened, and when its history became equally complicated as they detected evidence for several distinct periods of use, they realized the site had been occupied for a very long time, starting in the Stone Age, and they would have to create precise temporal subdivisions based on their observations of the stratigraphy, pieces from lower floors generally being older than those from higher up. But this was not always possible after the fact, given their presumptions at the time of original digging and given that their notes weren't detailed enough. The violent destruction of the Palace, which burned the tablets, was to become "a cardinal date in the prehistory of Europe," but archaeologists lamented the way Evans had recorded the primary evidence, which, by the very nature of excavation, could never be redone.[37]

Mackenzie's final entry for the season was on Saturday, May 26, when full-scale digging stopped and the three explorers began to sift through the masses of new information they had accumulated over the previous nine weeks. Mackenzie took charge of studying the pottery, which could give the historical framework in which to chart the building's construction, occupation periods, and final conflagration. Changes in the shapes and decorative styles of the pots together with their position in the stratigraphy allowed him to create a relative chronological sequence for the building; this would determine the dates for the finds within the building and could be applied to other sites with similar pottery. Fyfe completed a ground plan from hundreds of precise measurements of the building, while Evans synthesized their notes into his reports.

Evans followed his earlier hurried announcement about the palace archives with a second bulletin sent to the *Athenaeum* on June 8. The "palace of Mycenaean kings" of the previous dispatch was now conclusively identified as "the Palace of Minos," the title he had ridiculed Kalokairinos for using only six years earlier. His report concentrated on the discovery, made during the final week under the most chaotic conditions, of a group of four-sided clay bars and labels inscribed in the "hieroglyphic type of writing" he had first seen on his travels in eastern Crete, and he concluded that they were "in use among the ancient indigenous stock of Crete—the true Eteocretans of the Odyssey." The context of the discovery, which is now called the Hieroglyphic Deposit, seemed to be the final stages of the building's history, "marked by an overwhelming catastrophe and a subsequent complete abandonment of the palace site," and so Evans believed it to be contemporary with "the linear system of the true 'Minoan' archives," which, he felt, stood "on a far higher level of development." The age of this deposit continues to generate heated debate a century later, but there is now a consensus that it and the hieroglyphic script belong to a different period of destruction, probably about five hundred years earlier than Evans first placed it.

Mythical History

A week later, safely restored to the comfort of Youlbury, Evans began producing a series of glowing reports on what by any standard had been a truly remarkable first season. The principal themes were art, architecture, and, above all, writing—the key elements in his search for civilization. These were fully, even exaggeratedly, exploited for the benefit of the subscribers to the Cretan Exploration Fund, for he deemed it of prime importance to excite public interest in the Cretan work. George Augustin Macmillan—a partner in his family's London publishing firm, well known for their scientific books, and a close friend of the Evans family—took charge of the Cretan appeal. The Macmillan company produced a flyer designed to elicit support, which had on its cover a photograph of the diggers excavating the Throne Room, and included part of a text from one of Evans's highly animated lectures, which he illustrated with the latest technology of lantern slides: "There can be little remaining doubt that this huge building, with its maze of corridors and tortuous passages, its medley of small chambers, its long succession of magazines with their blind endings, was in fact the Labyrinth of later tradition which supplied a local habitation for the Minotaur of grisly fame." Evans truly believed that the Minotaur, which most analysts still considered to be a metaphor for the brutal side of man's character, had once lived in the building he was excavating, and that he was finding "the substantial truth of early tradition." This was a far cry indeed from his earlier admonitions about Schliemann's search for "poetical topography."

Evans prepared a serious and detailed report ostensibly for the scholarly community. In the *Annual of the British School at Athens*, he began with frank and grateful homage to those who preceded him at the Kephala, then paraphrased much from Mackenzie's records to elucidate the site and describe their finds. To help the uninitiated visualize the original building as he imagined it, he presented Gilliéron's reconstructed drawing of a fragment of a miniature wall painting depicting "a Mycenaean shrine," which, he insisted, "supplies indeed a vivid record of the kind of elevation which here would have confronted the spectator. This fresco," he decided, "shows clearly a substructure of large white gypsum blocks, resembling in character those of the western wall, while above . . . are the painted plaster fields enclosed by a skeleton of wood-work."[38] In other words, the wall painting was an illustration of the building itself, left behind for Evans and Fyfe to use as a crib, as it were; it was like an ancient postcard that showed the building, now deserted and collapsed, in its heyday. The façade shown in the painting became the palace of Evans's imagination, and the structure he was uncovering on the Kephala became the one in the painting. The Mycenaean shrine depicted at the center of the picture was a part of the whole, Evans reasoned—and so the concept of "the Palace-Temple" was born. But there was an even more intriguing feature: "In the case of this small Temple there were besides, three openings exhibiting pillars of the usual Mycenaean form, tapering downwards, the sanctity of which was shown by the horned cult object set before their bases." This horned cult object was like the figure depicted atop a built platform, on the relief vase he had acquired on his first visit to the site in 1894. Evans thus converted the symbol long known to Egyptologists as the hieroglyphic sign for the horizon into a new concept that he called the "Horns of Consecration."[39]

Exactly what Evans meant by this term was vague, but it implied stylized bovine horns symbolizing those from sacrificed beasts that were set into altars. The gender of the sacred beasts was also being altered: the stylized horns and bovine heads ceased to be those of cows (likened to the goddess Hera by Schliemann), or even of oxen, but, in keeping with the Greek legends that had led Evans to the Kephala, became those of bulls. Again, this was in contravention to the known bull representations in Egyptian art, in which the beasts were shown in full profile to demonstrate their male sex; for cows the artist needed only to show the animal's head.

The building's political authority also changed sex. The "superior size and elevation of the gypsum seat sufficiently declare it to be a throne," Evans stated, and given the intrinsic value of the artifacts in the chamber "a royal personage once sat here for council, or for the enjoyment of the oriental *kéif*," he fantasized, imagining a relaxed gathering around a smoldering *nargileh*, or hubble-bubble, as the British called the water pipe. Yet the small size and narrow proportions of the hollowed seat itself, the final clue, pointed to the inevitable conclusion, in Evans's mind, that the throne's occupant was a king rather than a queen.[40] On the grounds of male versus female dimensions, Ariadne's throne was transferred from the fully endowed Queen's bottom to the slighter seat of King Minos, even though Evans was fully aware that "the prominence of the female sex in the Mycenaean period—as illustrated by the cult-scenes on the signet rings—might in itself favour the view that a queen had occupied the throne here." He separated the political power, which he placed in the hands of his mythical king, from the religious authority, for which the art depicted the "leading part played by the Goddesses and female votaries in the cult-scenes," which, he believed, were "due to the longer survival in the domain of religious ideas attaching to the matriarchal system."[41] Thus, the prehistory of the matrilineal customs of classical Crete, as clearly decreed in the Law Code of Gortyn and suspected to have evolved from earlier matriarchal institutions, was now beginning to appear, or so it seemed to Evans, in the art of Knossos. Slowly, the aniconic cult of the "proto-Aryans" was giving way to "the Mother worship of Minoan Crete," as Joan Evans recalled, the mother figure whom Evans could barely remember in his own life but whom he never forgot.[42]

Gilliéron's reconstruction from fragments of the miniature frescoes offered a portrait of some of the more picturesque members of the romanticized royal court. Evans compared the painting style to the graceful sketches found on Athenian white-ground pottery of the classical period, but, he noted, his Cretan frescoes were "incomparably more modern and display a vivacity and a fashionable pose quite foreign to classical art." Revealing an unexpected knowledge of modern fashion, he continued, "At a glance we recognise the ladies in elaborate toilette. They are fresh from the coiffeur's hands with hair *frisé* and curled about the head and shoulders and falling down the back in long separate tresses." Mild Victorian shock may be detected in his description of their revealing costumes: "They wear high puffed sleeves joined across the lower part of the neck by a narrow cross-band, but otherwise the bosom and the whole upper part of the body appears to be bare . . . In the best executed pieces these *décolletées* ladies are seated in groups with their legs half bent under them, engaged in animated conversation emphasised by expressive gesticulation."[43] The full-sized wall painting once identified as "Ariadne" was now "a beautiful life-size painting of a youth, with an European and almost classically Greek profile."[44] When the British satirist and novelist Evelyn Waugh visited the Candia Museum in 1929 "to admire the barbarities of Minoan culture," he was less beguiled: "One cannot well judge the merits of Minoan painting, since only a few square inches of the vast area exposed to our consideration are earlier than the last twenty years," and the painters who had extended the fragments had "tempered their zeal for reconstruction with a predilection for covers of *Vogue*."[45]

The art of Knossos according to Evans depicted a brightly colored building peopled with well-mannered, courtly folk; yet for the readers of the popular *Monthly Review* Evans indulged in his reverie about the site's darker side:

> Everything around . . . the dark passages, the lifelike figures surviving from an older world . . . would conspire to produce a sense of the supernatural. It was haunted ground, and then, as now, "phantasms" were about. The later stories of the grisly king and his man-eating bull sprang, as it were, from the soil, and the whole site called forth a superstitious awe. It was left severely alone by the newcomers. Another Knossos grew up on the lower slopes of the hill to the north, and the old Palace site became a "desolation and a hissing."[46]

But this somber atmosphere came solely from his imagination and was based on later Greek myths, which continued to cast a shadow over his rational mind and impose themselves on the building he was uncovering.

A new myth was born in the same popular review: "There was no sign of an elaborate system of fortification such as at Tiryns and Mycenae," Evans reported. "The reason of this is not far to seek. Why is Paris strongly fortified, while London is practically an open town? The city of Minos, it must be remembered, was the center of a great sea power, and it was in 'wooden walls' that its rulers must have put their trust." The wooden walls were a clear reference to Britannia's "rule of the waves," and the comparison between London and Knossos was an obvious declaration of Minoan Crete's importance as a historical precedent for Victorian Britain's preeminence. The myth of peace-loving and seafaring Minoans thus began to take shape in Evans's mind and writings, and it was so appealing that it endured until the 1980s, when a Greek team revisited the forts and castles of Evans's earlier travels.[47]

In early September, Evans stood before admiring colleagues at the annual meeting of the British Association in Bradford, and of all the brilliant findings made that first season, he chose to publicize those dearest to the purpose of his Cretan work: his address was about "Writing in Prehistoric Greece." Evans reminded his listeners of the prophetic paper he had read to them in 1894, which very much anticipated his latest discoveries, and he was proud to recall Sir John Evans's prediction, at the Royal Institution in 1872, that Phoenician letters—important for European historians because of their adoption by the Greeks in the seventh century B.C.—were based on simple pictographs. Evans now had scientifically excavated proof in the form of "Hieroglyphic or Conventionalised Pictographic" signs, of which two-thirds matched those sketched a quarter of a century ago by his father. Not fully understanding the difference between pictographic and phonetic values, Arthur Evans fantasized: "The pictographic signs may be said to form an illustrated history of Cretan culture in Mycenaean times." He concluded that the pictographic script "itself shows a certain parallelism with the 'Hittite' inscriptions of Anatolia and Northern Syria. Its beginnings can, however, be traced very far back on Cretan soil, and it unquestionably represents the writing of the indigenous Cretan stock."

Evans compared the linear script and the tablets on which it was incised with those of Babylon, but asserted that in Crete "the letters themselves . . . are of a free, upright European character," in contrast to the Arabs' cursive script and the Assyrians' cuneiform letters, once described by a Western explorer as "chicken scratching." Evans remained wary of drawing too many parallels with the older scripts of Mesopotamia and the Middle East, lest he undermine his European agenda; any influence went from west to east and not the other way around. He insisted that his royal archive at Knossos belonged in the first half of the fifteenth century B.C. because "the Keft chieftains are seen bearing precious vases and ingots and golden oxheads as tributary gifts to Pharaoh . . . on the walls of the tomb of Rekhmara, the Governor of Thebes under Thothmes III," sixth ruler in Egypt's Eighteenth Dynasty. The gifts of the Keftiu were also depicted on his tablets, he explained, so the archive and the final destruction of the palace were a full century earlier than the heretic pharaoh Akhenaten and two centuries before the "latest prehistoric elements of Mycenae itself."[48] The diorite image that he had mistaken for Akhenaten at the time of excavation he now acknowledged to be that of one Ab-nub-mes-wazet-user, of the late Twelfth or early Thirteenth Dynasty, the time of the Cretan Kamares pottery in Egypt, and so even more important than previously imagined, as it secured the chronological as well as diplomatic link between Knossos and Middle Kingdom Egypt—in complete fulfillment of Petrie's prophecy of a decade earlier.[49]

So, on the basis of this great antiquity of the inscriptions at Knossos, Evans now postulated a Cretan ancestry for the Phoenician scripts, which grew out of the "powerful settlement of the Ægean island peoples on the coast of Canaan, represented by the Philistines and the abiding name of Palestine," though "we know that they shortly lost their indigenous speech and became Semitized . . . their Biblical names of Kaphtorim and Kerethim, or Cretans, sufficiently record their Aegean origin."[50] This conclusion makes it clear that Evans believed the Greeks came along very much later and used the Phoenician script to write their own language, which could not possibly be the language of the early Cretans, who, after all, were the "indigenous Eteocretans" of Homer. Salomon Reinach, who took everything Evans said quite literally, repeated this argument and further cautioned scholars who might dare to find Finnish, Hebrew, "bas-breton," or even Homeric Greek on the Knossos tablets.[51]

The Minoans, then, were cast back into the earliest times of Homer's Cretan genealogy. This adherence to the text of Homer, and Evans's possession of the inscribed tablets, created both intellectual and practical blocks to their decipherment. Now Evans had his own collection of "baneful signs," and, like Bellerophon in the *Iliad*, he was ignorant of their meaning, though he announced that "we have here locked up for us materials which may some day enlarge the bounds of history."[52] Unlike the Argive hero, however, he decided not to show them to anyone; he had every intention of being the first to read them, and so the inscriptions became "baneful" indeed and he suffered accordingly. Had Evans chosen to share transcripts of the tablets with scholars at an early stage, he might have averted what became the eventual downfall of much of his Minoan reconstruction, which was brought about much later when the tablets were deciphered. Instead, he guarded their secrets jealously and ignored the suggestions of amateurs like C. R. Condor, who proposed, "These texts will be found to be written in some Archaic dialect of Greek—a conclusion which seems to be supported by the accompanying art."[53] It was another fifty years before the dilettante philologist's prophecy, though itself based on flawed reasoning, was realized.

The British School at Athens benefited immensely from the popular success of the Cretan explorations. The annual general meeting of subscribers on October 30 promised to be so well attended, because of the excitement over the Cretan finds, that it had to be held in the large rooms of the Society of Antiquaries. In the chair was H. H. Asquith, M.P., soon to be Great Britain's prime minister. In a summary of the year's work, he touched on issues in a way that was both insightful and remarkably prophetic of the future of Aegean archaeology.[54] Recalling his own classical education, he ventured the guess that perhaps only one in a hundred of his fellow philologists read any archaeology. Now he mused that "the value of a particle, the nuances of an enclitic, the poetical or rhetorical intentions of the occasional lapses of some of the most famous Greek writers into what in lesser people would be called bad grammar, were of as much importance as, I imagine, to their successors of to-day are the large possibilities of truth or of error which hang on the proper classification of two or three ambiguous fragments of pre-Mycenaean pottery." Asquith cautioned that a due sense of proportion should be observed in the field, and that there was room for the philologist, the textual critic, the historian, and the antiquarian. But his words of warning went unheeded; pottery typology as the basis for history was already in full vogue and soon came to dominate Aegean studies, with Evans and Mackenzie in the forefront, for much of the remaining century.

"I gather that the mountain on which Zeus was supposed to have rested from his labour, and the palace in which Minos invented the science of jurisprudence, are being brought out of the region of myth into the domain of possible reality," Asquith remarked, perhaps with less zeal than Gladstone had spoken for Schliemann a quarter of a century earlier, but with the equally popular result of helping to transform myth into history. And he teased the excavators in his audience with a cutting appraisal of the weakened status of the modern archaeologist:

> It must make the mouth of Mr. Hogarth and his associates water to think of the days when Sir Charles Newton, with a Firman in his pocket, a Company of Royal Engineers and Sappers at his back, and a British man-of-war lying at a handy distance in a convenient bay, was able to rifle at his will the half-hidden treasures of Cnidus and Halicarnassus. These drastic proceedings belonged to the early fifties, to an era when what was called the Manchester School was in the ascendant in this country. In these later times, when, as we are told by the newspapers, we are all Imperialists, the British explorer proceeds upon his task with a humbler and more apologetic mien.

Some listeners may have been especially rankled as Asquith ended his lament: "There is no longer pride in his pick or defiance in his spade." But Evans had no intention of lowering the flag and proceeding "with a humbler and more apologetic mien." On the contrary, he treated Knossos as his foreign domain until such a time as he saw fit to give it up.

One inevitable motion of the meeting was to elect Evans to the managing committee of the British School, a position of some influence and one that he certainly used to benefit himself and those he favored for the rest of his life. It was Hogarth's last official function, as he retired from the school's directorship. His successor, Robert Carr Bosanquet, a sensitive, soft-spoken Cambridge man and veteran of the Phylakopi excavations, joined him and Evans as directors of the Cretan Exploration Fund.[55] As director of the School, Bosanquet was expected to open an excavation in Crete, and, on the strength of Evans's amazing discovery at Knossos, together with the statement in an inscription noted by Halbherr that there was a temple to Diktaian Zeus located at a place called in antiquity Elaia, he brought students of the British School at Athens in 1902 to Palaikastro, at the far eastern end of Crete, and began his search. Bosanquet was joined by Richard MacGillivray Dawkins, fellow of Emmanuel College, Cambridge, then at the beginning of a very successful career in Greek philology and archaeology, and Charles Currelly of Victoria College, Toronto.

Two days after the British School meeting, Evans addressed the Hellenic Society in London with his latest views on "Tree and Pillar Cult." The "true character of the Mycenaean religion," which he had predicted on the basis of his observations in 1894, was now confirmed by the pillars at the heart of the Palace-Temple, he thought, proudly displaying them both in their physical reality as columns and pillars within the Palace and in the ancient artist's impression of the Palace-Temple now restored to full color by Gilliéron. Evans went to great lengths to prove "that the cult objects of Mycenaean times almost exclusively consisted of sacred stones, pillars and trees." What made his case most convincing, in his mind, was the sanctity not only of the pillar itself but of the incised double-axe symbols, which, he proposed, "stood as the visible impersonation of the divinity. . . . His actual image in anthropomorphic shape was not needed by the religion of the time . . . Temple images in human shape were unknown."[56] This was a bold theory, and it did not appeal to many of his learned colleagues, though they remained silent for now to let him enjoy his moment of fame.

Evans became acutely aware that the expense of the first season at Knossos had been extravagant beyond the means at his disposal. He knew that whatever funds the Cretan Exploration Fund raised would be set against the coming year and he would be out of pocket for work already completed. He also began to worry about losing control of his most prized possession now that he had proven its worth. Upon hearing that his father planned to make a substantial donation to the Cretan Fund, Evans sent him a note in which he made the case for absolute control over his research:

> The Palace of Knossos was my idea and my work, and it turns out to be such a find as one could not hope for in a lifetime or in many lifetimes. That the Fund should help me is another thing. If you like to give me the money personally that would also be quite acceptable. But we may as well keep some of Knossos in the family! I am quite resolved not to have the thing entirely "pooled" for many reasons, but largely because I must have sole control of what I am personally undertaking. With other people it may be

different, but I know it is so with me; my way may not be the best but it is the only way I can work.[57]

As he expected, his father complied, and Evans succeeded in retaining control of his work and the excavation finances.

As the first year of the twentieth century closed, Evans stood on a pinnacle. It was far and away the most successful time of his life and, in his fiftieth year, he was ready for a second wind. In retrospect, we see 1900 as his summer solstice—the brightest and longest year of a life only half lived. He began it filled with great intentions and now ended it with the satisfaction of knowing he had accomplished everything he set out to do, and much more. Evans had found everything he had hoped for in one and the same place, on the Kephala hill, and all in the very first season. There was the Labyrinth of Daedalus built to house the sinister Minotaur; the Palace of King Minos; the main temple dedicated to the worship of the sacred tree and pillar; and the archives to attest to the civilized status of the occupants, the earliest bureaucrats in Europe. Evans had found not only the anticipated proofs of his earlier theories but also a painted representation of the building in its heyday, as well as portraits of the inhabitants themselves, a very cosmopolitan folk indeed and very much to his taste. The year 1900 was a pivotal one in the career of the explorer, who now joined Schliemann as one of the great architects of the Aegean past.

Art That Flusters and Scandalizes

Queen Victoria died on January 22, 1901, ending one of the longest reigns in Europe and one of the most productive and stable periods in British history. Victoria's death signaled the end of the British Empire's time of ascendancy. The British failure to defeat the Boers in South Africa brought an end to confidence and ushered in a feeling of impending decline, which was inevitable if, as the British believed, they were living out their own cyclical pattern of history, the three-part progression from birth to maturity to decay as outlined in General Pitt-Rivers's *Evolution of Culture* and many other essays of the time. The British had read of their birth as a nation outlined in countless approving histories, and many, like Evans, had witnessed for themselves the maturity of the mid-Victorian era. Now they progressed into what studies of previous high civilizations, like the Greek and Roman one, had shown was the third and final stage in a process as predictable as the sunset: decay always followed maturity. The ensuing Edwardian era, named for Victoria's son, who at the age of sixty-six was crowned King Edward VII, assumed an atmosphere of inevitable decadence and decline.[58]

Mackenzie, very much in tune with the social climate, wrote to Evans on February 5 with his conclusions as to the main historical periods at Knossos. The first period was that of a " 'Kamarais' palace . . . underneath the Mycenaean floor-level," corresponding to "the 'Kamarais' palace at Phaestos," and associated to the Egyptian Middle Kingdom; roughly 1800 B.C. The second period was that of the "Mycenaean palace" with its "Council Chamber," as he called the Throne Room; this was the zenith to which the finest architecture and paintings belonged, about 1550 B.C. To the third period he assigned "later constructions belonging to the periods of decline,"[59] after roughly 1400 B.C. This fundamental outline became the basis for Evans's Minoan chronological scheme, and, though he made amendments to the early and middle periods, to him the final stage was always degenerate, a label that more than any other distorted his perception of the later history of Knossos and Minoan Crete, and formed an early prejudice against the latest deposits in the palace.

Evans, Mackenzie, and Fyfe returned to Crete at the end of February to find that their palace, which had lain dormant under its protective blanket of soil for thousands of years until they exposed it to the elements, was now in a desperate state of disrepair. The winter rains, which in Crete have a way of coming down in sudden short bursts that create torrents and fill trenches to the brim, were vigorously dissolving the fragile mud-brick constructions. Even more distressing was the effect the rain was having on the gypsum throne and the nearby seats and parapet. Cretan gypsum is a crystalline alabaster that dissolves in water and so has to be regularly maintained with a coating of oil or wax to make it impermeable. As the building hadn't been maintained in more than three thousand years, and Evans wasn't certain how to treat it, his first act was to shelter the Throne Room. "The necessity and the desire to avoid the introduction of any incongruous elements" there forced him to "reproduce the form of the original Mycenaean columns" which, he believed, had stood in the balustrade opposite the throne and whose appearance he surmised from the architectural wall paintings from the previous season. This was how the process of "reconstituting" the building to its supposed former glory began, and it was accelerated by the imminent arrival of his most important bene-factor.

John Evans, at the age of seventy-seven, made the long journey across Europe and the Aegean Sea to witness for himself his son's tri-umph. John stayed in Candia and assisted with the excavations for a time, then traveled to Mount Ida to see the sacred cave of Zeus, and on to Phaistos to visit Halbherr. The hardship—beds made of simple wooden planks on trestles with thin mattresses, riding astride a donkey on a wooden saddle for three days over roughly eighty miles—was duly recorded in the elderly gentleman's diary but hardly deterred his excite-ment. Arthur, filled with the discoverer's conceit, led his proud father, once John Evans "the Great," but now, like Kronos, superceded by his son "Little" Arthur, to see grounds that had become as familiar to Arthur as those his father had taken him to half a century ago in England.

The second season on the Kephala began on February 27, and by June 17, when the stagnant malarial pools in the valley forced an end to the work, they had revealed more than half the building, with its as-tonishing complex of corridors and staircases connecting staterooms, storerooms, and shrines.

Evans could now imagine himself as an ancient visitor arriving at the West Court of the great king's Palace, where raised causeways guide the pedestrian to the entrance. The west façade was composed of gyp-sum slabs set back on a stone plinth, which, he surmised, "must at times have afforded an admirable sitting place for a large number of persons, and indeed was frequently used for this purpose by my Cretan workmen. It does not require a great stretch of the imagination to see the Elders of the Mycenaean Assembly seated in the same place, while the King himself sat at the gate in the Seat of Judgment in the stately portico beyond."[60] The West Portico gave access to a double entrance: one leading directly to what he called the Corridor of Procession, while the other opened onto a separate chamber, to which Evans assigned his "Royal use."

The Corridor of Procession, named for the discovery there of hu-man feet and occasional other body parts painted along either side of the corridor, led to where the "Cup bearer fresco," as the previous year's Ariadne had become, was found: it was now understood to be part of "the processional frescoes, with their apparently tribute bearing

Theatral Area

Royal Road

Throne Room
Central Stair
Repository

Grand Staircase

West
Court

Domestic Quarter

Central
Court

Procession Corridor

Shrine of the Double Axes

Stepped Portico

Early Hypogeaum

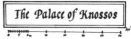

The Palace of Knossos

youths," for which Evans drew the analogy to "contemporary Egyptian monuments in which the representatives of various races bear tribute to Thothmes III," meaning the Keftiu.[61]

Where the corridor ends at the southern entrance to the large open area (54 by 24 meters) east of the Throne Room, which Evans called the Central Court, they found the fragments of what has become one of the best known of the modern Minoan personalities. The first piece to surface showed the back and ear of a male head wearing a crown, which, Evans hastily reported to the *Times*,

> supplies insignia of still more Royal support. It displays the upper part of a head wearing a crown, which terminates above in a row of five sloping lilies of varied metal-work with a higher one rising in the center. That the *fleur-de-lis* of our Edwards and Henrys should find a prototype in prehistoric Greece is a startling revelation; but it was perhaps fitting that, as last year's excavation in Knossos brought to light "the oldest throne in Europe," so the more recent researches should produce its most ancient crown.[62]

Then came a torso with a muscular right arm with clenched fist in *gesso duro*, hard plaster built up in low relief, imitating Egyptian stonework of the time. Eventually, parts of a leg and another arm appeared, which Evans initially thought were the parts of separate individuals, but later he and Gilliéron brought the plaster anatomy together to create one human figure, a bold move recently contested.[63] Given the Egyptian parallels, Evans concluded that "in these reliefs . . . we may also have to do with human personages," not divinities, and "these analogies afford a real presumption that in this crowned head we see before us a Mycenaean King."[64] This figure, whom we now revere as the "Prince of the Lilies" or Evans's "Priest-King of Knossos," was thus born of disparate limbs united to satisfy Evans's need for an earthly authority at Knossos.

Halfway along the southern part of the Corridor of Procession, the visitor had the option to turn left and proceed through a system of three doors between pillars into a colonnaded entrance which Evans dubbed the South Propylaeum, borrowing the term for "gateway" from classical Greek architecture, as Schliemann had done at Mycenae and Tiryns. Dörpfeld, when he visited again with his entourage, delighted in the identification and encouraged Evans to see a wide staircase beyond the Propylaeum, where the workers had found a great mass of sifted soil and so had called it the Central Clay Area. The clay was now interpreted as a collapsed earthen brick support for a "Grand Staircase," which Evans posited here as the main access for the next floor, the "*piano nobile*," as he referred to the first floor, using the Italian term denoting the principal story in a nobleman's house. Evans united the slender evidence of two fallen supports for wooden columns with his theory that pillars on the ground-floor level should support columns on the upper floor. He then borrowed from Phaistos the layout of what he termed the "Minoan Hall"—that is, a linear series of three rooms comprising a porch, antechamber, and inner hall, opening onto an open area or court—and created a perfect match at the head of the Grand Staircase, which became his Upper Western Megaron, though this was quite distinct from the Homeric Megaron of Mycenaean architecture, with its four columns around a central hearth; there was no hearth in the Minoan household.[65]

Exploration north of the Throne Room brought more frescoes, about a quarter life-size, which gave startling insights into the world of Minoan women. "*Mais, ce sont des parisiennes!*" exclaimed the visiting French scholar Edmond Pottier, when he first saw the fragments, which Gilliéron hastily restored, and so the principal female figure, in what we now call the Camp Stool Fresco, is still popularly known as "La Parisienne." Pottier suffered a *coup de foudre* (love at first sight) with his earliest glance at La Parisienne, with "that ruffled hair, that provocative lock on the forehead in a 'hook your heart' curl, that enormous eye and that sensual mouth . . . stained with violent red, that red, blue and black rayed tunic, that flood of ribbons tossed back in the manner of 'follow me, young man.' " Pottier spoke for modern males when he assumed, "This Pasiphae, who resembles a *habituée* of the Paris bars," belongs to "an art that flusters and scandalizes us."[66] Less passionate but equally enthralled in a boyish manner was Bosanquet, who, in a letter to his wife wrote falteringly of "a young lady—I don't know why my pen should blot the word there so guiltily—she isn't half so nice as another young lady I know: but there she is with her hair floating in the breeze, in several breezes blowing in different directions."[67] But Evans was reserved in his admiration, and noted "the bunched up dress over the shoulder suggests N. African comparisons," persisting in his hunt for the Libyan origins to his Minoans.[68] Still, he continued to be amazed at how animated Minoan women were as compared to their Egyptian and

Near Eastern contemporaries; and daring, as the next deposit showed.

It may have felt like déjà vu to Gilliéron when he pieced together a graphic scene with a dark-skinned figure leaping over the back of a raging bull, arms straddling the midsection of the beast in full gallop, for he had worked on a very similar painting for Schliemann at Tiryns. The Cretan scene included white-skinned figures at either end of the bull, one clutching at the beast's horns and the other standing ready to assist the leaper. Since in Egyptian art, gender is often indicated by skin tone—women are white and men are red—the figures at either side of the composition, which Evans called "girls attired like Mycenaean cowboys,"[69] quickly became the envy of the growing suffragette movement in Britain and America, where modern women competed with men for equality. But in certain functions the women may have preferred to remain segregated: "It may well be," Evans commented, "that long before the days when enslaved barbarians were 'butchered to make a Roman holiday,' captives, perhaps of gentle birth, shared the same fate within the sight of the 'House of Minos.' " For Evans, the figures "belong to the arena, and afford the clearest evidence that the lords of Mycenaean Knossos glutted their eyes with shows in which maidens as well as youths were trained to grapple with what was then regarded as the king of animals."[70] Here, then, were three of the seven youths and seven maidens of the Theseus tale, pictorial proof for Evans "that the legends of Athenian prisoners devoured by the Minotaur preserve a real tradition of these cruel sports." The sport of taurokathapsia, or bull-leaping, was thus fantasized by Evans to account for the scene, which he also found represented on seal-stones and their impressions.

Then came the epiphany. "Out of five different fragments of a clay seal belonging to as many different impressions, but overlapping one another in design, I have been able to reconstruct a wonderful religious scene," Evans wrote to his father on April 24, "a Goddess on a sacred rock or peak with two lions in heraldic attitudes on either side of it, her temple behind, and a votary in front."[71] He had wanted more concrete proof of the Mother Goddess cult, which he had predicted in his Mycenaean Tree and Pillar Cult of 1896 as the "prototype of the later Kybele and Rhea" (mythical wife of Kronos and mother of Zeus), and here was a female figure on the clay impressions of a gold ring bezel standing dead center and top register in a scene with two lions and one male, who were clearly subservient. No one could deny her superior status, and the staff that she held out vertically before her left no doubt as to her power.

Evans suggested that the goddess on the sealing was Rhea, or the " 'Idaean Mother' standing on her sacred peak,"[72] but the Greek Cretans had other ideas. They borrowed his reconstructed drawing of the scene for the next issue of Cretan postage stamps and adorned the 2-lepta denomination with the "pre-Hellenic" antecedent of the Greek goddess of the hunt: "Artemis (Mycenaean goddess) between two lions, drawing a bow," read the description.[73]

The male in the scene stood erect beneath the goddess in adoration, or so Evans postulated, thereby relegating males to mere mortality in Minoan art; to Evans, the male figure rarely rose above the role of priest, attendant, or votary to the much more impressive giver of life; his role was decidedly mundane. Then, behind the goddess on her sacred peak, was a structure with "horns of consecration . . . placed before the columns on the shrine . . . that . . . here represent the artificial pillar forms of the cult object as opposed to the holy mountain itself on which the Goddess stands." Thus "either the pillar or the sacred peak itself could be equally worshipped."[74]

The sealings came from an area in what Evans called the "Room of the Column Bases," halfway along the façade on the Central Court, and they further persuaded him that he had a shrine building here, as depicted in the "temple fresco" of the previous season. The new sealings with the goddess convinced him of the area's sanctity, and he posited a "Central Shrine" at this point. The new image also gave him "horns of consecration" on the entablature, the architectural space above the colonnade, to add to his hypothetical shrine. Gilliéron continued to work on the miniature frescoes, and Evans solidified his belief that the shrine fresco "depicts for us in all its brilliant colours" the Central Shrine he had uncovered, and that the illustrated sanctuary was "surrounded by a fashionable congregation."[75] But gathered in whose honor? To Evans, the building's dedication was obvious: "proofs of the cult of a similar Goddess supplied by other seal impressions found in the building, establish a real presumption that the shrine on the wall painting was in part at least dedicated to the cult of the same Mycenaean divinity." Tradition, Evans believed, supplied her name: "Diodorus records that in his day, there were still visible on Knossian soil, the site and foundations of the House of Rhea and a very ancient Cypress Grove (Diod. Sic. v. c. 66),"[76] to which Evans added the "straggling clumps of cypress-trees . . . still seen in the glen below the palace site—perpetuating thus the sacred tradition of the spot."[77]

The principal deity at Knossos, then, was a precursor of the Greeks' mother of Zeus. But another figure continued to raise his terrible head. A clay sealing preserved the impression of a scene with "a man clad in a kind of cuirass [defensive breastplate], with his body bent towards a monster seated on a cross-legged seat, with the legs of man, but the head, fore-legs and upper part of the body, including the tail, of an animal resembling a calf."[78] Evans combined this image with a number of seal-stones showing bovine heads on male bodies and started a corpus of ancient Minotaurs, to which Hogarth soon contributed.

Hogarth came to Crete in May 1901 looking for the Palace at the far limits of what he called the "Eteocretan country" of eastern Crete. His motives were clear: Homer and subsequent ancient authors explicitly located the land of the aboriginal Cretans in the east, and so modern archaeologists looking for the origins of the brilliant society illuminated by Evans at Knossos had to follow the word of the ancient bard and go east. Halbherr had noted inscriptions on his travels in 1892, and so it seemed all the more likely that the key to reading the documents that Evans gathered at Knossos was there. On Evans's recommendation, Hogarth chose the tiny bay of Kato Zakros, the last harbor on the maritime route to "the Cyrenaic shore"—the land of Petrie's New Race of Libyans in which Evans placed so much hope.* Six weeks of work produced little of architectural interest; the reason given was the "terrific denudation" from sudden storms, which caught on the eastern side of the Siteia Mountains and would have wiped away any substantial building. One deluge on May 15 had destroyed his storeroom with all his findings to date. It "swept the whole plain," Hogarth lamented, "and in two hours changed the face of the landscape, leaving stones and naked rock where fields, vineyards, and groves had been, and carrying to the sea 4,000 trees."[79] Perhaps it was this act of savage nature that inspired Hogarth to provide funds for the construction of a fountain at the head of a source in the upper village at Zakros, a fountain that still bears his name.[80]

But not everything was denuded. On a rocky spur above the marshland Hogarth located a rectangular building, identified by the Italian explorer Lucio Mariani as a temple, and dug deep into what he called "House A." Just inside a doorway to a small room near the entrance he

---

*Evans's instinct was correct, but Hogarth was the wrong man for the job. He came within a few meters of the rich palace, which was eventually discovered by Nicolas Platon in 1962.

found nearly five hundred well-preserved clay nodules impressed by seal-stones, like those at Knossos, but many with singularly disturbing images of monsters. The most comprehensible, which had bovine heads, fit well with Evans's Minotaur types, but both Evans and Hogarth were at a loss to explain the strange combinations of human and animal components depicted. Of one thing Evans was certain: they were "pure monstrosities and belong to no cult," though, he added, "the Minotaur himself makes his first appearance in their company."[81] When the Cretan government issued new stamps in 1905, they chose one of Hogarth's more disturbing images, which seemed to show a human hand falling limp from the mouth of the bull's head, to represent the Minotaur on the 3-drachma stamp.[82]

Evans's explorations opposite the Central Shrine building on the east side of the Central Court at Knossos brought even greater revelations. "It was at this point that the development of the excavation took an altogether dramatic turn," he later recorded.[83] On June 4 he wrote to his father,

> The architectural discoveries increase daily in importance. It is evident that we are only just coming to the real center of the Palace buildings. We have now a hall with two column-bases approached by a quadruple flight of stairs. Two of these, under the others, have had to be tunneled out. A gallery with a wooden colonnade ran round the west side of this room in two stages. Beyond the hall is a larger room, only partly excavated, with more column bases. It will probably prove to be the principal *megaron* of the Palace . . . Above the stairs are traces of a further higher flight having existed, and in parts we find evidences of two storeys above the basement. It is altogether unexampled and unexpected.[84]

But, as with many great discoveries, there were risks: "The excavation of this part was of extraordinary difficulty, owing to the constant danger of bringing down the staircase above. It was altogether miners' work," as they tunneled down the passage, eager to see where the steps would lead them. Two of the workers had in fact dug in the silver mines near Athens and used their experience to shore up the ceiling with wooden supports as they proceeded down the dark flight into the hillside. Four flights down they emerged into a hall, which from its tiers of pillars Evans called the "Hall of the Colonnades." A corridor took them farther east and into a long space, measuring eight by twenty-four meters with eight pillared pier-and-door partitions and very fine sandstone masonry blocks at the west end incised with the double-axe sign. Evans was inspired to name it the "Megaron [later the Hall] of the Double Axes."

The effects that Evans had seen on the single-story walls exposed for one winter was enough to convince him of the urgent need to intervene with this new and wonderful but very fragile subterranean structure of at least three stories. Theodore Fyfe rose to the challenge and began resetting some of the walls in place. They found that the ancient Cretans had built much of the structure with a framework of squared wooden beams packed with dirt and rubble and occasionally lined with well-finished cut sandstone blocks that gave an appearance of solidity and monumentality. Once the wood decayed, however, the whole lot would begin to crumble. What had kept it more or less upright was the fact that the beams had melted away only gradually, and so the collapse of debris from upper floors and the accumulation of earth in the rooms had settled against the walls, holding them in place. Now, once the excavators had removed the accumulation, the walls began to give way. Wherever there had been a wooden skeleton, Fyfe cleared the voids and filled them with modern beams carefully cut to copy the ancient ones. The process was essential for the building's survival, being a kind of architect's first-aid treatment. But before long Evans enjoyed the way the replacement looked and began to imagine other, less threatened parts of the palace where similar techniques might be equally pleasing aesthetically.

Full-scale excavation, with all its inherent tension and excitement, has a way of taxing even the most robust constitution, and three and half months, even today, is beyond the limits of most excavators. The digging stopped in mid-June, when the "fever season comes on" in Crete each year. Evans sailed to Athens almost immediately, leaving Mackenzie and Fyfe behind to put the finds in order and continue their studies of the pottery and architecture well into August, though they were both ill most of time. Evans was shocked to find one of his "antikas" dealers in Shoe Lane selling inscribed tablets exactly like those he'd just unearthed. On close inspection he recognized the group they likely belonged to and was able to prove the guilt of one Aristides, a temporary worker at the site, by producing copies of tablets from

Knossos very similar to those in Athens; the authorities arrested the man. Reports of the incident amused both Greek and foreign scholars, despite their surprise and dismay, because of the correspondence of the thief's name with the notorious fifth-century-B.C. Athenian politician "Aristides the Unjust," who was ostracized for collaborating with the Persians when they invaded Greece. More seriously, it alerted Evans to the fact that he must take greater precautions against theft in the future.

Mr. Evans with His Seven-Leagued Boots

Once again, Evans returned triumphant to Britain and was celebrated with the laurels bestowed upon a successful explorer and scholar. Dublin and Edinburgh universities conferred honorary doctorates on him, and the Royal Society elected him to a fellowship. Evans was the last archaeologist to join the Royal Society, which thereafter became the preserve of "hard" sciences; the "soft" science of archaeology came under the heading of the humanities, for which the British Academy was established that year and to which Evans was quickly elected. But all was not accolades.

Archaeology, like most scholarly pursuits, has its creators and destroyers. The former are those who originate theories and go into the field to find the tangible evidence to support them. The latter are those who nip at the explorers' heels from a cozy study or university library, demanding irrefutable proofs. In between are those who prefer to synthesize the results of their more adventurous colleagues, and who in doing so sustain the critical process necessary to screen doubtful or insufficiently supported conclusions. Not all these "armchair archaeologists"—as the diggers in the field dismiss those who stay at home—lose sight of their critical obligations and become full-time detractors, perpetually dissatisfied with the evidence. But a small number become such destroyers, insatiable critics with an overall negative attitude toward archaeologists and an indefatigable insistence on calling all of the evidence into question.

Evans's first major adversary was Sir William Ridgeway, Disney Professor of Archaeology at Cambridge University and a close friend of John Evans. Ridgeway combined philology and anthropology with archaeology in one of the first great syntheses of the "Greek problem," that is, "Who were the Greeks and where did they come from?" In his

1901 *The Early Age of Greece,* Ridgeway, citing Herodotus and Thucyd-ides, argued that the Pelasgians, the first race in the southern Balkan peninsula, were Greek speakers who lived "from time immemorial" in Greece and developed into the Mycenaean civilization. This was a view in sharp contrast to the "orthodox" belief held by classicists and ancient historians, and championed by Percy Gardner, that the Mycenaeans were Homer's Achaeans, the first Aryan invaders in Greece.[85] Ridgeway, like Evans, didn't subscribe to the need for migrations from central Europe or the Near East to explain the Mycenaeans. Where he and Evans crossed swords was Crete. Ridgeway adhered so closely to the ancient authors that he took literally Pausanias's statement that Daedalus—whom Homer in the *Iliad* (18: 591), credited with the "dancing floor of Ariadne at Knossos"—came from the Metionids, the royal house of Athens, and so concluded "the chief impetus in the development of Cretan art in the Mycenaean age came from continental Greece."[86] To Ridgeway, the palace that Evans revealed at Knossos with all its glorious paintings and artifacts was the result of an artistic impulse from the Greek mainland to Crete. Myres, in consultation with Evans, treated the Disney Professor as an amateur when it came to fieldwork, and he replied in his lengthy review of the book that "as it is only in the islands and in Crete that the adolescence of Mycenaean civilization can be traced in at all a continuous series . . . the center of origin, indeed, must be placed in the Cyclades and in Crete."[87]

Ridgeway's insistence that the Mycenaeans and not the Minoans were the originators of Greek culture led to a split in Aegean archaeology that appeared along university lines: Oxford supported Evans, and Cambridge followed "Ridgewayism," as Evans and his comrades dubbed the cause for Mycenaean hegemony. This schism in the British scholarly world, essentially Minoan versus Mycenaean, grew wider and deeper over time. But Evans held firm to his view that later Aegean societies, including the Mycenaean, were firmly rooted in his Cretan Minoans. As history credits its creators and not its detractors, its builders and not its destroyers, every encyclopedia reports Evans's accomplishments, but Ridgeway, though his views more closely fit the current consensus, figures in none.

A more vocal and potentially much more damaging campaign was launched by W. H. D. Rouse, a philologist of the Perse School at Cambridge, who took serious exception to Evans's classification of the double axe as a fetish for Zeus, chiding, "The Greeks would be as likely to worship a pair of top boots."[88] Evans's identification of the Knossian

Labyrinth relied heavily on the frequent occurrence of the double axe there, because he had adopted Schliemann's theory that the double-axe motif symbolized "Zeus Labrandeus," an early form of worship of Greece's greatest god at the Carian city of Labraunda, on the Turkish Aegean coast. Evans added that the Carian word for axe, *labrus*, was the basis for the Greek word "labyrinth," which thus meant "house of the axe." He was particularly eager to make the association with Zeus to prove that the Psychro Cave, where Hogarth found so many votive axes in gold and bronze, was linked to an early form of the cult of Zeus.

Rouse argued against this view: "Λαβύρινθος [*labyrinthos*] cannot be derived from λάβρυς [*labrus*] by any known laws of language. The derivation is a guess and no more, not supported even by the meaning, for a 'maze' has nothing to do with an axe [and] the axe was never at any time a symbol of Zeus in any part of the world." Rouse also ridiculed the way Evans jumped with such apparent ease across vast time periods:

> It should not be forgotten that we know λάβρυς only from the first century after Christ, and Mr. Evans with his seven-leagued boots has jumped from that date to the classical age, and thence to the second millennium B.C. . . . I have carefully examined [Knossos] twice, and I can testify that the evidence is stated incompletely, and in a manner which must mislead . . . This is no doubt unintentional, but none the less unfortunate, and the whole identification of Cnossos with the Labyrinth is childishly fantastic.

Finally, his most important point—"There is not a particle of evidence for a Zeus in Cnossos . . . The only deity of which evidence has been found is a female"—was one that even Evans had to concede.

But not to the attack on his Labyrinth. Evans stood his ground and upheld his "House of the Double Axe" identification, in spite of the soundness of Rouse's objections, which were the basis for an ingenious theory put forward by Ronald M. Burrows, professor of Greek at University College, Cardiff. Burrows, in his popular account *The Discoveries in Crete* (1907), proposed an Egyptian origin to the word, pointing out that the original labyrinth at Hawara was built for the Twelfth Dynasty pharaoh Amenemhat III, whose personal name was pronounced Nemarî, which, by the common interchange of *n* with *l*, was transliterated into Greek as *Labaris* or *Lamaris*. The title Labaris, then, would have applied to the prototype for the Cretan building, built at roughly the same time, around 1900 B.C., and it had nothing to do with axes. The Greek, Roman, medieval, and modern meaning of a maze, Burrows continued, could have come from the Greek word *labra*, which they took to mean a place of passage.[89] But no amount of contrary reasoning could convince Evans that his new etymology was false, for, as Rouse observed, he had "fallen so deep in love with it that he sees everything double-axes."[90] Though many scholars agreed with Rouse and Burrows, their voices were lost in the excitement created by the discovery of the fabled Labyrinth of Knossos. Recent etymological dictionaries accept Evans's proposed origins, and the Palace at Knossos has become the Labyrinth, against all previous logic, proving that the force of one man's will can and does change the course of history, ancient as well as modern.

When the British Association met in Glasgow in September 1901, Evans refrained from boasting of his recent discoveries of inscriptions and architecture. Instead he reported on the results of very deep trial trenches, in some places ten meters below the surface, into the Stone Age tell beneath the palace site. Drawing parallels for pottery and tools with the earliest cultures in Babylon, western Asia, and Egypt, Evans traced the origin of the clay figurines he had found, such as the "Aphrodite of Knossos," to the Babylonian Mother-Goddess. Then, he ended the address with his first public proposal, based on Mackenzie's framework, of three "distinct prehistoric classes" of building overlying the Neolithic tell: "The 'Kamares,' or Early Metal-age Period of Crete . . . the Mycenaean Period proper, the flourishing epoch of which is approximately fixed by the correspondence of some of the wall paintings with those representing the Keftiu on Egyptian tombs, c. 1550 B.C.," and what he called the "Transitional Period," between the two.[91]

Evans ended the year preoccupied with financial matters. He had spent more than £4,500 on Knossos, of which the Cretan Fund provided less than half. So he was particularly vexed by Mackenzie's report of January 6, 1902, outlining the questionable conduct of their foreman and muleteer, Alevisos, and an accomplice, Evangelis, who had arranged with local shopkeepers to pay a lower price for goods than that shown on their receipts and pocket the difference. Mackenzie recommended dismissal:

They form a pair who have worked together on a system of mutual profits for years, and they are now too old in the horn ever to be content with their wages or even moderate gains over and above that. If I can trust my experience of Greeks they (A. and E.) are not simple or unsophisticated enough even to turn over a new leaf, and for that reason they should not even be given the chance. When the chance is given to Greeks in such circumstances the result is invariably the same—renewed courage as Greeks themselves put it, and perseverance with renewed resource in the old tactics. Old dodgers like Alovisis and Evangeli could no more give up these than they could give up their long inbred habit of smuggling.[92]

Evans agreed that his old muleteer had exceeded "the permissible limits of peculation," and contacted Hogarth about securing the services of his legendary treasure hunter, Gregóri Antoniou. As Hogarth had given up digging in Crete after his disastrous season in Kato Zakros, Evans hired Gregóri and retained him throughout the remaining early campaigns at Knossos, thereby enhancing the quality of excavation enormously from 1902 on.

Hogarth, as a trustee of the Cretan Fund, was less than sympathetic to Evans's fiscal laments. "You are a rich man's son, and have probably never been at a loss for money," he wrote frankly. Like Mackenzie, Hogarth came from a large family of modest means and had to earn his livelihood and provide for his family largely through his archaeological fieldwork.[93] Evans would never comprehend this; he felt, as his half-sister recorded, about "a man who made his living out of excavation rather as a mystic feels about a man who makes a living, however honourably, out of religion."[94]

"You can hardly complain of 'paying for your whistle,' " Hogarth reproached Evans, "that is, for expenses avoidable had you so chosen. For example, the restorations and the very expensive building erected over the Throne Room." Hogarth accounted for the shortfall of the Cretan Exploration Fund by placing Evans's "expensive methods in digging . . . in collecting and in ordinary life" at the opposite extreme from those of Flinders Petrie, the very image of the ascetic archaeologist, and the successful Egypt Exploration Fund:

All P.'s "cave-man" plan of life has been deliberately adopted to convince the subscriber that every penny goes into the earth. The drawback in your method is that it does not appeal to people's pockets. I am not talking in the air for I am continually chaffed about the "princely" way things are done by us in Crete, and have lately heard that reports about our Cretan houses, brought back I suppose by big tourist parties, have decided some old subscribers, not to pay up again.[95]

So Evans continued to "pay for his whistle," which, though it seemed a bitter pill at the time, gave him free rein to conduct the excavation and restoration of Knossos exactly as he saw fit, and to justify the means and methods to no one.

The Queen's Megaron

The third season, intended as the last, began on February 12, 1902, and ran without pause until the end of June, during which time as many as 250 men were either reconstructing Evans's modern monument with masses of timber, brick, and iron, or revealing what remained of the ancient one.

"I am rather overwhelmed at the amount that still seems to remain to be done here," Evans wrote his father early in the season. "As to the Fund, nothing seems to be coming in now, so that I have to raise the wind considerably!" And so he did. After the workers lost several days to bitter cold and torrential rains, the mood changed on February 25 when Evans recorded "A day of fresco." At the west end of the South Portico of the Hall of the Double Axes came a large deposit of painted plaster fragments with "a lady in gay jacket with a very good profile, retroussé nose & slightly purple eyes, hair flying out & arm extended." The quick sketch in his notes shows a smiling, lighthearted maiden whom he imagined swirling in a dance. "It is not difficult to believe," he fancied, "that figures such as this, surviving on the Palace walls even in their ruined state, may lie at the root of the Homeric passage describing the most famous of the works of Daedalos at Knossos—the 'Choros' [dancing floor] of Ariadnê."[96] But there was little room for dancing in the small underground rooms where the fragments appeared. Instead, this "Dancing Lady," as she is now known, suggested to him that the area, approached by a private corridor, "evidently controlled by a strict system of guardianship and surveillance"[97] from the magnificent Hall of the Double Axes, was the women's quarters, though

to apply to this section indeed the oriental name of "Haremlik" might convey the wrong idea since there is no question—witness the miniature frescoes [e.g., the bull-leapers]—of a rigorous separation of the sexes in the "House of Minôs." We are at liberty to believe that this secluded quarter was in a special way the domain of the women, and the distinctive name of the "Queen's Megaron" has been accordingly given here to the most stately withdrawing room in this region.[98]

The same heap of painted plaster contained fragments showing fish and a seascape, which, when cleaned and mended, revealed one of the most enduring images of Minoan art. "Two large dolphins," Evans was thrilled to report, and "numerous smaller fry were most naturalistically rendered." He marveled at how "the spray and bubbles fly off at a tangent from the fins and tails, and give the whole a sense of motion that could not otherwise be attained," but "the spirited character of the designs, the prevailing colours of the fish, blue of varying shades, black and yellow, the submarine rocks with their coralline attachments, and still more the manner of indicating the sea itself," most struck him. He felt they "proclaimed identity of method," and he christened it the work of the "Knossian School" of painters.

A piece of plaster showing a bird's wing completed the composition, and he imagined this to be "the artistic substitute for a natural view, identical in intention with the landscape scenes that form such a favourite feature of the blind walls that shut in the smaller courts and areas of Italian villas, and which are supposed to cheat the eye with the illusion of a free outlook."[99] Thus the Queen's Megaron became the heart of an imagined "withdrawing room of the family quarter of the Palace," in the area still known as the "Domestic Quarter."

The excavation of such a deep and well-preserved monument taxed the skills and ingenuity of all concerned. When the collapsed brickwork, which had fallen into the open spaces, was removed, the stone walls, themselves reliant on a wooden infrastructure long since decayed, began to slip and crumble. But Evans never hesitated in the face of adversity. "I succeeded in a rather bold experiment the other day," he boasted to his father. "There was a much sloping wall of rubble masonry about a metre thick at the top of the main staircase, threatening destruction to all below it, as it was at an angle of about 75°. After due propping I had slits cut along the base on each side, its face was then planked over and roped and fifty men set to tug. It righted itself most gratefully against a stop temporarily erected for the purpose."[100] Fyfe quickly added wooden beams where they had rotted away, and the work went on.

Beneath the ground floor of the Domestic Quarter Evans found the openings into a system of stone-lined channels large enough for a man to crawl through, as he himself did as soon as the workers declared it sound. The rectangular channel was, Evans believed, designed to drain away the surface waters from the open courts near the Quadruple Staircase, as "the rains of Crete are often even now torrential, and in the Minôan Period, when the country was no doubt much better wooded, the rainfall must have been greatly in excess of what it is at the present time."[101] But the ancient architect added one further refinement, he believed, and it impressed the Victorian gentleman to no end. Near the Queen's Megaron, in a small closet about one meter wide and two long, Evans found openings into the drainage system in the narrow space defined by gypsum partition walls on either side and with a horizontal groove cut in the back wall a few feet above ground level—the exact height of the seat of the throne—from which he surmised that "there can be no doubt that this small chamber served as a latrine."[102] Not only was there an opening directly beneath the hypothesized wooden seat, but another one directly in front down which water could be poured to flush the toilet. Evans invited Captain T. H. M. Clarke, medical advisor to Prince George, to examine the sanitary marvel and to publish a report on it in the *British Medical Journal.* Clarke noted that the plumbing was cleverly placed on the side of the building that sloped toward the river, but what most astonished him was that the toilet was complete with a bend to "shut off the escape of sewer gas." Clarke recalled that when he had been sanitary advisor to Sir Herbert Chermside's administration in Candia, he "had a good opportunity of making the acquaintance of modern Cretan sanitation and of appreciating how far they have fallen from the standard of the Minôans," although he noted that it need not "astonish us who are aware of the attitude of some of our people at home on similar questions."[103] Evans had found the oldest flushing toilet in the world.

On March 1, Evans discovered what he recorded in his diary as "The Household Gods." In a tiny space south of the Domestic Quarter, on a stone bench along the north wall, he found a clay figurine of a male wearing a flat cap and holding out a dove with both hands. The object of this humble votary's devotion, Evans quickly guessed, was the female figurine on the opposite end of the bench, who "had a dove on head & both hands raised as an adorant—but doubtless here a Goddess receiving adoration." His earlier prediction of the religious sanctity of the dove was thus fulfilled and the indication of "the descent of the divine spirit" in bird form on the woman's head led him to call her the "Lady of the Dove."[104] Then the final confirmation of "the religious interest of the scene" that he needed appeared near the male figure: "a reduplicated double axe of grey steatite."[105] There were other figurines between the two end pieces, but also the remains of two "horns of consecration" in white plaster on a clay matrix. At the center of the dip in each horn was a drilled hole, which Evans concluded was to fit the "sacred Double Axe," as occasionally depicted on pottery fragments. Though the artifacts themselves had vanished, it was clear to him that the sockets could have no other purpose; the columns depicted in the miniature wall paintings weren't even considered, and the little space became "The Shrine of the Double Axes."

"The presence of female idols on the same base as the Sacral Horns and Double Axe seems to show that this symbolic weapon was associated here with the cult of a Goddess as well as a God," Evans conceded, but then recalled his earlier prediction that "the female aspect of divinity predominated" in the Mycenaean Tree and Pillar Cult, and "the male divinity is not so much the consort as the son or youthful favourite."[106] The pottery in the shrine dated it to Mackenzie's "periods of decline" after the great days of the Keftiu in 1550 B.C., and Evans ventured the idea "that the cult of Cretan Zeus was here linked with that of Rhea, the ruins of whose temple with its sacred Cyprus Grove was pointed out at Knossos in later days"—citing Diodorus once again.[107] Evans was so determined to have his Palace of Minos that it seems not to have occurred to him that the object of his full attention and resources might have been the same temple to the goddess as Diodorus described, though, when later musing on the absence of Greek and Roman habitation over the palace site, Evans admitted, "It almost looks as if some surviving tradition of the religious aspect of the Minoan building in its function of Sanctuary as well as Palace may have served to protect the site . . . It may well, indeed have been included in some late *temenos* like that of the Grove and Temple of Rhea."[108]

The season, though much longer and exhausting than intended, ended on a very high note. In a space in the Domestic Quarter, jokingly called "the Lair" because of the practical difficulties in excavating it and "a certain mystery attaching to it," Evans later reported without further explanation, he found a treasury of gold, bronze, ivory, porcelain, and rock-crystal objects. "Our last find here," Evans wrote in a final excited note to his father early in June, "is the remains of extraordinarily fine statuettes of ivory . . . the carving goes beyond anything that could have been imagined and is more like good Renaissance work than anything classical."[109] He later wrote:

> The life, the freedom, the elan of these ivory figures is nothing short of marvelous and in some respects seems to overpass the limits of the sculptor's art. The graceful fling of the legs and arms, the backward bend of the head and body give a sense of untrammelled motion . . . These youthful figures are athletic—not to say acrobatic—in their nature, and certain parallels presented by the Palace wall-paintings, as well as by a series of gem impressions, seems to connect them in the most unmistakable way with the favourite sport of the Minoan arena—the bull-grappling scenes.

The reference was to the "Toreador fresco," now fully restored by Gilliéron to show, as Evans described it, how "a girl toreador in cowboy costume is caught under the arm pits by the horns of a charging bull and is evidently in the act of being tossed. A youth, who seems already to have been thrown into the air, is seen performing a somersault over the animal's back, while a girl behind, perhaps intended to be standing in the middle of the arena, holds out both hands as if to catch the flying figure."[110]

Evans never doubted that these scenes were to be read literally. It did not seem to have occurred to him that there might be other explanations, less literal, more metaphorical, or even astral. Instead, this was the bull sport, the sacrifice of Athenian youths and maidens, which later Greeks recalled in the myth of the Minotaur. In this view he was supported by many idealists, like his colleague H. R. Hall, of the Department of Egyptian and Assyrian Antiquities in the British Museum and author of *The Oldest Civilization of Greece,* the first scholarly book to take account of Evans's discoveries.

Hall came by during the season and reported his revelations in the popular science review *Nature.* He encouraged readers to visualize his walk from Candia on which he passed "a couple of roadside wineshops, a house, and a path off to the left across the fields to a white patch with a wooden summer-house in the middle of it, from the top of which floats the Union Jack; this is Knossos, where Minos judged, where Theseus slew the Minotaur." Hall uncritically approved of Evans and his validations of mythical history: "Coming from the West, one enters first the great western court, which, if one is not a timid Dryasdust, but an archaeologist who takes pleasure in repeopling the ground on which he stands with those heroic figures which are associated with it in legend, one may call the Dancing-floor of Ariadne if one will."[111]

"It is a strange thing, this Cretan civilization," Hall wrote later that year, propagating Evans's concept of "peace-loving Minoans":

> Mycenae we know, but this is not Mycenae . . . Knossos is older, and Knossos is more civilised. Knossos is no hill fort . . . It seems a place of secure peace, apparently undefended by walls, a palace of luxurious baths and polished dancing-floors, inhabited by princes who seem to have taken their pleasure in leading the life of luxurious ease, surrounded by a court of ladies in most amazingly modern low-necked dresses and coiffures like the triumphs of a Regent Street window, and men with hair as long as the women's and almost as elaborately dressed, served by crowds of slaves and tribute bearers . . . This is all conjecture, but it conveys an impression . . . of an ancient culture, highly developed, peaceful, art-loving and luxurious, effeminate if you will; but brutal withal [a reference to the bull sports] and possessing sinister traits which oppress the mind.[112]

Hall, like Evans, was looking for the balance between a just society and a cruel one.

The winter passed quickly while Evans concentrated on preparing detailed preliminary reports, a "Bird's-eye View of the Minoan Palace at Knossos, Crete," which was an illustrated tour of the Palace for the scrutiny of Britain's most accomplished builders at the Royal Institute of British Architects in December,[113] and a series of lectures on "Prae-Phoenician Writing in Crete," delivered at the Royal Institution in London. By mid-February 1903 he was back in Crete, and on February 23 he hired fifty workers, believing "a relatively short Campaign would exhaust the resources of the Palace Site."[114] Again Duncan Mackenzie arrived from Italy and Fyfe came to supervise the plans and reconstruction. Halvor Bagge, about whom we are told only that he was a "Danish artist," was brought in to draw the year's finds. Neither Evans nor Mackenzie kept detailed notebooks from this year on, perhaps because they felt that they were merely supplementing the major work of the first three campaigns; their records are summaries, often written days after the discoveries were made.[115]

Excessive rain dampened the excavators' spirits and hampered large-scale work well into April, but it also revealed markings on the stone that previous dry brushing hadn't. On the thresholds of the doorways they observed scorings from the movements of the wooden doors, which showed that each passage had been closed by double doors with a vertical bolt that could secure one side. These elegant doors were part of an ingenious system of double doors between pillars which, when the doors were opened, appeared to be a line merely of pillars, as the leaves of the doors slipped perfectly into cuttings in the supports, but which could be shut one or more as desired. This "pier-and-door partition," as Evans called it, was another marvel of Cretan architecture, and it spoke of the Minoans' very high level of aesthetic sophistication; it was a design not seen again until the French doors of the eighteenth century.

When the weather cleared in April, Evans hired another hundred and fifty men and broke new ground northwest of the palace. "Things have taken—as usual—a much greater development than I had anticipated," he wrote to his father. "On the North West broad steps began to appear, going down in two flights at right angles . . . and have been found to lead to a paved area, which must have served for some kind of shows. In fact, it seems to me to be part of a primitive theatre," he concluded, estimating that between four and five hundred spectators could be accommodated in the large "gallery" above the southern flight of steps beside the "Royal Box," as he named a rectangular bastion at the convergence of the steps. "What performances," he asked, "are likely to have been given in the paved area? The favourite Minôan sport is ruled out, since the enclosure was in no wise adopted for a bull ring . . . In spite of its rectangular shape, when more level than at present and coated with cement, the area would have been well adapted for dances," a theory that tested positive when Evans invited the workers and their families to display their dancing skills before Dörpfeld and his party of German students on their annual visit. "It is difficult to refuse the conclusion that this first of theatres, the Stepped Area with its dancing ground, supplies a material foundation for the Homeric tradition of the famous 'choros.' " So it became the Theatral Area, though it might well have been an open market or public meeting place, and Evans again could cite material proof of the "truth in myth."[116]

The Snake Goddess

The season's greatest discovery, as usual, came at the end. "Noticing a slight depression in the pavement," Evans later reported, "I had some slabs raised" in a small chamber just west of the Central Court. Here he found to his delight ample evidence to confirm his designation of this suite of rooms as the "Central Shrine" with its cult statue of the divinity to whom the shrine was dedicated. Two stone-lined cists, like square boxes below floor level, were filled with gold, stone, and, especially, faience artifacts of such high quality that Evans extolled "the faience manufactory in the Palace of Knossos [as] the remote predecessor of that of Vincennes and Sevres, of Medicean Florence, of Urbino or Capodimonte, of Meissen, and of many other royal and princely fabrics of a similar kind."[117] Most important among these was the torso and head of a woman with "Matronly bosom. A mother Goddess," Evans noted.[118] The bodies of three snakes writhed about her arms and waist with their heads on her girdle, her right hand (the left was missing), and the high "tiara" towering above her head. Evans and Bagge restored this "Snake Goddess" to a standing position on the basis of a second female figure, also made of faience, who because of her smaller stature became the "Female Votary." This lesser figure, whose head and left arm were missing, held a curling length of twine in her upraised right hand, but Evans and Bagge, under the influence of the first figure, put snakes' heads on the lower part of the twine and in the fist of the left arm they replaced, ignoring the fact that no natural snake has peppermint stripes, which should have been well known to Evans, who had played with the reptiles since childhood.

But "the art reaches its highest level in certain small reliefs exhibiting groups of cows and goats suckling their young," Evans reported, "which makes it natural to detect in them a direct reference to the Mother Goddess of Minôan Crete." Then he made an interesting comparison: "the group of the cow and calf, in fact, presents essentially the same type as the Cow and Calf of Hathor and Isis."[119] Hathor, the Egyptian sky goddess symbolized as the cow who lifts the sun god into the sky with her horns, was most often depicted as a bovine head surrounded by stars. It was an obvious comparison for Evans to make; then he took a small marble cross that had been found with the faience figures and, observing that "the simple 'Greek' cross as a star symbol of religious import is found in Egypt as a mark of Hathor,"[120] set up the restored pieces as he imagined they might have once stood on a bench like that in the Shrine of the Double Axes, in the central place of worship with the goddess and her votaries on either side. But Hathor was Egyptian, and this was "pre-Hellenic" Crete, where a different body of myth existed. While acknowledging that Hera was the classical Greek equivalent to the bovine Egyptian goddess, Evans looked further into the past to identify his snake goddess, finally arriving at a nature goddess "of whom Aphroditê Ariadnê is a later transformation."[121]

The alleged sanctity of the Central Shrine, first indicated to Evans by its depiction in the miniature wall painting, was now assured by this new deposit, which Evans called the Temple Repositories; and the cult of the native Mother Goddess, the Lady of the Dove, and the Snake Goddess, all under the name of Ariadne, seemed proven. Yet, because Evans assumed a link between the double axe, so frequently seen carved as a mason's mark into blocks throughout the area, and Zeus and his offspring Minos, he concluded, "It would seem that there were here, as in early Anatolia, Priest-Kings; and the old tradition, that made Minos son and 'Companion' of Zeus and a Cretan Moses, is once more seen to have a basis in fact."[122] Evans was incapable of letting go of the concept of divinely inspired male authority.

Digging stopped during the first week in June, though it was clear that they had anything but "exhausted the resources" of the site. Evans wished to share his discoveries firsthand with the British public and set about trying to arrange for the movement of a selection of the artifacts to England, according to the clause in the antiquities law that allowed for the export of ἄχρηστα (*achrista*), or literally "useless" archaeological finds. He pressed R. W. Graves, the British consul in Crete, to arrange for the transfer of "duplicates and *objets sans valeur*" from Knossos to the Ashmolean Museum. Graves advised Evans "that a little in the way of exchanges for the benefit of the Candia Museum would greatly grease the wheels," a concept that was lost on Evans, and spoke to the high commissioner, getting Prince George's promise that the matter would be raised late in the legislative session so that it could be rushed through "by surprise, as he fears the Greek Chief Ephor [Kavadias, superintendent of antiquities in Athens], who is hostile to any such proposal," would exert his influence on the Cretan deputies. "I confess that I do not trust these people a bit, and shall not feel comfortable until it is a '*fait accompli*,' " admitted Graves.[123]

The mistrust between Evans and the Cretans was mutual. That year he had set up a display of the restored figurines from the Shrine of the Double Axes in a small room in the Palace to give visitors an impression of the atmosphere in the tiny Minoan shrine by looking through a hole in the door. Currelly later recalled:

> Unfortunately one of the boys from the British half-battalion that was stationed at Candia was small enough to squirm through the hole, and stole some antiquities. Evans got them back, but some of the Cretans insinuated that it had been an attempt on the part of the British to steal them. The Cretans would not allow a single object out of the country, and when any of us left it took about an hour for the customs officials, surrounded by admiring loafers, to go through a suitcase. Pillboxes were emptied, hair-brushes were combed. This was a bit of a comedy, as surely, if we had wanted to smuggle out small things, we would have had them in our pockets. But all Cretans wanted government jobs, and so the customs officers demonstrated their efficiency as dramatically as possible.[124]

The Cretans had good reason to doubt Evans's respect of their laws. In an interview in 1926, Evans related,

> One day I went to see an American who had been digging on a site on the east of Crete. He gave me an ancient Grecian vase. When I was leaving I wrapped the upper part of the vase in newspaper, and put it into the pocket of my knapsack. The body of the jar I put into my portmanteau. As a rule, Customs officials were most courteous and kind, but this time I was greeted by a newly-appointed man, who, finding the bottom of the jar in my knapsack, strongly demurred. I made up my mind he shouldn't have it. So I threw it into the sea. They did not find the bit in my portmanteau. When I got home I discovered that, as soon as I had left, there was an uproar in the Government. The Ephor (superintendent) of Antiquities went down to the port and instructed divers to fish for my wretched piece of crock at the bottom of the sea. All over Crete was broadcast the news that I had taken their greatest treasure, a golden boy with diamond eyes! Anyway, when the piece of the vase was rescued from the depths of the sea, it was taken in a procession to the museum. The next time I went back I

visited the Museum, and in the course of conversation I asked were my piece of crock was. "In the glass case," said the Ephor. He unlocked the case and I put the piece into my pocket and brought it home. It is now in the Ashmolean Museum.

Nonetheless, permission was granted for most of the objects that Evans applied for, but not for the inscribed tablets, as Hazzidakis informed him in a polite letter on June 26. Evans and Mackenzie packed up a modest selection of pottery shards, had plaster casts made of the most impressive artifacts, and shipped these to London, where they became the core of an exhibition including photographs and plans of finds from British excavations at Burlington House. It was twenty-six years since the newly-wed Evans, with Margaret, had traveled to London to see Schliemann's Trojan treasure, then scoffing at the amateur's pretensions about Troy and King Priam. Now, and in the same hall, he presented his own case to "those who wish to see with their own eyes that the 'myth' of Minos and Daedalos, and the Labyrinth had a very solid foundation," readers of the *Manchester Guardian* were told.[125]

Evans returned to Oxford in July to compose another detailed preliminary report and to consolidate his ideas on the Minoans, which he presented as the Yates Lectures at University College, London, in early November. Mackenzie provided a new chronological scheme of "three distinct strata of deposits" in the Palace. The first he now called the "prehistoric, neolithic stratum," which was "underlying the later deposit of the palace in what may be termed the Early and Middle Minoan classes." The third was "a 'late Minoan' stratum, represented all over the palace region . . . the later phase of this class covers the fabrics [pottery] elsewhere described as Mycenaean."[126] To this, Evans added the details that the pictographic script belonged to the "Middle Minôan Period," during which there was an "earlier Palace" (Mackenzie's "Kamarais" Palace of about 1900 B.C.) that was destroyed during "what seemed to have been a dynastic revolution." An important new refinement was "that the later Palace itself was divided by some internal disturbance, probably involving some change in the government, into two distinct periods."[127]

Evans elaborated on his ideas about the Cretan scripts in a lecture to the British Academy at the end of November. He proposed that two classes of linear script existed; the first, coming from early deposits in the late Palace like the Temple Repositories, had been "replaced by the other owing to a dynastic change"; and the second, examples of which now numbered about 1,600 tablets, belonged to the latest Palace period. He called these late Palace scripts Linear A and B.

Evans worked hard to translate his most famous discoveries. He found personal names with the "man" and "woman" signs attached, which allowed him "to trace the existence of male and female terminations and of changing suffixes, as well as compound formations of a similar type to Indo-Germanic." But he still couldn't read the tablets because of his insistence on the "unity of language in Minôan Crete going back to a remote period and probably corresponding to the Eteocretan language," and therefore certainly not Greek.[128]

Modern ethnic quarrels prompted the first serious attack on the growing body of Minoan artifacts at the end of 1903. Currelly recalled:

The Cretans had taken over the old Turkish barracks for a museum. Though the walls were stone, the timbers and wooden flooring made it a veritable fire-trap. Seven Cretan soldiers were on guard every night, but it is a question whether they were an advantage or not. As the Cretans were determined that anyone who saw any of this ancient civilization should come to Crete, it was a case of all the eggs being in one basket.[129]

Sure enough, in December someone did take advantage of the potential hazard and set fire to the barracks. Though the culprit was never brought to trial, the consensus was that it had been a Turk, jealous of the Cretans' history, who had tried to destroy it. Cretan newspapers demanded why a proper museum wasn't being built to house the island's treasures, and the suggestion was made that the delay in doing so, and perhaps the fire itself, was due to a conflict between Muslims and Christians. Both elements of the population were Cretan, but their beliefs and values were so far apart that the debate surrounding whose history was to be told in the museum had become explosive. Eventually, as the Muslim population dwindled, so too did their right to be represented in the island's history, and the new museum reflected the Christian majority's wishes.

Evans returned to Crete in March 1904 to find the fifth season in full swing under Mackenzie's supervision since February 15. Gregóri's talent at finding tombs was once again called upon, but this time they were rewarded, perhaps because he was joined by the equally sensitive Ioannis Papadakis, whom Evans credited with their first discoveries. "Unearthed remains of great stone mausoleum," Evans wired Macmillan, who submitted the hurried dispatch to the London *Times*: "Unique monument of its kind," the cable continued. "Nearly all metal objects removed in ancient times, but many scattered relics left. Repeated clay impressions Royal signet . . . Egyptian basalt bowl; many alabastra [Egyptian alabaster vases]; Egyptian necklace lapis lazuli with pendant figures." This was called the "Royal Tomb," a great rectangular chamber eight meters long and six meters wide lined with finely cut ashlar masonry, sited on a flat hilltop called Isopata overlooking the Venetian walls of Candia; it resembled in its rectangular layout the tombs of the Egyptian nobles at Thebes, and Evans, who had been expecting a circular beehive tomb like those found at Mycenae, remarked, "It is curious what an Egyptian element there is," in a letter to his father.[130] But for the press release he ventured, "Grave probably one of last Minoan Kings. Place for others never occupied. This great monument possibly represents traditional tomb of Idomeneus."[131] The Egyptian parallels were plentiful, but not enough to sway Evans from his pre-Hellenic Indo-European ideas.

At the Palace, "We have struck a continuation of the roadway west of the 'Theatre,' which promises to lead to something," Evans wrote to his father. Two hundred workers were engaged to remove "an enormous mass of earth including the remains of Greek and Roman habitation,"[132] which Evans later affirmed in his published report "proved to be of no importance in themselves."[133] The method used to remove the "unimportant" history was known as "the wager system." "They work in gangs on an ingenious system invented by Mackenzie, that of the στοίχημα [*stichima*] or match," Bosanquet recounted in a letter to his wife. "Two gangs of our men are each given an equal number of cubic metres, and a prize of a franc a head per day is paid to the team that finishes first. They work like heroes in these matches—and are paid at a higher rate than usual, apart from the trifling prize. Of course the system can only be used when there are masses of unproductive earth to be moved." The resulting ragged holes were known as "wager pits."

The pressure of large-scale excavation began to tell on Mackenzie. Later that year, when Mackenzie visited Saqqara in Egypt, his host, the

Egyptologist Arthur Weigall, expressed surprise at Mackenzie's ability to drink Scotch whiskey with dinner as if it were wine and asked if he wasn't afraid of getting drunk. "Intoxicated!" Mackenzie retorted, according to Weigall. "Ay, man, but the fear is I shall no' succeed in getting drunk on a wee bit whuskey like this. I want to be drunk if posseeble; for on a dark nicht like this, when the road gaes boomping alang before you, the blinder I am the swifter I'll ride." He added that he always drank four glasses of whiskey at Knossos before starting the ride home to Candia. "I have a wee bit pony there, by the name of Hell Fire," Mackenzie explained, "and I gallop home on him. Think, man, if I were sober—could I gallop unharmed though the streets of the city, and alang a road like a corkscrew, in much darkness?"[134]

Mackenzie's expressed need for whiskey was satisfied equally by raki, the Cretan spirit distilled privately every autumn in the months following the grape harvest from the must of wine pressings, similar to Italian grappa and French marc, which he found freely available in unlimited quantities in every Cretan household. His necessity for alcohol grew over the years and became one of the insurmountable obstacles to his success at finding a permanent post in archaeology and eventually led to his premature retirement from Knossos.

The success of the Knossos display at Burlington House, held over by popular demand until March 1904, prompted Bosanquet to inquire of Evans, "Would it be worth while to arrange an exhibition of Cretan antiquities in London?"[135] Both were eager to drum up much needed public support for the Cretan Exploration Fund, and so Evans remained in Candia well into July "chiefly in negotiations about what 'duplicates' I can get out," he wrote to his father. "I have a catalogue of objects, mostly broken, but I do not know whether they will be inclined to interpret the new law liberally." Though the Cretan Assembly agreed in principle to the demands, "A commission has to be appointed and all kinds of formalities had to be gone through." The Cretan Assembly acknowledged its debt of gratitude to Evans and the British government, and the commission eventually approved of the export of pottery shards to British museums, with the Ashmolean benefiting the most; it currently houses the most diverse collection of Cretan antiquities outside of Greece.

"At a time when the attention of the English public has just been rightly called to the successful explorations of Cnossus by Mr. Arthur Evans and his comrades," began an anonymous critique in the *Edin-*

burgh Review of how recent archaeological discoveries affected our understanding of Homer, "it may be well to consider the general value and extent of our knowledge about the Mediterranean in prehistoric ages, and about the Homeric poems which are our chief literary source."[136] Schliemann's discoveries were like those of Cuvier "digging up fossils of unknown animals" that meant nothing without knowledge of the earth's history but that had prompted the study of geology. Because Schliemann began at Mycenae, "we have at once a 'Mycenaean Age,' " the critic observed, but "Mr. Arthur Evans has given that name its death-blow" and "would substitute 'Minoan.' " Evans's discovery of Egyptian materials and influence at Knossos converted "the fleets of Minos," of Thucydides' famed "thalassocracy," to "a historical fact." These Bronze Age fleets, the critic went on, were "ready to carry on commerce and warfare in the Aegean Sea," followed later by the Phoenicians, who extended their control to include the western Mediterranean (both being obvious forerunners to "England of the present day," which "from Gibraltar to the Suez Canal, holds the coaling stations and strategic points, without caring for the interior districts"). The review concluded, "If Mr. Arthur Evans were merely a digger, this article would never have been written, for it would have been entirely useless. It is because of his profound and wide knowledge of prehistoric archaeology, of local antiquities, of museum-craft, of what may be summed up as 'ancient atmosphere,' that his work and that of Mr. Hogarth deserve the intelligent sympathy and the generous aid of every enlightened scholar."

In the autumn of 1904, the Cretan Assembly instructed the Cretan Post Office to issue a new series of stamps, which appeared the following February. Again, the Post Office turned to the numismatist J. Svoronos for inspiration, instructing him to depict scenes from Cretan history, mythology, or tradition. This time he had new representations to consider and decided to blend images from ancient Cretan coins with Evans's "impressions of the seals of the epoch of most remote antiquity," and Cretan scenes "celebrated for historical or archaeological reasons." Many of the objects that archaeologists uncover become the lasting icons, or visual reminders, for a period and place, the images we use in the present to associate with those times in the past we need to be in touch with. The selection of these icons is crucial to how the past is imagined in the present. The wide variety of images that Evans and his colleagues made available seemed, as far as the modern Cretans were concerned, a remarkably limited selection. One of the first finds, the "Aphrodite of Knossos," for example, could never evoke ancient Crete. It was primitive, Neolithic, tribal; it had little to do either with the concept of civilization at the turn of the century or with the Cretan Assembly's pre-Hellenic program. "La Parisienne" and even the "Prince of the Lilies" had a decidedly Egyptian look about them. But Evans's "Goddess standing on her sacred rock or mountain peak," whom the Cretans turned into "Artemis (Mycenaean goddess) between two lions, drawing a bow,"[137] was the perfect symbol to convey their link to the Minoans. So, too, was the archer on a stone vase fragment, as Crete in the classical Greek period was famous for her archers, and it was placed opposite one of Hogarth's "Minotaurs" from the Zakros sealings, in a border of continuous spirals around an engraving of Knossos at the end of the 1902 season.[138] The same impressions the Minoans had used perhaps to communicate their authority were thus used by the modern Cretan state for much the same reason. Once again, the present sifted through the past for symbols to guarantee its chosen future.

Evans returned to Crete in mid-March 1905, to find the island in a state of rebellion. Prince George had stood firmly by the principles of Cretan autonomy, still maintained by troops of the Great Powers acting as an international gendarmerie in the large towns. But the Christian Greeks weren't interested in Crete's independence—union with the kingdom of Greece remained their overwhelming desire—and they found their champion in the young lawyer Venizelos.

Venizelos objected to what he saw as Prince George's autocratic rule, and he openly declared that Cretans should have more say in their future; this led to his expulsion from the government in 1901. Venizelos's campaign against the prince's rule came to a head in February 1905 when members of the Cretan Assembly who favored Greek unity gathered in Therisos, near Canea, and declared their intentions to change the Cretan constitution and threatened armed insurrection if their demands weren't met. Venizelos placed himself at the head of a caretaker government, while Prince George declared martial law. By mid-March, the Therisos Rebellion, as it was known, had spread throughout the island and Crete was once again in a state of civil war. The rebellion lasted until November, when Venizelos met with the consuls of the Great Powers, who agreed to appoint an international commission to resolve the dispute. The commissioners arrived in 1906 and recommended the removal of the foreign troops and the establishment of a Cretan gendarmerie led by Cretan officers from the Greek army. It became clear that Prince George had lost the confidence that both the Cretans and the Great Powers had placed in him eight years earlier, and so he resigned in September 1906. Alexander Zaimis, a veteran Greek politician, replaced him and saw to the formation of the Cretan militia and the restoration of order.

The rebellion renewed the tension between Christians and Muslims, but also between the Cretans and their foreign overseers. "Palaikastro being remote from the large towns where foreign troops are stationed and the inhabitants being in sympathy with the revolutionary movement, the police had to be withdrawn," reported Bosanquet, who stayed in Athens, placing Dawkins in charge of the excavations there. "Once a party of malcontent workmen armed with rifles terrorized the rest into striking for higher wages." There were also sieges and countersieges of the local Toplou monastery, but "Mr. Dawkins stood his ground . . . and was able to keep his people in hand."[139]

Working under the Union Jack on his private estate, Evans was grateful for the close proximity of the British half-battalion at Candia, and he suffered little during the uprising. He lost the full-time commitment of Theodore Fyfe, who returned to Scotland to practice architecture instead of recording and rebuilding Evans's collapsed dreams, but gained in his stead Christian Charles Tyler Doll. Born in 1880 the son of a well-known architect in London's fashionable Bloomsbury district, Doll had studied architecture at Cambridge; articled to his father, then the British School's architect, he went to Crete in 1905 and found himself in charge of Evans's grandest scheme to date.[140]

The winter rains had undermined the second landing of the Grand Staircase in the Domestic Quarter, and the wooden supports inserted by Fyfe had rotted. Part of the landing had collapsed and the rest of the complex was on the verge of giving way. "To avert the ruin thus threatened demanded nothing less than heroic measures," Evans wrote with relish in his report. Doll supervised the removal of the entire upper flight of stairs, stone by stone, cleared the area of debris, then, with "the minimum of incongruity," replaced the wooden columns in the balustrade with stone ones coated in red plaster and put in iron girders where the wooden architraves and cross-beams had been. Evans found this pleasing:

> The effect of the legitimate process of reconstitution is such that it must appeal to the historic sense of the most unimaginative. To

a height of over twenty feet there rise before us the grand staircase and columnar hall of approach, practically unchanged since they were traversed, some three and a half milleniums back, by Kings and Queens of Minos' stock, on their way from the scenes of their public and sacerdotal functions in the West Wing of the Palace, to the more private quarters of the Royal household.[141]

The effect was indeed, and still is, truly remarkable. Evans later confessed to a malaria-induced vision one summer's eve in the Grand Staircase, when he was

tempted in the warm moonlight to look down the staircase well, the whole place seemed to awake awhile to life and movement. Such was the force of the illusion that the Priest King with his plumed crown, great ladies, tightly girdled, flounced and corseted, long-stoled priests, and after them a retinue of elegant and sinewy youths—as if the Cup-Bearer and his fellows had stepped down from the walls—passed and repassed on the flights below.

The illusion may have been inspired in part by Mackenzie's disgruntled report of a visit made by Isadora Duncan, the great American dancer noted for her re-creation of classical dance movements based on her study of Greek sculpture, but equally famous for dancing barefoot in translucent flowing garments like an ancient woodland nymph. He was shocked by her impromptu performance up and down the Grand Staircase.[142]

The Nine Periods of Minos

Evans tore himself away from Knossos in April for long enough to plead his case for the acceptance of the new chapter he was writing in world history at the international Archaeological Congress in Athens, where he was president of the prehistoric section. He appealed to his colleagues like a lawyer before the jury: "Are we not justified based on the archaeological evidence, to substitute the nine periods of Minoan culture for the nine 'years' of Minos of legendary tradition?" he asked, quoting Homer's phrase "Minos who ruled for nine years," though the Greek word translated as "years" referred to an indeterminate unit of time and so might have been months, seasons, or even periods, the last being how Evans understood it to justify his nine-period classification.[143]

Evans outlined the three main periods of Minoan civilization: Early, Middle, and Late, like the Egyptian kingdoms, each subdivided into I, II, and III, "tracing the birth, floruit and degeneration of each characteristic phase of Minoan culture." He believed they followed a continuous evolution, since the inscribed documents in the linear scripts "show linguistic unity," he affirmed, though he couldn't read them yet. The two greatest periods in the Palace, then, were the first palace of the Middle Minoan II period, which coincided with the long and stable reigns of the Egyptian Twelfth Dynasty of the eighteenth and nineteenth centuries B.C., and the second palace of Late Minoan II, roughly 1550–1400 B.C., when the "transformation of the palace was complete," the great vases of what he called the "Palace Style" were produced, Linear B was in use, and the wall paintings reflected those of the contemporaneous Eighteenth Dynasty in Egypt. "The great catastrophe of the Second Palace at Knossos marks the end of this period," he concluded. What followed was the period of decline during which he believed that squatters reoccupied the Palace. Evans defended his use of the term "Minoan" by pointing out that it was ethnographically neutral and so not to be confused with historical cultures like Pelasgians or Carians; the name "Minos," he recommended, "denotes the title of a dynast, rather like 'Caesar' or 'Pharaoh.' "

Evans's colleagues in the prehistoric section of the Archaeological Congress in Athens disagreed with his designations, however, and the organizers elected not to publish his full paper in their proceedings. The printed summary, which they allowed, was so filled with errors that Evans complained: "I was made to ascribe the chief masterpieces of Minoan Art to the last epoch of its decadence!"[144] He produced his own version privately, in French to mark his induction into L'Institut de France, the French equivalent of the Society of Antiquaries. Other excavators in Crete were for the most part opposed to the new classification. In a letter to Halbherr, Gaetano de Sanctis stated that he and Luigi Pernier, both of the new generation of Italian explorers in Crete, "agreed on two fundamental points, based on the examination of vases and fragments of vases found at Phaistos: in recognising the inaptness, uncertainty and artificiality of the tripartition of each of the great epochs of Cretan prehistory, and in holding it impossible that Mycenean pottery was the product of internal, autonomous development of Cretan pottery following the Kamares period."[145] But Evans stood his ground as dean of Cretan excavators, and his system prevailed.

Evans rushed back to Knossos following the congress, eager to see what lay on the hillside opposite the Theatral Area at the end of the well-built, perfectly aligned causeway, where he envisaged "some monumental structure." He engaged his own army of workers and followed the route as far as the track leading down from Candia, where it turned north. The men dug a long trench on the slope, 24 by 2.5 meters (enormous by today's standard of 4 by 4), which soon paid off. A baked tablet inscribed with Linear B was, to Evans, "the presage of the existence of some important building," which he assumed was the final destination of the Royal Road, as he called the causeway. A great complex appeared of paved courts with colonnades and pier-and-door partitions, recalling the Hall of the Double Axes, and a reduced version of the main Palace gradually emerged from the hillside. This "Little Palace," as Evans later called it, had been burned like the main Palace, but the architectural features were better preserved and included some not seen elsewhere, including columns with fluting in relief, "a moulding obviously taken over from Egyptian columns imitating clustered papyrus stems or sheafs of reeds."[146]

West of the Little Palace's hall, where Evans was struck by the "quasi-human aspect" of a natural lump of limestone found near the surface, "which indeed from its characteristic conformation might well be that of a Mother Goddess," excavation revealed a small room, roughly 2 by 2.5 meters, with a balustrade on three sides, upon which sat a plaster Horns of Consecration opposite the entrance—"the unfailing concomitant of Minoan sanctuaries," Evans proclaimed. Instead of recognizable images "made with hands," like those in the Shrine of the Double Axes and the Temple Repositories, here were "the fetish idols of a much more archaic cult," which inspired Evans to call the building the "House of the Fetishes," before settling later on the "Little Palace." Encouraged by Flinders Petrie, who had seen apes in the "bizarre flint forms" in the temple at Abydos in Egypt, Evans recognized that "the largest and principal figure was evidently chosen from its resemblance to a woman of ample matronly contours," while a "smaller nodule curiously suggested an infant," and a third looked like an Egyptian ape. "It is difficult not to conclude," he wrote in his report, "that we have here to do in its most primitive guise with the traditional Cretan cult of

Mother Rhea and the infant Zeus,—the divine offspring actually appearing in the form of his sacred stone or βαίτυλος [baetylos]." This was the stone given to Kronos to satisfy his infanticide, the baetyl of Evans's "Tree and Pillar Cult," which he no longer believed represented the supreme male. The new mother-and-child image haunted Evans, and he made the relationship the new main focus of his Minoan religion: "In the matronly fetish of natural stone we must certainly recognize the same Mother Goddess that we find so constantly recurring in Minoan religious art with her male satellite, her sacred Double Axe and her guardians, and the doves or snakes that alternately present her in a celestial or a chthonic aspect."[147] She was the Greek Rhea, Ops to the Romans, Hathor—later Isis—to the Egyptians, Cybele in Anatolia, and, according to Evans, Ariadne, Britomartis, or Diktyma to the Minoans.[148] Her unfortunate son, whose role was to die and regenerate yearly, was the classical Zeus Kretagenes (Cretan-born Zeus), an equivalent of the Greeks' Dionysus—as their Olympian Zeus, the Roman Jupiter, was immortal. The sacrificial youth was Osiris to the Egyptians and Attis or Adonis in the Anatolian cults. All were obvious precedents for the Christian Madonna and Child, and there was no doubt in Evan's mind that the human prototypes had once lived, like the Christian figures.

The great German philologist A. Fick had different ideas. In his book on pre-Greek place names, which appeared that year, Fick argued that the Minotaur was the sun and Pasiphae, which means either "the all shining" or "shining on all," was the moon. The labyrinth, to Fick, was the place where wise men traced the wanderings of the stars. But Evans had no patience for astral metaphors and "sun-myths" in his search for the literal truth behind the legends.

The Palazzo Evans

The 1905 campaign was the last major season in the Palace at Knossos. The greatest part of the two-acre building had been revealed, and what remained seemed to Evans minor by comparison. His preliminary report was concise because his mind was on the larger, much more detailed final publication that would follow once all the finds were studied. Evans had selected the finest examples of Minoan art to illustrate his reports and lectures, but in Aegean excavations these make up only a tiny percentage of the mass of everyday objects that pour from the ground by the ton. The thankless task of sifting through millions of broken pottery shards, essential for understanding the relative chronology of Knossos based on observations of stylistic change across stratified layers, fell to Mackenzie, who began to organize the pottery into crates stored in the newly roofed rooms behind the Throne Room.

Evans had opened a new chapter in world history, but he had exhausted himself and his assets in the process. "I do not think of doing any more excavation at Knossos," he wrote to Halbherr in July. "The work is too ruinous. I am between £700 and £800 out of pocket by this year's work and have had to sell part of my own collections to pay for it."[149] Never frugal with his assets, Evans had depleted his resources, drawing what little he could from the unsuccessful Cretan Exploration Fund, and he was forced to cancel the excavations in 1906. Instead, he used his allowance to bring another dream to fruition. Conceding that he should live nearer the Palace, with the prospect of many years of study and consolidation ahead, Evans returned to the hillside above the Kephala where he and John Myres had rested over a decade earlier. He and Doll drew up plans and ordered materials to be shipped to Candia, and Doll spent most of 1906 supervising the construction of what visitors to Crete at first called the Palazzo Evans, now famous as the Villa Ariadne. Doll worked throughout the year tirelessly chasing down customs officials to allow for the import of British steel girders so that this new building would survive whatever the Cretan climate could throw at it from above or below ground. By the early summer of 1907 Doll had created a building he boasted would make Youlbury pale by comparison, though Evans's new young American friend and colleague Richard Seager thought it "hideous."

Evans had taken to Seager instantly when this handsome, rich, twenty-one-year-old American arrived in Crete in 1903 to assist Harriet Boyd at Gournia; Seager was with him in England in the autumn of 1905 when Evans's car, a grand black Wolseley, crashed. "If old King Minos knew what was happening, I am sure he trembled for his reputation which lies so entirely in your hands," Harriet Boyd wrote when she heard the news, adding, "I am very glad my young compatriot escaped."[150] Evans and Seager developed a close personal relationship; Evans became one of Seager's prime supporters and mentors. Nonetheless, in 1907 Seager was repulsed by Evans's Cretan house and likened it, in private correspondence, to a cheap French villa.[151]

Bosanquet loved it. Writing to his wife from the Villa Ariadne, as

Evans "calls it in jest," he painted a picture of the place in its first incarnation:

> We drove out here between fields starred with big white anemones and blue iris. Near Cnossos, a short carriage drive bends off to the right; 50 yards of steep hill between young pines, and we are on a graveled terrace with flower beds marked out and shrubs newly planted, before a stately flat-roofed villa, irregular in plan, with one storey sunk for coolness, looking out over olive-trees, on the palace and the wide valley. From my room I have a glimpse of the sea. Wide corridors, cement floors and plain cement walls, bright brass handles on doors and windows and an English air of solidity about all woodwork and masonry. A big window seat to every window; just the necessary furniture, mostly from the Candia house; a real bathroom and capital servants.[152]

Manoli, or Manolaki, Akoumianakis—"my mountain wolf," as Evans affectionately called him[153]—became the groundskeeper, while Kostis Chronakis, a short-tempered man whose moodiness troubled Mackenzie, was butler, handyman, and cook, and his wife, Maria, housekeeper.[154] Life at Knossos changed overnight for Evans and Mackenzie now that they could enjoy the comforts of a large house and ordered garden with a full staff in the middle of the Cretan landscape. The Villa Ariadne became as much a part of Knossos as the antiquities were, and foreign visitors were treated to tea and sandwiches there after visits to the Palace. Evans continued to order provisions from England; preferring not to imbibe the local spirits, he maintained a stock of gin, whiskey, French wine, and, for special occasions, champagne. He insisted that the house be run on strict Victorian rules; once, Kostis recalled, when Evans entered his bath to find that the fresh bar of soap had been tampered with, he flew into a rage, stamping, waving his arms and shouting. "He used to strike me, he used to take me by the shirt and shake me," the Cretan confessed years later to the British film critic Dilys Powell, "a very strange man, a very strange man."[155]

Bosanquet's five-year term as director of the British School at Athens was due to end in 1906, and Evans, as a member of the subcommittee elected to find a successor, asked Mackenzie if he would consider the post. Mackenzie was reluctant to put in for the job, imagining that he would be more suitable as an assistant to the director. Nonetheless, Evans urged him to apply and kept him abreast of the developments and intrigues: John Myres was the Oxford favorite, who feared that a "combination of little Cambridgers" would elect Dawkins, Bosanquet's choice, as they had worked together at Palaikastro. Though "Mr. Duncan Mackenzie had had a long acquaintance with the practical side of archaeology of the prehellenic era and had also studied the art of the 'classical' age" and "he had also an exceptional experience of life in Greek lands," the committee conceded that "against this it was doubted how far he would be *d'accord* either with the type of students ordinarily sent out or with the Managing Committee. His literary style was also against him." They appointed Dawkins.[156] Mackenzie, disappointed and confirmed in his distrust of the British School, thus remained dependent on Evans for the foreseeable future.

Evans and Mackenzie returned to Crete in April 1907 to make modest "supplementary excavations in the west wing for the final publication" of the Palace.[157] "The great prehistoric Palace of Knossos is really inexhaustible," began the year's dispatch in the *Times*, where Evans published all his subsequent reports, forgoing the detailed scientific descriptions of the first campaigns, though little of consequence came from the site in 1907. The year's greatest discovery was made at the shop of a dealer in Athens, where Evans called in on his way home. It was a hematite bead seal engraved with a lion whose head is turned around, which reminded Evans of some of the sealings found in the Royal Tomb, and storerooms, of the West Magazines at Knossos, but above the lion on the seal stood "two guardian griffins on each side of a figure," which Evans "at once recognised as the ideogram of a kind of cereal that appears sometimes in connexion with a form of storehouse on a class of clay inventories specially connected with the Third Magazine—where, indeed, remains of burnt corn were also found." He concluded: "We have here, in fact, the actual signet of a Palace official—the steward of the Royal granaries."[158]

Evans reported that the seal had been recovered at Knossos by "a peasant hereabouts, while working his field a short time since," but that "the seal had naturally found its way out of the country" because of "the very stringent and childish native law by which the authorities have power to confiscate even such minor relics."[159] Evans's logic is difficult to follow, unless we postulate that he was annoyed because, having attempted to acquire the seal in Crete, he allowed his Athens dealer to take the risk of smuggling it to Greece, where export permits were possible but where Evans had to pay a premium for it. This resentment, combined with his firm opposition to the Cretan antiquities law, must have been seriously aggravated by the writ from Minos Kalokairinos issued against him on June 30, 1907.

Kalokairinos had returned to Athens University to complete a law degree and now brought his own case against Evans, claiming that Evans had "arbitrarily seized" his field at Hellenika on the slopes west of the Palace in 1904 and illegally exported the antiquities that he found there, "using them as if they were his own, while, according to the present law, these ancient heirlooms—with no exception—belong to the Cretan State." This suit refers to the period when Gregóri was searching for tombs well outside the limits of Evans's estate, and specifically to a grave, which Evans found and published a report on many years later, as having "come to light in the course of tillage on the ridge West of the Palace" and whose contents (now in the Ashmolean Museum) "were acquired some years since from their owner."[160] Kalokairinos pointed out that Hellenika was his property, which he gave over to the Cretan state, and he demanded that the finds be restored to Crete and that Evans be expelled from the country.

Evans hurriedly tried to solve the problem by offering to buy the land from Kalokairinos, but the root of the problem was deeper. Kalokairinos was bitter at having been left out of Cretan archaeology, which he considered himself to have founded. In 1905, he had begun publishing the *Archaeological Newspaper of Crete*, in which he reported on significant archaeological finds, beginning with his own, but in all the issues he never once mentioned Evans. Evans's Cretan lawyer assured him that Kalokairinos was known locally as a malcontent, but Evans feared the trouble that the case, in which he was clearly in the wrong, and the adverse publicity it would generate, could bring for him in Crete and Greece. But before the matter was discussed, Kalokairinos died and passed into obscurity. Years later Evans mentioned him briefly in a vague reference to "a native explorer," who had conducted a "promiscuous dig in search of ancient objects," at Knossos.[161]

Acutely aware of his insolvency, Evans took a small house near Boars Hill, planning to let Youlbury, which he could no longer afford to maintain.[162] In six major excavation campaigns, he had found what he was looking for, and he was known internationally for his revelations about early Crete, which made him a pivotal figure in the archaeological world, but he had ruined himself financially in the process. The Cretan Exploration Fund was a dismal failure, as the British public refused to support "a rich man's son" chasing his dreams on a faraway Mediterranean island, no matter how spectacular the discoveries.

Close friends and colleagues subscribed for a portrait by the British painter Sir William Richmond that was presented to the Ashmolean Museum at a grand ceremony in December 1907. The painting shows Evans as a handsome youth with a full crop of dark hair and a heavy mustache, draped with a loose-fitting white linen suit and open shirt tied with a red sash at his waist, sitting before a wall of ashlar masonry partially obscured by the Cup Bearer fresco on one side and, in the far background of the other, an Aegean backdrop of olive trees and hazy blue mountains in the distance. An English rose in his *boutonnière* indicates his nationality. Richmond's portrait encircled Evans with the plaster copies of his most famous finds, brought to London for the 1903 exhibition, and had him clutching an inscribed tablet in both hands, his thumbs gently tracing the characters on the surface as though he were trying to read the illegible script by touch, while gazing far off into the distance with a great sense of accomplishment gently radiating from his satisfied smile. Here was the brilliant creator surrounded by the re-creations of artifacts drawn from the fantastic world he had revived.

At the presentation ceremony, Evans thanked his Ashmolean colleagues for fulfilling his duties while he was in Crete, but he ended the year consumed with his financial troubles and wondering how he would accomplish the Herculean labor he had initiated at Knossos.

5

The Pan-Minoan School 1908–41

Some Hope of Minos

Public interest in archaeology rarely endures beyond the initial, star-tling discovery of a unique monument or brilliant artifact, which seems to appear as if by magic where fortunate explorers sink their spades. But "the real work of exploration begins where wholesale excavation ends," Evans wrote in the *Times* at the conclusion of the 1908 season.[1] The greater facts of Knossos and the Labyrinth had been established, as far as Evans was concerned, by 1905. Only the fine points, those minute details essential for writing history, remained to be ordered—by means of what Evans called the "wall analysis of the Palace."

Mackenzie arrived at Knossos in mid-March 1908 to supervise the excavation of small test pits below the lowest floor levels and beside walls of uncertain construction date. He carefully collected all of the tiny pottery shards from these tests to determine the stylistic date of the very latest piece, which he took to indicate the likely time period in which the wall was first built. But one of the unwritten laws of archae-ology states: the best things are always in the balks, which are the land divisions or scarps left untouched during large-scale clearing cam-paigns. So it was that after Evans's arrival they found "in a pit, perhaps the shaft of a drain," a spectacular steatite bovine head in the *Petit*

Palais, as Evans often called the Little Palace. This is a work that we now recognize as one of the great masterpieces of Minoan art.

"The modeling of the head and curly hair is beautifully executed and some of the technical details are unique," Evans marveled. The find measured twenty centimeters from chin to crown, or roughly half life-size. "The nostrils are inlaid with a kind of shell," he noted, and later identified the material as *tridacna squamosa*, from the Persian Gulf. But what most amazed him was the perfectly preserved rock-crystal right eye, slightly hollowed on the underside where the white cornea contrasts the black iris and brilliant scarlet pupil. This crystal is set in a border of red jasper "which surrounds the white field of the eye like the rims of bloodshot eyelids," Evans noted, adding that "the crystal lens of the eye both illuminates and magnifies the bright red pupil, and imparts to the whole an almost startling impression of fiery life." Gilliéron restored the missing eye and, on the basis of a sketch of a horned bovine head scratched onto the back of the vessel itself, restored both horns in shiny gold; pieces of gold foil found near the head had probably once coated wooden horns fixed above the ears. The overall effect was a spectacular work of lifelike art, which reminded Evans that one of the Keftiu craftsmen pictured with a Syrian prince in Egypt was described as "he who makes alive."[2]

Evans classed the head as a "rhyton," a vessel used for directing the flow of liquids poured as part of a ritual or ceremony (from the ancient Greek verb ρέω [*reo*], to flow). He made the allusion to bovine representations of the Egyptian goddess Hathor in his publication, but the Minoan cult of the Minotaur held sway in Evans's Crete, so the vessel became famous as a bull's-head rhyton.

Evans also recognized the bovine head as being like those carried by Keftiu emissaries in the procession of foreigners bearing tribute to the Egyptian pharaoh in nobles' tombs in Thebes; the date to which he ascribed it, the second palace period of Late Minoan II, "the last brilliant phase of the Little Palace before its partial destruction and reoccupation," fit perfectly with that of the Egyptian images, which were now also interpreted as rhytons. Their ancient worth and high quality of craftsmanship could be readily appreciated by this new discovery.[3]

The diggers in the Palace uncovered a southern entranceway with a small porch beneath which Evans noticed a circular cavity. He put some men to work clearing it out, but soon found that it was much larger and deeper than he would have expected. The pottery shards found in it were all of early types, and, as the digging continued day after day without reaching the bottom, Evans began to form the mental image of a very early "primitive beehive tomb," which would prove that the architectural form, identified with Schliemann's Mycenaeans in Greece, had a long ancestry in Crete. "No fresh news about the 'tomb,' " wrote Bosanquet to his wife in early April; he was recuperating from illness and enjoying the comforts of the Villa Ariadne. "The shaft is being continued downwards, slowly and without reaching solid rock— through later filling. It is certainly higher than the Treasury of Atreus at Mycenae—but one must not be too sure. It may have been a cistern, and no tomb at all." But Bosanquet shared Evans's excitement about the seemingly bottomless pit, adding, "If you find Kingsley's 'Heroes' do read Carol [their son] so much of Theseus and the Minotaur as is not too terrifying and tell him that I am now helping to dig up the ruins of the labyrinth."[4] The great "Hypogaeum," as Evans called this subterranean vault, turned out to be a massive water cistern, as Bosanquet had suspected, fifteen meters deep and eight meters wide at the base, cut into the soft bedrock with an internal staircase with inward-looking windows winding up the side: an amazing feat of engineering at the very beginning of the first palace period around 2000 B.C., but not the tomb that Evans sought.

Seager was digging early tombs on the tiny islet of Mochlos, on the northeast coast of Crete, and, in an unusual gesture of collaboration, Evans left Knossos briefly to join him. He reported their success in the *Times* and praised a "surprising series of small gold objects . . . as beautifully wrought as the best Alexandrian fabrics of the beginning of our era—artificial leaves and flowers, and (the distant anticipation, surely, of the gold masks of the Mycenae graves) gold bands with engraved and *repoussé* eyes for the protective blindfolding of the dead." Evans never concealed his wish to find the antecedents for every aspect of Schliemann's Mycenaeans, and every clue on Crete was exploited to the fullest. This suited Seager, who was having trouble raising money for his work because, like Evans, he was regarded as a rich man and expected to pay his own way. In addition, American excavators in Crete were not taken seriously by their academic institutions unless they could show they were helping to find the origins of classical Greece, an essential element in the United States' ideological identification with Periclean Athens and the world's first democracy. The Founding Fathers had consciously modeled themselves on the Athenian democracy, to such an extent that fifth-century-B.C. Attic Greek was suggested as the official language of the new democracy, as the architecture of its new state buildings reflected the appropriation of Attic ideals. American institutions were eager to be identified with the search for Greece's origins, which reminded Evans of the problems he was having in Britain trying to gain recognition for Aegean archaeology.

"I have some right to speak of Mr. Seager's work," Evans wrote a few months later in a testimonial to the American School of Classical Studies in Athens.

> Not only has he, as the French say, *"le main heureux"* with work of discovery but his excavations and researches are thoroughly well done from the scientific point of view . . . The methods by which he may best hope to recover the beginnings of an European Civilization in Crete & a great deal of the foundations on which the later Classical Culture rests are those which he pursues. They afford a great contrast to the tendency in certain quarters to deal even with these early monuments from the subjective point of view.[5]

Seager was delighted to have "the doyen of Cretan excavators," as he called Evans, publicize his discoveries. And so were Harriet Boyd and her husband, Charles Hawes, a Cambridge anthropologist[6] who asked him to write the preface to their general survey book entitled appropriately *Crete*, with a subtitle, *The Forerunner of Greece*, added to promote American sales.[7]

At Knossos, Doll carried on Fyfe's restoration work in the Domestic Quarter, finding that the wooden beams inserted in the Hall of the Double Axes in 1901 had "proved insufficient to withstand the violent extremes of the Cretan climate," and much of the upper floor had to be dismantled and rebuilt. Doll reconstructed most of the Queen's Megaron, and took the opportunity to open some of the blocked windows in the lower courts, allowing, as Evans imagined, "light to pour in between the piers and columns just as it did of old . . . In cooler tones it steals into the little bathroom behind." He shared this vision with the *Times*: "It dimly illuminates the painted spiral frieze above its white gypsum dado and falls below on the small terra-cotta bathtub, standing much as it was left some three and half millenniums back. The little bath bears a painted design of a character that marks the close of the great Palace Style. By whom was it last used?" In a revealing response to his own query, Evans ventured, "By a Queen, perhaps, and mother for some 'Hope of Minos'—a hope that failed,"[8] for the Palace was destroyed at the end of the Late Minoan II period. This sentimental allusion to "some hope of Minos," written in August 1908, may have come at the end of a pensive period during which Evans considered his own relationship to John Evans "the Great," who had died in his absence at the end of May. For his father he had been a hope, but one that triumphed.

Evans inherited "a considerable fortune" from his father, Joan Evans tells us, and then in October came into the entire Dickinson family estate when the last heir passed away. Evans was now richer and more celebrated than his father had been and he had his own hope, but it was unlikely to succeed as he had: Evans adopted Lancelot Freeman, a son of Margaret's brother who immigrated to America, and on him "lavished every advantage he could think of," his half-sister recalled. But Lance was "a delicate and unintellectual little boy," and not likely to succeed in academia.[9] Instead, he trained for a military career at Sandhurst.

Evans soon adopted another frail and simple boy, but this was a person whom Joan Evans deliberately excluded from her half-brother's biography, even though, or perhaps because, he became the focus of Arthur's most private devotion. James Candy, one of six children born to poor tenant farmers at the foot of Boars Hill in 1902, was a sickly child with a right ear infected after two unsuccessful mastoid operations (like the one which brought on Schliemann's early demise) when Evans first saw him at the flower show that he hosted annually at Youlbury. Evans noticed the little boy crying because he couldn't see the tug-of-war event between two local teams and, with his mother's permission, Evans had him hoisted onto his back for a better view. Later, when Candy joined some friends to found a Boy Scout troop on Boars Hill, Evans took greater notice of the fragile youth.

James Candy and his friends had elected Arthur Shepherd, an older boy from Boars Hill, to be their scoutmaster and lead them in a new movement which was sweeping Britain. Colonel Robert Baden-Powell, of Mafeking fame, founded the Boy Scouts in 1908 to combat what he saw as the state of social degeneration prevalent in Great Britain after the loss of the South African war. Under the simple motto "Be Prepared" (a play on his initials), Baden-Powell publicized a moral code called "The Scout Law" in a great newspaper and lecture campaign that quickly reached all levels of society. He promoted nine precepts based on honor, loyalty to authority (from God downward), charity, fraternity, chivalry, respect for the animal kingdom (though killing an animal for food was allowed), obedience, cheerfulness, and frugality (so that extra money could be given to others in need).[10] The positivist language of this Boy Scout Movement appealed to Evans, as did the outdoor activities designed to create healthy young men who loved and respected nature, and he instantly joined the movement, giving free use of his seventy-acre woods on Boars Hill and donating the pile house, which he had built for Margaret, for their headquarters.

Evans was a Boy Scout for the rest of his life, eventually achieving their highest award, the Silver Wolf, in 1938, and he took Scout Law very seriously, as Sir Mortimer Wheeler, one of the great pioneers of Indian archaeology, reported in his memoirs. Wheeler was a recent and penniless university graduate at the start of his career when he first met Evans on a formidable committee that awarded the young scholar a prestigious but meager fellowship of £50 a year:

> My future was indeed fixed, I was to be an archaeologist; but all else was quicksand. As I walked away slowly and thoughtfully down the long corridor, I became aware of light footsteps hurrying after me. I turned and found myself looking upon the small, slight form of Arthur Evans, a little breathless with his running. "That £50," he said in his quiet voice, "it isn't much. I should like to double it for you." And he was away again, almost before I could thank him. That characteristically generous act of Evans's changed the whole climate of the situation.[11]

Wheeler may not have realized that Evans was merely observing the third and ninth Scout laws.

The tenth law, "A Scout is pure in thought, word and deed," was soon added to remedy a specific moral dilemma that Baden-Powell, according to Tim Jeal, his most recent and convincing biographer, faced all his life. The "purity" clause probably came from Baden-Powell's attitude toward sex of any kind, but especially masturbation and "beastly" homosexual acts. Jeal agrees with the common view that Baden-Powell had an "emotionally intense" relationship with one Major Kenneth McLaren, who served with him at Mafeking and whom he described as "my best friend in the world," but he maintains it was "physically chaste." Baden-Powell's repulsion about masturbation is most graphically exhibited in the original text for his Scouting manual, which was censored by the publisher for being too explicit: "The result of self-abuse is always—mind you, always—that the boy after a time becomes weak and nervous and shy," began his attempt to terrify would-be offenders. "He gets headaches and probably palpitations of the heart, and if he carries it on too far he very often goes out of his mind and becomes an idiot. A very large number of the lunatics in our asylums have made themselves mad by indulging in this vice." Jeal suggests that "Baden-Powell's own sexual anxieties were responsible for the intensity of his attack on masturbation, since he found young men beautiful and women often the reverse . . . since interest in sex either seemed likely to lead boys to 'beastliness' with women, or to a propensity for 'the love that dare not speak its name,' it had to be curbed and crushed by iron willpower."[12]

There was also the matter of public opinion and the law. It was only twenty years since the Marquess of Queensberry had accused the Irish poet and playwright Oscar Wilde of sodomy, then a felony, and brought on a widespread discussion of the evils of homosexuality, resulting in Wilde's public humiliation, imprisonment, and early demise in 1900. Wilde's celebrated trial made it clear that homosexual behavior was considered to be degenerate and would not be tolerated by the British public. Many homosexuals, including Wilde, married and had families but repressed the true expression of their hearts. Evans confronted a similar personal issue: he had married Margaret out of friendship and admiration and had repressed his true longing for male companionship. I believe he continued to control his homosexual desires, as Baden-Powell did, but, unlike the "First Scout," he gave into them later when he began to lose his self-restraint.

When Arthur Shepherd marched his Scout troop up to the front door at Youlbury for inspection, he brought a new joy into Evans's life. "You can imagine our faces when we pressed the bell and there stood Sir Arthur, waiting to receive us," recorded Candy in his autobiography, "standing in his stately hall which was laid out in black and white marble in the form of a labyrinth with the Minotaur in the middle." Candy's loving memories of "the kindest man that I ever met" provide the most sincere glimpse of the personal side of Evans in his "lair."

"Looking back on those days," Candy reminisced, "I gradually became aware that he liked to talk to me and join in certain games, such as 'Flag Raiding,' which entailed crawling on one's hands and knees through the bracken in order to capture the opponents' flag . . . It seems that Sir Arthur had noticed that I was very pale and asked Arthur Shepherd if he knew the reason." Evans went to see Candy's parents and offered to be the boy's guardian, which they accepted because they couldn't afford to deal with his health problems and saw this as a great opportunity for the eight-year-old boy. "It was a case of farmyard to luxury," Candy recalled. "When the chauffeur rang the bell and Emma, the parlourmaid, took me to Sir Arthur with the words, 'Sir Arthur—Master Jimmie,' my whole life changed. The first surprise was that Sir Arthur kissed me," something Candy's father had never done. "To me, his house was out of this world. The luxury, the elegance, the vastness of the rooms, the pictures, the tapestries . . . but what impressed me most . . . was the number of bedrooms . . . the five bathrooms and, above all, a Roman bath with three steps going down into it." In recounting his spellbound first tour of Youlbury, he added the touching detail that the Victorian "Sir Arthur, with all these bathrooms, preferred to use, all his life, a large tin bath which was kept under his bed." Candy was shown to his room, next door to Evans's and equipped with a bell-pull "so that if I needed anything in the night he could come in to comfort me," Candy warmly recalled.[13]

The daily routine at Youlbury began at eight o'clock when Ada Porter, the housemaid, arrived in the bedrooms with a plate of fruit grown in the garden. She laid out Evans's clothes, all of which, Candy remembered,

> were made for him, and his trousers, regardless of the current fashion, had to be without "turn-ups." His boots (he would not wear shoes) had to be without laces, "waste of time," he said. So he had a tag at the front and one behind the heel which enabled him to pull his boots on in quick time. He could not bear to waste time, so his shirts were made with stiff turned down collars attached [and] he was never without his famous stick called Prodger.[14]

The breakfast gong went at nine. "What a spread!" Candy marveled in hindsight. "There was porridge, cold ham or kippers, eggs and bacon and kidney, all kept hot, and we could help ourselves to anything we wanted." After breakfast, Evans went to his library, where Mrs. Judd, the cook, followed him with her slate of the day's menus for his approval. She ran the kitchen with an assistant cook, a scullery maid, and a boy who cleaned the shoes and fetched the wood and coal. Four downstairs maids did the dusting and cleaning in their morning uniforms, while Evans spent the hours writing with a white goosefeather quill pen, which he used all his life, though the typewriter had been invented in 1873 and was in wide use at the time.[15]

At lunch, served by two maids, there was a menu with three courses and coffee, after which Evans had a siesta in the library. He awoke at three o'clock and often walked in the garden, immaculately kept by Mr. Osbourne, the head gardener, and four assistants. "He could tell you as easily of the life on the bottom of the lake as of the archaeology of Knossos,"[16] or of the taxonomy of butterflies, or of almost anything they encountered. Candy recalled that Evans "carried his own personal excavation tool; he allowed the nail on the little finger of his right hand to grow a quarter of an inch. This enabled him to remove dirt from his finds with it. I can see him now; bent over, his eyes close to some small object, working his nail into all the cracks and crannies."[17] Weather permitting, they played croquet on the lawn; it was one of the rare occasions when Evans wore pince-nez spectacles to see the ball. When he felt adventurous, Evans packed Jimmie and his nanny into the stately black three-seater Wolseley limousine maintained by the head chauffeur, Jim Wiblin, though more often driven by his assistant, Charlie Mott, and explored ruined abbeys or cathedrals, returning in time for tea in the magnificent drawing room, where Evans was master of ceremonies surrounded by his beloved paintings by Bronzino, Caravaggio, and Renaissance artists of the Venetian and Veronese schools, and embroideries from the Greek isles and the Balkans, while holding forth from his favorite chair.

At six o'clock sharp Evans returned to his library to write letters. Dinner was at seven "and woe betide you if you were late," Candy recounted. Candy wore an Eton jacket and followed Evans, clad in a dark suit, into the large dining room with a round table bright with fresh flowers in the center. There were never drinks before dinner, but always wine at the table, and champagne when there were guests. "A typical menu," Candy recalled, "was oysters, pheasant with all the trimmings, pudding and a savoury, followed by any fruit which was in season from the glasshouses." Coffee was taken in the drawing room, where Emma would bring a whiskey decanter for the master and a silver box of biscuits for his ward. This was the time for parlor games, and since Evans wasn't a skilled bridge player—he couldn't keep track of the numbers—the favorites were whist, patience, or charades. As Candy matured, Evans challenged him to billiards, a game he loved to play but always lost "due to his poor eyesight," Candy explained, eyesight so bad that in the evening he "would blunder into the trees and bushes unless he carried a lantern or had someone guide him." Finally, at nine-thirty sharp, guest or not, Evans retired to bed.[18]

Youlbury threw open its doors to the children of the community on Twelfth Night after Christmas—the Epiphany, the feast of celebrating the three wise men, or Magi, coming to pay homage to the baby Jesus. In Evans's version of Epiphany, he appeared as the Minotaur to devour the children who found their way to the center of the tiled maze pattern in the entrance-hall floor. There was a formal dance, which Evans called the "Cotillion," a French court dance performed by four couples standing in a square set (its patterns survive in the modern square dance). An orchestra set the tone and the young dancers presented each other with "little favours" provided by Evans. The festivities ended with the serving of slices from two large cakes, one for the boys and one for the girls, each cake containing a bean whose lucky recipient would be crowned King Minos or Queen Pasiphae, be placed on two mahogany replicas of the Knossian throne, and be honored in a final dance. It was regarded as *the* social event of the season for the children of Boars Hill and Oxford.[19]

"Kindness poured out of him; but, of course, when he told you to do something, by Jove, you had to comply." Candy recalled Evans's "volcanic nature," still intact in his sixties. "He was quick to anger, but just as quick to forgive, stubborn, and considered by some of his archaeologist colleagues to be a bit of tyrant," Candy admitted. "The first sign of his getting angry was when he started scratching the back of his head . . . Many a time at a hotel, Sir Arthur, after giving an order for lunch or asking for a knife or fork, and the waiter kept him waiting, would 'blow his top' and would tick him off left, right and center, with everyone watching."

"You know that I have really given Jimmie a little piece of my heart," Evans confessed to Candy's mother, and there is no doubt he meant it. Joan Evans, aware of her half-brother's proclivity toward young men, never mentioned Candy in her biography of Evans, perhaps suspecting either that Evans behaved illegally with the boy or that others might think so. Yet there is little doubt from Candy's affectionate memoirs that Evans's love for him was paternal.

In an unprecedented move, at the end of 1908 Evans announced his early retirement from the Ashmolean. But no one did this at Oxford, and Lord Curzon, chancellor of the university, wrote to him, "Your real monument is the Ashmolean itself . . . unrecognizable to the Oxonian of twenty-five years ago," and suggested, "though you may be resigning your post, I trust this will mean no severance between the University and yourself." So Evans accepted an honorary keepership of the museum, which meant he had a permanent seat on its governing body.[20] Hogarth became keeper of the Ashmolean in 1909, taking an active part in training students. In June, Evans was appointed Extraordinary Professor of Prehistoric Archaeology at the university, an honorary post with a token salary and few duties, and when John Myres accepted the recently created Wykeham Chair of Ancient History the following year, the three seasoned excavators began to play a major role in shaping the curriculum of a new generation of Oxford archaeologists.

Evans could now concentrate full-time on the publication of his work at Knossos and put the finishing touches to the first volume of *Scripta Minoa*, a full corpus of the hieroglyphic inscriptions from Crete, in which he argued for the Minoan origin of the Phoenician alphabet that later Greek colonists in the Levant adapted to write their language; this was the argument he had made more than a decade earlier in "Cretan Pictographs."[21] Armed with a much greater body of evidence, he successfully removed Egypt, hitherto regarded as the inspiration for the Phoenicians, from the line of descent that culminated in the great texts of classical Greece.

Evans spent the 1909 season at Knossos supervising Doll's "reconstitutions" in the Domestic Quarter of the Palace and searching the slopes near Isopata with Gregóri and Mackenzie for the predecessors to the Royal Tomb and the cemetery of the second great palace period. Evans assumed that a similar burial ground, with the remains of those who had built and had ruled in the first Palace, must be nearby. Instead they found more graves of the late period that, though also looted in antiquity, contained many small treasures overlooked by the clumsy grave robbers, including one that inspired Evans to consider a whole new aspect to Minoan religion.

The Isopata ring, a tiny gold signet Evans found in a corner of the first tomb they entered, has engraved on the bezel four mature women in characteristic flounced Minoan skirts in a field of lilies. Three of the women are in positions of worship, while the central figure has her head bowed with her right hand raised and her left hand down. Evans was struck by the similarity of the central figure's hand placement with a specific gesture he knew well from the contemporary religious dance performed not more than a kilometer from the tomb. The Dervish Academy at Tekke, which lay halfway between Knossos and Isopata on Evans's daily journey to Knossos, and whose abbot was a close friend of his and Mackenzie's, provided living parallels for this ancient scene. The dervishes are a mendicant Muslim sect best known for their "whirling dance," during which they spin on one foot, raising their right hands palm up and keeping their left hands down—a symbol of giving and taking—and, as the dance accelerates, they enter into a trance to lose their personal identities and to achieve union with their God. The placing of the hands of the ring's central figure and the gesture of the dervish dancers inspired Evans to interpret the women as votaries engaged in "a kind of orgiastic dance," designed to invoke the goddess, shown on the ring as a fifth tiny figure descending from the sky. He illustrated how the practice worked with the example from an Egyptian record of the Philistine prince Badira of Dor ("belonging," he surmised, "therefore to a colonial stock largely of Cretan extraction") making an offering to his god "who takes possession of his principal page and sets him into an ecstatic frenzy, indicated by the determinative of dancing. In this state he voiced divine commands."[22] The concept of ecstatic expression in Minoan religion thus became a part of the otherwise Teutonic construction that Evans had applied to early Crete.[23]

Perhaps this association with the modern male Muslim priesthood led Evans to concoct the ingenious theory that the Isopata ring and the others like it were specially made "*in usum mortuorum*, and that the rings were fitted to the fingers at a time when the flesh was decayed," because the ring's inner diameter, 1.4 by 1.2 centimeters, was "too small for any adult wearer."[24] What he rejected with this hypothesis was that the ring might have been worn by a slender adult female with small hands, perhaps because he found it difficult to accept that a woman might have held such an important office as to warrant both the ring and the well-built tomb. This would have meant that the sealings made from gold rings and found in the Knossos palace could have been stamped by female owners in positions of authority—a notion that was beyond the imagination of Evans or his society, which limited the rights of women, did not let them even vote, let alone hold political office.

In contrast, Evans's gender and international stature made him an attractive candidate for public office. That summer of 1909, he received a letter at Knossos asking him to stand as the Parliamentary representative for Oxford University at the next general election in 1910, so he spent the next six months campaigning for a political position that he didn't believe in and a post that he didn't want. "The comedy was over," Joan Evans commented, in December, when it was clear that he had insufficient backing and he withdrew his candidature. "None the less," she remarked, "it left Evans permanently disgusted with English politics."[25]

The Royal Institute of British Architects presented Evans with the Royal Gold Medal for the Promotion of Architecture at a grand ceremony on November 1, 1909. "While most of us are occupied with our personal aims and interests," the president began his introduction, "seeking our own profit or advancement, with some consideration for the greatness of our Art, and perhaps equal consideration for the necessary daily bread, there is among us a small band of workers moving on a higher plane, men who have set themselves to increase the sum of human knowledge." He cited scientists looking for cures to "sickness and pain" and explorers who cross deserts and mountains to "increase man's resources," but he pointed out that the inhabited world has a much deeper interest to architects and "we owe a great debt to those keen sportsmen who have set themselves to discover relics of past races . . . showing us how men have lived and fought and built." The first such "sportsman" to receive the medal had been Sir Henry Layard, whose great bulls of Nineveh still guard the entrance to the Assyrian collection in the British Museum; then came Schliemann with his "unflagging tenacity of purpose," which resulted in the discovery of Troy and Mycenae. Now the medal went to Evans, who "has devoted his mind, his time and his means" to discovering "the Palace of Minos," which, "it is no exaggeration to say, completely revolutionised our accepted ideas of the early civilizations surrounding the Mediterranean basin. He has converted myth into history and floating prehistoric tradition into established fact. He will tell us that Homer was not a Romanticist but an Historian."

Evans graciously accepted the medal, noting that the honor "really must be shared by those who have shared the work in Crete with me," naming Mackenzie, Fyfe, and Doll. He then presented his arguments for "The Palace of Knossos as a Sanctuary" with numerous lantern slides, urging the assembled architects to imagine Minoan Knossos like the Vatican in Rome, "for it swarmed with shrines and halls for ritual functions." In particular, he revived his arguments for identifying the area of the Temple Repositories as the Central Shrine depicted in the miniature fresco, his hypothesis from the very first dig season; Gilliéron had found more supporting evidence in the form of recently cleaned fresco fragments, which he restored onto the painting that now depicted the shrine at the center of a long, narrow composition with the stately ladies on either side and a throng of people in a rectangular court in the foreground (this is now called the "Grandstand fresco"). From the same "heap" of fresco fragments found in 1900, Gilliéron arranged a group into what Evans interpreted as "a crowd of spectators seated in a walled enclosure with olive trees—evidently the *temenos* (enclosure) of a sacred grove—overlooking an orgiastic dance, such as were held in honour of the Minoan Mother-Goddess."[26] And he topped this with a brilliant slide of the Isopata gold ring—his newest addition to Minoan devotion. As Evans believed that the Minoan Mother Goddess later became Aphrodite-Ariadne, he suggested, "The Court, with dancing votaries depicted on the fresco, which was obviously some part of the actual palace system, may be taken to represent the actual 'Dancing-place of Ariadne,' which Daedalos, according to the Homeric tradition, was said to have fashioned 'in broad Knossos.' "[27] For Evans, Ariadne's mythical dance was orgiastic and probably took place in the Theatral Area west of the palace.

The Illustrated Minoan Biography

Evans had indeed "converted floating prehistoric tradition into established fact," in the eyes of those who safeguarded knowledge, and so he was invited to write his new chapter in history for the eleventh edition of the *Encyclopaedia Britannica*—"a dictionary of arts, sciences, literature and general information." The Palace of Knossos, "with its wonderful works of art, executed for Minos by the craftsman Daedalos, has ceased to belong to the realms of fancy," he affirmed there. "With such remains before us it is no longer sufficient to relegate Minos to the region of sun-myths. His legendary presentation as the 'Friend of God,' like Abraham to whom as to Moses the law was revealed on the holy mountain, calls up indeed just such a priest-king of antiquity as the palace-sanctuary of Cnossus presupposes." Though the Cretan scripts were still undeciphered, Evans read the "titles of a succession of Minoan dynasts" in their recurring formulas and so took the next step of suggesting that two male profiles on clay sealings from the Temple Repositories, one of which was inscribed, were "portrait heads of a man and a boy, recalling the associations on the coinage of imperial Rome," citing the case of Severus, the second-century Roman emperor, and his son and successor, Caracalla, often pictured on the same coins.[28] Myres, in his 1911 *Dawn of History*, contributed to this imagined personification of "Minos of Cnossus," describing him as "a monarch who ruled the seas and terrorized the land, absolute and ruthless, if only because inflexibly just."[29]

As the Minoans entered history and Evans, with Myres, composed the illustrated biography of the ancient Cretans' best-known leader, an anonymous critic, taking stock of the first ten years of "Minoan Crete" in the *Edinburgh Review*, joined them in their fantastic re-creation, stating, "Minos holds in Greek story a position in some respects analogous to that of Charlemagne in the literature of the later Middle Ages," implying that there was a Cretan sovereign of similar stature to Charles I of France, crowned Holy Roman Emperor in 800, and the prototype of a Christian king and emperor throughout medieval Europe. The Cretan monarch's direct link to Western nations was traced "from Knossos to Mycenae, from Mycenae to Athens, from Athens to Alexandria, Rome to Byzantium . . . rising through the Middle Ages and the Renaissance to our day," and the physical evidence proving this linear cultural descent was "a triumph of the spade over the pen."[30] There was no sympathy for Fick's astral theories in this literal reading of the Greek legends and myths.

Evans returned to spade work in early 1910 and wearily reported to the *Times*, "There is no finishing a site like Knossos," adding that "the responsibilities that weigh on the explorer's shoulders are but little lightened as the years roll on."[31] He concentrated on "urgent works of conservation and reconstitution" in the Domestic Quarter, but his inquisitive spirit was drawn to the slopes north of the Royal Tomb, where Gregóri had found some "wild, long-rooted fennel, which seeks out by preference the spots above ancient cuttings [and which] served him, as often before, as a guide," to six new tombs. Evans still hoped they would find a cemetery of the earliest palace period, but the tombs they entered were a continuation of the same late cemetery, though one had exciting new features, which, Evans believed, vindicated his old argument with Rouse. The underground chamber was lined with benches, and not only was the cutting for the burial in the shape of a double axe, but two bronze votive double axes about twenty centimeters wide were lying on the ground amid scattered weapons and vases before the looted grave. This "Tomb of the Double Axes," as Evans called it, supplied parts of a second example of a "bull's head" rhyton, like the one from the Little Palace but with quatrefoil inlays that Evans again compared to "the conventional cruciform decoration which stands for spots on some of the cows of the Egyptian Goddess Hathor."[32] The tomb is comparable to those at Egyptian Thebes, where Hathor in bovine form was worshiped as a mortuary goddess—because the dead wished to be "in the following of Hathor"—who preserved the sun from the powers of darkness.[33] Nonetheless, Evans, satisfied that the sanctity of the double axe was once again proven, concluded, "The tomb, then, was at the same time a chapel where the protection of the Great Mother of the prehistoric Cretan cult was sought in the shades for the departed warrior."[34]

Gilliéron continued to work on the palace frescoes, adding upper bodies to the feet preserved in the "Procession Fresco" from what Evans now called the Royal Entrance Corridor. The principal figure was a woman in the Minoan flounced skirt faced on two sides by pairs of youthful adorants accompanied by "priestly players of the flute and lyre," inspired by the musicians depicted on a sarcophagus recently found at Ayia Triadha, near Phaistos.

Gilliéron's expertise was also employed that year at Tiryns, where Kurt Müller, of the German Archaeological Institute at Athens, found what Evans reported was "a heap of fresco fragments in a style almost exactly corresponding with that of the latest Palace period at Knossos," but, he observed, "[showing] a distinct divergence from the Minoan costume." This suggested to him that "the 'Mycenaeans' of the mainland represented an allied, but independent, element distinguished by certain national traits of their own from the people of contemporary Crete." The first Tiryns frescoes showed a life-size procession of warriors—unthinkable in Crete—and a miniature scene with dogs chasing wild boars as women looked on from their chariots, the latter recalling

Atalanta in the famed Calydonian boar hunt, described in the *Iliad* (9:529–99).[35] These could be read like illustrations to Homer, depicting his Achaeans, lords of Mycenae; Homer didn't place them in Crete until the very end of the Bronze Age, which proved to Evans that "the theory that the late Minoan civilization of Crete was an importation of 'Mycenaean,' or even Achaean conquerors [as Ridgeway persistently argued] thus loses whatever basis it ever had."[36]

Evans had another chance to argue his case for Minoan hegemony and the importance of Aegean archaeology when he accepted the presidency of the Hellenic Society in London upon Percy Gardner's retirement in April 1911. Evans agreed to the honorable duty "with considerable hesitation," as he confessed in his presidential address a year later: "I imagine that my presence in this Chair is due to a feeling on its part that what may be called the embryological department has its place among our studies." Standing before Britain's foremost classical scholars, Evans fought against the intellectual preference for "fruit over roots," stating, "The truth is that the old view of Greek civilization as a kind of '*enfant de miracle*' can no longer be maintained." Playing with the theme of origins, made fashionable by the recent announcement that the skull and ape-like jaw of the oldest European had been found in a ditch at Piltdown, near Lewes in Sussex—a British triumph of paleontology that stood for the next fifty years until it was proven a hoax[37]—Evans listed what he believed were the Minoan and Mycenaean origins for concepts generally associated with classical Greece. "I told them with pious unction," he wrote in a lighthearted vein to Charles Bell at the Ashmolean, "that Homer, properly speaking, was a translator, and that part of an illustrated edition of his original had lately come to light in Crete and Mycenae. In short, he worked up an older Minoan Epic and was after all somewhat of a 'literary dog.' "[38] Evans produced battle and hunt scenes from Minoan and Mycenaean art, which he read as scenes from the *Iliad* and *Odyssey*, then argued for a bilingual population in Greece able to translate from the original "Minoan Epos," as illustrated by the Cretan seals, into the Greek language of the Achaeans. This argument was necessitated by his belief that the language of the Knossos tablets could not be Greek: "To me at least the view that the Eteocretan population, who preserved their own language down to the third century before our era, spoke Greek in a remote prehistoric age is repugnant to the plainest dictates of common sense," he avowed. Evans defended his view that "the 'Mycenaean' is only a provincial variant of the same 'Minoan' civilization," arguing that the modifications in costume and the need for a fixed hearth were due to "a tendency among the newcomers [Cretans in Greece] to adapt themselves to the somewhat rougher climatic conditions . . . in this mainland plantation" in the Greek Peloponnese.[39] How his colleagues received such views is not recorded, but the public continued to respond favorably to Evans's imaginative reconstruction and rewarded him in the traditional British manner with a knighthood, bestowed during the Coronation Honours of King George V in 1911.

In 1912, Sir Arthur Evans was invited to stand for election as president of the Society of Antiquaries, an honor his father had held, but he pleaded overwork. Besides his duties to archaeology and Knossos, Evans had revived his old allegiance to the Serbs to assist them in their struggle for independence from the Ottoman Empire during the latest, most volatile stage of the Balkan conflict.

Westernized Turkish intellectuals, in a last-ditch effort to save the Porte, had joined forces with disgruntled military officers in July 1908 and staged a revolt in the Macedonian city of Salonika (modern Thessaloniki) against the Sultan Abd al-Hamid II, who had revoked the constitution. The sultan quickly ceded political power to these Young Turks, as the revolutionaries were known, retaining only a constitutional monarchy, but the resulting instability triggered a chain reaction beginning when Bulgaria declared its independence. Then Austria annexed Bosnia and Herzegovina, an illegal act designed to keep Bosnia from forming an alliance with Serbia, which was promoting a Yugo (southern) -slav federation; meanwhile the heir to the Habsburg throne, Archduke Franz Ferdinand, made it known that he favored an Austro-Hungarian Empire composed of a federation of national states, some of which would be Slav. The archduke was indulging proponents of the Pan-Slav movement, a cause that explored the common cultural heritage of the Slavs in eastern and east-central Europe and looked to the Russian Slavs for protection from their Austro-Hungarian and Turkish lords. Reading the daily newspapers must have given Evans a strange sense of déjà vu.

In September 1908, the Cretan Assembly declared its desire for union with Greece and its allegiance to King George I of the Hellenes. Fearing the wrath of both Constantinople and the Great Powers, the Greek Parliament rejected the Cretans' request, and the caretaker government in Crete resigned in 1909. A group of young officers in Greece, unhappy with their government's rejection of the Cretan demands, formed the Military League, which crippled the Greek Parliament until they summoned Venizelos to Athens to form a new government, which he did in September 1910. Venizelos proved to be such a popular leader that he was returned in the general elections of March 1912 with a five-sixths majority. This enabled him to reform the armed forces and establish cordial diplomatic links with Greece's Balkan neighbors Serbia and Bulgaria, which had secretly united to form a Balkan Alliance against Turkey (distracted at the time by the Italian invasion of Libya in 1911). Then, in the summer of 1912, Italy occupied Rhodes, Kos, and the ten other islands of the southeastern Aegean—the "Dodecanese."

Confident in the power of the new Greece and her allies, and the weak position of the pasha, Venizelos annexed Crete on Monday, October 14, 1912. Three days later Turkey declared war on the Balkan Alliance, and by the end of the week Greece entered what became known as the First Balkan War. In less than a month Greeks had marched into Salonika, hours before a Bulgarian division tried to claim the coveted Macedonian capital city, a major source of contention between the two nations. In a public lecture at the end of November, Evans proclaimed his astonishment "that Greek and Bulgarian should at last work together, and that rivalries and animosities of centuries should have been set aside in favour of joint action" that in a little more than a month had "changed the whole political configuration of the Balkan Peninsula." The "smiter of pashas" gloated: "An empire which has gone on for over five centuries has been deprived of its European provinces . . . by the small powers joined in an alliance which a few weeks ago must have been undreamt of by those who thought they knew the Balkan country and the Balkan people most thoroughly."[40]

When a truce was called and peace talks began in London in December 1912, Evans entertained Venizelos and the other Balkan delegates at Youlbury, where they discussed the common dream of independent Balkan states freed from Turkish rule. One dream was realized when the pasha ceded Crete to Greece with the signing of the Treaty of London to end the hostilities at the end of May 1913, but Evans's astonished disbelief at Bulgarian cooperation was justified in June, when Bulgaria deployed its armies to the west and launched an attack on Greece and Serbia to get a bigger territorial share of the winnings. Both former allies maintained their new frontiers, but Turkey reacted quickly and took back much of the land Bulgaria had recently gained.

This Second Balkan War ended in July with Greece and Serbia both 50 percent larger, sharing what had been Macedonia under the Ottomans. The Bosnian Slavs were now even more eager to join the victorious Serbs in their movement to create Yugoslavia, so the Austrian governor invited Franz Ferdinand to Sarajevo to tour the province and explain his nationalist intentions. That was when the Black Hand, a secret Serbian terrorist organization formed by military officers in 1911 to liberate Serbs under Ottoman or Austro-Hungarian rule, put a rapid end to the archduke's aspirations with his assassination on June 28, 1914. Austria declared war on Serbia a month later, which brought in Russia and her European ally, France. Germany joined Austria and set out to invade France, which had formed the Triple Entente with Great Britain and Russia in 1907. When Germany announced its intention to invade France by marching through Belgian Flanders on August 4, Britain entered the struggle, which spread to Asia and Africa and became the greatest war in history.

Archaeology in the Midst of Armageddon

Evans, who had never borne arms and was far too myopic and, at the age of sixty-three, too old for military service, joined the conflict on his terms and fought his own battles in the way he knew best. He accepted the presidency of the Society of Antiquaries in 1914 and his first duty was to send a fiery dispatch to the *Times*, published on September 1. On behalf of the Antiquarians, the Royal Academy, the British Academy, the Royal Institute of British Architects, the Society for the Protection of Ancient Buildings, the National Trust, and the Art Workers Guild, Evans protested against "the wholesale destruction wrought by the German troops, methodically and by superior orders, of ancient and beautiful buildings, libraries, institutions of learning, and works of art at Louvain, Malines, and other Belgian cities," with their overzealous use of bombardments, which, Evans asserted, went "beyond the ordinary license of warlike operations." He was particularly saddened to note that "thanks to the perfection of the new engines of destruction . . . the Cathedral of Rheims, 'the Parthenon of France,' " was lost in "the havoc . . . carried out to a degree hitherto unknown in the world's history." Evans restricted his venom, however, for the German armed forces. Against a consensus growing in favor of striking German and Austrian fellows from the rolls of British academic institutions, Evans, as president of the Antiquaries, reminded his members, "who stand on the neutral ground of science," that they "have not ceased to share a common task with those who to-day are our enemies," and who tomorrow "shall once more be labourers together in the same historic field."[41] Even in the darkest moments of the war, Evans resisted joining in the hysteria against German scholars and nationals.

At Youlbury, Evans erected a wooden watchtower 150 feet high with four flagpoles at the corners for each of the Allies, and when one of them reported a victory, he raised their national colors in tribute. Candy recalled that each morning at eleven o'clock Evans would go down to the kitchen, where the only phone in the house was (Evans rarely used the telephone, preferring instead the Victorian art of written correspondence), and stand on a crate to speak to the editor of the *Manchester Guardian* for news of the war. Since there was no radio, those who lived in view of Youlbury could, by reading the signals on Boars Hill, follow the Allies' progress a day earlier than those who waited for the newspapers.[42]

Evans concentrated his war effort on two fronts: the Slav bid for independent states, and what he believed was the preservation of civilization itself in the face of barbarism. On the former, Evans sheltered Tomáš Masaryk, who later became the first president of Czechoslovakia, during his exile from Moravia in 1915. One of the greatest leaders of the Pan-Slav movement, Masaryk, who was affiliated with the underground Czech liberation movement, was looking for French and British support to help restore Bohemia's independence, to establish a Czechoslovak state, to dismember the Austro-Hungarian Empire along ethnic lines, and to establish new nation-states between Germany and Russia as a cordon sanitaire drawn around the infection of German imperialism. Masaryk found a warm reception at Youlbury and a sympathetic ear in Evans, who championed his objectives in Whitehall and hosted clandestine meetings between the Slavs and influential members of the British Foreign Office. Candy recalled that groups of men dressed in dark suits and overcoats showed up at Youlbury close to midnight and crept into the library, where they spoke "foreign" and English until the early morning, "all very mysterious cloak and dagger stuff."[43] The meetings were part of the private negotiations for the April 1915 "Secret" Treaty of London, which brought Italy into the conflict on the side of the Allies in exchange for the promise of northern Dalmatia—but not the other Slav territories, which the Italians desired but Evans fought hard to keep independent.

In an extreme show of Balkan solidarity, Evans traveled across France in July 1917 and sailed from Marseilles to Corfu, one of the western Greek isles, where the Serbian government-in-exile was located. Evans arrived with the Yugoslav Committee, a London group comprising Serbs, Croats, and Slovenes, who, together with the exiled Serbs, declared their intentions for national unity and independence from Austria. And, as the war dragged on and the Austrians became desperate in their shortage of manpower, Evans made Youlbury's woodlands and scouting facilities available to hundreds of young boys fleeing the draft in Serbia and Montenegro.

Evans's second front was fought in the British Museum, where he was an ex officio trustee as president of the Antiquaries. As the war meant a cut in public expenditure, Evans directed his rage against what he felt were the tactics of bullies in the War Office. "The old idea on which civilized States have hitherto rested, that no mean function of the prowess of the fighting forces was to maintain the continuity of research, seems to have been thrown over by those who govern us," went his report to the Antiquaries in April 1918, after the galleries in the British Museum were closed to save money—enough to the British Treasury, as Evans calculated, for "three minutes of the War." The Air Board tried to requisition the building for their headquarters, but "against this proposal to make the Museum the seat of a Combatant Department and a legitimate butt for German bombs," Evans, as he reported, "raised a general storm of indignation throughout the Press and among the general public," as only he could, in what was called "a nine days' wonder"; the Air Board occupied the Savoy Hotel instead.[44] Nonetheless, civilian departments of government were moved into the galleries, which had to be hastily cleared, "to the final undoing of the work of a century and half." Evans warned, "The mushroom bureaucracy that is now springing up in every direction will stay if it can, and of the multiplication of public offices and 'Boards of Control' there seems to be no end." But he was most enraged by the way that the universities were being treated by

> those who control our Administration . . . [who are] inspired with a Philistine spirit for which we shall in vain seek a parallel among civilized Governments. Ruthless proscription, the result of panic action, threatens at every turn the very sanctuaries of learning. Those who represent its interests are doubtless a very inferior race in the eyes of politicians. We are not concerned to dispute their

verdict, but it is well to remind these that even the lowest tribes of savages are left their reservations.[45]

When the British Association met in Newcastle in 1916, Evans as president shared his anxieties and aspirations about the future of his branch of science:

Archaeology—the research of ancient civilizations—when the very foundations of our own are threatened by the New Barbarism! The investigation of the ruins of the Past—at a time when Hell seems to have been let loose to strew our Continent with havoc beyond the dreams of Attila! "The Science of the Spade"—at a moment when that Science confronts us at every hour with another and sterner significance! The very suggestion of such a subject of discourse might seem replete with irony.

But he defended archaeology "in the midst of Armageddon," because, he said, "it draws our minds from present anxieties to that still, passionless domain of the Past which lies beyond the limits even of historic controversies." Prehistory, to Evans, represented an undeniable continuum because it was built up stratigraphically, like geological layers, which could be checked and rechecked by excavation. "Thus evoked, moreover, the Past is often seen to hold a mirror to the Future—correcting wrong impressions—the result of some temporary revolution in the whirligig of Time—by the more permanent standard of abiding conditions, and affording in the solid evidence of the past well-being the 'substance of things hoped for.' " He cited the case of Serbia's great history as revealed by archaeological exploration, which formed the basis for the modern Serbs' nationalist aspirations.

But Evans's greatest concern was for the advancement of science through education, to ensure that "the lighted torch handed down to us from the Ages shall be passed on with a still brighter flame," for which, he advocated, "Let us go forward with our own tasks, unflinchingly seeking for the Truth, confident that, in the eternal dispensation, each successive generation of seekers may approach nearer to the goal."[46] Evans never doubted the existence of absolute truth and his role in its revelation. He believed that the revelation of knowledge was linear and that what he proved to be the case became the next step in an ascending process leading to wisdom, which made others' opinions needless and basically incorrect.

In the Mediterranean, Evans's colleagues carried out their duties with equal flair. In theory, Greece was neutral for much of the war but, in practice, King Constantine I supported the Central Powers and made life difficult for officials from Allied nations, who were busy either spying, like Dawkins, who returned to eastern Crete as a lieutenant in the Royal Navy to monitor Germany's latest weapon—the submarine—or actively engaged on Allied ships, like Myres, who took to the war more like a heroic figure from Homer's *Iliad* than a commander in the Royal Navy. The British novelist Compton Mackenzie, who served with Myres aboard the S.V. *Aulis*, once Prince George's private yacht and now chartered by the Royal Navy to gather Turkish intelligence, grumbled in his memoirs that Myres's "Assyrian" beard and Oxford professorship allowed him "a wider latitude than any temporary officer in the Eastern Mediterranean," which, combined with his cattle raids along the Turkish coast, familiar from his surveys in 1893, earned him the nickname "Blackbeard of the Aegean."[47] Myres's tendency "to change abruptly from a pirate into a don," Mackenzie lamented, made him the bane of many a professional sailor's existence. Hogarth, who in 1911 initiated the excavations at Carchemish, the great Hittite trading city on the Euphrates River in northern Syria, joined British intelligence at the outbreak of the war and controlled a band of young operatives in the Arab revolt against Ottoman rule, the most famous of whom was his protégé and assistant T. E. Lawrence, to whom he had become a mentor at Oxford. Lawrence played a major role in implementing Hogarth's dreams of Arab independence and unity. Another protégé was Leonard Woolley, a graduate of New College, Oxford, who had interned with Evans at the Ashmolean, worked under Hogarth at Carchemish, where he later took charge, and then served with him in Cairo. Woolley's memoirs illustrate how war service brought out a new appreciation for the archaeologist, whom he felt the general public regarded as a "ridiculous dryasdust" as "old as the pots which he unearths"—an opinion that was certainly held by officers of the British Army, who described Woolley and Lawrence as "doddering greybeards from the British Museum."[48]

The philologist J. C. Lawson, a fellow of Pembroke College, Cambridge, monitored Allied intelligence in Crete and was at the heart of one of modern Greece's most volatile transitions, the revolution that deposed King Constantine I and brought Greece into the war.[49] Venizelos, a keen advocate of Greek support for the Allies, confronted King Constantine about his sentiments and spurious stance of neutrality. A popular prime minister, Venizelos resigned twice in 1915; then, in 1916, with covert Allied help, detailed in Lawson's memoirs, he established a rival government in Salonika, until the Allies ousted the king in June 1917 and placed Venizelos as the head of a much divided nation. With the promise of territory for Greece on the Turkish Aegean coast once the Allies defeated the Central Powers, Venizelos brought Greece into the war on the side of the Entente in 1917.

In Athens, Alan Wace, another fellow of Pembroke, succeeded Dawkins as director of the British School at Athens in 1914. Described by Compton Mackenzie as "a tall slim man full of nervous energy, with a fresh complexion and an extraordinarily merry pair of light blue eyes,"[50] Wace had a solid grounding in the classics when he chose to study archaeology in 1901, the year that William Ridgeway's *Early Age of Greece* was published with the theory that so enraged Evans. "No one can deny the tremendous influence that Ridgeway's personality and methods exercised on his pupils," Wace admitted years later. Ridgeway taught them "not to be satisfied with superficial conclusions . . . to go back as far as possible to the first authority," which for the archaeologist was the artifact itself. They learned "the use of anthropological parallels, the value of self-criticism, detestation of humbug, caution against plausible theories, and the necessity of first collecting the evidence and then determining what conclusions can logically be drawn from it. Finally, if controversy were to arise they were counseled to reserve a few shots in the locker, so as to complete the discomfiture of the adversary if he were rash enough to reply."[51] Wace took the professor's lessons to heart and became a fervent practitioner of Ridgeway's methods as well as a staunch supporter of "Ridgewayism," opposing adherents of what became known as Evans's "Pan-Minoan" school. But Evans respected Wace's expertise, initially, and, as the British School's director, Wace in frequent correspondence kept Evans informed of personalities and events in Greece.

"He is unpractical, obstinate and sensitive," Wace wrote to Evans in March 1915 about Duncan Mackenzie, who was living in destitution in Athens.[52] Mackenzie had been hired by the London-based Palestine Exploration Fund to conduct excavations at a tell site near Jerusalem in 1910, but by 1912 he had so displeased his employers with his disdain for keeping accounts and writing reports that they had dismissed him. He then worked in the Sudan for a year and wound up in Athens unemployed at the outbreak of the war. Evans tried to coax him back to

Youlbury, not only because he commiserated with his old friend's situation but also because he needed his help preparing the Knossos publication. Mackenzie still hoped to find permanent work away from Evans, but his reputation as "a creature of moods and fancies," as Wace put it, had made him unemployable, and so eventually he gave in and returned to work for Evans.

In the same letter of March 1915, Wace told Evans about "one Gordon Childe, an Australian from Queen's and a pupil of Myres," in Greece during the Easter vacation for the first time. Destined to become one of the guiding lights of twentieth-century archaeology, Childe, as an undergraduate, was "doing Prehistoric Archaeology for Ethnological questions," Wace reported of him. "I sent him to Crete where he spent five days at Candia & Cnossus & saw today he is off to Nauplia, Tiryns, Argos & Mycenae. Then after Easter I am going to send him to Chaeronea and Thebes for two days & then he will have to dash back to Oxford. He seems keen and intelligent and I hope it will be possible for him to come out here later on, especially if we can do a prehistoric dig in Macedonia." Born in 1892, Childe read classics at Sydney University in 1911–14, where he came under the influence of a professor who directed him to the works of Hegel, Marx, and Engels and spurred his involvement in the labor movement. Childe was a confirmed socialist when he entered Queen's College, Oxford, in 1914 to read for the diploma in classical archaeology under John Myres's tutelage. He joined the Oxford Fabians (which became the Socialist Society in 1915) and was outspoken in his left-wing views until graduation in 1917, when he refused the draft and returned to Australia. The nickname "Handsome Childe," earned at Oxford, no doubt derided "his blue nose, like that of Cyrano de Bergerac," which, to Max Mallowan, made him "the ugliest man I ever met, indeed painful to look at."[53]

Childe was an outspoken opponent of the Great War and resisted forced conscription in Australia, which made a teaching post there out of the question. He joined the Industrial Workers of the World, and became the intellectual force behind its New South Wales chapter. (The "Wobblies" had been founded in the United States in 1907 to promote Marxist philosophy to laborers and to fight capitalism.) The transition from philosophical theory to political practice for the socialists took a giant step forward in October 1917, when the Bolsheviks, the hard-line faction of the Russian Social Democratic Labour Party led by Lenin, began the violent revolution in Petrograd that established the first government of the workers' councils, or "soviets," in Russia. "The shot heard around the world," as the first discharge came to be known, couldn't fail to impress the new generation of archaeologists, and when archaeological excavations resumed after the war, Gordon Childe and many of his generation set out to expose a very different set of historical precedents to explain their new perception of the world, vastly altered from that of their tutors.

The Bolsheviks took Russia out of the war when they signed an armistice with Germany in November 1917, allowing the Germans to mount a serious offensive against Paris in early 1918. But the arrival of re-enforcements from the United States, which declared war on Germany in 1917 after the latter's unrestricted use of submarines sank much neutral shipping, provided the Allies with the additional manpower of more than one million fresh troops to withstand the final German push. Nonetheless, the invaders came to within fifty kilometers of Paris—a tense time for all who watched the flags over Youlbury. Nationalist uprisings, inspired by the success of Russia's Bolsheviks, spread throughout the Austro-Hungarian Empire and weakened its armed forces, which included a significant number of Serbs. The war ended suddenly, soon after the Austrian army collapsed at the Adriatic port of Fiume in late October 1918, and the Allies quickly recovered most of German-occupied France and Belgium; popular unrest in Germany forced Kaiser Wilhelm II to abdicate, and Germany's generals signed an armistice with the Allies on November 11, formally ending the first great war of the twentieth century.

The armistice marked the beginning of many territorial disputes that arose as the Austro-Hungarian Empire disintegrated and the east European nations scrambled to define their frontiers. Evans saw the immediate threat of Italian imperialism on the Adriatic at Fiume, where, in December 1918, fresh Italian troops arrived to occupy what Britain and France had agreed in the secret Treaty of London was to be part of the new state of Jugo-Slavia. "A single spark may now create a conflagration which would spread from the Carinthian Alps to the borders of Albania and Greece," threatened Evans in a long letter to the *Manchester Guardian* on December 26. In a second letter two days later he pointed out that the French and British governments, in an attempt to placate Italy, censored their home press by not allowing the truth of the situation to be printed in the major newspapers. Both polemics were translated into French and made available to delegates to the peace conference in Paris, where Evans and Hogarth rushed to take part in the feeding frenzy of the victorious nations as they divided the spoils and set about trying to piece together the new map of Europe and the Middle East.[54]

Hogarth was the British commissioner in charge of Arab claims, while Evans worked behind the scenes as an unofficial delegate on the side of the Slavs. It was his forceful lobbying of Arthur Balfour, who had been British prime minister from 1902 to 1905 and was now foreign secretary, which finally swayed Lloyd George's ruling conservative British government to change its mind from supporting their Italian allies' claim to the southern Dalmatian coast to favoring the Slavic cause, thus forcing Italy to withdraw her troops.

The Paris delegates signed the Treaty of Versailles exactly five years after the assassination in Sarajevo. In theory it was a peace treaty, but in practice it was a cruel and vengeful document designed to castigate Germany and Austria by stipulating impossible terms of repayment for Allied war losses, and it ensured that hostility between the belligerent nations persisted into what should have been a period of reconciliation, as Evans found when he traveled overland to Stockholm in 1920 to receive the Great Gold Medal of the Swedish Society of Anthropology and Geography. He sensed that old friends in Germany were still willing, as scholars, to collaborate in research, but that friendship was not possible.[55]

The negotiations for the Slavic homeland dragged on fitfully into late 1920 when the Treaty of Rapallo finally established the new Jugo-Slavia. It was a rewarding, though exhausting, process for Evans, who was determined for the Slavs to triumph, even though their own leaders were often in discord. "The atmosphere of committee room and Council Chamber was always repugnant to Evans," Joan Evans recorded, "and the greed of nations horrified his moral sense as much as the geographical ignorance of politicians shocked his intellect."[56]

At Youlbury, Evans was "haunted by the memory of the boys who had once made holiday there, and would come no more," Joan Evans recalled. To men like Arthur Shepherd, the first Youlbury scoutmaster, killed in France, Evans built a semicircular seat with a sundial in the middle set to Summer Time and inscribed with: *Horas non numero nisi serenas* (I count the sunny hours) and the dedication:

In loving memory of a youthful band
Who played as children
Among these woods and heaths,

And shared, at Youlbury, in joyous hours:
In the Great War
For their country's sake and for mankind,
They fell before their time:
But, wherever they now lie,
Here they are never far.

For the pillars at the sides of the bench Evans wrote:

>   Not for their mother land alone
> Their youth, their love, their life they spent,
> The glorious halo round their brows
>   Shines in a wider firmament:
>   Theirs was a loftier sacrifice,
> For after years and all mankind,
> That for the Nations, as with Men,
>   Faith and humanity should bind:

> They fought that wars themselves should cease,
>   And *they* have entered into Peace.[57]

One of Evans's last duties as president of the Antiquaries was to attend the presentation ceremony at Stonehenge when this legendary property was given by its owner, Mr. C. H. E. Chubb, to the British nation in 1919. Evans used the occasion to offer his latest interpretation of the celebrated stone circle as a British Bronze Age grave-marker, adding, "At a time when so many of us are preoccupied with the memorials of our own dead on so many foreign fields this aspect of Stonehenge may be felt to have a solemn significance and the re-entrustment at such a moment to the guardianship of the nation of this great monument of remote predecessors must be recognized as singularly opportune."[58] Evans praised "the liberal and patriotic action of the donor" and began to reconsider his own ancient monument, now that his war duties had lapsed. He revised his notes for the annual meeting of the British Association at Bournemouth in September 1919 and read there a paper on "The Palace of Minos and the Prehistoric Civilization of Crete."[59]

Evans had intended to publish the results of the Knossos excavations as "The Nine Minoan Periods," but, as the goose-quill pen described the parallels for his finds throughout Crete and the Aegean and he drew on the results of others' work to fill the historical gaps at Knossos, the text became less of an excavation report than a synthesis of Minoan civilization as he saw it, which revolved around "The Palace of Minos," the title he settled on with George Macmillan, who agreed to publish the book at his own expense and split the profits (a first for Evans, who had paid for the printing of all his previous works). Evans insisted that the type be set at Oxford University Press, so that he could be in close contact with the printers, a convenience that Macmillan eventually regretted when, due to Evans's "sublime disregard for the cost of corrections," as Joan Evans recounted, "he not only corrected but rewrote" page proofs, driving the cost of alterations alone to £2,300, well beyond the original cost of typesetting.[60]

When *The Palace of Minos: A Comparative Account of the Successive Stages of the Early Cretan Civilization as Illustrated by the Discoveries at Knossos* appeared in 1921, it drew a mixed response. Bosanquet wrote a lyrical appraisal of Evans's "comparative account . . . which furnishes the European culture of to-day with the title deeds going back to the fourth millennium B.C.," praising his handling of "a great theme and beset with difficulty, but the author has gifts that fit him to act as guide through this labyrinth." He concluded eloquently, "The threads that archaeology has put in Sir Arthur Evans' hands are of necessity tangled, faded and broken; yet his learning and intuition have enabled him to weave them into a coherent whole that is almost history."[61] Hogarth, in the *Times Literary Supplement*, on the other hand, admonished Evans for "combining narrative and description with speculation," suggesting that it should have been two books; one of fact and one of fancy, and ending with a penetrating observation: "The limitations of archaeology are galling. It collects phenomena, but hardly ever can isolate them so as to interpret scientifically; it can frame any number of hypotheses, but rarely, if ever, scientifically prove." But, Hogarth conceded, "if any archaeologist is to pass the bounds of his science into the domain of speculative history, we had rather it were Sir Arthur Evans than another. He does it with an infectious enthusiasm, and his immense comparative knowledge tells us so many things by the way."[62]

Evans never felt that he was doing anything other than writing history where there had been none, and in *The Palace of Minos* he took the Minoan story up to the sack of the first palace at Knossos at the end of what he called the Middle Minoan III period, when, he suggested, the wealth of Knossos was carried off to fill the tombs of the mainland chiefs in the grave circle at Mycenae, thus explaining the Minoan manufacture of the finest works of movable art found at Mycenae, which were largely absent from Crete. The great palace of the Late Minoan I and II periods was promised for the next volume.

The Helladic Heresy

The same year that *The Palace of Minos* decreed Evans's "orthodox view" of the first half of the Greek Bronze Age, the modest publication of Carl Blegen's *Korakou*, the results of American excavations on a small tell near modern Corinth, in the Peloponnese, showed how far Ridgeway's "Mycenaean independence movement" had progressed during the war years under the leadership of one of his brightest disciples. Wace, as director of the British School at Athens, should have initiated a large field project but the war stopped that. Instead, he assisted Carl Blegen, secretary of the American School of Classical Studies at Athens, on his excavations at the small hillock called Korakou in 1915 and 1916.

Blegen, born in Minnesota in 1887, schooled in the classics and with a 1910 Ph.D. from Yale, believed that the Mycenaean site they uncovered at Korakou was Homer's "wealthy Ephyra." The period when it had been built (the "silver age," as they described it) came before the great days of Mycenae and Tiryns, and was characterized by a decorative pottery style, which they called "Ephyraean" and tried to explain in terms of local initiative under the minor influence of Cretan decorative styles. Blegen and Wace found evidence for well-stratified periods, and this gave them sound reason to suspect Schliemann's periods at Mycenae. Wace was eager to test their new theories with new fieldwork at Mycenae, but as the war intensified he was seconded to the British Legation in Athens as director of relief for British refugees from Turkey, and he couldn't take leave to excavate. Instead, he reinvestigated Schliemann's finds from Mycenae in the National Museum in Athens and, with Blegen, published a revolutionary paper in 1918 entitled "The Pre-Mycenaean Pottery of the Mainland," a work whose primary aim was to give Greece a pottery-based, relative chronology comparable to Evans's and Mackenzie's Minoan periods.

Blegen and Wace proposed "Helladic" as a Greek mainland equivalent to "Minoan," and "Cycladic" for the islands. Evans bridled at the suggestion that his "Minoan" terminology should be localized to Crete, and positively reared up in anger at their proposition that "the glory of Tiryns and Mycenae was the climax of prehistoric art on the mainland of Greece," which they called Mycenaean. They conceded this was "the fruit of the cultivated Cretan graft set on the wild stock of the mainland," but added that "the underlying mainland element influenced the dominant Minoan art so as to make it Mycenaean as opposed to Cretan."[63] This was pure Ridgewayism, but it was supported by concrete archaeological evidence in the form of well-stratified pottery, which Evans had to respect, so when Wace was freed of his embassy duties in November 1919, Evans intervened on his behalf with the British School, whose committee wanted to put their resources into a classical excavation, and used his seniority to convince them of the urgency and importance of Wace's long-standing desire to re-open the excavations at Mycenae, "in view of the great discoveries in Crete which have thrown an entirely new light on the origin and development of the Mycenaean civilization."[64] I think it was less the case that Evans was open-minded than that he fully expected Wace to confirm the Knossos stratigraphy at Mycenae.

Blegen's *Korakou* also displayed the new spirit in which young archaeologists were searching the past:

Agamemnon and his noble peers have long enjoyed the prominence that was their due; now light is shed on the conditions of the life of the humble commoner—the nameless τις ["someone"] of the Homeric poems, who with his fellows formed the bulk of the population and rendered Agamemnon's glory possible. We have recovered his modest house, though its clay walls have long since fallen away. We can picture him conducting his household worship about the pillar in his megaron. We have seen his simple bed, raised but slightly above the earthen floor. We have found the storage jars in which he kept his oil and grain; the quern on which he ground his flour; the hearth where he prepared his food; the vessels in which he cooked; and the dishes from which he ate his meals, and the cup from which he drank his wine. And in the disorder of his abandoned house we may recognize the haste with which he fled before that mysterious peril which, under the name of the Dorian Invasion, we believe engulfed his waning civilization.[65]

A new myth was emerging in archaeology, a glorification of the common laborer, like some sort of prehistoric noble savage. The archaeology of the commoner was part of the exaltation of the common worker as the backbone of society, which reflected the success of the Bolshevik Revolution in Russia and the growing appeal of socialism in Europe and North America.

Wace went to Mycenae in the spring of 1920 to initiate a program of "wall analysis" throughout the site comparable to what Evans had done at Knossos. By June he was able to report conclusively in the *Times Literary Supplement* that the sunken shaft graves beneath the Royal Grave Circle, where Schliemann thought he had gazed upon the gold mask of Agamemnon, were earlier than the vaulted, circular stone tholos tombs, for example the Treasury of Atreus, and he believed that the earliest burials in the shaft graves were those of an indigenous Helladic dynasty, which he placed much earlier in time than the great Homeric palace on the slope above them. The palace, he suggested, with the "best known monuments of Mycenae, the Lion Gate, the massive Cyclopean wall of the acropolis and the Royal Grave Circle marking the earlier shaft graves may well have been built, if we may assume that the ancient Greek legends contain a kernel of historic truth, by the princes of the dynasty which culminated with Agamemnon."[66]

Evans retorted three weeks later in the same newspaper: "With the exception of some insignificant native pottery almost every single article found in the tombs can now be thrown back to Minoan sources belonging to the close of the Middle Minoan Age," for which he hypothesized that the shaft graves were those of Minoan dynasts who had occupied the great palace during the Late Minoan I period. But Wace had shown that the palace and the great Treasury of Atreus and the other Mycenaean tholos tombs were almost three hundred years later than the shaft graves by finding pottery shards in Late Helladic III styles under threshold blocks and in the walls. Evans cautioned him "that sherds of pottery have a curious way of working in between blocks," and that the "disturbance due to later treasure seekers," a reference to Schliemann's excavation techniques, should be taken into account.[67]

Evans was indeed enraged by Wace's reports, and he sent copies of these with his reply to George Karo, the German scholar who had reinvestigated Schliemann's shaft graves at Mycenae and published a study of them in masterly detail, to elicit his support. But Karo replied:

I cannot agree with "Minoan dynasts at Mycenae," or elsewhere on the mainland. My theory is: 1) indigenous stock, Early and Middle Helladic, 2) towards the close of M M III (chronologically) immigration of a powerful, warlike, gifted, but primitive race, "Achaeans" or whatever you choose to call them. Occupation of the Peloponnesus, building of the Mycenaean palace after successful raids had provided the chiefs with plunder and slaves (including artists) from Crete: these raids . . . may account for the burning of the palaces of Knossos and Phaistos. But Minoan power was by no means broken, the invaders promptly expelled, a renascence follows these raids, Minoan civilization rules over them, as it usually does in such cases, but not Minoan military or political power. This theory explains the diversity of the finds from the Shaft Tombs, the differences in architecture, dress, cult (no chapels or sacred caves!), the absence of written documents or signets which would be incomprehensible if the dynasties were Minoan.[68]

Karo's view echoed that of archaeologists excavating on the Greek mainland, and it showed just how wide the rift had grown between those who subscribed to Evans's model of Minoan hegemony over the Aegean and those who favored the concept of independent local development.

Fresh from the council tables of Paris and the success of the Pan-Slavic movement, Evans pursued his ideal of a Minoan political unity based on shared principles of a common cultural heritage, and he did so with such single-minded determination that his critics called his vision the "Pan-Minoan school." As Evans began to lobby scholars the way he had lobbied politicians, the debate over national, or cultural, boundaries became the main theme of Aegean research in the era following the war, and it continues to divide the field of archaeology as much as it does modern nations.

The Minotaur's Lair

Mackenzie returned to Crete in September 1920 to find the Palace of Knossos "a perfect wilderness of weeds a meter high. This was true of the whole Palace with the exception of the covered part of the Domestic Quarter, and the Queen's Megaron, owing to its roof-pavement of

Maltese slabs, [which] was quite intact," he reported to Evans. Mackenzie blamed Hazzidakis, who was responsible for Knossos, while the sites elsewhere "are in quite good order." The union with Greece in 1913 had brought Cretan antiquities under Greek archaeological law, and the Greek government assumed responsibility for the protection of important ancient sites. Two ephorates, or offices, were established: one covered the Candia (now Herakleion) Museum and Knossos, with Hazzidakis in charge; the other comprised the smaller collections created at Canea and Rethymnon and all the other ancient sites on the island, which were put under the control of Xanthoudides, who had been secretary of the Syllogos.

"I beg of you to refrain from writing about it for the present," Mackenzie cautioned Evans. "Wace has told me that, as proprietor of Knossos, you are according to Greek law entitled to half the finds so that in view of future plans to secure at least part of these nothing should be meanwhile done to put people's backs up."[69] But Hazzidakis had other ideas, as Mackenzie's next letter reported:

> Hajidaki's visit to the Palace was somewhat distressing. He began by trying to bluff me but as he asked whether Wace had said anything at Athens about the condition of the Palace I told him frankly that they reported it to be in a wretched state. He has, however, the old fixed idea that the Palace is no longer your property and that it reverted to the Cretan Government automatically some years ago. I told him you entirely did not hold that opinion and that as long as you hold your rights of property it was natural you should be interested in the condition of the remains apart from your archaeological rights.[70]

The union with Greece had brought what Joan Evans called "a too Hellenic patriotism" to Crete.[71] National monuments with a direct bearing on Greek history were coveted to the exclusion of all others, which reminded Evans of the extremes of his "classical" colleagues in Britain. He and Dawkins had fought to stop the nationalistic Cretans from pulling down the Venetian walls of Heraklion in the summer of 1918, which they saw as reminders of an occupying force and inhibitors to their economic growth. And now Evans resisted the attempt by the new Greek authority to take Knossos away from him: he had fought hard for it and wasn't going to give it up easily.

Preparations for the second volume of *The Palace of Minos* and Wace's conflicting results from Mycenae made it clear to Evans that he had more questions to ask of Knossos. He set out for Greece early in February 1922 to call in at Mycenae, Tiryns, and Thebes to examine for himself the examples of the "Mycenaean" script, as Wace called painted graffiti found on coarse stirrup jars. He concluded that there may have been a "dialectic difference in the language," but "the linguistic forms must have closely resembled that of Minoan Crete"[72]—an extraordinary conclusion which, considering that the language itself continued to elude him, could be neither proven nor rejected.

At Knossos, Evans and Mackenzie welcomed the architect Francis G. Newton, who had worked with the latter in Palestine and then gone to Egypt, and Piet de Jong, an artist born in Yorkshire to Dutch immigrants, who had trained at the Leeds School of Art and was a master at reconstructed drawings of artifacts and architecture. De Jong was also a keen observer of human nature and didn't hide his feelings—sometimes whimsical, other times caustic—about his colleagues, who included the most illustrious of the British and American excavators in Greece.[73]

Gregóri Antoniou returned to the Middle East to dig with Hogarth and then Woolley at Carchemish, so Ali Baritakis, a Bektash Muslim who had been Gregóri's right-hand man since the Knossos excavations began, and who was always asked to excavate the exceptionally difficult or delicate deposits because of his dexterity and sensitivity, assumed the foreman's duties.[74] Known as Ali Aga, he always wore the Ottoman Cretan costume of dark baggy trousers and matching waistcoat with a spotless white shirt and red sash at the waist. Piet de Jong affectionately recalled him as "quite a philosopher, a typical Turk in his love of the countryside, of trees, flowers, running water. He was a great admirer of the beauty of cloud formation. He explained his weather forecasts by the way the clouds warred with the winds."[75]

The first great dig campaign to inaugurate the "New Era" of excavations at Knossos was a long affair starting in mid-February and running through to the beginning of July. "By means of indications followed with singular *flair* by my foreman, Ali Baritakis," Evans happily reported to the *Times*, the season began with the discovery of a great outer bastion at the North Entrance, then other structures surrounding the main building. At the southeast corner of the Palace they dug down into a collapse of huge building blocks, some weighing more than a ton, which had been hurled from the palace façade into private houses at the end of the first palace period, around 1750 B.C. Within the debris, Evans found two large ox skulls, and he was beginning to formulate a theory of seismic destruction, making the connection between the skulls and Homer's epithet for Poseidon, "in bulls doth the earth-shaker delight," when, as if on command, an earthquake struck on April 20, centered between Crete and Santorini. "The Earth-Shaker does not seem to have been pleased with our clearance work," Evans wrote, "for just as the evidences of his former havoc were beginning to come out, a sharp shock, accompanied by a deep rumbling sound, was felt on the site."[76]

The shock gave Evans a new appreciation of nature's destructive force and a novel theory to explain the end of the first palace period, which he changed from "a dynastic revolution" to "the great earthquake at Knossos." He contacted the National Observatory in Athens for confirmation of the epicenter and to learn whether or not a volcanic eruption might not have similar consequences. The reply confirmed the quake but denied the link to volcanic eruptions.[77] The latter had become a possibility since 1909, when K. T. Frost, an imaginative young philologist at Queen's University, Belfast, launched a theory that the prehistoric eruption of the island of Santorini, also called Thera, brought about the end of the Cretan palaces and the subsequent "submergence" of Minoan civilization, and was at the root of the ancient Greek and Egyptian tales of the lost continent of Atlantis.[78] Frost's article in the Times received little notice and, though he published a more detailed version for scholars, he perished in the Great War, leaving no one to defend his case. Evans, on examining the pottery found by earlier explorers at Santorini, pointed out that, though it was executed under strong Cretan influence and even included pieces of Cretan manufacture, it was stylistically later than that in his "seismic deposits" at Knossos, and so it belonged to "a later ceramic phase than that represented by the filling in of the Knossian houses."[79] Evans thus dismissed the Cretan connection to Atlantis.

Near the "House of the Sacrificed Oxen," as the crushed building became known, the workmen dug down into a great vault about thirty feet deep going beneath the corner of the palace. "Here were no signs of human occupation," Evans told the Times, "but on the South side appeared the opening of an artificial cave, with three roughly cut steps leading down to what can only be described as a lair adapted for some great beast," he teased, adding "but here perhaps it is better for imagination to draw rein." However, Evans let his imagination roam further when he addressed the Antiquaries in London on his return in July: "Is it possible that lions . . . were kept for show [at Knossos]?" he asked his learned colleagues. Evans was certain that he had a found a monster's lair, and there was only one monster associated with the Knossian Labyrinth: "The traditions of such an usage—doubtless with other accretions," he suggested, "may well have contributed to the origin of the later tales of the Minotaur that haunted the site in historic times."[80]

A monster of a different sort soon raised its ugly head in the Aegean. Greek troops had landed at Ismir, ancient Smyrna, on Turkey's Aegean coast in May 1919 and claimed the lands promised by the Allies, who occupied Istanbul. At the same time, the Turkish war hero General Mustafa Kemal (Atatürk) landed at Samsun, on the Black Sea, and began the revolt against the sultan that led to the formation of the modern Turkish republic. Atatürk's nationalists attacked Smyrna in August 1922 and set fire to the port city, which resulted in the rapid evacuation of Greek forces, soon followed by one and a half million refugees: this completely changed the cultural makeup of modern Greece. The Asia Minor Disaster of 1922, as the defeat came to be known in Greece, was complete in January 1923 with the signing of the Treaty of Lausanne, whereby an exchange of populations was ordered. In Crete, roughly thirty thousand Christians from Turkey arrived to take the place and property of the thirty thousand Muslims who were forced to leave their homes. One man who was caught in the middle was Ali Aga. Evans and Mackenzie fought to try to keep him and his property intact, but their remonstrations with the British Embassy brought only the partial victory of allowing him to stay in Crete; he lost all of his land and died a few years later.

Evans and Mackenzie returned to Crete for four months of excavation and exploration in spring and summer 1923. Ali Aga was replaced in the field by Manoli, Evans's "Old Wolf," who, later generations reported, knew "as much about archaeology as Evans himself," given his close association with Knossos since the early excavations.[81]

They began the season with the continued exploration of the "Minotaur's lair," which they now recognized as an underground quarry, and the neighboring slopes on the south side of the Palace, which produced evidence for an ancient road arriving near the South Porch. But further exploration there was cut short and all subsequent fieldwork redirected to a new area because of the unexpected discovery of a great "heap" of decorated fresco fragments—enough to fill more than eighty, meter-long wooden trays—found in an unusual manner. Piet de Jong recalled:

> Sir Arthur became very enraged on hearing that a man had decided to build a tavern quite near to the entrance to the excavation near David's house. He had unfortunately for himself deposited several tons of tiles and bricks on the south side of the little path, whereas his site was to be on the north, on land which Sir Arthur had not been able to buy. He immediately called all the workmen off the dig and made them carry the material to the taverna for "safety" he said. He then locked it up, and over it hoisted a Union Jack. At the same time he started excavations on the man's land on the wager system. He found the frescoes and site now known as the House of the Frescoes. He could then of course confiscate the land or buy it at a very low price.

The House of the Frescoes produced wonderful paintings of "wild nature," Evans reported, "where blue birds appear here and there, amidst a wilderness of grotesque rocks overgrown with flowers and creepers." One species in particular surprised him, and he excitedly reported the identification of "apes of the *cercopithicus* genus, not found nearer than the Sudan," depicted so vividly that he felt the artist must have studied them at first hand. Equally impressed was de Jong, who used the little blue monkey in the Minoan painting as the theme for his wicked caricature of Evans, recalling Mackenzie's guarded references to his employer as "that monkey."[82]

Evans regaled the annual meeting of the British Association in the autumn with his new examples of Minoan art, and outlined his ideas about Crete as a stepping stone of early culture, suggesting that trade connections with Africa would be found where the road he had discovered leading south from the Palace ended up in the Mesara, which he promised to explore further.

Evans was excited about his work and showed no signs of slowing down the pace of excavation and exploration in Crete, so it must have come as a surprise to his colleagues when the *Times* of February 5,

The tiny Shrine of the Double-Axes, cleared and restored in 1902, pictured with its finds recomposed and set on the restored bench opposite the entrance. Evans believed that metal "double-axes" stood in holes drilled in the center of the two plaster "horns of consecration" (ASHMOLEAN MUSEUM)

Contents of the Temple Repositories, cleared in 1903, recomposed, and ordered as Evans imagined they might have stood in a shrine with the "Snake Goddess" and her headless votary flanking "the simple 'Greek' cross," which, he declared, was "a star symbol of religious import . . . found in Egypt as a mark of Hathor" (ASHMOLEAN MUSEUM)

Musée de Candie

The Cretan government gave the Candia Syllogos a new museum in the old Turkish barracks to display the over-abundant first harvest of the foreign excavators who eagerly joined in the search for Crete's historical treasures; the finds from Knossos, in the foreground, took pride of place

Fyfe stands in a light well in the Domestic Quarter contemplating the imminent collapse of the stone walls because the wooden framework that once supported them had rotted away (ASHMOLEAN MUSEUM)

"I succeeded in a rather bold experiment the other day," Evans boasted in a letter to his father. *"There was a much sloping wall of rubble masonry . . . threatening destruction to all below it, as it was at an angle of about 75° . . . I had slits cut along the base on each side, its face was then planked over and roped and fifty men set to tug. It righted itself most gratefully against a stop temporarily erected for the purpose"* (ASHMOLEAN MUSEUM)

Wherever there had been a wooden skeleton, Fyfe cleared the voids and filled them with modern beams carefully cut to copy the ancient ones. This essential process for the building's survival—an architect's first-aid treatment— is shown here in the area of the Queen's Megaron in the Domestic Quarter (ASHMOLEAN MUSEUM)

The wooden supports rotted, so Doll (in the straw hat and waistcoat, to the left of Mackenzie and Evans) used reinforced concrete and cement to rebuild the Grand Staircase, shown here in 1905 (ASHMOLEAN MUSEUM)

Romantic portrait of Evans in 1907 by Sir W. B. Richmond. Here was the brilliant creator surrounded by the re-creations of artifacts drawn from the fantastic world he had revived

Doll designed and completed the Villa Ariadne in 1906 (ASHMOLEAN MUSEUM)

The "Palazzo Evans," as some preferred to call the Villa Ariadne, boasted the only Edwardian garden in the Balkans (ASHMOLEAN MUSEUM)

Evans and Mackenzie, lower right, paid the workers in a weekly ceremony in the Villa garden (ASHMOLEAN MUSEUM)

"It is difficult to refuse the conclusion that this first of theatres, the Stepped Area with its dancing ground, supplies a material foundation for the Homeric tradition of the famous 'choros' "—the dancing ground that Daedalus built for Ariadne at Knossos, Evans mused. He called the stepped area north of the Palace the Theatral Area
(ASHMOLEAN MUSEUM)

The road from the Theatral Area led Evans to the Little Palace buried under the slopes northwest of the main Palace
(ASHMOLEAN MUSEUM)

Mackenzie (right center) monitors men digging with his "wager system" in the Little Palace. "Two gangs of our men are each given an equal number of cubic metres," Bosanquet explained, *"and a prize of a franc a head per day is paid to the team that finishes first. They work like heroes in these matches —and are paid at a higher rate than usual, apart from the trifling prize." The resulting ragged holes were known as "wager pits"*
(ASHMOLEAN MUSEUM)

Fetish stones found in the Little Palace struck Evans by their "quasi-human aspect . . . which indeed from its characteristic conformation might well be that of a Mother Goddess," in the center, with what Evans conjectured was an infant (left) and an Egyptian ape (right)
(ASHMOLEAN MUSEUM)

Gilliéron's restoration of the stone bovine head found in the Little Palace in 1908. Evans marveled at how "the crystal lens of the eye both illuminates and magnifies the bright red pupil, and imparts to the whole an almost startling impression of fiery life" (Evans 1914, Fig. 87a)

Doll reconstructed most of the Queen's Megaron in 1908, and took the opportunity to open some of the blocked windows in the lower courts, allowing, as Evans imagined, "light to pour in between the piers and columns just as it did of old . . . It dimly illuminates the painted spiral frieze above its white gypsum dado and falls below on the small terra-cotta bathtub, standing much as it was left some three and half millenniums back. The little bath bears a painted design of a character that marks the close of the great 'Palace Style.' By whom was it last used? . . . By a Queen, perhaps, and mother for some 'Hope of Minos'—a hope that failed." (ASHMOLEAN MUSEUM)

Drawing of the scene on the bezel of the Isopata gold ring found in 1909. Evans was struck by the similarity of the central figure's placement of the hands with a specific gesture he knew well from the contemporary dance performed at the nearby Dervish Academy (after Evans 1914, Fig. 16)

Renewed digging on the south side of the Palace in 1922 produced "the opening of an artificial cave, with three roughly cut steps leading down to what can only be described as a lair adapted for some great beast," Evans first reported, later suggesting that it "may well have contributed to the origin of the later tales of the Minotaur that haunted the site in historic times" (ASHMOLEAN MUSEUM)

Mackenzie's health declined as his drinking increased, and Evans forced him to retire at sixty-eight years old; he died in an asylum in 1934 (ASHMOLEAN MUSEUM)

John Pendlebury (second from the left, atop the wall) arrived at Knossos in 1930 and directed the excavations at the so-called Temple Tomb, shown here, in 1931
(ASHMOLEAN MUSEUM)

Evans was so convinced that the structure, which included a pillar crypt and paved courtyard, was the cenotaph of King Minos that he called it the "Temple Tomb" and restored it, complete with horns of consecration, during the course of the excavation, which Pendlebury felt was "playing about with the tomb in an abominable way"
(ASHMOLEAN MUSEUM)

Evans was honored for his discovery of the "pre-Hellenic Minoan Culture" at the Jubilee Celebrations of the British School at Athens in London in 1936 (ASHMOLEAN MUSEUM)

Evans in his library at Youlbury in 1935 surrounded by books and papers and clutching in his right hand the ivory Adonis, almost certainly a forgery (pencil sketch by Francis Dodd)

Evans (seated center) joined the Boy Scout movement in 1908 and remained active in it for the rest of his life, eventually achieving its highest award, the Silver Wolf, in 1938 (ASHMOLEAN MUSEUM)

1924, reported the startling news that he was handing over his estate at Knossos, which included the Palace, Villa Ariadne, and vineyards to the British School at Athens. "It is my idea that the property might become quarters for the British School in Greece and my villa might become a place of study for students of the school," Evans told reporters. "So much has been discovered lately that it is essential for students to spend some weeks at a time on the island. I believe there is an enormous field for research work for the next 100 years in Crete, and that we are at the beginning of a new era of discovery there."[83] The same paper included a letter from Macmillan reporting on "Evans's Munificence": "High on the roll of benefactors of the School, as on that of our greatest British scholars and explorers, will stand to all time the name of Arthur Evans."[84] As we have seen, a major factor that gave Evans more than the usual proprietary rights over the Minoans that all archaeologists feel for those aspects of the past to which they dedicate their lives was the extra dimension of ownership. And now, suddenly, he was relinquishing his grip.

The real reason, perhaps, for his generosity became clear to outside observers the following day. The press releases of February 5 were intended to circulate on the same day that Evans appeared at the Marlborough Street Police Court with George Cook, a seventeen-year-old "hawker" (someone who will sell anything for a profit), as described in a brief notice in the *Times* on February 6, who gave his address as the Waterloo YMCA. The pair were "charged on remand with being concerned together in committing an act in violation of public decency in Hyde Park on the night of January 29." Evans's lawyer stated that both defendants "denied some of the incidents deposed by the police, who did not probably know the fact, undisputed, that the elder defendant was 'night blind,' and had to be led about." However, he agreed that an offense may have been committed and proposed that the case be left as it stood before the magistrate and called no witnesses. The magistrate felt "the less he said about it the better," and "the evidence satisfied him beyond all doubt that there was an infringement." Evans was fined £5 and paid costs; the boy was told to reside out of the county of London for twelve months, presumably to keep him from talking to the press. Evans's positive act of a substantial gift to the state was, I believe, a public act of contrition, and perhaps recommended by his legal counsel.

This is the first conclusive evidence the biographical record contains that Evans had physical relations with a young man. Perhaps it was the

first time and he bungled it, or perhaps it was something he did often
when in London and this was the first time he got caught. Either way, it
showed that Evans, at the age of seventy-three, was slipping, losing his
grasp on his private life. It may well have been part of a larger issue; either he was relaxing his guard or he had lost control of it.

The January newspapers were filled with photographs of Howard
Carter's amazing finds from Tutankhamen's tomb in the Valley of the
Kings in Egypt; not a day passed without some new revelation while
Carter stage-managed the unwrapping of the young pharaoh's mummy
as the grand finale to his brilliant discovery of the previous year. Then,
on January 19, Leonard Woolley announced his discovery of Ur of the
Chaldees, the great Sumerian city of the Bible, with photographs of exquisite jewelry and gold statuary inlaid with semiprecious stones.[85]
Evans felt more than a little left behind and was decidedly envious, as
his paper on "Recent Light on the Minoan Art of Crete," read at the
Royal Institution on February 8, showed. He started out by stressing
the common Libyan origin of the ethnic Egyptians and Cretans, closely
connected throughout their history, but then he criticized the pre-
dictability of Egyptian art in an attempt to minimize Carter's success,
asking, "How much might not a skilled Egyptologist have drawn be-
forehand of the inexhaustible treasures of the Tomb of Tutankhamen?"
He contrasted this with the excited prediction that "were ever an intact
Royal Tomb of the great days of Knossos to be discovered, who would
venture to forecast the artistic revelations that it might bring to light?!"
As an appetizer, Evans then projected slides of the "famous ivory Goddess now in Boston—so modern in its expression that many had
doubted its genuineness," he admitted, but then showed slides of "a figure of a Boy-God, apparently by the same hand and unquestionably
genuine, who seems to be in the act of adoring his Lady Mother." This
was the first public revelation of his latest acquisition, an ivory statuette
which, he claimed, "showed a delicate and sympathetic execution more
suggestive of Leonardo than of any ancient models."[86]

The Boston Goddess was the first of a dozen examples of Minoan
ivory figures to appear during and after the war years. Recent investigations cast serious doubt on most if not all the ivories that appeared on
the art market, because the culprits were well known to many archaeologists, including Evans.[87] Woolley tells the story of staying at the Villa
Ariadne when they were called upon by the police: "Evans for years had
employed two Greeks to restore the antiquities which he had found.

They were extraordinarily clever men—an old man and a young one—and he had trained them, and they had worked under the artist whom he had employed there, and they had done wonderful restorations for him. Then the old man got ill and at last the doctor told him he was going to die." The man sent for a policeman, not a doctor, as he wanted to confess that for years with his younger partner, George Antoniou, he had been forging antiquities. The police summoned Evans and Mackenzie, who invited Woolley to join them, to inspect the premises:

> I never saw so magnificent a collection of forgeries as those fellows had put together. There were things in every stage of manufacture. For instance, people had recently been astounded at getting what they call chryselephantine statuettes from Crete; statuettes of ivory decked out with gold—there is one in the Boston Museum and one at Cambridge, and one in the Cretan Museum at Candia. These men were determined to do that sort of thing and they had got there everything, from the plain ivory tusk and then the figure rudely carved out, then beautifully finished, then picked out with gold. And then the whole thing was put into acid, which ate away the soft parts of the ivory giving it the effect of having been buried for centuries.* And I didn't see that anyone could tell the difference! I said to Evans, "I shall never buy a Greek antiquity." He said, "Well, even I feel rather doubtful now," and he was a marvelous judge.[88]

The men had worked for Gilliéron, and so they were very well versed in the intricacies of Minoan art and how to reproduce it. Indeed Gilliéron, now joined by his son (also called Emile), had a thriving business selling "museum copies" of Minoan and Mycenaean metal and ivory objects, specializing in gold jewelry. The curious truth is that Evans was indeed the marvelous judge Woolley said he was—yet from that time on he insisted on including many obviously modern pieces in his reconstruction of the past and used them to bolster his arguments on Minoan religion.

---

*A variation on the acid technique was to bury the recently manufactured "artifacts" in a spot in the garden where the household was instructed to dispose of their bodily fluids, thereby "contributing to the family business." This was related to me by Vangelis Kyriakides, of Herakleion, Crete, who heard it from his grandfather.

Karo in his memoirs, published after Evans's death, recalled that Gilliéron had offered him the Boston Goddess in 1914 but that he'd turned it down. Karo added this insight:

Only during the years of war 1915–1918 did gold and ivory stat-uettes richly embellished with gold "from Crete" first come to light. These skillfully produced works always had to fit excellently with the results of Evans' research regarding Minoan religion. And he had no doubts as to their genuineness because—as he wrote to me once—nobody yet had knowledge of the still unpub-lished results. That men to whom he must, after all, have indi-cated some of those results would repay his benevolence over many years in such a way was to a man of his character wholly in-comprehensible. And the successful efforts of Spyridon Mari-natos, while he was Ephor (i.e., provincial curator in Crete) to expose bit players, goldsmiths working on order as forgers, did not reach the men behind the scenes.[89]

All suspicion fell on Gilliéron and his assistants, but few raised their voices, in deference to his eminent employer. Again one has to wonder whether this was not a part of a larger picture of Evans slowly losing touch with his critical faculties, becoming less able to distinguish fact from fiction or life from fantasy.

Also on the wane, I believe, was Evans's willingness to support young scholars, unless, of course, they subscribed to his views. "My digging days are over," Wace wrote in desperation to Blegen in April 1924. "Nei-ther Macmillan & Co (nor A.J.E. also I fear) will allow me to dig again!" Wace's refusal to give in to Evans's arguments over the dates of the main architectural features at Mycenae had finally turned Evans against him. What had started out as a scholarly debate took a serious turn for the worse when Evans and Mackenzie realized that the "Helladic heretics" couldn't be bullied into changing their minds. In the summer of 1923 both Mackenzie and Evans had been on speaking terms at least, as Blegen, who took a lighter view of the situation, reported in letters to his fiancée. Mackenzie had arrived in Athens ahead of Evans at the end of March and Wace had taken him to see the Mycenae plans with Ble-gen at the American School, across the garden from the British School. "Old Duncan seemed to think he was in a dangerous place in the mid-dle of the enemy's camp. His manner was more than usually shy and frightened and he received every remark from Wace and me with the caution and suspicion of the canny highlander that he is," Blegen reported with glee, adding, "You know (according to Seager) Duncan thinks (or thought) I am the wicked villain in the background who incites and encourages Wace to put forth all those heretical views on Mycenaean chronology!" But the true nature of Mackenzie's strict adherence to his master's reconstruction of history left no room for dialogue. "Needless to say the discussion led to no conclusion," Blegen grieved.

Mackenzie was inexpressibly shocked at the late date (Late Helladic III) Wace gives the hearth in the Megaron at Mycenae and his remark about that was rather good. He said, "Dear me, We can't possibly accept that. We're absolutely committed on that as dating from LM I. We have it down in black and white. It's in the book." ("We" means Mackenzie & Sir Arthur Evans & the book is the "Palace of Minos"). This seemed rather characteristic of his attitude on a good many points.

Evans showed up a week later, and Blegen observed his declining tolerance for debating their new ideas. "It seems that Evans, encouraged by Mackenzie, disagrees violently with many of our chief theories about the chronology of things at Mycenae, though last year he seemed very reasonable and we thought he had accepted most of them." Nonetheless, Blegen felt, "He is really a delightful old boy and I like him very much. I think he would be extremely glad if Wace and I would abandon the Mycenaean field with its difficulties and dangers and take up instead the neolithic or at least the Early Helladic Periods which are certainly not Cretan anyway and in which heretical views are comparatively harmless!"

A year later, however, the debate had grown into an acrimonious feud in which Evans publicly attacked Wace's excavation methods in the *Times* and privately referred to him as writing "like a pettifogging lawyer rather than a judicial investigator," making "everything fit a preconceived and impossible theory."[90] "You know old Foxy suggested ages ago that A.J.E. was jealous of Mycenae," Wace confided to Blegen. "I'm coming much against my will to believe it." Foxy was the popular nickname for Edgar John Forsdyke, keeper of Greek and Roman Antiquities at the British Museum and, as a graduate of Keble College, Oxford, very much an adherent of Evans's Pan-Minoan school.[91] Evans's jealousy and ire may also have been heightened by Wace's being asked to write the entry on the Aegean civilizations for the *Cambridge Ancient History*, in which he boldly stated, "The great outstanding fact is that Crete, then at the beginning of the second climax of its Bronze Age civilization, was so superior in all arts and crafts, that her domination of her neighbours was a foregone conclusion. He would have been a bold man to prophesy that before the end of the Bronze Age the newly founded stronghold of Mycenae would eclipse the power and riches of Cnossos."[92]

As in many disciplines, accomplished men of forceful character find it difficult to tolerate younger scholars who threaten to overturn their ideas, forgetting that they were once young and rebellious themselves. Evans supported the succeeding generation only so long as they toed the line; when Wace refused to subscribe to Evans's desired history, Evans did everything in his power to have him removed, and his power was great. The managing committee of the British School decided not to reappoint Wace to the directorship in 1923, and he left Greece to search for work; he became a deputy keeper in charge of textiles at London's Victoria and Albert Museum in 1924. He continued to present his views on pre-Hellenic Greek archaeology and Evans continued to fight them. But Wace didn't return to excavate in Greece until after Evans's death.

An Archaeological Jules Verne

Evans and Mackenzie were back at the head of a huge workforce chasing the first indications of a paved route south from Knossos in May 1924, and by early June, Evans cabled the *Times* to report that he had found "the most imposing structure that has yet come to light in Crete."[93] Beneath a dense alluvial deposit from the Vlychades river, skirting the south side of the Palace hill, Evans found the huge, roughly hewn blue limestone piers of a viaduct and bridgehead, which he imaginatively restored in an artist's reconstruction as a grand bridge across the river. This convinced him that the main entrance to the Palace, which he hadn't found at the north or the west, must have been at the south side, where erosion had swept any traces into the river. Spurred by this great idea, Evans organized a series of grand expeditions to the potential harbors on the south coast of the island. Piet de Jong recalled,

In those days our excursions were made on horses and mules and always in great style. Sir Arthur always led, followed by myself, because Mackenzie did not like to be too near such an electric and erratic personality as Sir Arthur and be obliged to talk to him; he, therefore, always followed me. I acted as a buffer. Mackenzie was followed by more agreeable company, but always in the same order. Manolaki, then Kronis who took care of the animals, Kosti the butler, Hassan his assistant, and lastly a donkey which carried samples of wine as we went along.[94]

Evans wrote up the journeys for the *Times*, and his dispatches read like those describing the trips he had undertaken with Myres thirty years earlier, but with a different kind of excitement. The wonder and speculation of the earlier reports were replaced with confidence based on his own immense experience of Cretan antiquities of all periods, combined with "the lynx eyes of my foreman Manolaki, whom nothing Minoan escapes." But there was still room for adventure. At Kali Limenes, the "Fair Havens" cited in the New Testament, where St. Paul is reputed to have been delayed by bad weather and where Evans noted "the shore was plentifully strewn with fragments of Roman wine jars that may have supplied the crew of the Apostle's ship with good cheer," Evans pitched his tent on the beach:

There suddenly arose about sundown a truly "typhonic" south wind, with a touch of the east, which brought up a heavy sea, and in the small hours of the morning when, fairly roused at last by the thuds and buffetings, I unfastened the door of my tent, a great wave burst in, swamping everything within. For one who suffers from complete night blindness it was an awkward quandary, but, happily, some sailors engaged in salvaging their half-sunken boat helped me out. Next morning the breakers rolled over the spot where my tent had been.

Evans found numerous important sites on these journeys, including the Minoan settlement at Trypiti, recently excavated by the Greek Archaeological Service,[95] but the greatest of all was the principal object of his exploration, the main southern port for Knossos, which he found covered by sand dunes at Kommos, on the shores of the Mesara. Recent American excavations have confirmed Evans's impressions that Kommos had a Cretan customs house where "export duties were levied by the officers of the Minoan Priest-Kings."[96] Later that year, Evans showed the Egypt Exploration Society his evidence for what he now called "The Great Transit Route" connecting the Libyan Sea with the Aegean at Knossos, where the counterpart to the "processional groups of Minoan envoys bearing their characteristic fabrics as offerings," or Keftiu, "was the Procession fresco of Knossos, the gifts in this case being offered to the Minoan Goddess." He further highlighted this intercourse with examples of "wall paintings with Sudan monkeys amidst papyrus thickets, and the remarkable scene in which a Minoan captain was depicted leading black troops: a practice clearly borrowed from contemporary Egypt."[97] Yet he continued to maintain that Minoan culture was independent of Egypt, even as he personally continued to gather evidence to the contrary.

Simultaneous with Evans's real discoveries on the ground was an increasing number of spectacular "revelations" from objects that surfaced far from his watchful gaze. "I used to dream of an archaeological Jules Verne," wrote Salomon Reinach in his review of Evans's publication of the first group of jewels from clandestine sources, "a story for eight to twelve-year-olds, making the most marvelous finds beneath the ground. But could I have imagined anything more marvelous than Sir Arthur Evans has to show?"[98] A wave of engraved gems and gold rings whose miniature scenes fit perfectly with Evans's theories about Minoan myth and religion, beginning with a group said to be from Thisbe, near Thebes, joined the influx of statuettes of doubtful antiquity. Since Evans had predicted a "Minoan Epos" on which Homer and the later Greeks based their heroic tales, he willingly overlooked their questionable authenticity and published them with full scholia. This "Thisbe treasure" included engraved scenes of bull sacrifice and the Minoan goddess in a variety of predictable poses, but there were also pictures that recalled episodes from the Theban tale of Oedipus Rex, the young hero who unwittingly killed his father and married his mother.

With the Thisbe jewels, Evans published two newly discovered gold rings, one said to have been found in a cave-like tomb near Archanes, south of Knossos. The Archanes ring showed a bull-leaper flying over the back of a galloping bull: a scene almost identical to the one restored from painted plaster fragments in the Palace. The second gold ring, which Evans called the "Ring of Nestor" because he was told that it came from the Mycenaean cemetery at Kakovatos, near Nestor's "sandy" Pylos, on the western coast of the Peloponnesus, depicted parts of another myth that had been dear to Evans's heart since he first predicted the Aegean Tree and Pillar Cult: at the center of the engraved scene on the ring bezel, dominating the composition, was a rambling tree which Evans likened to "the old Scandinavian 'Tree of the World,' the Ash of Odin's steed, Yggdrasil."[99] Many reviewers were skeptical about the authenticity of the pieces, but Gordon Childe was delighted to write an extensive appraisal in *Nature*, playing up Evans's evidence for the Minoan epic—probably because he was himself busy mythmaking in his own right.

Childe had returned to England after the war and, impressed with the workings of the Soviet state in the USSR, he began to glorify what we now regard as the mass destruction of nature for surplus and profit. Childe incorporated Karl Marx's principles of praxis—that change comes about through actions, not thoughts or words, and that the forces of production are fundamental to the economic structure on which all society rests—into a materialist fundamentalism, the living embodiment of which, for Childe, was Soviet Russia.

Childe outlined his ideas on the origins of the Indo-European languages in his 1926 book *The Aryans: A Study of Indo-European Origins*. He dismissed Gobineau's ideas outright, but then went on to picture the arrival of a group of rough and ready savages who had only their language to recommend them, sweeping through Europe in a wave of destruction, but "from the fields they had wasted chosen blossoms grew." The Aryans' mixture with the "Nordics" gave them the physical qualities "to conquer even more advanced peoples and so to impose their language on areas from which their bodily type has almost completely vanished. This is the truth," Childe concluded, "underlying the panegyrics of the Germanists: the Nordics' superiority in physique fitted them to be the vehicles of a superior language."[100] Unintentionally, Childe's work provided the historical precedent and material evidence for the strident anti-Semitic sentiment shared by dispossessed German war veterans meeting in the beer halls of Munich, and it was quickly incorporated into the recently founded National Socialist German Workers Party's effort.

It was a period of mythmaking, and the gold rings, like the ivories, were too convenient. Though there is still a group of scholars stubbornly clinging to their veracity,[101] the fact that a second identical copy of the Archanes ring appeared in Evans's collection at the end of his life confirms a suspicion that it was the product of a modern workshop able to churn out such items on demand. There was just such a workshop in Athens, which was world-renowned for its gold copies of Minoan and Mycenaean jewelry, and it was run by the two men closest to the excavated originals: Gilliéron *père et fils*. Though it may never be proven conclusively, the glare of suspicion falls firmly on the father and son during what might be called a "neo-Daedalic period" in Minoan art.

"I had a very sad arrival here," Evans wrote to his cousin Josephine Phelps from Knossos in June 1925. While in Athens he had heard through Blegen that Richard Seager had taken ill on the boat from Egypt to Crete. Evans arranged for a Greek naval boat to rush to Crete and take Seager to Athens, but they were too late. Evans arrived in time for the funeral, where he got out of the carriage to walk bareheaded behind the coffin; "he felt the death," witnesses said.[102] Evans had been very close to Seager and characterized him to his cousin as "the most *English* American I have ever known."[103]

Seager's premature death added to the popular speculation that those who visited the tomb of Tutankhamen, which he had done shortly after its discovery, were "cursed by the mummy." Less than five months earlier, Francis Newton, recently appointed to the Egyptian Exploration Fund, had died at Assiut in Egypt at the age of forty-six. Newton had also been one of the early visitors to Howard Carter's excavations in the Valley of the Kings and so his mysterious death, attributed to sleeping sickness *(encephalitis lethargica)*, fed the popular fear of the Egyptian malediction.

Evans did little digging in 1925, instead employing a work team to rebuild parts of the west wing of the Palace and supervise Gilliéron *fils* on the restoration of the thousands of plaster fragments from the House of the Frescoes. Evans continued to explore Crete and visited Malia, where Hazzidakis, in 1913, had discovered a new palace about twenty miles east of Knossos on the north coast. Hazzidakis retired from archaeology and invited the French School to come and excavate the site, which they did beginning in 1919. Evans was most impressed by the finds, which he used to liven up his lecture to the Hellenic Society in London that November, but was critical of the French methods: "they let it drag on and on, with only a few men and boys at work and continual changes in direction."[104]

The Royal Anthropological Institute presented Evans with the celebrated Huxley Medal for distinguished service to anthropology in the autumn, and he responded with a paper on the racial origins of his Minoans. Evans suggested that the earliest inhabitants had come from Anatolia and the east, as evidenced by similarities in the steatopygous (from the Greek *steatopygia*, meaning fatty buttocks) Neolithic figurines; but that Libyan customs "took root" at Knossos late in the Neolithic period, around 3000 B.C., at the same time as they affected pre-Dynastic Egypt. "The Libyan Delta Goddess appeared to have been, in part at least, incorporated in the Cretan Mother Goddess," Evans surmised as he continued to search for the origins of his Nature Goddess.[105]

Daedalic Deco

Evans returned to Knossos in mid-March 1926 with Theodore Fyfe, who took Newton's place, and worked for a month to complete the rebuilding of the South Propylaeum so that Gilliéron's full copies of the Priest-King and Cup-Bearer frescoes were set in place just before the "Earth-Shaker" roared again. "My own mind was full of past earthquakes," Evans wrote to his cousin, "when on June 26 last, at nine-forty-five in the evening of a calm, warm day, the shocks began." He was reading in bed in his basement room in the Villa Ariadne and looked on as "small objects were thrown about, and a pail, full of water, was nearly splashed empty. The movement, which recalled a ship in a storm, though only a minute and a quarter's duration, already began to produce the same physical effect on me as a rough sea. A dull sound rose from the ground like the muffled roar of an angry bull."

Delighted with this encounter, Evans mixed experience with imagination: "It is something to have heard with one's own ears the bellowing of the bull beneath the earth who, according to a primitive belief, tosses it with its horns. It was doubtless the constant need of protection against these petulant bursts of the infernal powers that explains the Minoans' tendency to concentrate their worship on the chthonic aspect of their great goddess, wreathed with serpents as Lady of the Underworld." Again mixing reality with fantasy, Evans reported, "One consolation is that the Palace with its reconstituted upper floors has resisted well. The copy of the Cup-Bearer, with the other processional figures, now appear in their proper places on the walls, and the Priest King looks down again on the Corridor approaching the Central Court. It is a wonderful effect."[106] He had done one better than Daedalus: he had built a labyrinth that survived the wrath of the "Earth-Shaker."

The Palace of Knossos and Villa Ariadne were formally handed over to the British School in 1926, after a long delay during which the British and Greek governments debated the issue of taxes, finally agreeing to waive them. Evans, who normally fumed when things progressed slowly, was content to let the procedure linger on. He was surprised and disappointed that the students of the British School didn't come to use the facility, but, as Piet de Jong recalled, "the hesitation to come was due to the fact that students did not wish Sir Arthur to feel that he was no longer owner of Knossos, and this was not comprehended by him." Mackenzie was installed as the first "Knossos Curator of the British School," a post funded from a generous endowment that Evans provided. But Mackenzie's health was in a rapid state of decline after years of unhappiness and alcohol abuse, so the first year of his appointment was spent in the Swiss Alps recovering from influenza. In order to keep up Knossos, Evans had to let go of other parts of the past and sold a large part of his coin collection to "a Cambridge man" in September 1926 for £18,000, and then put his prized collection of Cretan coins at auction in Geneva in October. He had acquired many coins during his early travels in Crete, and many of these have now been traced to the Ashmolean Museum. The coins sold in Geneva were probably those from the Greek and Roman levels of his excavations at Knossos, especially where Mackenzie's wager system had been employed.

The focus of the work at Knossos in the late 1920s was on what Evans called "reconstitutions" of the Palace and surrounding buildings. "It is not too much to say that in the last few years the site of Knossos has renewed its life," Evans began his address to the Royal Institute of British Architects in November 1928 in which he illustrated the latest constructions in the Domestic Quarter that he had completed that year. Christian Doll responded: "It is a long time since I was at Knossos, and what I have seen tonight on the screen has, in one sense, rather taken my breath away; and yet, in another sense, I can faithfully say that nothing at Knossos would surprise me, and nothing in Sir Arthur Evans' work would surprise me." Doll then slipped into affectionate yet telling reminiscences of working with Evans: "before you half recovered some object, he would come to you and say 'You will find so and so there,' and every time it turned out to be so; he was never wrong." Doll was emphatic in his praise of Evans's work, though he acknowledged, "No doubt many of you object very much to restoration, I know that most antiquaries object to it; but it is impossible to avoid it at Knossos," and pointed out that there would be little to see there if Evans hadn't rebuilt as he did.

The fact was, though, that even some of Evans's close friends and colleagues were taken aback by the scale of the "reconstitutions," though few would dare to voice disapproval in public. Halbherr, in a private letter to a colleague, captured the mood of Evans's closest supporters: *"L'Evans continua le sue ricostruzioni a Cnosso, molto istruttive per i profani, ma molto ardite."* (Evans continues his reconstruction at Knossos, very instructive for the layman but very daring [*ardito* can also mean presumptuous].)[107]

Evelyn Waugh, on a cruise with friends in February 1929, gave one of the most astute impressions of Knossos during the restoration. Waugh and some friends

chartered a Ford car with a guide to Cnossos, where Sir Arthur Evans (our guide referred to him always as "Your English Lord Evans") is rebuilding the palace. At present only a few rooms and galleries are complete, the rest being an open hillside scarred with excavation, but we were able to form some idea of the magnitude and intricacy of the operation from the plans which were posted up for our benefit on the chief platform. I think that if our English Lord Evans ever finished even a part of his vast undertaking, it will be a place of oppressive wickedness. I do not think that it can be only imagination and the recollection of a bloodthirsty mythology which makes something fearful and malignant of the cramped galleries and stunted alleys, these colonnades of inverted, conical pillars, these rooms that are mere blind passages at the end of sunless staircases; this squat little throne set on a landing where the paths of the palace intersect; it is not the seat of a lawgiver nor the divan for the recreation of a soldier; here an aging despot might crouch and have borne to him, along the walls of a whispering gallery, barely audible intimations of his own murder.[108]

The British historian and philosopher R. G. Collingwood was equally disturbed by what he saw. "The first impression on the mind of a visitor is that Knossian architecture consists of garages and public lavatories," he wrote, though he acknowledged this might be due to the restorations done in concrete, "which may in this respect give a false idea of the original." But Collingwood found that the utilitarian aspect of the buildings left him cold, and the fact that there was "no taste, no elegance, no sense of proportion," in comparison to the mathematical perfection of ancient Greek and Roman architecture.[109] He came closer to the point when observing that Minoan architecture, like that of his own time, was an architecture of "comfort and convenience—a trade, not a fine art." But he failed to realize that his criticism was not of Minoan work but of Evans's vision and re-creation of Knossos and, as such, was exactly to the point.

The most sagacious observer of Knossos I myself have known was Pierre Elliott Trudeau, then Canadian prime minister, whom I had the pleasure of escorting through the Palace in 1983. Trudeau marveled at how the Minoan architect had predicted the shapes and colors of Art Deco, then caught himself, looked at me, and asked, "*When* did you say this place was restored?" He cracked a knowing smile, which he kept throughout the remainder of the visit. Perhaps Trudeau's attitude is the healthiest to adopt when viewing Knossos.

Of all of Evans's colleagues, Bosanquet best saw the future worth of the immense, thirty-year undertaking when he pointed out that Evans had created a precedent which "has immensely raised the standard of an excavator's duty." Indeed, Evans's restorations are the first steps toward what we now call "archaeological parks." The "re-constitutions" have come to symbolize Knossos, more than the original walls, and they themselves are the present focus of a huge conservation program.[110]

Cambridge Blue

Mackenzie's mental health went into a rapid decline after his first bout of illness in 1926. He had once enchanted young James Candy with tales of woodland fairies, but as he gave way to deeper depression and heavier drinking, Mackenzie would go into the garden and throw stones at the nightingales, complaining that their song kept him awake. Evans planned for his lieutenant's retirement in Scotland at the end of 1929, but Mackenzie precipitated events by going on drunken binges and feigning illness. Then early one morning in June 1929 at Knossos,

Evans, "seeing that there was still a light," he reported to the director of the British School, "roused de Jong & we two went up to investigate. We found that besides the lamp there was a candle burning in the dining room & on going in were very much shocked. I saw at first, besides three bottles, what looked like a large pumpkin on a dish. On going nearer I found that it was Mackenzie's head, with his nose on his plate, & at first we both thought he had had a mortal stroke." But Mackenzie had been drinking heavily. He was sixty-eight years old and had devoted almost half of those years to Evans and Knossos. Much recent scholarship points out the debt we owe to Mackenzie's records and judgments, a debt never recognized in his own lifetime; he stood by as Evans received countless awards. Mackenzie's was a life of service, which in the end he found too difficult to sustain. Evans relieved him of his duties and sent him off to Athens with the hope that he would journey on to stay with his sister in Italy, which he eventually did, and died in a sanatorium in 1934.

Mackenzie's departure from Crete left a vacuum that could hardly be filled by one man. His devotion to Knossos and Evans would be impossible to re-create. But a new kind of dedication to Knossos and Crete, both ancient and modern, appeared in the person of John Pendlebury. Born in London on October 12, 1904, Pendlebury was a forthright man of action and intellect, a graduate of Pembroke College, Cambridge. (He had represented the university against Oxford in the hurdles and got his blue for the high jump in 1926 and 1927; he was the first Cambridge man to reach six feet in the varsity sports.) Pendlebury had arrived at the British School at Athens in November 1927, where he began a study of Egyptian artifacts in the Aegean, but he instantly felt out of place with his own countrymen. "I only wish everyone here wouldn't be so obviously learned to the eyebrows," he reported to his father in a regular correspondence that he maintained throughout his life.[111] "It makes me feel such an imposter being here at all. Most of them feel I think that a blue has put me beyond the pale!" The description of his fellow students was most telling: "The party consists of a chap called Davies, a dreadful lantern jawed Oxford man the reason for whose existence is I suppose one of the secrets of the universe." Others fare little better. Sylvia Benton, the excavator of Ithaca, in the young man's eyes was "an elderly school marm, tough as nails and hard as rock." The others were "Miss Whitfield another of Oxford's gems, so conceited she hardly knows what to do with herself. Miss Roger, an inefficient South African just down from Oxford. Miss Turnbull, an almost non-existent New Zealander." Only one of his peers seems to have struck the right chord: "Miss White . . . alone of the lot strikes one as being at all human . . . the rest are definitely sub-human."[112]

Pendlebury traveled to Crete in early 1928 with Hilda White and saw Knossos for the first time. "Very confusing," he reported to his father, and "spoilt in places by Evans' restorations."[113] He was duly invited to stay at the Villa Ariadne, but not Hilda, who resented that "no women folk are asked to stay in that bachelor haunt."[114] Pendlebury seems to have hit it off quite well with Evans, as he wrote home, "The Cretan trip was an immense success. There are certainly chances there! Evans suggested—secretly of course—either digging for Neolithic below the Central Court at Knossos or else going down to Komo on the south coast which was the port on the Libyan Sea." He also quickly changed his tune on the reconstruction work: "Evans seems to be rebuilding the palace completely in the most splendid style!"[115]

John and Hilda were married in September 1928 and spent the winter excavating at Luxor in Egypt. Then, in early May 1929, Pendlebury received a telegram from the Villa Ariadne asking if he would be willing to carry on the work of curator at Knossos in the event of Mackenzie's retiring in the autumn.[116] He accepted, and the Pendleburys arrived at Knossos in mid-March 1930. In anticipation of female students coming to Knossos, Evans had asked Piet de Jong to draw up plans to add a second story to the taverna at the foot of the driveway. But, as de Jong recalled, Evans

always liked to have things go quickly and be done immediately; he could not wait for preliminaries. The restoration of the taverna was an example. He called me one afternoon to discuss what could be done to make it habitable; an amenity to the villa. We examined the walls, roof, etc. and the next day I started on one or two schemes to show what could be done to get a nice lay out and generally make a pleasant living house. During my studies I went down to have a look at something and found the place already being altered. When I told Sir Arthur I was getting out a plan for the arrangement, he said it was quite unnecessary, he had told them what to do, illustrating the desired changes with the aid of his

walking-stick. The result was truly awful. When Pendlebury came
and took up residence in it he got someone to alter it, but the opportunity of making anything of it had been lost.[117]

Pendlebury's first task was to clean up the estate and then to catalogue the mountains of pottery from thirty years of excavation. "A very
long job and difficult," he explained to his father, "considering that all I
have to go on are the labels (written in pencil on worm-eaten wood in
1901 by a Greek foreman who can't spell and who called the places by
quite different names)!"[118] Pendlebury lacked Mackenzie's reticence
and so found relations with Evans difficult, but he brought a new air of
liveliness to the task, and never lost his sense of humor, as expressed in
an "air," which he sent to his father:

Evans had a son
Who married Wace's darter
And nearly spoilt the feud
By mixing up the strata
    (*to the tune of Phairson's Feud*)[119]

Evans never gave up hope that he would find the "Royal Tomb" at
Knossos, and the best chance presented itself in 1931 when, so he reported, a priest from Fortetsa tried to sell him a huge gold ring, like the
ones from Archanes and Pylos, engraved with a religious scene. Evans
balked at the price, but learned that it had been picked up by a boy in a
vineyard south of the Palace. Evans and Pendlebury went to the spot
and found a small early Greek cemetery on a steep hillside above traces
of a large Minoan structure, which they started clearing in April.

"The dig is turning out a tremendous affair," Pendlebury eagerly informed his father at the beginning of his collaboration with Evans. "We
have got what certainly looks like a royal tomb with side chapels and
pillared halls." Then, a nearby sounding produced "what seems to be a
sort of Cathedral, at any rate a most important temple or shrine. Unfortunately it is running under the modern road. I only hope Evans
won't do a lot of tunneling & then clear off leaving one to deal with in-
furiated road inspectors."[120]

As Pendlebury refused to bow to Evans's whims, he found him increasingly difficult to work with. At the end of May 1931 he wrote,
"The digging is finally over, and we are getting a bit of a grip on the

pottery. Evans is worse than ever and I really don't see how we're to stand him even another year."[121] Evans was convinced that the structure, which included a pillar crypt and paved courtyard, was the cenotaph, or empty tomb, of King Minos; Greek legend says Minos died in Sicily chasing Daedalus to the ground, and so, Evans reasoned, a temple was built in his honor at Knossos. He called the building the "Temple Tomb" and restored it, complete with horns of consecration, during the course of the excavation, which Pendlebury felt was "playing about with the tomb in an abominable way."[122]

Evans finally had his Royal Tomb, though the inner "sepulchral crypt" contained material of the Mycenaean period and not Minoan, and Pendlebury had learned what it was like to work with "little Arthur," as he began to refer to him. One last insult came when Evans received the Flinders Petrie medal for the discovery and excavation of this tomb, which Pendlebury preferred to call "our tomb."[123]

It was evident that Pendlebury wasn't willing to stand by as Mackenzie had done and watch Evans take all the credit for his work. Evans didn't go to Crete for the next few years, so the inevitable clash was postponed until 1934, when the British School's committee told Pendlebury that he must work full-time at Knossos and stop traveling around Crete the way he did. Pendlebury was compiling a gazetteer of archaeological sites to accompany a general book on the archaeology of Crete, so his travels were a combination of adventure and discovery; he came to love Crete and the Cretans as Evans never had. But Evans resented what he regarded as his paid servant being away from Knossos for such long periods, not to mention his excavations in Egypt. Pendlebury left the Knossos curatorship but returned to Crete each year to conduct his own excavations in Lasithi.

The Ring of Minos, which had led Evans to the Temple Tomb, was bought by the Herakleion Museum, but it was later judged to be a fake and returned to its owner, whose wife purportedly lost it—but not before it had been drawn, photographed, and cast so that Gilliéron *fils* could make a copy. The engraved scene once again illustrated scenes from Evans's "lost Minoan Epos," this time including a ship in the form of a *hippocamp*, or sea horse, with horns of consecration set on the ship's cabin and the craft steered by the Minoan goddess. Like the Archanes ring, two copies currently exist and neither is convincing, though they will always have their supporters.

Evans's goose-quill pen ceased to transcribe his formal vision of the

Minoans with the completion of the fourth and final volume of *The Palace of Minos* on September 4, 1934. Like the second and third volumes, the last book's free admixture of modern and ancient artifacts make it almost impossible to take the analysis seriously. The ivory statuettes and the gold rings figured prominently, along with lengthy reports on the architectural restorations. But Evans had accomplished what he had set out to do when he first went to Crete forty years earlier, and the Cretans were grateful to him. He returned to Knossos for the last time in April 1935 to become an honorary citizen of Herakleion. Ten thousand people turned up to see the man who had given them the monument at the heart of modern Crete and in return offered him the brazen image that stands like a sentinel in the open court near the entrance to Knossos. Seemingly endless addresses citing the work he had done and the gratitude of the Cretans for his gift were read out in the hot sun for his benefit. Evans gave in his turn an address in a mixture of ancient and modern Greek to those who had benefited most from his discoveries. His emotional valediction to the site of his greatest achievement concluded with a clear statement of his dominant life themes; he reminded his audience of the value of human accomplishment as reward for hard work and perseverance, but also, as he put it, of humility in the presence of a power greater than man:

> We know now that the old traditions were true. We have before our very eyes a wondrous spectacle—the resurgence, namely, of a civilization twice as old as that of Hellas. It is true that on the old Palace site what we see are only the ruins of ruins, but the whole is still inspired with Minos's spirit of order and organisation and the free and natural art of the great architect Daedalos. The spectacle, indeed, that we have before us is assuredly of world-wide significance. Compared with it how small is any individual contribution! So far indeed, as the explorer may have attained success, it has been as the humble instrument, inspired and guided by a great Power.

When all the celebrations were over Evans bade his final farewell to Knossos.

Pendlebury was moved by the passing of generations. "Evans left yesterday," he wrote his father. "There has been a sad break in the continuity of splendour since our day. It was rather depressing."[124]

Evans was acutely aware of his failures, especially his inability to decipher the inscribed tablets, as he admitted in 1935:

> The discovery of these documents attesting an advanced system of writing in Minoan Crete—which in its earlier phase had preceded the Greek by some seven centuries—at the time excited more general interest than any other found within the Palace walls of Knossos. But the widespread hopes of its early interpretation were not verified. No one, indeed, who understood the real conditions could expect such a speedy solution of the problem . . . Of the Minoan script, not only the language but the greater part of the phonetic values of its characters are both lost.[125]

Lost, we know now, because of the limits Evans had imposed upon them. The primary obstacle to decipherment was that Evans never fully published them. Some drawings appeared in that fourth volume, but the years of notes, tracings, and photographs of the roughly 1,800 tablets in Linear B script remained locked away in his study at Youlbury. The tablets were the single most important find of his career, and even in the last years of his life he couldn't bear to give them up. He must have continued to hope that he would stumble upon a solution to their meaning and startle the world with one final revelation, but no matter how long he held them he would never read them. What he couldn't realize was that his lifelong anti-classical bias and a firm belief in the pre-Hellenic and Eteocretan status of his Minoans, as decreed by Homer, would ensure that he could never know what those little characters, now as firmly etched in his mind as they were in the soft clay, longed to tell him.

Evans repeated his lament to a public audience in London in 1936, and there, a new generation, unaffected by the blinkers he himself had imposed, took up the inquiry and succeeded where the discoverer had failed. Fourteen-year-old Michael Ventris was taken by his mother to the Jubilee celebrations of the British School at Athens that year, and they listened to Evans speak of the discovery that had been both the glory and the bane of his life. After the lecture, the boy was introduced to the grand gentleman and took Evans's urging seriously. Ventris was determined to read the texts, and so he did, but not in Evans's lifetime.

A Minoan Madonna

The fiftieth anniversary of the British School at Athens was celebrated in grand style with a public exhibition and lecture series in the Royal Academy of Arts in October and November 1936. Despite the numerous important and eminent projects and personalities of the school who had taken part in revealing "All periods of the History of Greek Lands and Greek people," and though his work was not connected directly with the school, pride of place was given to the eighty-five-year-old Evans, who sat full center at High Table for the Jubilee Dinner on October 13, Alan Wace to his far right and Bernard Ashmole, an authority on classical Greek sculpture and collateral descendant of Elias Ashmole, at the other end on the left. John Myres, in his opening remarks as chairman of the school, placed Evans's work "on one side of the central classical studies," with his discovery of the "pre-Hellenic Minoan Culture," and Byzantine civilization on the other.[126] The public perception of the time is nowhere more clearly and concisely stated than in the reply given by the Greek minister, Simopoulos, "The excavations at Knossos have made famous the name of Sir Arthur Evans, who had the unique distinction of turning into authentic history what had previously been considered as mythology."[127] Not wishing to disappoint, Evans used the first of the public lectures, on "The Minoan World," designed to initiate the layman to aspects of Greek art and archaeology as elucidated by the activities of the school, to reaffirm his own place in relation to Schliemann's, to demonstrate the importance of his discovery by relating it closely to Egypt, and, most important of all, to validate the connection between scenes in Minoan art and scenes from Greek myths (and, by extension, the authenticity of the doubtful ivory figures and gold jewels—all part of the large display he showed to interested parties at the end of the address).

The transcribed lecture is the last of Evans's publications on the Minoans. It was certainly written by him, yet the references to his actions are in the third-person singular. Like Julius Caesar writing a history of his own deeds, he recalls how Evans had first "stumbled" onto the Minoans: "He had observed in the Athens Museum and in private possession certain early seals found in Crete." While this may be excused as the work of a diligent scribe of the Royal Academy forgetting to personalize the speech before sending it to the printers, less forgivable is the use of a capital *E* when he describes himself as the "Excavator" (perhaps we are meant to consider "Creator" as an alternative?) who proposed the subdivision of the Minoan periods some thirty-five years before.

Evans's final thoughts on the underworld and Minoan religion, issues that had clearly preoccupied him greatly in recent years, exposed one of the main themes of his life: "As a whole the Minoan signet-rings supply a principal source of our knowledge of the Minoan Religion. Judged from a Christian standpoint, this was on a distinctly higher level than the classical form that succeeded it. It included . . . a primitive element in which 'Bethels,' in the form of pillar shrines, are by due ritual infused with the divine spirit, often descending in dove form." There is little doubt that a parallel was being drawn between the Minoan dove and the Holy Spirit of the Christians, often pictured as a dove. The successful completion of his search for Christian roots in the prehistory of Crete was further elucidated:

> The old Cretans themselves belonged to an ethnic stock . . . which can be traced east through a large part of Anatolia and Northern Syria, and the Religion itself belonged fundamentally to Western Asia. It is not strange, therefore, that the form of Christian belief that we still see to-day throughout the Mediterranean area should find some interesting anticipations in that of Minoan Crete. The root idea was matriarchal and the Mother Goddess presides. The adoration of Mother and Child on a Minoan signet-ring, with the Magi in the shape of warriors bringing their gifts, is almost a replica of that on a Christian ring-stone of the Sixth Century of our era. The mother here with the Child on her lap is a true Madonna. In another interesting scene the death of a youthful God is clearly referred to . . . the idea of resurgence after death also repeats itself in these scenes, symbolized by the chrysalis as well as the butterfly . . . But though in such scenes the parallelism with Thammuz and the Great Mother on the Syrian side is unmistakable, the outlook in the Minoan World was purer, and in all branches of its art—extending over so many centuries—no single representation has been brought to light of an indecent nature.

Thus not only were the motifs of Christian worship found in Minoan art but the spirit of "decency" could also be attributed to the Cretans of his mind. Primarily, though, the motif of the Madonna and Child, mother and son, both divine, absorbed him in his last years.

Historical imperatives based on the Aryan myth in Germany and nostalgia for the Roman Empire in Italy, both encouraged by the intransigence of modern politicians, brought Europe to war again when Germany, under Hitler's leadership, invaded Poland in 1939 as a first step to creating a new, third variant of the Germanic Kingdom. The Allies came together again, this time without Italy, which under Mussolini's Fascist government sided with Hitler; archaeologists once again performed as military liaisons in the field of operations. Captain John Pendlebury returned to Crete as British vice-consul, but his true mission was to train and direct a band of Cretan guerrillas to raid Italian possessions in the Dodecanese.

Pendlebury took to the task with his indomitable spirit of adventure and trooped around Herakleion with his carefree manner and a sword-stick, a short walking stick or crop concealing a steel blade, tucked under his arm. He thrived on the experience of training his old friends in the mountains he loved, but the war eventually caught up with him. He wrote to Hilda on March 7, 1941, asking after "Little Arthur, Myres . . . all the rogues of yester year." But the letter ends with, "At present we seem as safe as you, though by the time this gets to you we may not be so!" It was the last time she heard from him. On May 21, Hitler sent his newest secret weapon against Crete, light infantry paratroopers, and Pendlebury vanished amid the dark clouds of battle and rumor.

Pendlebury had loved Crete and the Cretans too much. That he had given his heart and soul to the islanders and their natural paradise was obvious; the introduction to his last text on ancient Cretans, his 1939 book, *The Archaeology of Crete*, concludes with an emotional acknowledgment to the living:

> And last but not least come all those companions of our travels and the hospitality of the Cretans themselves. A journey is pure joy, whether accompanied by a vigorous young Kourete of Dikte or by an equally vigorous but more reminiscent elderly Idaean Daktyl, whether one's lodging is with the village schoolmaster, in a monastery, or on the bare hillside with the raggle-taggle gypsies. To have stood on Ida, on Dikte and on Aphendes-Kavousi in the

clear shrill wind and to have toiled through the hot little valleys with that unforgettable smell of herbs is an experience the memory of which nothing can ever take away from you.[128]

But now he and his memories were gone. The world learned later that Pendlebury was wounded during the fighting after the first wave of German paratroopers initiated the Battle of Crete, then executed the following day. Within a few days, the main centers of Crete were taken and the conquering general of the occupying forces installed himself in the only suitable lodging on the island: the Villa Ariadne.

Evans took the news of the Battle of Crete and Pendlebury's death severely. It was as though all that he had done at Knossos was lost to the new barbarians, and the death of Pendlebury, at the age of thirty-five, seemed to eclipse the bright future of Cretan archaeology. Evans would never have sacrificed himself the way Pendlebury had. He saw himself as a savior who could bestow goodness through his mere presence, rather than join in a movement on a personal level like Pendlebury. Even in the Balkans, Evans saw himself as a translator through whom oppressed peoples might voice their deepest anxieties but not as someone who would take an interest in them personally. Pendlebury was a man of his time, one who chose action over words, and he identified so closely with the passionate Cretans, in both their euphoria and their pain, that in the end he became one of them and paid the price with his life.

On the morning of July 8, 1941, Myres, Dawkins (now Emeritus Bywater and Sotheby Professor of Byzantine and Modern Greek at Oxford), and Edward Thurlow Leeds, keeper of the Ashmolean, motored to Youlbury to congratulate Evans on his ninetieth birthday. They found him in a frail state and fretting that he should move to the lodge gatehouse of Youlbury because he "had spent all his money on Knossos and there was nothing left."[129] But his spirits were lifted when, on behalf of the Hellenic Society, they presented him with an ornate scroll to "honour his contributions to learning," and "above all" to commemorate "his never-failing inspiration and encouragement to all workers in these wide fields, his initiative and wise counsel in the advancement of learning and research on many occasions, and his lifelong and strenuous devotion to the cause of freedom in thought and in action."[130] Had such a scroll been delivered on his seventieth birthday, the bearers might have felt less guilt at representing the hypocrisy with which the academic establishment treats senior scholars. Like most prestigious prizes, it came twenty years too late. Evans had become a nuisance to the young scholars he had vowed to assist; many felt that he had positively destroyed Wace's career. But it was not the time to be truthful; respect was demanded and given to one of the most influential archaeologists of the twentieth century.

Three days after the visit, Arthur John Evans passed away in his sleep. He was cremated in the cleansing fire of the Greeks and his mortal remains were taken to the churchyard at Abbot's Langley where they lie with those of his father and mother, far from Youlbury's viewing platforms, which looked down along the Vale of White Horse where this story began with the birth of Arthur Benoni Evans in 1781. Three full generations of Evans men in one and a half centuries helped to rewrite world history, but the most substantial contribution came from the third and last of the line.

6

The Minoan Maze

Epitaph

Sir Arthur Evans's death brought both sadness and relief to his friends and colleagues. Myres wrote the obituary notices for the British Academy and Royal Society, based on his own experience and his personal knowledge, but also on letters that he solicited from associates who conveyed their own impressions. Bell, from the Ashmolean Museum, suggested that Myres take the opportunity to set the record straight: "You especially are able to differentiate more justly than anybody between the different shares of the various partakers in the discovery of Minoan civilization (a thing which needs doing very badly), providing you take care not to minimize your own share, which everybody who was about at the time knows to have been a very large one."[1] Instead, Myres wrote a hero's epitaph for his tutor, mentor, and colleague, and lectured in a similar vein on Evans's life and work to the Hellenic Society in the autumn of 1941. But when asked by the London publishers Chatto and Windus, he declined to turn his notes into a book. For whatever reasons—perhaps because he knew he couldn't maintain the mask of uncritical praise any longer, with Bell's words and his own memories having played too long on his subconscious—Myres passed the offer on to Evans's half-sister, Joan. No one immersed in the discipline could have written a biography without references to actions that almost certainly would have been considered disrespectful to the recently departed.

As the war intensified in Europe, the War Office requisitioned Youlbury in the autumn of 1941 for billeting a regiment of the Royal Air Force and ruined the house; it was almost as if they were getting back at Evans for his 1917 campaign against them. Joan Evans undertook the task of dealing with his estate and of putting order in the mortal records of a long, active, and complex life. She and Myres established a correspondence in which it is quite clear that she found the task daunting. She was the ideal choice in many ways, though she may not have thought so at the time. She had come to know Evans's scholarly work through the index volume she compiled for *The Palace of Minos* in 1936, but, as with the index, she became highly selective about what she chose to draw attention to in her half-brother's intellectual history. The biography she composed set in order the lifetime and career of a man whose life was a series of powerful episodes. She did not touch on certain topics and personalities, and not because they were unimportant. The adoption of James Candy, a contemporary of hers, was not referred to at all even though he occupied a special place in Evans's heart and was part of the Boy Scout movement—an important aspect of Evans's later life. She avoided the stormy side of Evans's character and deemed his public dispute with Wace unworthy of her posthumous portrait. Instead, she painted her half-brother in much the same light as his commissioned portraits had shown him: as a formidable figure surrounded by his greatest finds. She sanitized his story, like the mother in J. M. Barrie's *Peter Pan* who enters the children's brains as they sleep and tidies their thoughts into an order she approves of, discarding anything she thinks doesn't belong.

Yet what didn't belong in Joan's reconstruction was in many ways more interesting than what she thought did. Her performance as biographer may be compared to what a strict wife might have been during Evans's life: someone to temper his childlike enthusiasm and creative reconstructions with her logical reasoning. But Evans's popular success was largely due to the fact that he didn't allow anyone to check his theories, and so he was able to assert their "correctness" without too much opposition. Joan may have felt it her duty to make posthumous corrections to the life of one she admired. Unfortunately, her depiction lacks depth and reads as flatly as Sir William Richmond's portrait. By relegating Evans's successful discoveries to the result of being in the right place at the right time, or "Time and Chance," and by explaining his insights as mere intuition, she denied what made Evans worthy of her biography in the first place: his strength of character, his stamina in the face of contrary circumstance or opinion, and, above all, his enormous creative ability.

Arthur Evans did not stumble upon Knossos by some happy circumstance. He set his mind on acquiring the rights to a well-documented site and spent seven full years in preparation by visiting similar sites, making detailed notes on the finds and conclusions of his predecessors in the field, and becoming an active participant in the modern politics of Crete. Like any architect of the past, he knew he also had to be an architect of the present and future, and secured the expertise he lacked in the person of a site foreman, architects, and conservators, and he sought the funds necessary to give him the freedom to reveal Knossos as his personal vision dictated.

Michael Ventris, the young man who had heard Evans mourn over the silence of the Knossos tablets in 1936, announced to a startled world in 1952 that he had deciphered Linear B: the tablets were written in an early form of ancient Greek. Ventris attributed his success to the ready availability of transcriptions of the tablets from new excavations that Carl Blegen had undertaken at Pylos, in Messenia, and to Myres's finally making the Knossos tablets available, a full half-century after Evans should have distributed his notes. More tablets became available from Mycenae itself, when Wace returned there, after thirty years in exile, vindicated by the proof that Mycenaean Greeks were in charge of Knossos when the great fire that baked the tablets swept through the Palace at the end of Evans's second palace period.

Scholars quickly accepted Wace's theory of the Mycenaean domination of Crete, but Blegen soon pointed out that Evans's date, roughly 1400 B.C., was two centuries earlier than the very similar tablets at Pylos and Mycenae.[2] Leonard Palmer, professor of comparative philology at Oxford, who wrote a synthesis of the tablets and their contents for the general reader in 1960, showed that the language of the tablets from the three sites was uniform and must have been written about the same time. He began a meticulous reinvestigation of the Knossos tablets to verify their date, and found compelling evidence to show not only that

Evans's date was wrong but that Evans had deliberately falsified the records to suit his desire for the tablets to belong to the acme of Minoan civilization, before his squatter reoccupation—the time period to which Palmer now assigned the archives. In 1961 Palmer launched a vicious radio and newspaper campaign against Evans, highlighting inconsistencies and contrasting his notes with Mackenzie's.[3] Sir John Boardman, then Oxford University Reader in Classical Archaeology, stepped in to defend Evans, and many others have since joined what has become a seemingly inextricable issue, important because it figures prominently in the basic question at the heart of Greek archaeology and history: Who were the Greeks and where did they come from?[4] Two camps continue to argue for either the early or late date,[5] and a third option—that the tablets belong to more than one period—was recently thrown into the arena.[6]

One constructive result of Palmer's inquisition has been the refinement of Evans's LM II date by his supporters to the later LM IIIA period, roughly 1350 B.C. Another is the recognition of the major contribution that Mackenzie made to the excavation and publication of Knossos; he is the subject of a recent biography.[7] Perhaps now his ghost, reputed to wander the lower corridors of the Villa Ariadne, may leave Evans's shadow forever.

Gordon Childe was dismayed to see how quickly and easily Evans's Pan-Minoan School was overthrown, and disillusioned to witness the failure of the "grand and hopeful experiment,"[8] as he called Soviet authority, when the grisly details of Joseph Stalin's despotic rule emerged after his death in 1953, followed in 1956 by his public denunciation. With de-Stalinization in full swing, Childe retired himself from archaeology and life by leaping from a cliff to his death in October 1957. He rationalized his suicide in a note complaining of "inefficient teachers" and "distinguished professors mumbling lectures ten years out of date" at British universities. "But even when retired, their prestige may be such that they can hinder the spread of progressive ideas and blast the careers of innovators who tactlessly challenge theories and procedures that ten or fifteen years previously had been original and fruitful (I am thinking for instance of Arthur Evans)."[9] Childe asked his successor not to open the note for a decade, "as it may cause pain and even provoke libel actions,"[10] but he wanted it known eventually that he had made his choice while still of sound mind not to join the ranks of distinguished but doddery emeritus professors. Yet one can't but observe that he had backed losing horses all his life, and may have seen fit to end it before making any further blunders.

Black Ariadne

The Mycenaean Greek takeover of Knossos has become an accepted historical fact based largely on the language of the Linear B texts. But the strong Egyptian element there, as Evans consistently noted, is only very recently being reconsidered. A German geologist named Hans Georg Wunderlich proposed that Knossos was an Egyptian-style funerary temple in his 1972 book, *Wohin der Stier Europa trug* (published in English in 1974 as *The Secret of Crete*). This pragmatic scientist couldn't conceive of anyone's using Cretan gypsum, which disintegrates rapidly when exposed to the elements, to build a functional structure. Knossos, according to Wunderlich, was occupied by the dead, not the living. His theory was quietly dismissed without debate and he died soon after its publication; Wunderlich was an outsider, and his suggestion was much too far from Evans's understanding of the building. Even the American philologist Martin Bernal, who pointed out in his 1987 book *Black Athena* (essentially a historiography of the ancient and modern theories about the origins of the Greeks) that there was plenty of evidence for Egyptian sovereignty over Crete and parts of Greece, failed to mention Wunderlich's theory, though it fit well with his own.

Bernal's view—that the ancient Greeks never concealed their indebtedness to Pharaonic Egypt but that modern scholars denied it in favor of the Aryan origin of Greek society and language—received a great deal of scholarly and public attention because it chronicled the racial and ethnic prejudices inherent in the writing of ancient history and prehistory. The book's subtitle, *The Afroasiatic Roots of Classical Civilization*, guaranteed it a swift and largely negative response from academic circles in Europe and North America. But the question remains how much the ancient Greeks owed to the Egyptians, whom many black scholars consider to have been black Africans and, therefore, a source of ancestral pride to all blacks.

Bernal's assertion that a "huge number of Egyptian objects [were] found at every level in Crete"[11] is an exaggeration; and his thesis that the strong Egyptian element in the early Aegean—which Evans explained as "a real religious syncretism," a fusion of beliefs—was due to Egypto-Phoenician invasions around 1550 B.C. is problematic. The

Hyksos, a Semitic group who founded the Fifteenth Egyptian Dynasty when they forcibly occupied the eastern Nile Delta in around 1650–1550 B.C., blocked regular intercourse between the Theban pharaohs and Crete. In fact, the great majority of Egyptian artifacts in Crete belong to the end of the second palace period, in which Evans recognized the marked Egyptian influence in Minoan art.

Evans had declared: "As regards Egypt, Minoan Crete did not find itself in the position in which Palestine and Phoenicia, having only land frontiers, stood towards the great border Powers of the Nile and of the Euphrates." He had maintained that "with the sea between, it could always keep the foreign civilization at arm's length. Its enterprising inhabitants continually absorbed and assimilated Egyptian forms and ideas, developing them on independent lines. They took what they wanted," he had fantasized, "nothing more, and were neither artistically nor politically enslaved."[12] But we see now that this was just a part of Evans's vision of the Minoans' "free and independent spirit," as he saw it, an idea that has suffered much from the proof of the Mycenaean conquest of Crete. There may well have been Egyptian rule in Crete, whether economic, political, or both, but not until the dynamic pharaohs of the Eighteenth Dynasty repossessed the Nile Delta around 1550 B.C. and extended their control over their neighbors to create the largest and most powerful empire of its day.[13]

If we consider the possibility that Knossos came under Egyptian authority at some point in the second palace period, when Mycenaean Greek mercenaries established control there, we could justify Evans's frequent identification of Aphrodite-Ariadne with the Egyptian Hathor-Isis, and his first impression that a woman sat on the throne at Knossos. Indeed, the British scholar Rodney Castleden, in his 1989 book *The Knossos Labyrinth*, proposed that a female representative of the Minoan nature goddess occupied the throne in what he preferred to call a temple-complex.[14] Castleden's theory may be linked to the movement for empowering women in prehistory, spearheaded since the early 1970s by the late Lithuanian archaeologist and philologist Marija Gimbutas. Gimbutas maintained that there was a time during the European Neolithic period when men and women lived in peace and harmony worshiping nature goddesses until around 4000 B.C., when Indo-European invaders, perhaps the Aryans, imposed their patriarchal rule and warlike gods.[15] She believed that Minoan Crete was one of the survivals of what she called "Old European Matriliny" in the

Bronze Age, ending with the Mycenaean conquest of Knossos. Its transfer from a nature goddess to the Egyptian goddess of the underworld
could have been plausible and even attractive to Evans, had he not insisted on giving it to Minos.

The thalassocracy of Minos itself, which Evans and his generation
never thought to question, was attacked by the American historian
Chester Starr, who in 1955 suggested that Thucydides, an Athenian,
used the myth as a historical imperative for his native city when they
established their own maritime rule over the Aegean islands.[16] Then, in
1979, the "wooden walls" of Evans's Minoan thalassocracy came under
attack by the Greek archaeologist Stylianos Alexiou, who pointed out
that there was plenty of stone military architecture in Minoan Crete,
much of which Evans himself had observed during his early travels
with Myres.[17] Alexiou's observations were added to by another Greek
archaeologist, Stella Chryssoulaki, who recalled seeing plenty of strong
walls as a young girl when she traveled the hills of Crete with her father,
who engineered the new roads built after the Second World War.
Chryssoulaki gathered convincing evidence that the Cretan countryside—in the early palace period, at least—was controlled from the
small forts that Evans chose to forget about once he found Knossos.[18]

But Crete is inextricably linked to myth. In the summer of 1979 the
British archaeologist Peter Warren and his Greek colleagues Efi and
Iannis Sakellarakis confronted macabre scenes at their excavations,
the former in the town of Knossos, and the latter on a windswept
northern spur of Mount Juktas called Anemospilia, meaning "caves of
the winds."

The Knossos team found a jumbled deposit of butchered human
bones, sometimes semiarticulated, scattered throughout a small house
burned during the second palace period. Osteologists identified the remains of at least four children in good health at the time they were
butchered in much the same way the Minoans slaughtered their sheep
and goats, suggesting they had been sacrificed and eaten.[19] Warren used
this conclusion, unsavory to modern tastes,* to propose that the Minoans practiced ritual human sacrifice and cannibalism—which the
Greeks recalled in their myth of Kronos, who devoured his children.[20]

---

*The senior Cretan archaeologist Nicolas Platon was so horrified at this suggestion
that he insisted the bones must be those of apes, not humans.

Elsewhere on the site, Warren identified three circular structures as "the dancing-place of Ariadne," based on Homer's description of the one wrought by Daedalus.[21]

At Anemospilia, the Sakellarakis team found four skeletons pinned down when a small building, described as a shrine, had collapsed; they identified them as a priest, a priestess, another functionary, and a youth. The youth lay on a stone table, which they assumed was a sacrificial altar. This sensational discovery was argued as the strongest evidence for human sacrifice in Minoan Crete, where the bull sports may not have been enough to quench the Minoans' appetite for blood. Again the myth of Kronos and Zeus was brought into the otherwise scientific discussion.[22]

It was a bad year for Evans's aesthetic Minoans, once described by Leonard Woolley as "the enchantment of a fairy world," and "the most complete acceptance of the grace of life the world has ever known,"[23] but now accused of murder and cannibalism. Perhaps the 1979 discoveries could be read otherwise: as the preparation of human remains for excarnation, the practice of exposing the deceased for consumption by birds and beasts so the flesh may be recycled in a pure and natural manner. But even this suggestion comes at a time when archaeologists are obsessed with environmental issues and trying to convince wary governments of the need to look at ecological change over the long term.

In the end, only Knossos itself and the artifacts unearthed there during controlled excavations remain as solid proof of Evans's Minoans, but these, too, have become problematic. The Palace and surrounding buildings are crumbling as fast as Evans's intellectual reconstruction of his ancient Minoan society. The building techniques of this century have not withstood the rigors of the Cretan climate or of the relentless passage of the more than one million visitors who flock to Knossos each year in search of a part of their history. This influx has necessitated a major new campaign of restorations, and these value the modern architecture as much as the ancient vestiges. Perhaps the time has come to accept that Knossos is no longer ancient, no longer either Minoan or Mycenaean, but timeless—as important to us now as it was to those who built it four thousand years ago.

In restoring the Palace at Knossos, we are now not trying to re-create some past golden age but preserving a building that has taken on a series of new meanings in this century. The Labyrinth-Palace-Temple at Knossos has become the symbol of our greatest aspiration, a site where we understand the transformation of ideas and the relative nature of history and archaeology. And where better to realize our purpose in that fluid interplay of the past with the future than in the Minoan maze at Knossos, revealed and crafted by Evans.

Notes

1. Apprentice Archaeologist 1851–83

1. Joan Evans 1943, 13.
2. Joan Evans reported her grandmother's actions with approval as she performed a similar though much less drastic cleansing process for her half-brother Arthur over a century later, 1943, 24.
3. Daniel 1981a, 34.
4. Joan Evans 1943, 50.
5. Ibid., 67.
6. Thomson 1950, 102–3.
7. Joan Evans 1943, 83.
8. Ibid., 83.
9. Ibid., 65–66.
10. Ibid., 93.
11. Ibid., 93–94.
12. Ibid., 99.
13. Ibid., 83.
14. Ibid., 55.
15. Ibid., 64.
16. Newton 1850, 1.
17. Frere 1800, 204. For summary and results of recent work see R. Singer and others 1993.
18. Daniel 1981a, 49.
19. Joan Evans 1943, 100.

20. Ibid., 101.
21. Ibid., 103.
22. Prestwich 1860.
23. Daniel 1967, 13–14.
24. Joan Evans 1943, 104.
25. Ibid., 144.
26. Ibid., 130.
27. Myres 1942, 324.
28. Turner 1981.
29. Brown 1993, 13.
30. Grimm, *Geschishte der deutsche Sprache*, 1848, 6, 162.
31. Joan Evans 1943, 165.
32. Brown 1993, 13.
33. J. L. Myres 1942, 325.
34. Joan Evans 1943, 163.
35. Ibid., 163.
36. Ibid., 176.
37. Ibid., 176–77.
38. Brown 1993, 17, Fig. 12.
39. Joan Evans 1943, 177.
40. Ibid., 178.
41. Evans 1876.
42. Ibid., 308.
43. Stillman's dispatches appeared in *The Nation* 3, 1866, 275–77; 4, 1867, 54–55, 76, 318–19, 459; 5, 1867, 337–38; 7, 1868, 10–11, 290–91, 366–67; 8, 1869, 48–49. His later recollections are in Stillman 1901, ii, 21–45.
44. A. D. Momigliano 1994.
45. Stephens 1895, ii, 152.
46. Poliakov 1974, 299.
47. Gossel 1965, 109–10.
48. Joan Evans 1943, 190.
49. Stephens 1895, ii, 163.
50. Macmillan 1929.
51. Joan Evans 1943, 221–22.
52. Ibid., 227.
53. Ibid., 252.
54. A. D. Momigliano 1994, 203.
55. Stephens 1895, ii, 223.
56. Ibid., 259.
57. Joan Evans 1943, 267.
58. Traill 1995, 229.
59. Finlay 1974, 6–7.
60. Grote 1846–56, I, 434–35.
61. Traill 1995, 112–21.
62. Duchene 1996, 92.

63. Newton 1878.
64. Traill 1995, 207.
65. Joan Evans 1943, 261–62.
66. Mallowan 1977, 26.
67. Joan Evans 1943, 262–63.
68. Evans 1931b, 21.
69. Evans 1901a.
70. Traill 1995, 231–33.
71. Evans 1883c, 438.
72. Ibid., 439.

2. The Ancient Labyrinths 1883–93

1. Joan Evans 1943, 269.
2. Ibid., 271.
3. Bowden 1991, 163, Figs. 59–60.
4. Allen 1883, 236–37.
5. Joan Evans 1943, 156.
6. Pitt-Rivers 1906.
7. Schliemann 1875, 363.
8. J. L. Myres 1942, 354 n. 1.
9. Macmillan 1929, xvii.
10. *Times*, April 24 and 29, 1886; Traill 1995, 254.
11. *Academy*, July 10, 1886, 31; *JHS* VII, 1887.
12. Joan Evans 1943, 276.
13. Evans 1888b.
14. Evans 1891b.
15. Evans 1889a.
16. Flinders Petrie 1931.
17. Flinders Petrie 1901.
18. N. Momigliano 1999, 5; Lock 1990, 177.
19. Hogarth 1910, 19.
20. Flinders Petrie 1888, 402.
21. *Hist. Nat.* xxxvi, 13, 19, 85.
22. Flinders Petrie 1890, 271.
23. Ibid., 275.
24. Fitton 1995a, 114.
25. Flinders Petrie 1890, 276.
26. Ibid., 275–77.
27. Flinders Petrie 1892b, 152.
28. Dunbabin 1956, 351.
29. Brown 1986, 41.
30. Joan Evans 1943, 291–92.
31. Traill 1995, 293–97.
32. Lambros 1891, 95.

33. Joan Evans 1943, 309.
34. Hoeck 1823–29.
35. Grote 1846–56, I, 311.
36. Hirst 1887a, 230–31; Hazzidakis 1931.
37. Hazzidakis 1881.
38. Di Vita 1985, 17.
39. Hirst 1885, 128.
40. Thénon 1866–68.
41. Hirst 1887b, 157.
42. Halbherr and Fabricius 1885.
43. Willetts 1955, Chap. IX.
44. Detorakis 1994, 265.
45. Warren 1972.
46. Fowler 1984, 66.
47. Falkener 1854, 24.
48. Warren 1972, 80.
49. There is some confusion over the exact dates: see Hood 1987, 86; Kopaka 1990, 19.
50. Kopaka 1990, 1995.
51. Aposkitou 1979, 83; Hood 1987, 88–89.
52. M.S.F. Hood 1987, 87–8.
53. P. Gardner 1894, 476.
54. Macmillan 1929, iii.
55. Haussoullier 1880.
56. M.S.F. Hood 1987, 90.
57. Stillman 1881; repeated in Driessen 1990, 17–18.
58. Stillman 1901, ii, 220.
59. Brown 1986, 37.
60. Stoll 1961, 53; Hood 1992, 224–25.
61. Traill 1995, 226.
62. Halbherr 1893, 110–12; Di Vita 1984, 33 with plan.
63. Wroth 1886.
64. *Athenaeum* 3077, Oct. 16, 1886, 507.
65. Driessen 1990, 24–25; Hood 1992, 226–27.
66. Fabricius 1886.
67. M.S.F. Hood 1992, 226.
68. *Athenaeum* 3077, Oct. 16, 1886, 508.
69. *Athenaeum* 3080, Nov. 6, 1886, 607.
70. Stoll 1961, 66; Hood 1992, 226.
71. Driessen 1990, 26–27.
72. *Antiquary*, Sept. 1891, 95.
73. Homolle 1891, 452.
74. Millington-Evans 1894.
75. Horwitz 1981, 76.
76. Stephens 1895, ii, 420.

77. Joan Evans 1943, 306.
78. A. Brown 1986, 39.
79. Joan Evans 1943, 304.
80. Evans Archive, Ashmolean.
81. Traill 1995, 228–29.
82. Perrot 1891.
83. *Iliad* 13:570, 20:403.
84. Evans Archive, Ashmolean.
85. Ibid.
86. Joan Evans 1943, 304.
87. Stephens 1895, i, vi.
88. Joan Evans 1943, 305.
89. A. Brown 1993, 34, Fig. 30.
90. Joan Evans 1943, 304.
91. Evans 1893b.

3. Candia 1893–1900

1. Brown 1986, 39.
2. J. L. Myres 1950.
3. J. N. L. Myres 1980, 10.
4. Brown 1986, 39.
5. S. Reinach in *Revue Archéologique* 1884, I, 336–43; *AJA* 1, 1885, 225.
6. Brown 1986, 41.
7. J. L. Myres 1895.
8. Brown 1986, 42.
9. Ibid., 42–43.
10. Ibid., 43.
11. *Times*, Sat. Sept. 23, 1893.
12. Higgins 1979.
13. Joan Evans 1943, 316 n. 1.
14. Evans 1893a, 195.
15. Fitton 1995, 141–43.
16. *Academy* 1156, June 30, 1894, 540.
17. *JHS* 14, 1893, xi, 266; Macmillan 1929, xix; Pope 1975, 146 n. 1.
18. Brown 1993, 37.
19. Evans 1935b, ix.
20. *Acts* 27:8.
21. *Athenaeum*, Nov. 21, 1885, 675; Hirst 1887, 231.
22. *Times*, Aug. 29, 1894.
23. Foundoulaki 1996, 177–78.
24. Joan Evans 1943, 311.
25. Randolph 1687; Warren 1972, 77.
26. Joan Evans 1943, 311.
27. Ibid., 312.

28. Ibid.
29. Ibid.
30. Ibid.
31. Ibid., 314.
32. Ibid., 313–14.
33. *Times,* Aug. 29, 1894.
34. Ibid.
35. Joan Evans 1943, 314.
36. *Odyssey* 19: 172–79
37. *Iliad* 2:645–52.
38. Joan Evans 1943, 315.
39. Ibid.
40. *Iliad* 5:43.
41. Hirst 1887c.
42. Brown 1993, 47.
43. Halbherr 1892, 215.
44. Brown 1993, 48.
45. Halbherr 1892, 115.
46. Joan Evans 1943, 316.
47. Ibid.
48. *Times,* Aug. 29, 1894.
49. E. S. Bosanquet 1938, 147.
50. Brown 1993, 50.
51. Halbherr 1893, 198; Brown 1993, 51–52.
52. *Times,* Aug. 29, 1894.
53. Evans 1894c.
54. *Times,* Aug. 29, 1894.
55. Evans 1894e, 270–74.
56. Evans 1883c, 438.
57. Evans 1894e, 357.
58. Ibid., 367–68.
59. Herodotus *Histories* I, 173.
60. Evans 1894e, 358, 362.
61. Flinders Petrie 1892b, 356–57; 1894.
62. Evans 1894e, 370.
63. Ibid., 369–71.
64. Ibid., 372.
65. Ibid., 358.
66. *Oxford Magazine,* quoted in *Academy* 1175, Nov. 10, 382.
67. Joan Evans 1943, 307.
68. Evans 1889a.
69. Joan Evans 1943, 318.
70. Ibid., 318.
71. Brown 1993, 54.
72. Halbherr 1893, 13–14.

73. Brown 1993, 55.
74. Evans 1896a.
75. Evans 1888b.
76. Schliemann 1878, 252–54.
77. Evans and Myres 1895, 469.
78. Evans 1896h, 173 fig. 1.
79. Evans and Myres 1895.
80. Ibid.
81. *Academy* 1210, July 13, 1895.
82. Helbig 1896; see also Myres's review in *Classical Review* 10, 1896, 350–57.
83. Evans 1895d.
84. Reinach 1895.
85. Reinach 1892, 90.
86. Renfrew 1987, 14.
87. Reinach, "Chronique d' Orient" in *Revue Archéologique* 27, 1895, 357 n.2, 384.
88. J. L. Myres 1942, 335.
89. Ibid., 332.
90. Joan Evans 1943, 307.
91. Evans 1897a, 351.
92. Evans 1896a.
93. Evans 1896a; 1897a, 351.
94. Evans 1897a, 354–55.
95. Evans 1896a.
96. *Odyssey* 10:519–20.
97. Evans 1897a, 358.
98. Ibid., 355 Fig. 26.
99. Pendlebury and Money-Coutts 1938, 57, 101.
100. Evans 1896b, 513.
101. Ibid.
102. Evans 1921a, 632–33 fig. 470.
103. *Diodorus* V. c. 70, 6.
104. Halbherr 1893, 198.
105. Evans 1896h, 170–71.
106. Ibid., 170.
107. Evans 1896c, 18.
108. Brown 1993, 74 fig. 63.
109. Evans 1896d, 54.
110. Ibid.
111. Ibid.
112. E. L. Godkin, "Crete in England," *The Nation*, March 25, 1897, 217–18.
113. Evans 1896b, 512.
114. Ibid.
115. Evans 1896g.
116. Taylor 1890, 310.
117. Evans 1901c, 112.

118. Schliemann 1878, 252–54.
119. Evans 1901c, 100.
120. Ibid., 105.
121. Evans 1896b, 513.
122. Evans 1896f, 919.
123. Ibid.
124. Evans 1897a, 389–90.
125. Ibid., 361.
126. Evans 1898a, 14–15.
127. *Illustrated London News*, June 20, 1896, 776.
128. Hogarth 1910, 21.
129. Ibid., 21–22.
130. Ibid., 25.
131. Ibid., 23.
132. Ibid., 41.
133. "The restless isle," *Dundee Advertiser*, Feb. 21, 1913.
134. J. L. Myres 1942, 335, n.7.
135. Evans 1897a, 367.
136. Ibid., 379. McIver and Wilkin made a journey to Algeria in 1900 "the main object of which was to investigate the evidence for the Libyan origin of Prof. F. Petrie's 'New Race.'" They concluded "the Berbers are essentially a white race, with brown-black hair and hazel eyes, and a skin which is really red-white. They are, therefore, the true representatives of the white Libyans of the Egyptian wall-paintings." *Athenaeum*, Dec. 1, 1900, 728–29.
137. Poliakov 1974, 68.
138. Brown 1993, 75.
139. Hogarth 1910, 66.
140. Evans 1898a, 29.
141. Ibid., 30–32.
142. Ibid., 37–38.
143. Ibid., 18.
144. Currelly 1956, 60–61.
145. Evans 1898a, 12–13.
146. Ibid., 46ff.
147. Kalopothakes, "Crete under Prince George," *The Nation*, Nov. 13, 1899, 386.
148. Letter of 3/15 January, 1899, Evans Archive, Ashmolean Museum.
149. Demargne 1902; Boardman 1961, 63–64 No. 270.
150. Brown 1983b, 14.
151. Hogarth 1910, 66–67.
152. Ibid.
153. E. Capps, "A New Archaeological Law for Greece." *The Nation*, Aug. 3, 1899, 88–90.
154. Joan Evans 1943, 327.
155. Brown 1983b, 15.

4. Knossos 1900–1907

1. Poole 1922.
2. Apollonius Rhodius, *The Argonautica* iv, 1639–50.
3. Joan Evans 1943, 329.
4. Letter from Hogarth to Evans, April 6, 1899, Evans Archive, Ashmolean Museum.
5. N. Momigliano 1999, 39.
6. Joan Evans 1943, 330.
7. N. Momigliano 1999, 28–32. Hogarth's testimonial for Mackenzie: Wellcome Papers W/24 (October 1912).
8. N. Momigliano 1995, 165.
9. *Builder* 168, Jan. 19, 1945, 59.
10. Hogarth 1910, 20.
11. J. L. Myres 1942, 337.
12. Hogarth 1910, 68.
13. Candy 1984, 21; perhaps the same incident as the one recounted in Evans 1928b, 546–47, in which case it refers to 1906 or later.
14. J. L. Myres, *Oxford Magazine*, May 9, 1900.
15. N. Momigliano 1999, 67.
16. Allsebrook 1992, 88.
17. Hawes, 1965, 97.
18. Evans 1921a, 688 fig. 507.
19. Evans 1901a.
20. Evans 1900f, 56.
21. Joan Evans 1943, 333.
22. J. L. Myres 1900.
23. It was in the collection of Antonios Zacharakis. Evans 1900f, 18 n. 1.
24. Published by Reinach in *Le Petit Temps*, May 6, 1900.
25. Kopaka 1990; 1995.
26. Lapatin forthcoming.
27. Rizzo 1985, 29, quotes a letter from Halbherr to Comparetti in 1886 stating his worries over Gilliéron's fees.
28. Traill 1995, 238.
29. Evans's 1900 notebook, 40, Evans Archive, Ashmolean Museum.
30. Hogarth 1900a, 85.
31. Joan Evans 1943, 334.
32. Hogarth 1910, 69.
33. Hogarth 1900b, 100–101.
34. Simply stated in a *mantinada*, a popular form of Cretan lyric, by Spiros Voskakis of Epano Zakros:

   Ο κερατάς ο Κόγκαρυς
   που ήρθ' απ' την Αγγλία
   μας έκανε ερείπια
   τα εθνικά μνημεία

roughly translated:

> That cuckold, that Hogarth
> who from England came
> turned our national heritage
> into a ruinous shame

35. Hogarth 1926.
36. Letter from C. F. Bell, Budapest, May 26, inquiring after his health, reads, "I do hope that you have been feeling somewhat better—that you have shaken off the malaria for the time." Evans Archive, Ashmolean Museum.
37. Palmer 1961, 357.
38. Evans 1900f, 10.
39. Ibid., 11. See B. B. Powell 1977 for a recent reappraisal.
40. Ibid., 42.
41. Ibid., n. 1.
42. Joan Evans 1943, 389.
43. Evans 1900f, 47.
44. *Man* I, 1901, 5.
45. Waugh 1946, 51–52.
46. Evans 1901a, 132.
47. Tzedhakis et al. 1989.
48. *Times*, Sept. 15, 1900.
49. Evans 1900c.
50. Evans 1900d; Letter to *Times*, Sept. 15, 1900.
51. Reinach 1902, 8.
52. The Cretan Exploration Fund, 1900. First report to the subscribers, privately circulated.
53. Published in letter to the editor of the *Times*, April 2, 1901, followed by a second letter of April 12, published April 16.
54. *Annual of the British School at Athens* 6, 1900, 135–37.
55. *Athenaeum*, Nov. 10, 1900, 621.
56. Evans 1901c, 100, 106; *Athenaeum*, Nov. 10, 1900, 620.
57. Joan Evans 1943, 335.
58. MacEnroe 1995, 11.
59. N. Momigliano 1999, 154–55; Evans Archive, Ashmolean Museum.
60. Evans 1901d, 6.
61. Ibid., 15.
62. Horwitz 1981, 138.
63. Neimeier 1988.
64. Evans 1901d, 15.
65. Ibid., Fig. 8.
66. Farnoux 1993, 105.
67. E. S. Bosanquet 1938, 106.
68. Evans 1901 Notebook.

69. *Times*, June 14, 1901, 8.
70. Evans 1901d, 94–95.
71. Joan Evans 1943, 337.
72. Evans 1901d, 30.
73. B. T. K. Smith, *Philatelic Record*, March 1905.
74. Evans 1901d, 30.
75. *Times*, July 15, 1907, 8.
76. Evans 1901d, 30.
77. Evans 1921a, 344.
78. Evans 1901d, 18 fig. 7a.
79. Hogarth 1901, 123.
80. Papadakis 1992, 55–56.
81. Evans 1921a, 707–8; see Weingarten 1983 for a comprehensive study of the Zakros sealings with bibliography.
82. Poole 1922, 14.
83. Evans 1901d, 102.
84. Joan Evans 1943, 338.
85. Gardner 1892.
86. Ridgeway 1901, 202.
87. Myres's review of Ridgeway 1901 is in the *Classical Review* 16, 1902, 70.
88. Rouse 1901, 272.
89. Burrows 1907, 117.
90. "The Double axe and the labyrinth" in the *Saturday Review*, July 26, 1902, 105–6.
91. Evans 1901b.
92. N. Momigliano 1999, 162.
93. Lock 1990, 177.
94. Joan Evans 1943, 340.
95. Ibid., 341.
96. Evans 1902b, 58.
97. Ibid., 54.
98. Ibid., 45.
99. Ibid., 59.
100. Joan Evans 1943, 344–45.
101. Evans 1902b, 89.
102. Ibid., 86.
103. Clarke 1903, 598.
104. Evans 1902b, 100.
105. Evans 1902 notebook, 31.
106. Evans 1901c, 168.
107. *Diodorus* V. c. lxv.I.
108. Evans 1904c, 51.
109. Joan Evans 1943, 345.
110. Evans 1902b, 73–74.
111. Hall 1902b, 57.
112. Hall 1902a, 393.

113. Evans 1903d.
114. Evans 1903b, 1.
115. N. Momigliano 1999, 42.
116. Evans 1903b, 111.
117. Ibid., 67.
118. Panagiotaki 1993, 54.
119. Evans 1903b, 71.
120. Ibid., 89.
121. Ibid., 111.
122. Ibid., 38.
123. Letter from R. W. Graves to Evans June 6, 1903, Evans Archive, Ashmolean Museum.
124. Currelly 1956, 63–64.
125. Brown 1983a, 11.
126. Duncan Mackenzie 1903, 157–58.
127. Evans 1904b, 137.
128. Ibid., 138–39.
129. Currelly 1956, 65.
130. Joan Evans 1943, 347.
131. *Times*, April 25, 1904.
132. Joan Evans 1943, 348.
133. Evans 1904c, 51.
134. N. Momigliano, 1999, 71.
135. Letter from R. C. Bosanquet to Evans, Nov. 18, 1903, in Evans Archive, Ashmolean Museum.
136. "Homer and his commentators," *Edinburgh Review*, Jan. 1905, 189–215.
137. B. T. K. Smith, *Philatelic Record*, March 1905.
138. Poole 1922, 16.
139. "Recent work in Crete and elsewhere," *Times*, Aug. 7, 1905.
140. *Builder*, May 6, 1955, 761.
141. Evans 1905a, 26.
142. Candy 1984, 26.
143. *Odyssey* XIX, 178, 179.
144. Evans 1921a, vi.
145. Di Vita 1985, 33–34.
146. Evans 1905a, 7.
147. Ibid., 9–11.
148. See Warren 1990 for a recent reaffirmation of the Baetyl = Rhea formula.
149. N. Momigliano 1999, 75.
150. Letter from Harriet Boyd to Evans, Oct. 7, 1905, Evans Archive, Ashmolean Museum.
151. Becker and Betancourt 1997, 74.
152. E. S. Bosanquet 1938, 169.
153. J. L. Myres, *Times*, July 14, 1951.
154. N. Momigliano 1999, 68.

155. D. Powell 1973, 42–43.
156. N. Momigliano 1999, 78–79.
157. *Times,* July 15, 1907, 8.
158. Ibid.
159. Ibid.
160. Evans 1935b, 849 fig. 832; Hood and Smyth 1981, no. 149.
161. Evans 1935b, 621.
162. Joan Evans 1943, 354–55.

5. The Pan-Minoan School 1908–41

1. *Times,* Aug. 27, 1908, 6.
2. Evans 1914, 93 n.6.
3. Ibid., 89.
4. E. S. Bosanquet 1938, 170–71.
5. Sept. 20, 1908. AJE/Youlbury—J. R. Wheeler, American School of Classical Studies at Athens Archives, Athens.
6. Allsebrook 1992, 126.
7. Evans 1909b.
8. *Times,* Aug. 27, 1908, 6.
9. Joan Evans 1943, 349.
10. Jeal 1989, 392–94.
11. Wheeler 1956, 34.
12. Jeal 1989, 107–8.
13. Candy 1984, 15–16.
14. Ibid., 27.
15. Beeching 1990.
16. Candy 1984, iii.
17. Ibid., 27.
18. Ibid., 17, 25, 27.
19. R. Hood 1998, 6–7.
20. Joan Evans 1943, 356.
21. Evans 1909a.
22. Evans 1914, 12.
23. See Warren 1988 for a recent reappraisal.
24. Evans 1914, 13.
25. Joan Evans 1943, 357–62.
26. Evans 1911a, 289.
27. Evans 1909c, 7.
28. Evans 1909a, viii; 1910b, 422.
29. J. L. Myres 1911, 184.
30. "Minoan Crete," *Edinburgh Review,* April 1910, 459–60.
31. *Times,* Sept. 16, 1910.
32. Evans 1914, 83.
33. Lurker 1980, 58–59.

34. *Times*, Sept. 16, 1910.
35. Rodenwaldt 1912, 121 Pl. 14, 1.
36. *Times*, Sept. 16, 1910.
37. Spencer 1990.
38. Joan Evans 1943, 365.
39. Evans 1912b, 281–82.
40. Joan Evans 1943, 366–67.
41. *Times Literary Supplement*, May 18, 1916, 237.
42. Candy 1984, 22–23.
43. Ibid., 36.
44. Joan Evans 1943, 369.
45. Evans 1918a, 205–7.
46. Evans 1916b, 23.
47. C. Mackenzie 1940; J.N.L. Myres 1980.
48. Woolley 1920.
49. Lawson 1920.
50. C. Mackenzie 1931, 194; R. Hood 1998, 45.
51. Wace 1931, xxiii.
52. A. J. B. Wace to Evans, March 3, 1915, Evans Archive, Ashmolean Museum.
53. Mallowan 1977, 235.
54. Evans 1919a.
55. Joan Evans 1943, 373.
56. Ibid., 372.
57. Ibid., 374.
58. Evans 1919b, 192–93.
59. Evans 1919c.
60. Joan Evans 1943, 363–64.
61. R. C. Bosanquet 1922, 51, 70.
62. *Times Literary Supplement*, Dec. 29, 1921, 869.
63. Blegen and Wace 1918, 188.
64. Waterhouse 1986, 26, 108.
65. Blegen 1921, 125–26.
66. Wace 1920a.
67. *Times Literary Supplement*, July 15, 1920, 454.
68. Karo to Evans, Aug. 27, 1920, Evans Archive, Ashmolean Museum.
69. Letter to Evans, Sept. 14, 1920, Evans Archive, Ashmolean Museum.
70. Mackenzie to Evans, Oct. 2, 1920, Evans Archive, Ashmolean Museum.
71. Joan Evans 1943, 372.
72. *Times Literary Supplement*, Nov. 16, 1922, 747.
73. R. Hood 1998, a collection of de Jong's caricatures, is presented with frank comments.
74. See Mackenzie's testimonial on Ali's behalf in the Evans Archive, Ashmolean Museum.
75. Piet de Jong to Myres, Evans Archive, Ashmolean Museum.
76. Evans 1922, 326.

77. D. Eginitis to Evans, June 14, 1922, Evans Archive, Ashmolean Museum.
78. Frost 1909; 1913.
79. Evans 1922, 328.
80. Ibid., 329.
81. Waterhouse 1986, 95.
82. R. Hood 1998, 11.
83. *Times*, Feb. 5, 1924.
84. Ibid.
85. *Times*, Jan. 19, 1924.
86. Typescript in the Evans Archive, Ashmolean Museum.
87. Lapatin 1997, 663–82, esp. 664, n. 7; Hemingway 2000.
88. Woolley 1962, 21–23.
89. Karo 1959, 41–42.
90. *Times*, April 8, 1924, 10; Koehl 1990, 48.
91. R. Hood 1998, 28–32.
92. Wace 1923, 615.
93. *Times*, June, 11, 1924.
94. Letter to J. Myres, Evans Archive, Ashmolean Museum.
95. Vasilaki 1989.
96. Shaw 1995.
97. *Times*, Dec. 19, 1924.
98. Hughes-Brock 1994, 7.
99. Evans 1925b, 51.
100. Childe 1926a, 212.
101. Noted in Hughes-Brock 1994.
102. D. Powell 1973, 41.
103. Joan Evans 1943, 379.
104. Ibid., 380.
105. Evans 1925a.
106. Joan Evans 1943, 382–83.
107. Accame 1984, 209–10.
108. Waugh 1946, 52.
109. M. S. F. Hood 1995.
110. Harrington 1999.
111. Pendlebury Archive, British School at Athens.
112. Letter of Nov. 20, 1927, Pendlebury Archive, JP/L/268.
113. Letter of Feb. 12, 1928, to father, Pendlebury Archive, JP/L/292.
114. Letter of May 10, 1928, Pendlebury Archive, JP/L/313.
115. Ibid., JP/L/314.
116. Ibid., JP/L/405.
117. Letter to Myres, Evans Archive, Ashmolean Museum.
118. Pendlebury Archive, JP/L/425.
119. Letter to father, Pendlebury Archive, JP/L/451.
120. May 19, 1931, Pendlebury Archive, JP/L/458.
121. May 31, 1931, Pendlebury Archive, JP/L/464.

122. June 9, 1931, Pendlebury Archive, JP/L/465.
123. Dec. 10, 1931, Pendlebury Archive, JP/L/477.
124. April 23, 1935, Pendlebury Archive, JP/L/646.
125. Evans 1935, xix.
126. British School at Athens Annual Report for the session 1936–37, 14.
127. Ibid., 15.
128. Pendlebury 1939, xxix.
129. Candy 1984, 82.
130. Joan Evans 1943.

6. The Minoan Maze

1. E. Bell to Myres, Sept. 5, 1941, Evans Archive, Ashmolean Museum.
2. Blegen 1958.
3. Palmer 1961.
4. Palmer and Boardman 1963.
5. The most comprehensive survey of the problem is Niemeier 1982.
6. J. M. Driessen 1990.
7. N. Momigliano 1999.
8. Green 1981, 103.
9. Daniel 1980.
10. Green 1981, 152.
11. Bernal 1987, 385.
12. Evans 1921a, 19.
13. MacGillivray et al. 2000.
14. Castelden 1989; 1990.
15. Gimbutas 1974; 1989; 1991.
16. Starr 1955.
17. Alexiou 1979.
18. Tzedhakis et al. 1989; MacGillivray 1997.
19. Wall et al. 1986.
20. Warren 1981.
21. Warren 1984.
22. Sakellarakis 1981.
23. Quoted in Gimbutas 1991, 344.

Bibliography

Sir Arthur Evans's Scholarly Writings

1870a. "Greek Epigrams" (Oxenham Prize), *Prolusiones Harrovianae,* Harrow, 1869–70.

1870b. "The Life and Character of John Howard" (Prize essay), *Prolusiones Harrovianae,* Harrow, 53.

1871. "On a Hoard of Coins Found at Oxford, with Some Remarks on the Coinage of the First Three Edwards," *Numismatic Chronicle,* 2nd ser., XI, 264–82.

1873. "Over the Marches of Civilised Europe," *Fraser's Magazine,* May, vol. 7, no. XLI, 578–96.

1876. *Through Bosnia and the Herzegovina on foot, during the Insurrection, August and September 1875, with an historical review of Bosnia* (reprint of letters to the *Manchester Guardian*), London. (2nd ed. revised and enlarged, 1877.)

1878a. *Illyrian Letters: a revised selection of correspondence from the Illyrian provinces of Bosnia, Herzegovina, Montenegro, Albania, Dalmatia, Croatia and Slavonia, addressed to the* Manchester Guardian *during the year 1877,* London, Longmans, Green.

1878b. "The Slavs and European Civilization" (lecture delivered at Sion College, February 23), London, Longmans.

1880a. "On Some Recent Discoveries of Illyrian Coins," *Numismatic Chronicle,* 2nd ser., XX, 269–302.

1880b. "The Austrian Counter-Revolution in the Balkans," *Fortnightly Review.*

1880c. "Herzegovina," *Encyclopaedia Britannica,* 9th ed.

1881. "Christmas and Ancestor-Worship in the Black Mountains" [offprint].

1882a. "The Austrian War against Publicity," *Fortnightly Review.*

1882b. "A Series of Ancient Gems from Dalmatia," *Proceedings of the Society of Antiquaries,* 1st ser., X, 175–78.

1883a. "Roumania," *Encyclopaedia Britannica,* 9th ed.

1883b. "Bronze Weapons Found near Oxford and from the Wrekin," *Proceedings of the Society of Antiquaries,* 1st ser., IX, 8.

1883c. Review of Schliemann's *Troja* in *Academy,* 24, Dec. 29, 437–39.

1884a. *The Ashmolean Museum as a Home of Archaeology in Oxford,* Oxford, Parker.

1885a. "Antiquarian Researches in Illyricum, I–II," *Archaeologia,* 48, 1–105.

1885b. "Megalithic Monuments in Their Sepulchral Relations," *Lancashire and Chestershire Antiquarian Society* (Manchester), 3, 1–31.

1886a. "Antiquarian Researches in Illyricum, III–IV," *Archaeologia,* 49, 1–167.

1886b. "Recent Discoveries of Tarentine Terracottas," *Journal of Hellenic Studies,* 7, 1–50.

1887a. "On the Flint-Knappers' Art in Albania," *Journal of the Anthropological Institute* 16, 65–67.

1887b. "On a Coin of the Second Carausius, Caesar in Britain in the Fifth Century," *Numismatic Chronicle,* 3rd ser., VII, 191–219.

1888a. "The Vlachs," *Encyclopaedia Britannica,* 9th ed.

1888b. "The Hallstatt Period in Upper Bavaria," review of J. Nane, *Die Hügelgräber zwischen Ammer- und Staffelsee,* Stuttgart 1887, *Archaeological Review,* 1, 119–23.

1889a. "Stonehenge," *Archaeological Review,* 2, 312–30.

1889b. *The "Horsemen" of Tarentum,* London, Quatrich (reprinted from the *Numismatic Chronicle,* 3rd ser., IX, 1–228).

1890a. "Some New Artists' Signatures on Sicilian Coins," *Numismatic Chronicle,* 3rd ser., X, 285–310.

1890b. "Ancient British Antiquities" (syllabus of three lectures), Oxford University Extension, summer meeting.

1891a. *Syracusan "Medallions" and Their Engravers,* London, Quatrich (reprinted from the *Numismatic Chronicle,* 3rd ser., XI, 205–376.

1891b. "On a Late-Celtic Urn-Field at Aylesford, Kent, and on the Gaulish, Illyro-Italic, and Classical Connexions of the Forms of Pottery and Bronze-Work There Discovered," *Archaeologia,* 52, 315–88.

1892a. "A Roman Bronze Lamp from South Italy," *Proceedings of the Society of Antiquaries,* 2nd ser., XIV, 155.

1892b. "Entdeckung von drei menschlichen Skeleten in der Höhle Barma Grande zwischen Mentone und Ventimiglie," Munich.

1893a. "A Mykênæan Treasure from Ægina," *Journal of Hellenic Studies,* 13, 195–226.

1893b. "On the Prehistoric Interments of the Balzi Rossi Caves near Mentone and Their Relation to the Neolithic Cave-Burials of the Finalese," *Journal of the Anthropological Institute,* 22, 287–307.

1893c. "Introductory Note on the Vases from Gela," in P. Gardner, *Catalogue of Greek Vases in the Ashmolean Museum,* Oxford.

1893? "Notes on the Origins & Affinities of Mycenaean Culture," unpublished ms. in Evans Archive 0009.

1894a. "Contributions to Sicilian Numismatics 1," *Numismatic Chronicle,* 3rd ser., XIV, 189–242.

1894b. *History of Sicily,* edited by E. A. Freeman, Oxford.

1894c. "A Mycenaean System of Writing in Crete and the Peloponnese," *Athenaeum,* June 23; see also *Times,* August 29.

1894d. "On a New System of Hieroglyphics and a Præ-Phoenician Script from Crete and the Peloponnese," *Proceedings of the British Association* (Oxford), 776–77.

1894e. "Primitive Pictographs and a Præ-Phoenician Script from Crete and the Peloponnese," *Journal of Hellenic Studies* 14, 270–372. Reprinted as *Cretan Pictographic and Præ-Phoenician Script,* London 1895.

1895a. "A Mycenaean Military Road in Crete" (with J. L. Myres), *Academy,* 1204, June 1, 469.

1895b. "Greek and Italian Influences in Præ-Roman Britain," *Arch. Oxon.,* London 159–64; reprinted letter from the *Times,* September 23, 1893.

1895c. "The Rollright Stones and Their Folklore," *Folklore,* 6, 6–51.

1895d. "On Primitive European 'Idols' in the Light of New Discoveries," *Proceedings of the British Association* (London), 834–35.

1896a. "Explorations in Eastern Crete. I. A Mycenaean Dedication," *Academy,* 1258, June 13.

1896b. "Explorations in Eastern Crete. II. A 'Town of Castles,' " *Academy,* 1259, June 20, 512–13.

1896c. "Explorations in Eastern Crete. III. Mycenaean Dikta," *Academy,* 1261, July 4, 17–18.

1896d. "Explorations in Eastern Crete. IV. Above the Libyan Sea," *Academy,* 1263, July 18, 53–54.

1896e. "Mycenaean Fluted Columns," *Academy,* 1264, July 25, 70.

1896f. " 'The Eastern Question' in Anthropology," *Proceedings of the British Association* (Liverpool), 906–22.

1896g. "Pillar and Tree Worship in Mycenaean Greece," *Proceedings of the British Association* (Liverpool), 934.

1896h. "Goulàs, the City of Zeus," *Annual of the British School at Athens,* 2, 169–94.

1896i. "Contributions to Sicilian Numismatics 2," *Numismatic Chronicle,* 3rd ser., XVI, 101–43.

1897a. "Further Discoveries of Cretan and Aegean Script, with Libyan and Proto-Egyptian Comparisons," *Journal of Hellenic Studies,* 17, 327–95.

1897b. "A Roman Villa at Frilford," *Archaeological Journal,* 45, 340–54.

1897c. "A Votive Deposit of Gold Objects Found on the North-West Coast of Ireland," *Archaeologia,* 55, 391–408.

1897d. "Two Fibulae of 'Celtic' Type from Aesica," *Archaeologia,* 55, 179–94.

1898a. Letters from Crete, private circulation, Oxford 1898; reprinted from the *Manchester Guardian,* May 24 and 25, June 13.

1898b. "The Athenian Portrait-Head by Dexamenus of Chios," *Revue Archéologique,* 32, 337–55.

1899. "On the Occurrence of 'Celtic' Types of Fibula of the Hallstatt and La Téne Periods in Tunisia and Eastern Algeria," *Proceedings of the British Association* (Dover), 872.

1900a. "Mycenaean Cyprus as Illustrated in the British Museum Excavations," *Journal of the Anthropological Institute,* 30, 199–221.

1900b. "The Palace Archives of Mycenæan Cnossus," *Athenaeum,* May 19.

1900c. "The Palace Archives of Cnossus: A New Series in Hieroglyphic Characters," *Athenaeum,* June 23.

1900d. "Writing in Prehistoric Greece," *Proceedings of the British Association* (Bradford), 897–99.

1900e. "The Palace of Knossos in Its Egyptian Relations," *Archaeological Report of the Egyptian Exploration Fund,* 1–7.

1900f. "Knossos, I. The Palace," *Annual of the British School at Athens,* 6, 3–70.

1901a. "The Palace of Minos," *Monthly Review,* no. 6. II. 3, March, 115–32, reprinted in Deuel 1961, 284–300, and Daniel 1967, 150–65.

1901b. "The Neolithic Settlement at Knossos and Its Place in the History of Early Aegean Culture," *Proceedings of the British Association* (Glasgow), 99–204.

1901c. "Mycenaean Tree and Pillar Cult and Its Mediterranean Relations," *Journal of Hellenic Studies,* 21, 99–204; also published separately, London, Quatrich.

1901d. "The Palace of Knossos," *Annual of the British School at Athens,* 7, 1–120.

1902a. "The Labyrinth and the Palace of Knossos," *The Speaker,* July 19.

1902b. "The Palace of Knossos," *Annual of the British School at Athens,* 8, 1–124.

1903a. "Præ-Phoenician Writing in Crete" (syllabus of three lectures on January 2, 15, 29), Royal Institution, London.

1903b. "The Palace of Knossos," *Annual of the British School at Athens,* 9, 1–153.

1903c. "The Minoan Civilization of Crete, and Its Place in the Ancient World" (syllabus of the Yates Lectures, November 3–18), University College, London.

1903d. "A Bird's-Eye View of the Minoan Palace of Knossos, Crete," *Royal Institute of British Architects,* 3rd ser., X, 97–106.

1904a. "The Significance of the Pottery Marks," in Atkinson et al., *Excavations at Phylakopi in Melos* (*Journal of Hellenic Studies,* Suppl. 4), London, 181–85.

1904b. "The Pictographic and Linear Scripts of Minoan Crete and Their Relations," *Proceedings of the British Academy,* 1903–1904, 137–39.

1904c. "The Palace of Knossos," *Annual of the British School at Athens,* 10, 1–62.

1905a. "The Palace of Knossos and Its Dependencies," *Annual of the British School at Athens,* 11, 1–26.

1905b. "The Prehistoric Tombs of Knossos," *Archaeologia,* 59, 391–562.

1905c. "Excavations at Knossos in Crete," *Proceedings of the British Association* (S. Africa).

1905d. *Preliminary scheme for the classification and approximate chronology from the close of the Neolithic to the Early Iron Age,* privately printed, Oxford.

1906a. *Essai de classification des époques de la civilization Minoenne,* London.

1906b. "Minoan Weights and Mediums of Currency, from Crete, Mycenae and Cyprus," *Corolla Numismatica in Honour of Barclay V. Head,* Oxford, 336–67.

1908. "The European Diffusion of Pictography and Its Bearings on the Origin of Script," in R. R. Maret (ed.), *Anthropology and the Classics,* Oxford, Clarendon, 9–43.

1909a. *Scripta Minoa* I, Oxford.

1909b. Preface to C. H. Hawes and H. B. Hawes, *Crete the Forerunner of Greece*, London, 1909–11.

1909c. "The Palace of Knossos as a Sanctuary," *Royal Institute of British Architects*, 3rd ser., XVII, 6–7.

1910a. "Notes on Some Roman Imperial 'Medallions' and Coins," *Numismatic Chronicle*, 4th ser., X, 1–13.

1910b. "Crete-Archaeology," *Encyclopaedia Britannica*, 11th ed., 421–26.

1911a. "Restored Shrine on Central Court of the Palace of Knossos," *Royal Institute of British Architects*, 3rd ser., XVIII, 288–310.

1911b. "On the Ancient Engravers of Terina, and the Signatures of Evaenetus on Late Tetradrachm Dies," *Numismatic Chronicle*, 4th ser., XII, 21–62.

1912a. *The Nine Minoan Periods, a summary sketch*, privately printed for the International Archaeology Congress, Rome.

1912b. "The Minoan and Mycenaean Element in Hellenic Life," *Journal of Hellenic Studies*, 32, 277–97.

1913. "The Ages of Minos," Huxley lecture to the University of Birmingham, privately printed.

1914. "The 'Tomb of the Double Axes' and Associated Group and Pillar Rooms with Ritual Vessels of the 'Little Palace' at Knossos," *Archaeologia*, 65, 1–94.

1915a. Presidential address to the Society of Antiquaries (on the German destruction of ancient monuments), *Proceedings of the Society of Antiquaries*, 2nd ser., XXVII, 227–29.

1915b. Presidential address to the Numismatic Society, *Numismatic Chronicle*, 4th ser., XV, 27–41.

1915c. "Cretan Analogies for the Origin of the Alphabet," *Proceedings of the British Association* (Manchester), 667.

1915d. "Diagramatic Map Illustrating the Ethnic Relations between the Adriatic, Drave, and Danube," *Proceedings of the British Association* (Manchester), 673–74.

1916a. "The Adriatic Slavs and the Overland Route to Constantinople," *Geographical Journal*, 241ff.

1916b. "New Archaeological Lights on the Origins of Civilization in Europe: Its Magdalenian Forerunners in the South-West and Aegean Cradle," *Proceedings of the British Association* (Newcastle), 3–25.

1916c. Presidential address to the Society of Antiquaries (protest against the "removal" of honorary fellows of enemy nationality), *Proceedings of the Society of Antiquaries*, 2nd ser., XXVIII, 205–87.

1916d. "Commemorative War Medals," *Morning Post*, June 21.

1916e. Presidential address to the Numismatic Society, *Numismatic Chronicle*, 4th ser., XVI, 22–36.

1916f. "Notes on the Coinage and Silver Currency in Roman Britain from Valentinian I to Constantine III," *Numismatic Chronicle*, 4th ser., XV, 433–519.

1917a. Presidential address to the Society of Antiquaries (on the history of the Society), *Proceedings of the Society of Antiquaries*, 2nd ser., XXIX, 155–82.

1917b. Presidential address to the Numismatic Society, *Numismatic Chronicle*, 4th ser., XVII, 20–41.

1917c. "Greece," *New Europe*, May–June.

1918a. Presidential address to the Society of Antiquaries (on the requisition of the British Museum by the Air Board), *Proceedings of the Society of Antiquaries*, 2nd ser., XXX, 189–207.

1918b. Presidential address to the Numismatic Society, *Numismatic Chronicle*, 4th ser., XVII, 14–22.

1919a. *L'Italie et les Yougoslaves, Une Situation Dangereuse*, Paris, Lang, Blanchong (trans. of letters to the *Manchester Guardian*, Dec. 26 and 28, 1918).

1919b. Presidential address to the Society of Antiquaries (New fields of research, protection of antiquities, reorganization, Stonehenge), *Proceedings of the Society of Antiquaries*, 2nd ser., XXXI, 188–95.

1919c. "The Palace of Minos and the Prehistoric Civilization of Crete," *Proceedings of the British Association* (Bournemouth), 416–17.

1919d. "A Recent Find of Magna-Graecian Coins of Metapontum, Tarentum, and Heraclea," *Numismatic Chronicle*, 4th ser., XVIII, 122–54.

1921a. *The Palace of Minos at Knossos* I, London, Macmillan.

1921b. "On a Minoan Bronze Group of a Galloping Bull and Acrobatic Figure from Crete," *Journal of Hellenic Studies*, 41, 247–59.

1922. "New Discoveries at Knossos," *Antiquaries Journal*, II, 319–29.

1924. Preface to S. Xanthoudides, *The Vaulted Tombs of the Mesara*, Liverpool.

1925a. "The Early Nilotic, Libyan, and Egyptian Relations with Minoan Crete," Huxley lecture of the Royal Anthropological Institute, *Journal of the Royal Anthropological Institute*, 55, 199.

1925b. "The 'Ring of Nestor': A Glimpse into the Minoan After-World, and a Sepulchral Treasure of Gold Signet-Rings and Bead Seals from Thisbê, Boiotia," *Journal of Hellenic Studies*, 45, 1–75.

1926. "The Shaft Graves of Mycenae and Their Contents in Relation to the Beehive Tombs" (paper read to the British Association in Oxford, Aug. 6), privately printed.

1927a. "A Coin of the Second Carausius," *Numismatic Chronicle*, 5th ser., V, 138–63.

1927b. *Catalogue of savage implements and antiquities comprising the collection of savage implements formed by Sir John Evans, the property of Sir Arthur Evans*, sold at auction, July 12, London.

1927c. "Work of Reconstruction in the Palace of Knossos," *Antiquaries Journal*, VII, 258–66.

1928a. "The Glozel Forgeries," *Manchester Guardian*, Jan. 7.

1928b. *The Palace of Minos at Knossos* II, London, Macmillan.

1928c. "A Forged Treasure in Serbia," *Edinburgh Review*, 247, 287–300.

1928d. "Select Sicilian and Magna-Graecian Coins," *Numismatic Chronicle*, 5th ser., VI, 1–19.

1928e. "The Palace of Knossos and Its Dependencies in the Light of Recent Discoveries and Reconstitutions," *Royal Institute of British Architects*, 36, 91–102.

1929. *The Shaft Graves and Bee-hive Tombs of Mycenae and Their Inter-relations*, London, Macmillan.

1930a. *The Palace of Minos at Knossos* III, London, Macmillan.

1930b. "Some Notes on the Arras Hoard: Inception of *Solidus* Standard on British Model in Medallions of Constantius Chlorus," *Numismatic Chronicle,* 5th ser., X, 221–74.

1931a. *The Earlier Religion of Greece in the Light of Cretan Discoveries,* Fraser Lecture at Cambridge, London, Macmillan.

1931b. Introduction to Emil Ludwig, *Schliemann of Troy: The Story of a Gold-Seeker,* London and New York.

1931c. "Discovery of the Temple-Tomb of the House of Minos," *Proceedings of the British Association* (London), 447.

1933a. Foreword to J. D. S. Pendlebury, *A Handbook to the Palace of Minos Knossos,* London, Macmillan.

1933b. *Jarn Mound, with Its Panorama and Wild Garden of British Plants,* Oxford, Vincent.

1934. "Knossos and Mycenae: The Great Cleavage of L. M. II and Evidences of the Continued Reaction of Minoan Crete on the 'Mycenaean' World after the Fall of the Palace," *Proceedings of the First International Congress of Prehistoric and Protohistoric Sciences* (London), August 1932, 192–94.

1935a. "The Historic Beacon," *Scouter,* 39, 72–73.

1935b. *The Palace of Minos at Knossos* IV, London.

1936a. Special sections classified in detail for Joan Evans 1936, *Index to the Palace of Minos,* London, Macmillan.

1936b. "The Minoan World," Lecture at the Royal Academy of Arts, Oct. 16, privately printed.

1936c. "Minoan Culture on Display at the Royal Academy," *Illustrated London News,* Nov. 7, 808–9, 842.

1937. *Holland and the Dutch for the British Contingent, Boy Scouts,* London.

1938. *An Illustrative Selection of Greek and Graeco-Roman Gems, to Which Is Added a Minoan and Proto-Hellenic Series,* Oxford University Press.

Biographies, Obituaries, and Memoirs of Evans and Knossos

Brown, A. 1983a. *Arthur Evans and the Palace of Minos,* Ashmolean Museum, Oxford.

———. 1983b. "Arthur Evans at Knossos," *Ashmolean,* Summer, 14–17.

———. 1993. *Before Knossos . . . Arthur Evans's Travels in the Balkans and Crete,* Ashmolean Museum, Oxford.

———. 1994. "Arthur Evans" *Ashmolean,* 2–4.

Candy, J. S. 1984. *A Tapestry of Life,* Braunton, Devon.

———. 1989. *Silver Threads,* Abingdon, Fine Print.

Casson, S., ed. 1927. *Essays in Aegean Archaeology Presented to Sir Arthur Evans in Honour of His 75th Birthday,* Oxford, Clarendon.

Evans, Joan. 1943. *Time and Chance: The Story of Arthur Evans and His Forebears,* London.

Harden, D. B. 1951. *Sir Arthur Evans Centenary Exhibition,* Ashmolean Museum, Oxford.

———. 1983. *Sir Arthur Evans 1851–1941, "A Memoir,"* Ashmolean Museum, Oxford.

Honour, A. 1961. *Secrets of Minos: Sir Arthur Evans' Discoveries at Crete,* New York, Whittlesey House.

Horwitz, Sylvia L. 1981. *The Find of a Lifetime: Sir Arthur Evans and the Discovery of Knossos,* New York, The Viking Press, and London, Weidenfeld and Nicolson.

Hutchinson, R. W. 1947. "Sir Arthur Evans," *Kritika Chronika,* A, 453–57.

MacEnroe, J. 1995. "Sir Arthur Evans and Edwardian Archaeology," *Classical Bulletin,* 71, 3–18.

Myres, J. L. 1941. "Sir Arthur Evans," in *Obituary Notices of Fellows of the Royal Society,* III, no. 10 (Dec.), 941–68.

———. 1942. "Sir Arthur Evans," in *Proceedings of the British Academy,* XXVII, 323–57.

Powell, Dilys. 1973. *The Villa Ariadne,* London, Hodder and Stoughton.

Wilkes, J. J. 1976. "Arthur Evans in the Balkans 1875–81," *Bulletin of the Institute of Archaeology,* University of London, 13, 25–56.

General

Accame, S. 1984. *F. Halbherr e G. DeSanctis. Pionieri delle Missioni Archeologische Italiane a Creta e in Cirenaica,* Rome, La Roccia.

Alexiou, S. 1979. "Fortifications and Acropolises in Minoan Crete," *Kretologia,* 8, 41–56.

Allen, J. Romilly. 1883. "The Past, Present and Future of Archaeology," *Archaeologia Cambrensis,* 1, 231–43.

———. 1889. "On the Organisation of Archaeological Research," *Archaeologia Cambrensis,* 7, 274–82.

Allsebrook, M. 1992. *Born to Rebel: The Life of Harriet Boyd Hawes,* Oxford, Oxbow.

Alsop, J. 1964. *From the Silent Earth,* New York.

Aposkitou, M. 1979. "Μίνως Καλοκαιρινός, Εκατό χρόνι α από την πρώτη ανασκαφή της Κνωσού," *Kritologia,* 8, 81–94.

Avgouli, M. 1994. "The First Greek Museums and National Identity," in F. E. S. Kaplan (ed.), *Museums and the Making of "Ourselves,"* Leicester University Press, 246–65.

Becker, M. J., and P. P. Betancourt. 1997. *Richard Berry Seager: Pioneer Archaeologist and Proper Gentleman,* University of Pennsylvania Museum of Archaeology and Anthropology, Philadelphia.

Beeching, Wilfred A. 1990. *Century of the Typewriter.* Bournemouth, British Typewriter Museum.

Bender, H. H. 1922. *The Home of the Indo-Europeans,* Princeton University Press.

Berard, V. 1898. *Les Affaires de Crète,* Paris.

Bernal, M. 1987. *Black Athena: The Afroasiatic Roots of Classical Civilization:* I, *The Fabrication of Ancient Greece, 1785–1985,* New Brunswick, Rutgers University Press.

Bickford-Smith. 1897. *Cretan Sketches,* London.

Bintliff, J. L. 1983. "Structuralism and Myth in Minoan Studies," *Antiquity,* 58, 33–38.

Blegen, C. W. 1921. *Korakou: A Prehistoric Settlement near Corinth,* New York, American School of Classical Studies at Athens.

———. 1923. "Corinth in Prehistoric Times," *American Journal of Archaeology*, 27, 151–63.

———. 1958. "A Chronological Problem," *Minoica: Festschrift zum 80. Geburstag von J. Sundwall*, Berlin, 61–66.

Blegen, C. W., and J. Haley. 1928. "The Coming of the Greeks," *American Journal of Archaeology*, 32, 141–54.

Blegen, C. W., and A. J. Wace, 1918. "The Pre-Mycenaean Pottery of the Mainland," *Annual of the British School at Athens*, 22, 175–89.

———. 1939. "Pottery as Evidence for Trade and Colonisation in the Aegean Bronze Age," *Klio*, 32, 131–47.

Boardman, J. 1961. *The Cretan Collection in Oxford*, Oxford, Oxford University Press.

Bosanquet, E. S. 1938. *Robert Carr Bosanquet: Letters and Light Verse*, Gloucester, John Bellows.

Bosanquet, R. C. 1900. "Archaeology in Greece 1899–1900," *Journal of Hellenic Studies*, 20, 167–81.

———. 1901. "Archaeology in Greece 1900–1901," *Journal of Hellenic Studies*, 21, 334–52.

———. 1922. "Realm of Minos," *Edinburgh Review*, 236, July, 49–70.

Bowden, M. 1991. *Pitt-Rivers: The Life and Archaeological Work of Lieutenant-General Augustus Henry Lane-Fox Pitt-Rivers, DCL, FRS, FSA*, Cambridge, Cambridge University Press.

Bradley, R. 1983. "Archaeology, Evolution and the Public Good: The Intellectual Development of General Pitt-Rivers," *Archaeological Journal*, 140, 1–9.

Brown, Ann. 1986. " 'I Propose to Begin at Gnossos.' John Myres's Visit to Crete in 1893," *Annual of the British School at Athens*, 81, 37–44.

Burrows, R. M. 1907. *The Discoveries in Crete and Their Bearing on the History of Ancient Civilization*, London, John Murray.

Bury, J. B. 1920. *The Idea of Progress*, London.

Butcher, K., and D. W. J. Gill. 1993. "The Director, the Dealer, the Goddess and Her Champions," *American Journal of Archaeology*, 97, 383–401.

Caskey, L. D. 1914. "A Statuette of the Minoan Snake Goddess," *Museum of Fine Arts Bulletin* (Boston) XII, no. 73, December, 51–55.

———. 1915. "A Chryselephantine Statuette of the Cretan Snake Goddess," *American Journal of Archaeology*, 19, 237–49.

Castleden, R. 1989. *The Knossos Labyrinth*, London, Routledge.

———. 1990. *Minoans*, London, Routledge.

Childe, V. G. 1925a. *The Dawn of European Civilization*, London.

———. 1925b. "Greek Myths and Mycenaean Realities" (review of Evans, *Ring of Nestor*), *Nature*, 116, 635–36.

———. 1926a. *The Aryans: A Study of Indo-European Origins*, London.

———. 1926b. "The Origin of European Civilization" (review of Glotz, *Aegean Civilization*), *Nature* , 117, 716.

———. 1927. "The Minoan influence on the Danubian Bronze Age," in S. Casson, ed., *Essays in Aegean Archaeology*, Oxford, Clarendon, 1–4.

———. 1928. *The Most Ancient East: The Oriental Prelude to European History*, London, Kegan Paul.

———. 1936. *Man Makes Himself*, London, Watts.

———. 1942. *What Happened in History*, Harmondsworth, Penguin.

———. 1951. *Social Evolution*, New York, Schuman.

———. 1956. *Piecing Together the Past: The Interpretation of Archaeological Data*, New York, Frederick A. Praeger.

———. 1958a. "Retrospect," *Antiquity*, 32, 69–74.

———. 1958b. "Valediction," *Bulletin of the London Institute of Archaeology*, 1, 1–8.

Clarke, M. L. 1954. *Classical Education in Britain, 1500–1900*, Cambridge, Cambridge University Press.

Clarke, T. H. M. 1903. "Prehistoric Sanitation in Crete," *The British Medical Journal*, Sept. 12, 597–98.

Collingwood, R. G. 1946. *The Idea of History*, Oxford, Oxford University Press.

Cook, R. M. 1955. "Thucydides as Archaeologist," *Annual of the British School at Athens*, 50, 266–70.

Cottrell, L. 1953. *The Bull of Minos*, London.

Currelly, C. T. 1956. *I Brought Home the Ages*, Toronto, Ryerson Press.

Daniel, G. E. 1950. *A Hundred Years of Archaeology*, London, Thames and Hudson.

———. 1962. *The Idea of Prehistory*, London, C. A. Watts.

———. 1967. *The Origins and Growth of Archaeology*, Harmondsworth, Penguin.

———. 1975. *150 Years of Archaeology*, 2nd ed., London, Thames and Hudson.

———. 1980. Editorial, *Antiquity*, 50, 1–3.

———. 1981a. *A Short History of Archaeology*, London, Thames and Hudson.

———. 1981b. *Towards a History of Archaeology* (ed.), London.

Daressy, G. 1895. "Une flottille phénicienne," *Revue Archaéologique*, 3rd ser., 27, 286–92.

Darwin, C. 1859. *On the Origin of Species by Means of Natural Selection, or, the Preservation of Favoured Races in the Struggle for Life*, London.

———. 1871. *The Descent of Man, and Selection in Relation to Sex*, London.

Dawes, M. C. 1888. "Excavations at Mycenae," *Athenaeum*, 3179, 423–24.

Demargne, J. 1902. "Psychro," *Bulletin de Correspondance Hellénique*, 26, 580–83.

Detorakis T. 1994. *History of Crete*, Herakleion, Geronymaki.

Deuel, L. 1961. *The Treasures of Time*, New York, World.

Dillon, E. J. 1897. "Crete and the Cretans," *Fortnightly Review*, May.

Di Vita, A. 1985. "1884–1984: A Hundred Years of Italian Archaeology in Crete," in *Ancient Crete: A Hundred Years of Italian Archaeology*, Rome, de Luca, 17–25.

Dörpfeld, W. 1942. "Uber die Kunst der 'altesten Indogermanischen Hellenen,' " in *Επιτύμβιον Χρίστου Τσούντα*.

Driessen, J. M. 1990. *An Early Destruction in the Mycenaean Palace at Knossos (Acta Archaeologica Lovaniens Monographica)*, Louvain.

Driessen, J. M., and C. F. Macdonald. 1997. *The Troubled Island (Aegaeum 17)*, Liège.

Drower, M. S. 1985. *Flinders Petrie: A Life in Archaeology*, London, Gollancz.

Duchene, H. 1994. *Notre Ecole Normale*, Paris, Belles-Lettres.

———. 1996. *Golden Treasures of Troy*, New York, Abrams.

Dunbabin, T. J. 1956. "Sir John Myres" (obituary), *Proceedings of the British Academy*, 41, 349–65.

Dussaud, R. 1905. "Questions mycéniennes," *RHR* 51, 32–43.

———. 1914. *Les civilisations préhelleniques*, 2nd ed., Paris.

Edwardes, C. 1887. *Letters from Crete*, London, Richard Bentley.

Evans, J. 1936. *Index to the Palace of Minos*, London, Macmillan.

———. 1956. *A History of the Society of Antiquaries*, London, Society of Antiquaries.

———. 1964. *Prelude and Fugue: An Autobiography*, London.

Fabricius, E. 1886. "Alterthümer auf Kreta, IV: funde der mykenäischen Epoche in Knossos," in *Mitteilungen des Deutschen Archäologischen Instituts*, 11, 135–49.

Falkener, E. 1854. *A Description of Some Important Theaters and Other Remains in Crete, from a MS. History of Candia by Onorio Belli in 1586*, London.

Farnoux, A. 1993. *Cnossos. L'archéologie d'un rêve*, Paris, Gallimard.

———. 1996. *Knossos: Searching for the Legendary Palace of King Minos*, New York, Harry Abrams.

Fick, A. 1905. *Vorgriechische Ortsnamen*, Göttingen.

Finlay, M. I. 1974. *Schliemann's Troy—One Hundred Years After*, London, British Academy.

Fitton, J. L. 1991. *Heinrich Schliemann and the British Museum*, London, British Museum.

———. 1995a. *The Discovery of the Greek Bronze Age*, London, British Museum.

———. 1995b. "Charles Newton and the Discovery of the Greek Bronze Age," *Klados: Essays in Honour of J. N. Coldstream*, BICS Suppl. 63, London, 73–78.

Flinders Petrie, W. M. 1888. "Excavations in the Fayum," *Academy*, 33, June 9, no. 840, 402.

———. 1890. "The Egyptian Bases of Greek History," *Journal of Hellenic Studies*, XI, 271–77.

———. 1892a. *Ten Years Digging in Egypt 1881–1891*, London.

———. 1892b. "Excavations at Tel El-Amarna," *Academy*, April 9, no. 1040, 356–57.

———. 1894. *Tell el Amarna*, London, Methuen.

———. 1901. *Methods and Aims in Archaeology*, London, Macmillan.

———. 1931. *Seventy Years in Archaeology*, London, Sampson Low, Marston.

Forsdyke, E. J. 1911. "Minoan Pottery from Cyprus, and the Origin of the Mycenaean Style," *Journal of Hellenic Studies*, 31, 110–18.

———. 1925. *Catalogue of the Greek and Etruscan Vases in the British Museum, Vol. 1, Part 1, Prehistoric Aegean Pottery*, London.

———. 1929. *Minoan Art* (Annual Lecture on Aspects of Art at the British Academy), London.

Foundoulaki, I. 1996. Κρήτη [Crete] 1893, Rethymnon.

Fowler, R. 1984. *The Cretan Journal by Edward Lear*, Athens, Denise Harvey.

Freeman, E. A. 1877. *The Ottoman Power in Europe*.

Frere, J. 1800. "Account of Flint Weapons Discovered at Hoxne in Suffolk," *Archaeologia*, XIII, 204–5.

Frost, K. T. 1909. "The Lost Continent," *Times*, Jan. 19.

————. 1913. "The *Critias* and Minoan Crete," *Journal of Hellenic Studies,* 33, 189–206.

Fyfe, T. 1903. "Painted Plaster Decoration at Knossos," *Royal Institute of British Architects,* 3rd ser., X, 107–31.

Gardner, P. 1892. *New Chapters in Greek History,* London, John Murray.

————. 1894. "Sir C. T. Newton," *Academy,* Dec. 8, 1179, 476.

————. 1911. "Presidential Address," *Journal of Hellenic Studies,* 31, lii–lxi.

Gimbutas, M. 1974. *Goddesses and Gods of Old Europe,* Berkeley, University of California Press.

————. 1989. *The Language of the Goddess,* San Francisco, HarperCollins.

————. 1991. *The Civilization of the Goddess,* San Francisco, HarperCollins.

Glotz, G. 1925. *The Aegean Civilization,* London, Kegan Paul, Trench, Trubner.

Gosset, T. F. 1965. *Race: The History of an Idea in America,* New York.

Grant, M. 1916. *The Passing of the Great Race; or the Racial Basis of European History,* New York, Scribner.

Green, S. 1981. *Prehistorian: A Biography of V. Gordon Childe,* Bradford-upon-Avon, Moonraker Press.

Grimm, J. 1882–88. *Teutonic Mythology,* trans. J. S. Stallybrass, London.

Grote, G. 1846–56. *History of Greece,* 12 vols. London.

Halbherr, F., and E. Fabricius. 1885. *Le leggi antiche della città di Gortina,* Florence.

————. 1888. "Scavi e trovamenti nell'antro di Zeus sui monte Ida in Creta," and "Scoperte nel santuario di Hermes Craneo," *Museo Italiano di Antichità Classica,* II, 689–768, 913–16.

————. 1890. "Iscrizioni cretesi," *Museo Italiano di Antichità Classica,* III, 559–750.

————. 1891. "Researches in Crete. I. Itanos," *Antiquary,* 24, Nov., 201–3; Dec., 241–45.

————. 1892. "Researches in Crete. II. Palaekastron of Sitia," *Antiquary,* 25, March, 115–18; "III–IV. The Praesian Peninsula," *Antiquary,* April, 152–55; May, 214–17.

————. 1893. "Researches in Crete. V. The Isthmus of Hierapytna," *Antiquary,* 27, Jan., 10–14; "VI. From Hierapytna to Lyttos," *Antiquary,* May, 195–99; "VII Lyttos," 28, *Antiquary,* July, 12–15; "VIII. Cnossos," *Antiquary,* Sept., 110–12.

Halbherr, F. and P. Orsi. 1888. "Scoperti nell'antro di Psychrò," *Museo Italiano di Antichità Classica,* II, 905–12.

Hall, H. R. 1901a. *The Oldest Civilization of Greece,* London, David Nutt.

————. 1901b. "The Older Civilization of Greece," *Nature,* 64, May 2, 11–15.

————. 1902a. "The Older Civilization of Greece: Further Discoveries in Crete," *Nature,* 66, Aug. 21, 390–94.

————. 1902b. "The Mycenaean Discoveries in Crete," *Nature,* 67, Nov. 20, 57–61.

————. 1913. *The Ancient History of the Near East,* London, Methuen.

————. 1915. *Aegean Archaeology,* London, Philip Lee Warner.

Hampson, N. 1982. *The Enlightenment,* Harmondsworth, Penguin.

Harrington, S. P. M. 1999. "Saving Knossos," *Archaeology,* 52, 1, 30–40.

Harrison, J. E. 1909. "The Influence of Darwin on the Study of Religions," in Seward 1909.

Haussoullier, B. 1880. "Vases peintes archaïques découvertes à Knossos," in *Revue Archéologique*, 40, 359–61 (reprinted from *Bulletin de Correspondance Hellénique*, 4, 1880, 124–27).

Hawes, C. H., and H. B. Hawes. 1909. *Crete: The Forerunner of Greece*, London and New York, Harper.

Hawes, H. B. 1965. "Memoirs of a Pioneer Excavator in Crete," *Archaeology*, 18, 94–101.

Hazzidakis, J. 1881. *Περιήγησις εις την Κρήτην*, Ermopolis.

———. 1931. *Ιστορία του Κρητικού Μουσείου και των αρχαιολογικών ερευνών εν Κρήτη* [*History of the Cretan Museum*], Archaeological Society.

Heaton-Comyn, N. 1911. "Minoan Lime Plaster," *Royal Institute of British Architects*, 3rd ser., XVIII, 697–710.

Helbig, W. 1896. *Sitzungsber. d. Mün. Acad.*, 539–82.

Hemingway, S. A. 2000. "Minoan Bone and Ivory Scupture," in MacGillivray, Driessen, and Sackett, 2000.

Higgins, R. 1979. *The Aigina Treasure: An Archaeological Mystery*, London, British Museum.

Hirst, J. 1885. "Notes from Athens," *Athenaeum*, 2987, 128.

———. 1887a. "Notes from Crete," *Athenaeum*, 3094, 230–31.

———. 1887b. "Notes from Crete," *Athenaeum*, 3118, 157–58.

———. 1887c. "Notes from Crete," *Athenaeum*, 3135, 718–19.

———. 1888. "Notes from Crete," *Athenaeum*, 3152, 378–79.

Hoeck, K. 1823–29. *Kreta. Ein Versuch zur Aufhellung der Mythologie und Geschichte, der Religion und Verfassung dieser Insel, von den Ältesten Zeiten bis auf die Römer-Herrschaft*, I–III, Göttingen.

Hogarth, D. G. 1896. *A Wandering Scholar in the Levant*, London, John Murray.

———. 1900a. "Knossos II: Early Town and Cemeteries," *Annual of the British School at Athens*, 6, 70–85.

———. 1900b. "The Diktaian Cave," *Annual of the British School at Athens*, 6, 94–116.

———. 1901. "Excavations at Zakro, Crete," *Annual of the British School at Athens*, 7, 121–49.

———. 1902. "The Zakro Sealings," *Journal of Hellenic Studies*, 22, 76–93.

———. 1910. *Accidents of an Antiquary's Life*, London, Macmillan.

———. 1926. *Twilight of History*, London.

Homolle, T. 1891. "Nouvelles et correspondance," *Bulletin de Correspondance Hellénique*, 15, 441–58.

Hood, M. S. F. 1987. "An Early British Interest in Knossos," *Annual of the British School at Athens*, 82, 85–93.

———. 1992. "Schliemann and Crete," in J. Herrmann (ed.), *Heinrich Schliemann: Grundlage und Erlebnisse moderner Archäologie 100 Jahre nach Schliemanns Tod*, Berlin, 223–29.

———. 1995. "Collingwood on the Minoan Civilisation of Crete," in D. Boucher and B. Haddock (eds.), *Collingwood Studies*, vol. 2, 175–79.

Hood, M. S. F., and D. Smyth. 1981. *Archaeological Survey of the Knossos Area*, British School at Athens Suppl., Vol. 14, Oxford.

Hood, M. S. F., and M. Cameron. 1967. *Catalogue of Plates in Sir Arthur Evans' Knossos Fresco Atlas,* Farnborough, Gregg Press.

Hood, R. 1998. *Faces of Archaeology in Greece,* Oxford, Leopard's Head.

Hudson, K. 1981. *A Social History of Archaeology,* London.

Hughes-Brock, H. 1994. "Les révélations de Sir Arthur Evans," *Ashmolean,* 27, 7–9.

Huxley, T. H. 1909. *Evolution and Ethics: Collected Essays.* London.

Jeal, T. 1989. *Baden-Powell,* London, Hutchinson.

Kabbani, R. 1986. *Europe's Myths of Orient: Divide and Rule,* London, Macmillan.

Kalokairinos, M. 1901. *Νομοθεσία του βασιλέως της Κρήτης Μίνωος,* Athens.

Karo, G. 1959. *Greifen am Thron,* Baden-Baden.

Koehl, R. 1990. "A Letter from Evans to Droop on the 'Problem' of Wace," *Classical Journal,* 86, 45–52.

Kopaka, K. 1990. "Μίνωος Καλοκαιρινού Ανασκαφές στην Κνωσό," *παλ–ίμψηστον,* 9–10 (Herakleion), 5–69.

———. 1995. "Ο Μίνος Καλοκαιρινός και οι πρώτες ανασκαφές στην Κνωσό," *Proceedings of the 7th Cretological Congress* (Rethymnon), 501–11.

Lambros, S. 1887. "Notes from Athens," *Athenaeum,* 3099, 390–91.

———. 1891. "Heinrich Schliemann," *Athenaeum,* 3299, 94–95.

Lapatin, K. 1997. "Pheidias ελεφαντουργός," *American Journal of Archaeology,* 101, 663–82.

———. forthcoming. "Mysteries of the 'Snake Goddess' and Other Unprovenienced 'Minoan' Statuettes."

Laroche. 1898. *La Crète ancienne et moderne,* Paris.

Lawson, J. C. 1920. *Tales of Aegean Intrigue,* London, Chatto & Windus.

Levi, D. 1960. "Per una nuova classificazione della civiltà minoica," *Parola del passato,* 15 (71), 81–121.

Levine, P. 1986. *The Amateur and the Professional: Antiquarians, Historians and Archaeologists in Victorian England 1838–1886,* Cambridge, Cambridge University Press.

Lock, P. 1990. "D. G. Hogarth (1862–1927): '. . . A Specialist in the Science of Archaeology,' " *Annual of the British School at Athens,* 85, 175–200.

Lorimer, D. 1988. "Theoretical Racism in Late Victorian Anthropology, 1870–1900," *Victorian Studies,* 31, 405–30.

Lubbock, Sir J. 1865. *Pre-historic Times, as illustrated by ancient remains and the manners and customs of modern savages,* London, William and Norgate.

Luce, J. V. 1969. *Lost Atlantis: New Light on an Old Legend,* London, Thames and Hudson.

Ludwig, E. 1931. *Schliemann: The Story of a Gold-Seeker,* London and Boston.

Lurker, M. 1980. *The Gods and Symbols of Ancient Egypt,* New York, Thames and Hudson.

Macalister, R. A. S. 1923. "Exploration and Excavation," *Cambridge Ancient History* I, Chapter III, 112–44.

MacGillivray, J. A. 1997. "The Cretan Countryside in the Old Palace Period," in R. Hägg (ed.), *The Function of the Minoan "Villa,"* Stockholm, 21–25.

———. 1998. *Knossos: Pottery Groups of the Old Palace Period (British School at Athens Studies,* 5). London.

MacGillivray, J. A., J. M. Driessen, and L. H. Sackett, eds. 2000. *The Palaikastro Kouros (British School at Athens Studies 6)*, London.

Mackenzie, C. 1931. *First Athenian Memories*, London, Cassel.

———. 1940. *Aegean Memories*, London, Chatto & Windus.

Mackenzie, Donald A. 1919. *Myths of Crete & Pre-Hellenic Europe*, London.

Mackenzie, Duncan. 1903. "The Pottery of Knossos," *Journal of Hellenic Studies*, 23, 157–203.

———. 1905. "Cretan Palaces and the Aegean Civilizations," *Annual of the British School at Athens*, 11, 181–223.

———. 1906a. "Cretan Palaces and the Aegean Civilizations II," *Annual of the British School at Athens*, 12, 216–48.

———. 1906b. "The Middle Minoan Pottery of Knossos," *Journal of Hellenic Studies*, 26, 243–67.

———. 1907. "Cretan Palaces and the Aegean Civilizations III," *Annual of the British School at Athens*, 13, 423–45.

———. 1908. "Cretan Palaces and the Aegean Civilizations IV," *Annual of the British School at Athens*, 14, 343–422.

Macmillan, G. A. 1911. *A Short History of the British School at Athens*, London.

———. 1929. *A History of the Hellenic Society*, London.

Mallowan, M. 1977. *Mallowan's Memoirs*, London, Collins.

Mariani, L. 1895. "Antichità cretesi," *Monumenti Antichi*, 6, 156–347.

McDonald, W. A., and C. G. Thomas. 1990. *Progress into the Past* (2nd ed.), Bloomington and Indianapolis, Indiana University Press.

McNeal, R. A. 1972. "The Greeks in History and Prehistory," *Antiquity*, 46, 19–28.

———. 1974. "The Legacy of Arthur Evans," *California Studies in Classical Antiquity*, 6, 205–20.

Meyer, E. 1962. "Schliemann's Letters to Max Müller in Oxford," *Journal of Hellenic Studies*, 82, 75–105.

Michaelis, A. 1908. *A Century of Archaeological Discoveries*, London, John Murray.

Milchhöfer, A. 1883. *Die Anfänge der Kunst in Griechenland*, Leipzig, F. A. Brockhaus.

Millington-Evans, M. 1894. *Chapters on Greek Dress*, London, Macmillan.

Momigliano, A. D. 1994. "Liberal Historian and Supporter of the Holy Roman Empire: E. A. Freeman," in G. W. Bowersock and T. J. Cornell (eds.), *A. D. Momigliano: Studies on Modern Scholarship*, Berkeley, University of California Press, 197–208.

Momigliano, N. 1995. "Duncan Mackenzie: A Cautious Canny Highlander," *Klados: Essays in Honour of J. N. Coldstream, BICS* Suppl. 63, London, 163–70.

———. 1996a. "Evans, Mackenzie, and the History of the Palace at Knossos," *Journal of Hellenic Studies*, 116, 166–69.

———. 1996b. "Duncan Mackenzie and the Palestine Exploration Fund," *Palestine Exploration Quarterly*, 128, 139–70.

———. 1999. *Duncan Mackenzie: A Cautious Canny Highlander and the Palace of Minos at Knossos*, London, Institute of Classical Studies.

Montelius, O. 1899. *Der Orient und Europa*, Stockholm, Konigl. Akademie der schöne Wissenschaften, Geschichte und Altertumskunde.

———. 1903. *Die typologische Methode: Die alteren Kulturperioden im Orient und in Europa*, I, Stockholm, Selbstverlag.

Morley, J. 1903. *The Life of William Ewart Gladstone*, I, London.

Mosso, A. 1907. *The Palaces of Crete and Their Builders*, London, Fisher Unwin.

Myres, J. L. 1895. "On Some Polychrome Pottery from Kamarais in Crete," *Proceedings of the Society of Antiquaries*, 15, 351–56.

———. 1896. "Mykenaean Civilization: Helbig's 'La Question Mycénienne,' " *Classical Review*, 10, 350–57.

———. 1900a. Notice in *Oxford Magazine*, May 9.

———. 1900b. "On the Plan of the Homeric House, with Special Reference to Mykenaian analogies," *Journal of Hellenic Studies*, 20, 128–50.

———. 1902. "Ridgeway's *Early Age of Greece*," *Classical Review*, 16, 68–77, 91–94.

———. 1911. *The Dawn of History*, Oxford, Oxford University Press.

———. 1933. "The Cretan Labyrinth: A Retrospective of Aegean Research" (Huxley memorial lecture for 1933), *Journal of the Royal Anthropological Institute*, 63, 269–312.

———. 1950. "Easter in a Greek Village," *Folklore*, 61, 203–8.

Myres, J. N. L. 1980. *Commander J. L. Myres, R.N.V.R. The Blackbeard of the Aegean* (Tenth J. L. Myres Memorial Lecture, London).

Newberry, P. E. 1908. "Two Cults of the Old Kingdom," *Liverpool Annals of Archaeology*, 24–29.

Newton, C. T. 1850. "On the Study of Archaeology," *Archaeological Journal*, 8; reprinted in Newton 1880, 1–38.

———. 1878. "Dr. Schliemann's discoveries at Mycenae," *Edinburgh Review;* reprinted in Newton 1880, 246–302.

———. 1880. *Essays on Art and Archaeology*, London, Macmillan.

Niemeier, W.-D. 1982. "Mycenaean Knossos and the Age of Linear B," *Studi Micenei ed Egeo-Anatolici*, 23, 219–87.

———. 1988. "The Priest-King Fresco from Knossos," in E. B. French and K. A. Wardle (eds.), *Problems in Greek Prehistory*, Bristol.

———. 1995. "Die Utopie eines verlorenen Paradieses: Die Minoische Kultur Kretas als neuzeitliche Mythenschöpfung," in R. Stupperich (ed.), *Lebendige Antike*, Mannheim, Palatium.

Nixon, L. 1983. "Changing Views of Minoan Society," in O. Krzyszkowska and L. Nixon (eds.), *Minoan Society* (Bristol), 237–43.

———. 1994. "Gender Bias in Archaeology," in L. J. Archer, S. Fischler, and M. Wyke (eds.), *Women in Ancient Societies*, London, 1–23.

Orsi, P. 1888. "Studi illustrativi sui bronzi arcaici trovati nell'antro di Zeus Ideo," *Museo Italiano di Antichità Classica*, II, 769–904.

Palmer, L. R. 1961. *Mycenaeans and Minoans*, London, Faber.

———. 1980. "The First Fortnight at Knossos," *Studi Micenei ed Egeo-Anatolici*, 21, 273–93.

Palmer, L. R., and J. Boardman. 1963. *On the Knossos Tablets*, Oxford.

Panagiotaki, M. 1993. "The Temple Repositories of Knossos: New Information from the Unpublished Notes of Sir Arthur Evans," *Annual of the British School at Athens*, 88, 49–91.

Papadakis, N. 1992. *Οι Κρήνες της Σητείας*, Siteia.

Parabeni, R. 1904. "Ricerche nel sepolcreto da Haghia Triada presso Phestos," *Monumenti Antichi*, 14, 677–756.

Pashley, R. 1837. *Travels in Crete*, Cambridge and London, John Murray.

Peet, T. E., A. J. B. Wace, and M. S. Thompson. 1908. "The Connection of the Aegean Civilization with Central Europe," *Classical Review*, XXII, 233–38.

Pendlebury, H. W., J. D. S. Pendlebury, and M. B. Money-Coutts. 1938. "Excavations in the Plain of Lasithi. III. Karphi: A City of Refuge of the Early Iron Age in Crete," *Annual of the British School at Athens*, 38, 57–145.

Pendlebury, J. D. S. 1930. *Aegyptiaca*, Cambridge, Cambridge University Press.

———. 1933. *A Handbook to the Palace of Minos at Knossos*, London, Macmillan.

———. 1939. *The Archaeology of Crete*, London, Methuen.

———. 1948. *John Pendlebury in Crete, Comprising his Traveling Hints and His First Trip to Eastern Crete (1928) together with appreciations by N. Hammond and T. J. Dunbabin* (privately circulated, University Press, Cambridge).

Perrot, G. 1891. "Les vases d'or de Vafio," *Bulletin de Correspondance Hellénique*, 15, 493–537.

Perrot, G., and C. Chipiez. 1894. *Histoire de l'art dans l'antiquité, vol. vi: La Grèce primitive, l'art mycénien*, Paris.

Philips, E. D. 1964. "The Greek Vision of Prehistory," *Antiquity*, 38, 171–78.

Picard, C. 1932. "Au pays du griffon: Cnossos ressuscitée," *La Revue de L'Art*, LXI, 3–18, 49–60, 105–16.

Pitt-Rivers, A. H. L.-F. 1906. *The Evolution of Culture and Other Essays*, Oxford, Oxford University Press.

Poliakov, L. 1974. *The Aryan Myth: A History of Racist and Nationalist Ideas in Europe*, New York, Basic Books.

Poole, B. W. H. 1922. *The Postage Stamps of Crete*, Beverly, Mass., Severn-Wylie-Jewett.

Pope, M. 1975. *The Story of Decipherment*, London, Thames and Hudson.

Pottier, E. 1897. *Vases antiques du Louvre: Salles A-E*, Paris.

Powell, B. B. 1977. "The Significance of the So-called 'Horns of Consecration,' " *Kadmos*, 16, 70–82.

Prestwich, J. 1860. "On the occurrence of flint implements associated with the remains of animals of extinct species in beds of a late geological period at Amiens and Abbeville and in England at Hoxne," *Proceedings of the Royal Society* (London), X, 50.

Radet, G. 1981. *L'Histoire et l'oeuvre de l'Ecole française d'Athènes*, Paris, Albert Fontemoig.

Randolph, B. 1687. *The Present State of the Islands of the Archipelago*, Oxford.

Raulin, C. 1869. *Description physique de l'Ile de Crète*, 3 vols. and atlas, Paris.

Rehak, P. 1995. "The Use and Destruction of the Minoan Stone Bull's Head Rhyta," *Aegaeum*, 12, 435–60.

Reinach, S. 1892. *L'Origine des Aryens: Histoire d'une Controverse*, Paris.

———. 1893. *Le Mirage oriental*, Paris, G. Masson.

———. 1895. *La sculpture en Europe avant les influences Gréco-romaines*, Angers, Burdin.

———. 1896. *Chronique d'Orient: Documents sur les fouilles et découvertes dans l'orient hellénique*, II, Paris.

———. 1901. "La découverte de la Crète préhellénique. La Crète avant l'histoire," *Chronique des Arts*, 181–256.

———. 1902. "La Crète avant l'histoire," *L'Anthropologie*, 13, 1–8.

———. 1909. *Orpheus: A General History of Religions*, London.

Renfrew, C. 1987. *Archaeology and Language*, London, Jonathan Cape. Reissued Penguin 1989.

Ridgeway, W. 1896. "What People Made the Objects Called Mycenaean?," *Journal of Hellenic Studies*, 16, 80.

———. 1901. *The Early Age of Greece*, I, Cambridge.

———. 1909. "Minos: The Destroyer Rather Than the Creator of the So-called 'Minoan' Culture of Cnossus," *Proceedings of the British Academy*, 97–129.

———. 1931. *The Early Age of Greece*, II, Cambridge.

Rizzo, M. A. 1985. "The First Explorations," in *Ancient Crete: A Hundred Years of Italian Archaeology*, Rome, de Luca, 27–38.

Rodden, J. 1981. "The Development of the Three Age System: Archaeology's First Paradigm," in Daniel 1981b, 51–68.

Rodenwaldt, G. 1912. *Tiryns II. Die Fresken des Palastes*, Athens.

Rouse, W. H. D. 1901. "The Double Axe and the Labyrinth," *Journal of Hellenic Studies*, 21, 268–74.

Sakellarakis, J. and E. 1981. "Drama of Death in a Minoan Temple," *National Geographic*, 159, 2, 205–22.

Sayce, A. H. 1923. *Reminiscences*, London.

———. 1927. "David George Hogarth," *Proceedings of the British Academy*, 381–83.

Schliemann, H. 1875. *Troy and Its Remains*, London.

———. 1878. *Mycenae*, London.

Schrader, O. 1890. *Prehistoric Antiquities of the Aryan People*.

Seaman, L. C. B. 1973. *Victorian England*, London, Methuen.

Settegast, M. 1990. *Plato Prehistorian*, Hudson, N.Y., Lindisfarne.

Seward, A. C., ed. 1909. *Darwin and Modern Science*, Cambridge.

Shaw, J. W., and M. C. Shaw, eds. 1995. *The Kommos Region and the Houses of the Minoan Town*, Princeton, Princeton University Press.

Simonelli, V. 1897. *Candia Ricordi di Escursione*, Parma.

Singer, R., B. G. Gladfelter, and J. J. Wymer. 1993. *The Lower Paleolithic Site at Hoxne, England*, Chicago, University of Chicago Press.

Smith, G. E. 1923. *The Ancient Egyptians and the Origins of Civilization*, London, Harper.

Spanaki, S. G. 1960. "Η οικογένεια των Καλοκαιρινών της Κρήτης," *Kritika Chronika* ΙΔ 271–307.

Spencer, F. 1990. *Piltdown: A Scientific Forgery*, London, Natural History Museum.

Spratt, T. A. B. 1865. *Travels and Researches in Crete*, London.

Starr, C. G. 1955. "The Myth of the Minoan Thalassocracy," *Historia*, 3, 282–91.

———. 1984. "Minoan Flower Lovers," in R. Hägg and N. Marinatos (eds.), *Minoan Thalassocracy: Myth or Reality?*, Stockholm, 9–12.

Stephens, W. R. W. 1895. *The Life and Letters of Edward A. Freeman* (in two vols.), London, Macmillan.

Stewart, J. G. 1959. *Jane Ellen Harrison: A Portrait from Letters*, London.

Stillman, W. J. 1874. *The Cretan Insurrection of 1866–7–8*, New York.

———. 1881. "Extracts of letters from W. J. Stillman, respecting ancient sites in Crete," *Archaeological Institute of America: Appendix to the Second Annual Report of the Executive Committee*, Cambridge, Mass., 41–49.

———. 1901. *The Autobiography of a Journalist* (in 2 vols.), London, Grant Richards.

Stocking, G. W. 1987. *Victorian Anthropology*, New York, Free Press.

Stoll, H. A. 1961. "Schliemann und die Ausgrabungen von Knossos," in V. Georgiev and J. Irmschen (eds.), *Minoica und Homer*, Berlin, 51–70.

Stubbings, F. H. 1958. "Alan John Bayard Wace" (obituary), *Proceedings of the British Academy*, 263–80.

Svoronos, J. N. 1890. *Numismatique de la Crète ancienne*, Maçon.

Taylor, I. 1890. *The Origin of the Aryans*, London, Walter Scott.

Thénon, L. 1866–68. "Fragments d'une description de l'île de Crète," [series of brief reports in] *Revue archéologique*, Paris.

Thompson, M. W. 1977. *General Pitt-Rivers: Evolution and Archaeology in the Nineteenth Century*, Bradford-upon-Avon, Moonraker Press.

Thomson, D. 1950. *England in the Nineteenth Century (1815–1914)*, Harmondsworth, Penguin.

Traill, D. 1985. "Schliemann's 'Dream of Troy'—The Making of a Legend," *Classical Journal*, 81, 13–24.

———. 1995. *Schliemann of Troy: Treasure and Deceit*, New York, St. Martin's.

Trigger, Bruce G. 1980. *Gordon Childe: Revolutions in Archaeology*, London, Thames and Hudson.

———. 1989. *A History of Archaeological Thought*, Cambridge, Cambridge University Press.

Tsountas, C., and J. I. Manatt. 1897. *The Mycenaean Age: A Study of the Monuments and Culture of Pre-Homeric Greece*, London.

Turner, V. 1981. *The Greek Heritage in Victorian Britain*, New Haven and London, Yale University Press.

Tyler, E. B. 1865. *Researches into the Early History of Mankind and the Development of Civilization*, London, John Murray.

———. 1871. *Primitive Culture*, London, John Murray.

———. 1881. *Anthropology: An Introduction to the Study of Man and Civilization*, London.

Tzedhakis, I., S. Chryssoulaki, S. Voutsaki, and Y. Venieri. 1989. "Les routes minoennes: un rapport preliminaire. Défense de la circulation ou circulation de la défense?," *Bulletin de Correspondance Hellénique*, 113, 43–75.

Vasilaki, A. 1989. "The Early Minoan Settlement at Trypeti, South Crete," *Archaeologia*, 30, Athens, 52–56.

Ventris, M. 1952. "Deciphering Europe's Oldest Script," *Listener*, July 10, 57–58, reprinted in Deuel, 1961, 305–12.

Wace, Alan J. B. 1920a. "Excavations at Mycenae," *Times Literary Supplement,* June 24, 398.

———. 1920b. "Excavations at Mycenae. II," *Times Literary Supplement,* Aug. 19, 530.

———. 1923. "Early Aegean Civilization," chapter xvii in *Cambridge Ancient History,* 1st ed., I, 589–615.

———. 1927. *A Cretan Statuette in the Fitzwilliam Museum,* Cambridge.

———. 1931. Introduction to Ridgeway 1931.

———. 1932. "Chamber Tombs at Mycenae" (*Archaeologia,* 82), Oxford, Society of Antiquaries.

———. 1940. "The Date of the Treasury of Atreus," *Antiquity,* 233.

———. 1949. "The Greeks and Romans as Archaeologists," *Société royale d'archéologie d'Alexandrie,* Bulletin 38, 21–35.

Wall, S. M., J. H. Musgrave, and P. M. Warren. 1986. "Human Bones from a Late Minoan IB House at Knossos," *Annual of the British School at Athens,* 81, 333–88.

Walters, H. B. 1934. *The English Antiquaries of the Sixteenth, Seventeenth and Eighteenth Centuries,* London, Walters.

Warren, Peter M. 1972. "16th, 17th and 18th Century British Travelers in Crete," *Kritika Chronika,* 24, 65–92.

———. 1981. "Minoan Crete and Ecstatic Religion," in Hägg and Marinatos, eds., *Sanctuaries and Cults of the Aegean Bronze Age,* Stockholm, 155–66.

———. 1984. "Circular Platforms at Minoan Knossos," *Annual of the British School at Athens,* 79, 307–23.

———. 1988. *Minoan Religion as Ritual Action,* Gothenburg, University of Gothenburg.

———. 1990. "Of Baetyls," *Opuscula Atheniensa,* 18, no. 14, 193–206.

Waterhouse, H. 1974. "Priest-Kings?," *Bulletin of the Institute of Classical Studies* 21, 153–55.

———. 1986. *History of the British School at Athens,* London.

Waugh, E. 1946. *When the Going Was Good,* London, Duckworth.

Weingarten, J. 1983. *The Zakro Master and His Place in Prehistory,* Göteborg, Paul Aström.

———. 1991. *The Transformation of Egyptian Taweret into the Minoan Genius, Studies in Mediterranean Archaeology,* 88, Partille, Paul Aström.

Weiss, R. 1969. *The Renaissance Discovery of Classical Antiquity,* Oxford, Basil Blackwell.

Wheeler, E. R. M. 1956. *Still Digging,* New York, Dutton.

Willetts, R. F. 1955. *Aristocratic Society in Ancient Crete,* London, Routledge and Kegan Paul.

Wilson, D. 1851. *The Archaeology and Prehistoric Annals of Scotland,* London and Cambridge, Macmillan.

Winckelmann, J. J. 1764. *History of Ancient Art,* Germany; English editions from 1850.

Wood, M. 1985. *In Search of the Trojan War,* London, BBC Publications.

Woolley, C. L. 1920. *Dead Towns and Living Men,* Oxford, Oxford University Press; reissued London, Jonathan Cape 1932.

———. 1953. *Spadework,* Lutterworth Press, London.

———. 1958. *History Unearthed*, London, Benn, reissued New York, Frederick A. Praeger 1962.

———. 1962. *As I Seem to Remember*, London, George Allen and Unwin.

Wroth, W. 1886. *Catalogue of the Greek Coins of Crete and the Aegean Islands*, London, British Museum.

Wunderlich, H.-G., 1974. *The Secret of Crete*, New York, Macmillan.

Xanthoudides, S. 1904. *Ο Κρητικός Πολιτισμός*, Athens.

———. 1924. *The Vaulted Tombs of the Mesara*, London, University Press of Liverpool.

Zoes, A. 1996. *Κνωσός το Εκστατικό Οραμα*, Herakleion, University of Crete.

Acknowledgments

The inspiration for this book came in 1992 when Bob Cornfield and I waited to play at New York's Central Park tennis courts. I tried to convince him that Arthur Evans had created, not discovered, the Minoans and he urged me to take my case to a wider audience than my classes, where I worked through a detailed critique of Evans in directed readings at Columbia University. During the spring term of 1993, two graduate students, Senta German and Paul Christenson, met with me every Monday night at my apartment on Riverside Drive; I cooked and they presented their reports on the previous week's readings on Evans's early writings. But it wasn't until the autumn of 1994 that I was convinced to take Bob's suggestion seriously. A year later, while I was in Oxford on a visiting fellowship at All Souls College, I began to write this book. During the subsequent migratory period, I was pampered in the homes of Steve MacGillivray and Hannah McCouch, Judith Weingarten, Bob Cornfield, and Ann and Gordon Getty, and blessed with long stretches of solitude to work through the complex details of Evans's life, and my own.

Many friends and colleagues helped with this project. In the Ashmolean Museum, Michael Vickers drew my attention to Charles Kingsley's *Heroes*, Sue Sherratt gave access and guidance to the Evans Archive, and Julie Clements provided copies of Evans's excavation photographs—reproduced here by kind permission of the Visitors of the Ashmolean Museum. The British School at Athens kindly granted access to the Pendlebury Archive there. Cindy Ciparelli took the time to copy Evans's reports to the *Times* in the New York Public Library. Jan Driessen helped with papers on Kalokairinos's Knossos excavations. Iannis Kaphesakis and Nikos Papadakis in Siteia introduced me to Cretan postage stamps. Ariane Marcar shared her novel theories about the Egyptian basis for much of Minoan religion. Nico Momigliano offered many insights into the complex relationship between Evans and his "first lieutenant," Duncan Mackenzie, and very kindly sent me an advance copy of her book on the "cautious and canny highlander." Natalia Vogeikoff, archivist of the American School of Classical Studies in Athens, very kindly sent me the correspondence from and about Evans in the Blegen Archive. S. J. Berwin and Company in London most efficiently researched the legal matters pertaining to Evans's arrest and trial in London. Juanita Wichienkuer drew the maps and the Palace plan. Alisia Margolis, Delia Riccardi-Percy, and Maria Xanthopoulou inked the line drawings. To all I am most grateful.

First drafts of parts of this book were read by Ann Brown, Bob Cornfield, Ruth Davis, Trinity Jackman, Steve MacGillivray, Hannah McCouch, and Spencer Harrington, but the major editorial credit goes to Elisabeth Sifton, who slashed and burned early drafts and helped to convert them into the book's present form. What a privilege it has been to work with her!

Three collegiate soundings for some of the ideas expressed herein were given in January and May 1996; the first in London organized by Cyprian Broodbank, the second in Cambridge by Sophia Voutsaki and Tod Whitelaw, and the third by Nico Momigliano at Balliol College, Oxford. The positive responses at the first two followed by a decidedly negative reaction at the third indicated that I was moving forward and breaking new ground.

The sustained freedom required to research and compose this book, as well as the commitment to its theme, came from Bob Cornfield's powers of persuasion over the past seven years. This book wouldn't exist without him.

Index